D0091764

Praise for
YOUNG TITAN

"Perceptive and entertaining."
—Jonathan Yardley, *The Washington Post*

"A vivid portrait of a young man on the make, as ambitious as he was gifted . . . Enthralling."
—Newsweek digital edition

"Entertaining and erudite. . . . Shelden is full of sharp literary insights about Churchill, as one would expect from a biographer of his rank."
—*The Wall Street Journal*

"[As this] glowing portrait makes clear, the young Churchill was as beloved as he was despised: his intelligence, industry, and wit made him a darling of the press, and he was often seen as a future Prime Minister."
—*The New Yorker*

"Much has been written about Winston Churchill, but there is still much to learn, especially about those early years when he seemed destined for greatness. Michael Shelden now thoughtfully explores those years in *Young Titan*. . . . An engaging as well as perceptive take on the man who believed that while we are all worms 'he was a glowworm'—a belief history would splendidly vindicate."
—*Richmond Times-Dispatch*

"Just when you think there can be nothing fresh to be said about the long life of Winston Churchill, along comes biographer Michael Shelden's page-turner about Churchill from age 26 to 40. . . . many readers who assume they've read it all will find Mr. Shelden's lively account a must-add for their groaning shelves."

—*The Washington Times*

"Swiftly narrated. . . . Shelden, a noted biographer whose 1992 *Orwell* was a Pulitzer Prize finalist, explores the young titan in entertaining depth, with deep regard for Churchill's achievements and no end of colorful detail."

—*USA Today*

"A biographer of note, [Shelden] actually found a fresh angle on England's man with the big cigar that should appeal to avid history fans."

—*Ft. Worth Star-Telegram*

"In sparkling prose, Shelden explores the tendentious world of high-level Edwardian politics as Churchill worked with and competed against the likes of Herbert H. Asquith, David Lloyd George, and other notables."

—*Library Journal*

"A fluid and informative examination of the early career of one of modern Britain's most outstanding political leaders."

—*Publishers Weekly*

"[A] charming new biography. . . . Shelden has capitalized on an understudied period of an iconic life and proved that such a study can still surprise."

—*New Criterion*

"[A] solid biography covering the first four decades of Winston Churchill's life, marked by both ambition and heartbreak. . . . Shelden offers an unadorned account of Churchill's dogged pursuit to build his legacy against some long odds."

—*Kirkus Reviews*

"Michael Shelden has done the nigh-impossible: he has found original things to say about the man Isaiah Berlin called 'the largest human being of our time'—Winston Churchill. In this entertaining and deeply researched book, Shelden paints a memorable portrait of the young Churchill's life and loves."

—Jon Meacham, author of *American Lion*

"*Young Titan* gives us an exciting, needed look at Winston Churchill in his years as a Liberal. Breaking with the Conservatives, he battled for better working conditions, for unemployment insurance, for improvements in education. He waged a two-front war: against the Tories on the right, the socialists on the left. It is the young Churchill at his best, a great foretelling of what was to come when Britain and the world needed him most."

—Chris Matthews, author of *Jack Kennedy: Elusive Hero* and anchor of MSNBC's *Hardball*

"For history buffs, Winston Churchill is the gift that keeps on giving, and in *Young Titan* Michael Shelden has given us the gift of Churchill's fascinating formative years. It's all here—the boy wonder, adventurer, romantic, orator, and eloquent man in the arena. I didn't want it to end."

—Tom Brokaw, author of *The Greatest Generation*

ALSO BY MICHAEL SHELDEN

Mark Twain: Man in White

Graham Greene: The Enemy Within

Orwell: The Authorized Biography

Friends of Promise: Cyril Connolly and the World of Horizon

YOUNG TITAN

• THE MAKING OF •
WINSTON CHURCHILL

———⊸⊱◦⊰⊶———

MICHAEL SHELDEN

SIMON & SCHUSTER PAPERBACKS
New York London Toronto Sydney New Delhi

Simon & Schuster Paperbacks
A Division of Simon & Schuster, Inc.
1230 Avenue of the Americas
New York, NY 10020

Copyright © 2013 by Michael Shelden

All rights reserved, including the right to reproduce this book or
portions thereof in any form whatsoever. For information address
Simon & Schuster Paperbacks Subsidiary Rights Department,
1230 Avenue of the Americas, New York, NY 10020

First Simon & Schuster paperback edition March 2014

SIMON & SCHUSTER PAPERBACKS and colophon are registered trademarks
of Simon & Schuster, Inc.

For information about special discounts for bulk purchases,
please contact Simon & Schuster Special Sales at
1-866-506-1949 or business@simonandschuster.com.

The Simon & Schuster Speakers Bureau can bring authors
to your live event. For more information or to book an event,
contact the Simon & Schuster Speakers Bureau at
1-866-248-3049 or visit our website at www.simonspeakers.com.

Designed by Renata Di Biase

Manufactured in the United States of America

10 9 8 7 6 5 4 3 2 1

The Library of Congress has cataloged the hardcover edition as follows:
Shelden, Michael.
  Young titan : the making of Winston Churchill / Michael Shelden.
      p.   cm.
1. Churchill, Winston, 1874–1965. 2. Great Britain—Politics and govern-
ment—1901–1936. 3. Cabinet officers—Great Britain—Biography. 4. Prime minis-
ters—Great Britain—Biography. I. Title. II. Title: Making of Winston Churchill.
  DA566.9.C5S446 2013
  941.084092—dc23
[B]   2012017488
ISBN 978-1-4516-0991-2
ISBN 978-1-4516-0992-9 (pbk)
ISBN 978-1-4516-0993-6 (ebook)

To my daughters, Sarah and Vanessa

The force of character is cumulative.

—RALPH WALDO EMERSON

CONTENTS

YOUNG TITAN

Near midnight on a Saturday in May 1941 a great wave of planes appeared over London, their silhouettes against a moonlit sky. As they roared past Westminster Bridge, whole streets were set ablaze, fires broke out at Westminster Abbey, and shrapnel pounded the tower of Big Ben. Soon flames were sweeping through the debating chamber of the House of Commons. Its roof fell away, the galleries collapsed, and a shower of twisted steel and masonry buried the rows of green leather benches where so many famous debates had raged over the decades. Only the scorched walls were left standing.

The next afternoon, while parts of London were still burning and the smell of smoke was everywhere, Winston Churchill came to Parliament to inspect the damage. This was the second spring of Adolf Hitler's war against Great Britain, and Churchill was just completing his first year as prime minister. To everyone's surprise, the clock tower—though blackened and pockmarked—withstood the raid, and Big Ben was continuing to strike the hours. Because the attack had come late at night, only a few people had been in the building, and the death toll was limited to three, including two policemen. Over the whole of London, however, the casualty rate was appalling, with more than three thousand killed or injured. It would prove to be the worst night of the Blitz.

As he poked through the rubble, Churchill paused beside some charred beams and cast a solemn gaze over the destruction. With its roof gone, the wrecked chamber was illuminated by a pale shaft of sunlight, and the air was thick with dust. There were no relics to salvage, nothing new to learn about the enemy's methods. At one level this was simply the latest in a long list of venerable buildings to suffer the fury of modern war. But, of course, there was a greater casualty here—a direct hit on the very heart of British political life. In a flash Hitler's bombers had gutted the home of one of the world's most important democratic assemblies. As Churchill would later put it, "Our old House of Commons has been blown to smithereens."[1]

The loss was personal. The prime minister had spent much of his life in this chamber, beginning with his appearance on its floor as a new member forty years earlier, when he was a slender young man with fine, reddish hair, sharp blue eyes, and a boy's freckled face. Here, as he would say, "I learnt my craft." On this ground his father—Lord Randolph Churchill—had stood as an ally of Disraeli and an adversary of Gladstone. In the Ladies' Gallery his American-born mother—the indomitable Jennie—had watched proudly as her son gave his maiden speech. He had sparred with friends and enemies here—from the early days of the century when he matched wits with the political powerhouse Joseph Chamberlain, to more recent times when he challenged the judgment of Joe's younger son, Neville, who so badly misjudged Hitler in the 1930s.[2]

Here he had enjoyed moments of triumph and endured defeats; given brilliant speeches and, occasionally, a dull one; earned the admiration of many; and enraged not a few. On one memorable occasion early in his career an opponent had jumped up during a raucous debate, grabbed the Speaker's bound volume of the rules of the House and thrown it at him, hitting him in the face and drawing blood. During the abdication crisis of 1936, when he had tried to offer words of support for Edward VIII, howls of protest had filled the chamber, silencing him and causing some to predict that his political career was at an end.

Just three days before Hitler's planes dropped their bombs on this spot, Churchill's old friend and rival from the early years—David Lloyd George—had risen in the debates to paint a bleak picture of the progress of the war, complaining of "discouraging" setbacks. In what was to be his last speech in the old chamber Churchill responded to Lloyd George's pessimism with an impassioned declaration of his faith in the war effort. "I feel sure we have no need to fear the tempest," he said on Wednesday, May 7. "Let it roar, and let it rage. We shall come through."

Little did anyone suspect that the tempest would soon roar and rage in the very place where he spoke.

Now, as he surveyed the damage of that fiery Saturday night, tears began to trickle down his cheeks, and then to flow. "He did not try to stop them," noted a reporter standing nearby, "or even wipe them away." Motionless in the sunlight—one hand in his overcoat, his feet planted firmly on a mound of rubble—he looked for a second like a statue that had miraculously survived the bombing.

The next moment, however, he pulled himself together and declared decisively, "The Chamber must be rebuilt—just as it was."

Then he turned and walked carefully back to his waiting car. A crowd had gathered outside, where debris from the bombing was spread in all directions, "with burned bits of paper blowing in gutters." In the background could be heard what an observer later called "one of the most horrible sounds" of the war—"the tinkle of glass being swept up." Yet Churchill showed no sign of indecision or gloom. He waved confidently and a rousing cry greeted him.[3]

History likes winners, and the image of the older, victorious Churchill has long overshadowed the story of the eager younger man who soared to prominence only to find he had overreached, and who left office with his reputation in tatters. Yet in many ways the early period is the most colorful of his career and the key to his character. It was an exhilarating time full of high drama, political intrigue, personal courage, and grave miscalculations.

Churchill thought his chance for greatness on a grand scale would come early in life, and for such a restless, ambitious man the long wait was difficult to bear. By the time he became prime minister at sixty-five, he was more than ready for the job and was able to offer the world much of what it expects from its heroes—except the excitement and glamour of youth.

No doubt the great man weeping among the ruins of his parliamentary past was a better leader because he had spent a lifetime preparing for his part. But there was a period in his twenties and thirties—in the distant Edwardian past—when success had beckoned on the world stage, and when the vigor of a more dashing, youthful character was at his command. The adventures and ordeals of those early years were essential to the making of the man who triumphed in the Second World War. Young Winston's career began with dreams of success that fueled a spectacular political rise, but which ended in dramatic failures, creating an equally spectacular fall. At forty he was largely written off as a man whose best days were behind him.

As Churchill confessed in old age, he had felt so misunderstood in those younger days that he thought he had become in the eyes of many "a freak—always that—but much hated & ruled out." Redeeming the promise of his youth became the great challenge of his later life.[4]

INTRODUCTION:
THE YOUNG TITAN

Winston Churchill didn't stumble into greatness. In a conscious and methodical way, he set out as a young man to become the hero that he believed his era of "great events" demanded. He fashioned his career as a grand experiment to prove that he could work his will on his times, persevering in that approach despite repeated setbacks and the often harsh ridicule of those who didn't share his high opinion of himself. Many of his contemporaries accepted that history is "the Biography of great men," as the Victorian sage Thomas Carlyle put it, but whether Churchill belonged among the great was always a subject of hot debate, and—for some—it still is. He had few doubts about his destiny, however, and raced to establish himself as the most dynamic and imaginative politician in the British Empire.

At the heart of his story is an irrepressible spirit whose tough character was shaped in part by a romantic temperament that flowered in his youth and never entirely disappeared. It arose from a powerful concept of personal will that Churchill embraced early in adulthood. "I believe in personality," he declared in one of his earliest political speeches, confidently endorsing the notion that the heroics of great leaders—not vast movements or impersonal systems—shape history. "We live in an age of great events and little men," he said, "and if we are not to become the slaves of our own system . . . it will only be by the bold efforts of originality, by repeated experiment, and by the dispassionate consideration of the results of sustained and unflinching thought."

The details of party platforms and manifestos were never as important to him as the larger issue of providing vigorous national leadership equal to any challenge. Almost from the start, critics saw him as a power-hungry egotist, calling him "the embodiment of pugnacity" and "a hustler of the first class." He saw himself as an imaginative figure of high purpose and decisive action. "Little men," he argued, let events take their course. "I like things to happen, and if they don't happen I like to make them happen."[1]

As one political opponent observed, his ear was "sensitively attuned to the bugle note of history." He heard it loud and clear in the heroic story of his legendary ancestor, John Churchill, first duke of Marlborough—the victor of the Battle of Blenheim in 1704—whom he called an "Olympian figure," boasting that the duke "never fought a battle that he did not win, nor besieged a fortress he did not take." Inspiration came as well from the ambitious ideals of his father's early supporter, Benjamin Disraeli. His praise for one of Disraeli's most admirable qualities as a leader could also be applied to him: "He loved his country with a romantic passion."[2]

Like the young Disraeli, he found encouragement for his passionate nature in the writings of the Romantic poet who created a veritable blueprint for the heroic life—Lord Byron. In old age Churchill often surprised admirers by suddenly declaiming from memory long stretches of Byron's verse. He could do it by the hour, as his daughter Sarah discovered to her amazement on a trip in 1945: "My father, relaxed and fortified, recited for an hour from *Childe Harold* by Byron and then had about thirty minutes' sleep." When Franklin Roosevelt suggested in 1941 that the Allied powers should call themselves the "United Nations," Churchill was quick to agree and just as quick to quote a relevant verse from Byron about the Battle of Waterloo: "Here, where the sword united nations drew, / Our countrymen were warring on that day!"

Churchill was not merely showing off. From early youth he was drawn to Byron as a stirring example of the man of action who was also a man of ideas. He was so intimately acquainted with the poet's work that it became deeply embedded in his mind and always seemed close at hand to supply a reference for any idea or event. One of his most resounding statements—his great rallying cry for wartime sacrifice in 1940, "I have nothing to offer but blood, toil, tears and sweat"—has its parallel in Lord Byron's scathing attack on the lack of sacrifice in an earlier war when Britain's landed gentry sent "their brethren out to battle" and enriched themselves with millions in wartime profits. "Safe in their barns," Byron's *The Age of Bronze* says of the gentry, they grew fat from their "blood, sweat, and tear-wrung millions."

To young Winston, the poet's career as an eager adventurer, defiant freethinker, and proud visionary was partly an inspiration, and partly a warning against the dangers of living at such a high pitch. The two had several things in common, beginning with their aristocratic backgrounds, and their experiences—many decades apart—as pupils at Harrow. Both men were dazzled by the story of Napoleon's rise and fall, and both kept cherished busts of the great French leader on their desks. Churchill was especially fascinated by Byron's poetic meditation on Napoleon's un-bounded ambition ("a fever at the core," the poet called it). Between the two world wars Churchill was a member of the Byron Society, and one of his most treasured possessions was a seventeen-volume edition of By-ron's works he purchased in 1906. In his only novel, *Savrola*—published when he was twenty-five—Churchill created an imaginary state to serve as the backdrop to the Byronic escapades of his young protagonist, a val-iant defender of liberty and romance whose cast of mind is described as "vehement, high and daring."[3]

Like Byron, Churchill was the chronicler of his own history. In a series of books written at a rapid pace in his early twenties he created vivid descriptions of his early adventures as a soldier and war correspon-dent. "When I was 25 years old," he said in old age, "I had, I believe, written as many books as Moses." Thanks to this torrent of prose in five books and many newspaper articles, almost everyone in Britain knew of young Churchill's brave deeds on three continents between 1895 and 1900. He lived the adventures of a storybook character—fighting with the Bengal Lancers on the Indian frontier; scouting for rebels with the Spanish army in Cuba; traveling along the Nile to take part in what was to prove the last great cavalry charge of the British Army in the nine-teenth century; and, most dramatic of all, surviving capture by the Boers in South Africa, and then making his escape across hundreds of miles of unfriendly territory. As a prominent magazine of the day remarked, "He has both acted his romance and written it."[4]

Young Churchill lacked the rugged good looks of a Byronic hero—his pale, round face was no match for the poet's dark, chiseled features—but he played the part with enthusiasm. He enjoyed taking risks, loved dramatic gestures, brooded intensely but not long over his failures, and often wore his heart on his sleeve. He thought playing for high stakes was the only way to live. This path had been blazed by his father, whose impetuous character, volatile career, and early death at forty-five had inspired at least one prominent eulogist to compare Lord Randolph to Lord Byron.

"The two men resembled each other," the editor of the *Saturday Review* wrote of Randolph and the poet shortly after the statesman's death in 1895. "Mr. Matthew Arnold said of Lord Byron that he was the greatest elemental force in English poetry since Shakespeare; and it would be as true, we think, to say that Lord Randolph Churchill was the greatest elemental force in English politics since Cromwell." Such praise, exaggerated though it was, made a great impression on Winston, who later called the whole tribute in the *Saturday Review* "the best article" on his father that "had appeared anywhere."[5]

Young Winston Churchill succumbed to Byron's political romanticism with all his heart. Many of his Edwardian contemporaries perfectly understood its effect on him. Admirers saw Churchill as a reformer determined to improve the lives of ordinary people, and his words and manner reminded them of a misty past when the poor and the weak had gallant champions. As one newspaper editor remarked, young Churchill's dashing style brought to mind "the clatter of hoofs in the moonlight, the clash of swords on the turnpike road. It is the breath of romance stirring the prosaic air of politics." A friend said of him, "His world was built and fashioned in heroic lines. He spoke its language."[6]

Believing himself a hero, Churchill worked the magic of making others believe it, too. Byron's verse—so full of energy, passion, and political idealism—provided a spur for the young man's imagination, giving him a way of seeing the world, and also a way of understanding how the world would see him.

Churchill's romanticism was not confined to affairs of state. Biographers have often dismissed the notion that he thought much about falling in love, portraying him as a young man who was awkward around women, and whose occasional efforts at flirtation were the halfhearted actions of someone merely "going through the motions."

The reality is much different. Far from being shy or inexperienced, he was still in his teens when he became an enthusiastic champion of the music-hall beauties in London, risking a scandal one night at the Empire Theatre when he started a riot after standing up in the festive crowd and launching a rousing tribute to the charms of the assembled women, who were then under attack from anti-vice campaigners. "Where does the Englishman in London always find a welcome?" nineteen-year-old Winston Churchill asked his fellow revelers before he was thrown out. "Who is always there to greet him with a smile and join him in a drink? Who is ever faithful, ever true?—the Ladies of the Empire Promenade."

From the comfort of middle age, Churchill recalled this outburst as his first public address, wryly remarking, "In these somewhat unvirginal surroundings I . . . made my maiden speech."[7]

During his twenties and early thirties he pursued three of the most beautiful women of his time, and made such a powerful impression on each that even though they declined his marriage proposals they remained his devoted friends far into old age. All three remembered him not as a callow, uncertain youth, but as a stylish character who played polo, was fond of visiting galleries and museums, often attended plays in the West End, read voraciously, and pursued women with great passion.

The elegant young beauty Consuelo Vanderbilt—his cousin by marriage—described his character in those days as "ardent and vital" and said he had "every intention of getting the most out of life, whether in sport, in love, in adventure or in politics."[8]

He was so "ardent" that when he finally decided to marry, he spent a week away from his fiancée to undertake an eleven-hundred-mile round-trip to a remote Scottish castle, where another young woman equally devoted to him was waiting for an explanation of his decision. The story of that emotionally fraught journey—made only three weeks before his wedding in London—is the subject of a later chapter, where it is told for the first time.

As a bachelor, he made an effort to play the dandy, carrying a walking stick and wearing a glossy top hat, starched wing collar, and frock coat with a sleek watch chain. His taste for fine clothing extended even to his choice of underclothes, which were made of an expensive silk weave. "It is essential to my well-being," he said in defense of his yearly expenditure on silk underwear. It was a typical extravagance for him, along with his fondness for other luxuries like champagne and fine cigars. "There has never been a day in my life," he reflected, "when I could not order a bottle of champagne for myself and offer another to a friend."[9]

Even at the outset of his career his well-chosen words and ready wit drew attention. In 1900, as he was on the verge of winning his first election to Parliament, he defined a political candidate as someone "who is asked to stand, wants to sit, and is expected to lie." The young man could also be amusingly satirical about the competitive nature of his glittering Edwardian era, judging the bejeweled women of his social circle as though each aspired to be another Helen of Troy. When a friend suggested that a certain young lady's face might launch at least two hundred ships, Churchill replied, "By no means. A covered sampan or small gunboat at most."[10]

In his fifties Churchill gave his own account of his life up to the beginning of his political career. *My Early Life* ends as the Edwardian age is beginning and does so abruptly, leaving the reader to wonder how this remarkable young man—still unmarried, and still untested as a politician in 1901—will make his way to the front ranks in a system dominated by much older, and much more experienced, men. In the following pages I take up the story where Churchill left off, tracing his progress from a novice politician to one of the most prominent members of the British Cabinet, a journey that will take him from the beginning of his twenty-sixth year to the end of his fortieth year. In the last chapters of the story, when the new century was facing its first assault from Germany, all eyes were on him as he served as First Lord of the Admiralty and readied the British fleet for action. In those heady days his was still the face of youth in the government, and many expected him to emerge from the war as the next prime minister.

But, within a year, everything went wrong. One by one his plans met with failure or stagnated for want of support. Friends turned against him, and enemies rejoiced in his downfall. Too late, the young politician discovered that he had placed too much faith in men who let him down, and in big ideas that didn't work.

Blamed for the disastrous Gallipoli campaign in the eastern Mediterranean, he was attacked in the British press as "a danger to this country" and soon lost his high position in the government. The German press mocked him by suggesting that the title "Earl of Gallipoli" should be given to him, and joked that he was London's modern Lucifer: "He has fallen from the heavens—the most beautiful morning star of some London seasons." In late 1915 he shed the last trappings of power and went to France to fight in the trenches, humbly donning the uniform of a major. What he learned from failure was crucial to his later success, but it was a devastating setback whose sting he would feel for years.[11]

Between his rise and fall he built a modern navy, experimented with radical social reforms and did battle with others who thought he wasn't radical enough, survived various threats on his life, made powerful enemies and a few good friends, fell in love (several times), became a husband and father, annoyed and delighted two British monarchs, took the measure of the German military machine as he rode at the side of Kaiser Wilhelm on maneuvers, risked his life in the air as a pilot in training, authorized executions of notorious murderers, and faced deadly artillery barrages on the Western Front.

Proud and exuberant, he delighted in his ability to master the art of politics and proved time and again that he could outwit older and much more experienced rivals. His impressive skills as a legislator and administrator surprised both admirers and critics and taught him how to overcome bureaucratic and political obstacles to get things done quickly. Embracing the new reforming spirit of the Edwardian age, he learned to question the easy assumptions of his own aristocratic upbringing and to explore fresh approaches to old problems. Professional and personal disappointments schooled him in the virtue of patience and the dangers of overconfidence. In his friendships he came to treasure loyalty and to be wary of betrayal.

By the end of his first forty years he had a good understanding of how far his talents could take him, and how far he could fall. While political ideas changed with the times, what remained constant was his obedience to that bold, early declaration, "I believe in personality." Exploring the heart of that personality is the aim of this biography.

In a lifetime that stretched from November 30, 1874—when Disraeli was prime minister—to January 24, 1965—when the music of the Beatles was Britain's most famous export—Winston Churchill played many parts on the world stage. If he had died when he was forty—when his fortunes were low, and his youth behind him—his story would still be one of the best of the century, in part a riveting drama of ambition, in part a sobering tragedy. Fortunately, there was a second act.

PART I

1901—1905

I

A NEW WORLD

On a frigid winter night at the turn of the last century a young man of twenty-six sat in a stuffy railway carriage writing to a beautiful woman. The view from his window was of a dark, snow-swept prairie that seemed to go on forever under a vast, starless sky. More than four thousand miles from home, he was tired and lonely. His last stop had been St. Paul, Minnesota, and straight ahead was the Canadian border.

"In the train to Winnipeg," Winston Churchill noted in black ink at the top of his stationery, then added the date, "20 Jan. 1901," and—skipping the salutation—began simply "Pamela." He was writing to the great love of his young life, a glamorous figure back home whose charm and good looks had earned her praise as "the brightest star in London's social firmament." As he told her early in their relationship, she exercised "a strange fascination" over him. Unfortunately for him, many other men felt the same way.

For at least two years Winston had been sending her long letters full of devotion. "My love is deep and strong," he declared in one letter. "Nothing will ever change it." They had become acquainted in India, when both were twenty-two. He was a cavalry officer and she was the daughter of a colonial official. They took an elephant ride together, dined at her home, and made polite conversation at parties. Then, about a year and a half later, when they were both back in England, Winston resolved to capture her heart. But he found the beauty, with her seductive gray eyes, porcelain complexion, and smooth dark hair, besieged by other suitors. She was the center of attention at every ball and managed her time with various men so successfully that one of her society friends later referred to her lightheartedly as "the most accomplished plate-spinner" of her day.

Undeterred by competition, Churchill tried to impress her with the power of his words. One morning a heavy bundle arrived at her door containing the manuscript of his novel, *Savrola,* and a letter explaining that the story offered "a mirror" of the author's mind. If she honored him by looking into it, he wrote, "I am sure it will gain beauty by the reflection." When this and similar tactics failed to win her over, he raised the stakes. "Marry me," he wrote a few months later, "and I will conquer the world and lay it at your feet."[1]

He may have taken this extravagant promise seriously, but Pamela Plowden didn't. So, for the time being, he went back to pursuing his passions for soldiering and writing, and hoped for another chance to impress her. Separated from her by thousands of miles in South Africa during the Boer War—Britain's fight with the fiercely independent Dutch settlers over gold, diamonds, and empire—Churchill kept his love alive by periodically gazing at three different portraits of Pamela tucked into a special wallet. During his imprisonment by the Boers in late 1899, he wrote her a brave, jaunty note from Pretoria: "Among new and vivid scenes I think often of you." His plight couldn't help but move her. When his mother gave Pamela the news that he had escaped from prison and was safe, she responded with a two-word telegram: "Thank God."

Returning home a hero, he was emboldened to try his luck with her again, thinking that he knew her heart. "No one would understand her as I do," he told his mother. On a fine October day in 1900 he proposed. He chose a suitably inspiring spot. His friend the Countess of Warwick invited Pamela to spend a weekend amid the medieval grandeur of her home at Warwick Castle. With soaring towers and battlements as a backdrop, the hopeful suitor asked Pamela to go punting on the River Avon, which flows majestically beside the castle. Everything went well until they were gliding along and he asked the question. She turned him down and broke his heart.[2]

He was still under her spell—still convinced that she was "the only woman I could ever live happily with"—when he left home in December to lecture on his South African adventures in a hastily arranged tour of Canada and the United States. Now—three months after his proposal—here he was in the dim light of the railcar writing yet another letter to her. As his train sped across northern Minnesota toward the Canadian border, his heartbreaking experience at the romantic castle must have seemed like something out of a bad dream. Perhaps he was thinking that one more letter from a remote part of the globe would catch her fancy and soften her resistance.

In the few years since his first acquaintance with Pamela in India, he had become an international celebrity, a "boy wonder" who could fight and write, and whose future seemed glowing. The newspapers in Winnipeg were trumpeting his visit as a major event, and a record crowd was expected at his lecture. In big black letters one ad for his forthcoming appearance at the Winnipeg Theatre began: "Winston Spencer Churchill. The War As I Saw It." Ticket prices started at fifty cents and went all the way up to a dollar and a half.

Besides *Savrola*, other titles on display in the shop windows of Winnipeg were *London to Ladysmith Via Pretoria*, the tale of his flight to freedom in South Africa; and *The River War*, his two-volume account of the British campaign in the Sudan, where he had fought so bravely. Of this last book, published in 1899, the American war correspondent Richard Harding Davis wrote, "It was a work that one would expect from a Lieutenant General when, after years of service in Egypt, he laid down his sword to pen the story of his life's work. From a Second Lieutenant, who had been on the Nile hardly long enough to gain the desert tan, it was a revelation."

Winston had promised the world to Pamela, and he was the kind of man who thought he could give it to her. Yet she had turned him down. And now, no matter where he was, her image still haunted him, and he still believed that she had a place in the grand future he envisioned for himself. "There is that between us," he wrote her on the train, "which if it should grow no stronger, will last forever."[3]

Money was one of the major obstacles in their relationship. Society expected a woman of Pamela's great beauty to marry a man with an impressive fortune. "She ought to be a rich man's wife," declared the urbane Colonel John Brabazon—commander of Churchill's cavalry regiment—when he heard that Pamela and Winston were not going to marry. Churchill, though he was the grandson of a duke, had inherited relatively little money. Lord Randolph left many debts behind, and Winston's fun-loving, gregarious mother was a hopeless spendthrift. (As a friend said of Jennie, "Life didn't begin for her on a basis of less than forty pairs of shoes.")

The Marlborough fortune—greatly enhanced by a few million dollars when Consuelo Vanderbilt married into the family—was in the hands of Winston's cousin "Sunny," otherwise known as Charles Richard John Spencer-Churchill, 9th Duke of Marlborough. For a couple of years—until Consuelo gave birth to the first of her two sons in 1897—Winston was next in line to inherit the title and all the riches that came with it, including his birthplace, Blenheim Palace. But he didn't show much interest in becoming a mere duke when so many other paths of glory seemed open to him. Even his own grandmother—a Victorian relic who wore lace caps and used an ear trumpet—didn't think he would make a good nobleman. He was too ambitious and driven. "Your first duty," the old dowager duchess had solemnly informed Consuelo when she married Sunny, "is to have a child, and it must be a son, because it would be intolerable to have that little upstart Winston become Duke."[4]

To most people, Sunny seemed a prickly and condescending character, but Winston—who was three years younger—was one of his few loyal friends and always tried to see the best in him. "Sunny and I were like brothers," Churchill later said of their early relationship. The young duke was proud of his cousin and was happy to allow him the freedom to come and go at Blenheim more or less as he pleased. In 1900 he even allowed him to take over his old bachelor chambers in fashionable Mayfair at 105 Mount Street. Churchill moved there just one month before proposing to Pamela.[5]

A new job also came to Winston at this time, but it didn't do anything to improve his financial prospects. In fact, it didn't pay a penny. At the beginning of October the young hero of the Boer War successfully launched his political career by winning a seat in the House of Commons as a Conservative member for the Manchester suburb of Oldham. Churchill's victory was an early signal of the party's great triumph in the autumn general election of 1900, and he was immediately hailed as a rising political star who would do much to enliven the Commons when it met in February. In these circumstances proposing to Pamela may have seemed a good idea.

But with no sign yet that MPs would one day be paid for their work, he couldn't offer a new bride much in the way of security.

Pamela's close friend and great benefactor in society, Lady Granby, later Duchess of Rutland—and a second mother to Pamela, whose own mother had died of a snake bite in India several years earlier—had no doubt advised her to wait for a proposal from a more prosperous suitor. Churchill knew that he was at a disadvantage. Before he went to South Africa, he wrote Pamela in reference to their relationship, "For marriage, two conditions are necessary—money and the consent of both parties. One certainly, both probably are absent." Unable to win her consent, he did at least make a gallant effort to prove he could earn a small fortune if he needed to. He devised an ambitious plan immediately on his return from South Africa.

In demand as a speaker, he arranged to spend an entire month after the general election giving talks on the Boer War in more than two dozen British towns. He boasted that he could make £2,000 from the tour, which in those days was equal to the annual salary of the typical editor of a London newspaper. As it happened, the audiences were so large in November that he earned twice that figure. And this paled beside the riches he hoped to make from his North American tour, which began that December and was nearing its conclusion when he boarded the train taking him to frosty Winnipeg.[6]

Wearing a derby and a stylish double-breasted overcoat with a fur collar, Churchill arrived in Winnipeg around lunchtime on Monday, January 21, 1901. He was welcomed by a small committee that included a dapper grain tycoon who had become the province's lieutenant governor. The temperature was around ten degrees Fahrenheit, a bitterly cold wind was scattering snow in the streets, and the mood of the city was grim. The weather wasn't the cause of the long faces among the residents. They were used to the cold.

It was the latest news of the day that had cast a shadow over this remote outpost of the empire—"fourteen hundred miles from any British town of importance," as Churchill described it. The big headline in the morning paper announced the impending event that had unsettled so many loyal Canadians: QUEEN VICTORIA ON DEATHBED. HER LAST HOURS.

News of the eighty-one-year-old monarch's failing health had spread widely during the last few days, and now that her end seemed near, the queen's many subjects in the empire were trying to come to grips with the realization that the old order was fading fast. "It appeared as if some monstrous reversal of the course of nature was about to take place," one historian later observed. "The vast majority of her subjects had never known a time when Queen Victoria had not been reigning over them." Her death was seen as a monumental event even by those who watched at her bedside as she endured the common suffering of a last illness. Her final hours, said the Duke of Argyll, were "like a great three-decker ship sinking. She kept on rallying and then sinking."[7]

Before starting off on his journey to Canada, Churchill had seen the first reports that the queen was gravely ill, and he had mentioned this in his letter to Pamela. Though he knew only a few details of the unfolding drama back home, he was already trying to imagine what lay in store for the post-Victorian world.

In the short term he worried that Parliament would be dissolved and that he would have to stand for election again in the coming weeks. That would mean canceling what remained of his tour and losing the lecture fees. He was trying to put a lighthearted spin on this unhappy prospect when he wrote Pamela: "See how [the queen's death] complicates and clouds all my plans, disturbing not only nations but Winstons."[8]

For the moment, however, the imperial drama was good for business at the Winnipeg Theatre's box office. In a city of only fifty thousand people, more than a thousand tickets had been sold for Churchill's evening lecture, and so few regular seats were left that extra chairs were being added at the back of the hall and down in the orchestra pit. For these Canadians living so far away from the little world of British royals, aristocrats, and MPs, Lord Randolph's son represented the closest link to the ruling class of the empire. It was worth a hard-earned dollar to listen to this celebrated figure who had traveled five hundred miles overnight to speak to them at a time when great change was in the air.

The high expectations of his visit delighted Churchill, for his lectures had not gone well on the other side of the border. Instead of improving on what he had earned from his talks in Britain, his American tour had experienced so many setbacks that he was making less than half of what he had collected at home. In some cities the audiences had been sparse or unsympathetic, or both. In Washington, D.C., his share of the box office receipts was the equivalent of only £50; in Baltimore it was £35; in Hartford it was an embarrassing £10.

Many Americans of German and Dutch descent identified with the independent Boers and didn't look kindly on an Englishman who had made a name for himself fighting for the colonial power. As for Irish-Americans, many of whom nursed long-standing grievances against the English, Churchill found that they "showed themselves actively hostile. . . . In Chicago I encountered vociferous opposition." On more than one occasion an audience cheered when Churchill's illustrated lecture included a "magic-lantern" slide of a fearsome-looking Boer farmer armed for battle. Churchill's response was to admit the fighting prowess of the old Dutch settlers, but also to point out that he had not been able to admire the Boer warriors at a safe distance. "You are right to clap them," he said, "[but] you haven't got to fight them."[9]

(Churchill proved early on that he could handle disruptions. During his election campaign in October someone had made fun of his youth by shouting, "Does your mother know you're out?" to which he replied, "Yes, sir, and what is more, when the poll is declared, my mother will know that I am in.")[10]

Churchill's tour was managed by a flamboyant American promoter named Major James Pond, who was himself a war hero (he won the Medal of Honor in the Civil War). The old major had a habit of making exaggerated promises to his star lecturers, boasting of full houses and rich returns, and then offering elaborate excuses when the results proved otherwise. His most famous client, Mark Twain, once remarked to another lecturer, "If you got half as much as Pond prophesied, be content & praise God—it has not happened to another." But Churchill learned the truth the hard way, discovering too late that he wasn't being properly promoted, and that the major was taking an unfair share of the ticket sales. A quarrel broke out between the two, and the young lecturer threatened to abandon the tour when it was only half finished. For his part, "the vulgar Yankee impresario," as Churchill called him, complained that his client was taking advantage of him by living lavishly on the road and sticking him with the bills.

"Do you know what that young man did?" an indignant Major Pond asked a friend. "He drank a pint of champagne for breakfast every morning, and I had to pay for it."[11]

The feud escalated on Churchill's December tour of eastern Canada. Thinking that he now enjoyed a "home" advantage over his Yankee impresario, he made it clear that he wouldn't come back to finish the tour in the States unless he received more of the profits. The major surprised his rebellious client by showing up at the lecture in Ottawa on December 27 and confronting him backstage.

A tall man with broad shoulders and a long gray beard, he looked like a biblical patriarch towering over a cornered sinner as he wagged his finger at Churchill (who was just under five feet, eight inches tall) and demanded that the tour continue without any interruptions. The young man's response was to dig in his heels, declaring that he was canceling his sold-out appearance the next night in the Ontario city of Brantford.

"Pond, I won't go," he said. "There's nothing in it for me. Look at this great affair [his lecture in Ottawa], and I only get $300 out of it."

"Do you refuse to go to Brantford?" asked Major Pond.

"I do. . . . I will not go there or anywhere else under present arrangements."

The old major wasn't used to such insubordination. He had won his Medal of Honor in brutal hand-to-hand combat with the band of Confederate raiders led by William Quantrill, a ruthless enemy, and he wasn't about to defer to young Churchill without a fight.

He poured out his complaints to the press, and soon newspapers on both sides of the border were casting Pond as the victim of an ungrateful English aristocrat who cared for nothing but money, and who wouldn't honor his obligations. "Winston Churchill is a thoroughly unpopular man in this city tonight," wrote a Canadian reporter after refunds were given to the disappointed audience whose evening had been ruined.[12]

"Your statements to the press did considerable harm," Churchill angrily told Pond, who quickly realized that the wave of bad publicity was threatening to get out of hand and damage his own reputation on the lecture circuit. In this standoff between the old war hero and the new, the old one finally blinked and surrendered to Churchill's demand for a fair share of the profits.

"Peace has . . . been patched up on my terms," Winston proudly reported in a letter to his mother, "and I propose to go through with the tour."

Gritting his teeth, he prepared to resume the grueling schedule that would take him to Michigan, Illinois, Missouri, and Minnesota before returning him to Canada for his talk at Winnipeg. In the end he couldn't afford to give up the fees for his remaining lectures. What he couldn't fix was the damage done by Pond's false portrayal of him, which was especially regrettable because there was one person in Canada whose good opinion he was desperate to have.

At the very time he was engaged in this public feud, he was staying at the governor general's official residence in Ottawa, and among the other guests was Pamela Plowden, who was visiting her friend Lady Minto—wife of the governor general. Winston had known for weeks that he and Pamela would be in the same place in Canada at the same time, and that, if all went well in his tour, he would have another chance to show her that his success wasn't fleeting, and that the problem of earning money was one he could easily solve. Instead, when he arrived for his stay with Lord and Lady Minto at elegant Rideau Hall, the tour was limping along, and he was caught in the unexpected storm of criticism over his dispute with Pond.

During their brief time together Pamela was polite but distant. "Very pretty and apparently quite happy" was Winston's general observation of the woman who had turned down his proposal only two months earlier. "We had no painful discussions" was the best he could tell his mother when he wrote her about his talks with Pamela. He had been expecting to share a moment of triumph and wanted Pamela to see him basking in the praise of his Canadian audiences, and living well on a steady flow of dollars from his lectures. But, thanks to Pond, that triumph was diminished. Churchill left Ottawa under a cloud, and Pamela soon returned to her busy social life in London. The old major—who was to die less than three years later—never knew how much he had bungled his young Englishman's tour.[13]

The long journey that took Churchill halfway across North America to Winnipeg also had its share of disappointments, including a controversy sparked by charges that he was rude to callers at his hotel in St. Paul. Without bothering to get his side of the story, a local newspaper called him a "cad of first water" and suggested that he suffered from "boyish petulancy." For many Americans, Churchill was too sure of himself, and too proud of the British Empire, to be likable, and they were quick to find fault. Even the bighearted Theodore Roosevelt took an instant "dislike" to him when they met in the first week of his tour, later criticizing young Churchill for showing "an inordinate thirst for that cheap form of admiration which is given to notoriety." It was an odd charge coming from a man so fond of the attention given to his presidency that he famously exclaimed, "I have got such a bully pulpit!" When she was asked in old age why her father didn't care for Churchill, Alice Roosevelt Longworth said, "Because they were so alike."[14]

Though Winnipeg's size and location may have seemed unpromising, the city proved to be the best stop on Churchill's tour because it finally gave him the chance to address a large and fully sympathetic audience. When he arrived in the snowy darkness to give his lecture at the Winnipeg Theatre, he was encouraged by the sight of five hundred people waiting outside for standing-room tickets. Few noticed his arrival, but then he was almost unrecognizable bundled up inside a heavy fur coat he had purchased that afternoon at the Hudson's Bay Company store on Main Street.

Backstage, he rushed to the curtain and peeked out to get a preview of his audience. As the manager would later determine, it was the largest crowd in the theater's history, and included all classes, from the civic leaders comfortably seated in the boxes to the farm laborers pressed against the back walls. The cream of society who sat closest to the stage presented an impressive view. Churchill joked that the men were in evening dress, and the "ladies half out of it."[15]

"Crowds stirred his blood," Churchill wrote of his hero in *Savrola*, and no doubt there was a stirring in his own veins as the lights went down, the curtain rose, and he took the stage. After "a liberal outburst of applause," he began to tell the extraordinary story of how he had sailed to South Africa as a war correspondent, come under attack from well-armed Boer fighters while accompanying British troops on an armored train, been taken prisoner after a fierce battle, and escaped on his own after only three weeks in captivity. Caught up in the drama of the tale, the audience made hardly a sound as Churchill described his efforts to find his way to freedom by using the stars to guide his escape while the Boers searched for him in vain. Finding a temporary safe haven among civilian workers secretly supporting the British, he hid out for a few days in a coal mine.

"My only companions," he told the hushed crowd, "were numbers of white rats with pink eyes. However, I was furnished every morning with copies of Boer newspapers in which I read accounts of my own capture in different disguises each day. The Boers have been reputed to be an ignorant and uncivilized lot, but in the respect of intelligent anticipation and fertile imagination I can say as a journalist that their newspapers are the equal of anything produced in the civilized world."

Witty at times, melodramatic at others, he kept the audience in suspense as he described being smuggled aboard a train headed to Portuguese East Africa, where he showed up a free man—though weary and unkempt—at the British consulate. Even now, he was still relishing his feat, obviously pleased with himself for having beaten the odds. "The stars in their courses," he said of his escape in the darkness, "fought for me." When his lecture came to a close, and the cheers and applause died away, some in his audience must have been wondering what the stars had in store for him next. At twenty-six he had already done enough to fill several lives.

That he was expecting big things, there can be no doubt. He knew from the news of the queen's illness that great changes were coming soon. To his audience, he read out the latest bulletins about her condition, and when the lecture ended late that night, many expected to wake the next morning to hear Victoria was dead. Anxious for more news, Churchill went home with the lieutenant governor to spend the night at Government House. He was a good guest, singing the praises of Winnipeg. It was "a great city," he said, and was vital to the empire's future. "The Canadian west is Britain's bread shop," he declared, "and when I go back I shall tell the electors of my constituency that I have spoken to those who supply them with their bread." These words, he later noted with satisfaction, made his listeners "purr" with pride.[16]

* * *

It was one o'clock the next afternoon when Winnipeg received the news by wire from Ottawa that the queen had died at her home on the Isle of Wight. "Our Good Queen Is Dead," began one announcement. Mourning bells were already ringing when Churchill made his way to the station, where he was scheduled to leave town shortly after two on a train of the Great Northern Railway that would take him back to the States. Some merchants had placed black-bordered portraits of the queen in their shop windows. On a pillar in the city hall square a stone bust of her was draped in black.

Churchill was touched by the quick response to the news. "This city far away among the snows," he later remarked, "began to hang its head and hoist half-masted flags."

He had received word that Parliament would not be dissolved, and that he would be able to complete the remaining ten days of his tour. His passage was booked on a ship leaving New York at the beginning of February. For two months of work his total earnings would amount to £1,600—far below the £5,000 he had hoped for at the outset. Yet, when all his lecture money was combined with payments for his writing over the past two years, he had every reason to be happy with the total sum. "I am very proud of the fact," he wrote his mother, "that there is not one person in a million who at my age could have earned £10,000 without any capital in less than two years."[17]

This was the money that would sustain him over the next few years as he worked to establish himself as a prominent figure in the House of Commons. He now seemed to have everything he needed to rise in the new age of Victoria's successor, King Edward VII—talent, ambition, courage, connections, a small fortune, and one or two lucky stars. Only Pamela—or perhaps someone very like her—was missing from the picture.

In New York a reporter asked him to clarify a detail in the story of his South African escape: "It has been said that a Dutch maiden fell in love with you and assisted you to flee. You yourself have said it was the hand of Providence. Which is true?"

Churchill was prompt in his reply. "It is sometimes the same thing," he said, laughing good-naturedly over the intriguing link between love and the stars.[18]

II

A Family Affair

After five years of chasing adventure in various parts of the globe—with more than sixty thousand miles of travel behind him—Churchill returned home exhausted on the night of February 10, 1901. His cozy chambers were waiting for him at the stately terra-cotta building in Mayfair where cousin Sunny was the leaseholder, and there were bundles of mail and newspapers needing to be sorted and read. He deserved a few weeks of leisure to catch up on his affairs and renew his acquaintance with life in London—"that great rain-swept heart of the modern world," as H. G. Wells called it. There was also the novel pleasure of regularly occupying the same bed. As he later observed, "For more than five months I had spoken for an hour or more almost every night except Sundays, and, often twice a day, and had travelled without ceasing, usually by night, rarely sleeping twice in the same bed. And this had followed a year of marching and fighting with rarely a roof or bed at all."[1]

But he had timed his return so that there was little chance of enjoying anything more than a brief rest. When King Edward—bearlike in his huge ermine cape—opened Parliament four days later, Winston was there looking appropriately solemn and dignified in mourning clothes for the late queen. After taking the oath as a new member that afternoon, he waited less than a week to deliver his maiden speech. For less celebrated newcomers, months and even years might pass before they dared address the House, but Churchill couldn't wait to capitalize on the whirlwind of publicity that preceded him and to show that he was worthy of the attention. After all, he had spoken to much larger audiences in recent times, so he wasn't daunted by the glare of the Parliamentary spotlight.

This, however, was an audience like no other. The House of Commons was home to many of the best speakers in the land, sophisticated debaters who knew all the rhetorical tricks, and who had been sharpening their skills against each other for years. Some of the most distinguished had given their own maiden speeches when Churchill was no more than a toddler. The leader of the House of Commons, the lean, unflappable patrician Arthur Balfour, had won his first election just before Winston was born and had long ago established his reputation as a sophisticated debater whose nimble reasoning could quickly cause an opponent's argument to unravel. On the opposition bench the generally acknowledged master was forty-nine-year-old Herbert Asquith, an Oxford-educated barrister whose blunt, methodical style had prompted his fellow Liberals to call him "the sledgehammer."[2]

Having demonstrated on his lecture tour that he could spin a good tale, Churchill now meant to show how well he could drive home an argument. He had been looking forward to this moment for years and spent the days leading up to it polishing his remarks and committing them to memory, making sure that nothing would go amiss. At his chambers he stood before a mirror pretending he was addressing the House. This became a common method of preparation for him, to the annoyance of others nearby. "All day," recalled a friend, "he might be heard booming away in his bedroom, rehearsing his facts and flourishes to the accompaniment of resounding knocks on the furniture."

Everything had to be perfect, from the way he tugged at the lapel of his long frock coat to his manner of beating the air with a clenched fist. As a final safeguard, he decided to write out a short list of his major points and keep them handy while he spoke. But he had great confidence in the power of his memory. "If I read a column of print four times over," he boasted to a parliamentary sketch writer, "I commit it so perfectly to memory that I could forthwith recite it without an omission or error."[3]

A few years earlier, he had put together some of his views on oratory in a manuscript he called "The Scaffolding of Rhetoric," concluding that all great speeches use common words in pleasing rhythms to cast complex ideas in memorable images. He was especially fond of William Jennings Bryan's impassioned criticism in 1896 of the gold standard:

"You shall not press down upon the brow of labor this crown of thorns; you shall not crucify mankind upon a cross of gold." From early adulthood to old age, Churchill's eye and ear were attuned to the discovery of arresting analogies that might become, as he put it in his essay, "the watchwords of parties and the creeds of nationalities."

Though proud of his reputation as a young man of adventure, he also wanted to earn respect as a man of learning. He regretted not having a university education, but he was always his own best teacher, and had made good use of his independent reading. In political battles he wanted to excel by making knowledge his sword, entering each fray with more facts and a deeper understanding of the issues than his opponents. While other politicians were content to get their information from a scattering of newspapers and party pamphlets, he devoured whole shelves. As an early observer of his career amusingly noted, Churchill began "living with Blue Books and sleeping with encyclopedias." And some of those close to him doubted that he slept much. "His power of work is prodigious," wrote a family friend, "almost commensurate with his passion for it. Whether he ever rests or ever sleeps I do not know."[4]

On February 18 both Asquith and Balfour were in their usual places in the House when MPs began returning from dinner for the evening session. Gaslights hidden behind glass panels high overhead illuminated the narrow debating chamber, dominated at one end by the canopied Speaker's chair and the long table with its books and brassbound oaken boxes. Debates could last until midnight—or much later on occasion—and some visitors to the House thought it looked best at night with "lights blazing and the Chamber full of warmth and glow and animation." When word circulated that Lord Randolph's son was going to speak, the five rows of benches on either side of the floor filled quickly, as did the surrounding galleries for journalists and guests.

Entering the chamber, Churchill found that everyone was watching him closely, curious stares following him as he walked toward his seat clutching a single page of handwritten notes. A reporter thought that the new man was being "eyed as a new actor is eyed on the stage during rehearsals, and of whom a great deal is expected." Several members took note of Winston's choice of a corner seat in the second row behind the government bench, where they had once been accustomed to seeing his father. The son was happy to invite the inevitable comparison with Lord Randolph, whose marble bust adorned a spot only a short distance away in the entrance to the members' lobby.[5]

In his maiden speech Churchill wisely chose to play it safe, avoiding any appearance of a forced effort at eloquence. As friends and family had advised him, it was best to stick to a single subject he knew well and to seem modest in manner and tone if not in fact. The Boer War was continuing to drag on, so he addressed the problem of bringing the struggle to a swift conclusion and creating a just peace. First, the remaining pockets of resistance had to be subdued. He urged a renewed effort that would overwhelm the diehards with greater force and cut off their supplies. It was a reasonable strategy, but he found a way to make it seem the only natural response by describing the effects in terms that anyone in an island nation could understand.

"The Boers," he said near the end of his speech, "will be compelled, with ever-diminishing resources, to make head against ever-increasing difficulties, and will not only be exposed to the beating of the waves, but to the force of the rising tide."

He made it clear, however, that he had no interest in humiliating or wiping out the enemy. Any plan to make their resistance "painful and perilous," he declared, should also "make it easy and honourable for [them] to surrender." He was willing to concede that the other side had its own sense of duty to consider. "If I were a Boer," he said, "I hope I should be fighting in the field." This provoked a few muttered complaints among fellow Tories, but his was a balanced view that won him respect from critics of the war on the opposition benches.

For the close of his speech, he put aside politics to pay tribute to his father's memory, and his words were widely praised afterward as a touching expression of filial piety. He didn't mention Lord Randolph by name, but his reference was all the more effective because it assumed a shared awareness of the Churchill legacy. "I cannot sit down," he said, pausing to look around the packed chamber after speaking for almost three-quarters of an hour, "without saying how very grateful I am for the kindness and patience with which the House has heard me, and which have been extended to me, I well know, not on my own account, but because of a certain splendid memory which many honourable members still preserve."[6]

All in all it was a promising debut and was judged a success by many. The *Daily Telegraph* said that Churchill "satisfied the highest expectations," and the *Daily Express* reported that "he held a crowded House spell-bound." After getting into the flow of his speech he was fine, but he struggled a little at first, folding his arms to hide his nervousness. Some observers were struck by the youthfulness of his appearance, noting that with his smooth, fair complexion he could easily be mistaken for "a lad of eighteen." Others were disappointed to find that he showed few traces of the heroic figure whose adventures they had followed in the press. "There are dozens of men in the House of Commons who look more like the ideal of a daredevil fighter and traveller," complained one reporter. "Perhaps his tailor does not do him justice, but as he stood up in the House of Commons tonight he certainly had little of the taut smartness of the well-knit soldierly figure one expected to see. To be quite frank, he was scholarly and limp."

It didn't help that the young man also had trouble pronouncing the letter *s,* despite taking great pains to overcome the problem. He would struggle with it for years, seeking advice from specialists and endlessly rehearsing tongue-twisters such as "The Spanish ships I cannot see, for they are not in sight."[7]

It was easy to underestimate Winston Churchill. Anyone who knew him well understood that there was much more to him than met the eye. Those who found little evidence of the hero in his appearance couldn't see, for example, that under the supposedly ill-fitting frock coat was a scar on his arm where a doctor at a dusty field hospital had removed a strip of flesh after the Battle of Omdurman. A fellow officer who had suffered what was later called a "shocking sword cut on his right arm" needed a skin graft, and Churchill had volunteered a piece of his own flesh. It was done with a razor, and without anesthesia, and "hurt like the devil." Winston rarely mentioned it, but there had been nothing "scholarly and limp" about his bravery on that day. By comparison, addressing the House was a picnic, and he later described it as an experience both exhausting and inspiring—"terrible, thrilling yet delicious."[8]

* * *

Several spectators who had paid especially close attention to Winston's speech watched him from a cramped row of seats behind a brass screen high above the floor in a gallery reserved for female visitors. Accompanied by Consuelo Marlborough and other women of the Churchill clan, Winston's mother had come to the House to show her support; but in accordance with the rules, her group was tucked away almost out of sight behind the grille of the Ladies' Gallery. It was a dark area filled with grand women in silks and satins and plumed hats—some occupying a "privileged section . . . to which only the Speaker's order admits." But to the members below all these female spectators were merely, as one contemporary novelist put it, "dusky forms, invisible, save as a dim patchwork."

Jennie Churchill knew this spot well, having come to it frequently to hear Randolph in his heyday. She had learned to live with the inconvenience and indignity of the gallery, but was outspoken in her disapproval. "Hidden in Eastern fashion from masculine sight," she wrote in 1908, "fifty or more will sometimes crowd into the small, dark cage to which the ungallant British legislators have relegated them. The ladies in the first row, in a cramped attitude, with their knees against the grille, their necks craned forward, and their ears painfully on the alert if they wish to hear anything, are supposed to enjoy a great privilege. Those in the second row, by the courtesy of the first, may get a peep of the gods below. The rest have to fall back on their imagination or retire to a small room in the rear, where they can whisper and have tea." [9]

Asked in 1885 if the gallery could have its own lights, Herbert Gladstone—the prime minister's son—advised against it. According to the official record of the debate in Parliament, he dismissed the request because "ladies came to the Gallery to hear and see what was going on in the House, and he did not think that the question of light applied in the matter." The record doesn't include what the women sitting in darkness thought of this observation. [10]

For some bachelor MPs the dark remoteness of the Ladies' Gallery had become part of their courtship rituals. Attendants in the corridor separating the tea room from the "cage" were sometimes kept busy exchanging notes between members on the floor and the women they wanted to impress behind the grille. With a fanciful touch, one Edwardian authority on the House described a young member receiving a note after giving a

strong speech: "On reading it he looks up with a pleased smile to the Ladies' Gallery, where two bright eyes are gleaming through the grille."

The women were not supposed to talk in the gallery. No fewer than four
notices commanding silence were posted there. But the whispered conversations were always a source of interest to Jennie. She thought they were an
excellent guide to the changing fortunes of the politicians below and would
listen carefully as society hostesses plotted their next dinner party or young
beauties their next conquest. She had a good ear and, to the amusement of
her friends, could mimic the conversations with devastating accuracy:

> "Is that Mr. ————?" exclaims a pretty blonde to her neighbor.
> "Do lend me your glasses. Yes, it is he. I wonder if he would dine
> with me tonight." ("Sh!" comes from a relative of the man who
> is speaking.) "We are thirteen—so tiresome. I think I must send
> him a note by the usher." ("Sh!") "I can get the answer at once—*so*
> convenient." ("Sh! Sh!") "*Who* is that odious woman hushing me?"[11]

It was partly to encourage an attentive and respectful audience
among the ladies that Jennie arrived early in the gallery with a formidable party of titled relatives to hear Winston's speech. In addition to Consuelo, Duchess of Marlborough (stunning, as always, in her Vanderbilt
jewels), she brought along four of Winston's aunts in all their aristocratic
finery. In youth these sisters of Lord Randolph—Cornelia, Rosamund,
Fanny, and Georgiana—were much admired beauties, and each had
married well. The one who held Winston in the highest regard was Cornelia, Lady Wimborne, a wealthy and influential political hostess whose
invitations to dinners at her London mansion overlooking Green Park
were highly prized. In time Jennie and her well-connected relatives and
friends would prove so effective in promoting Winston's career behind
the scenes that a political rival would complain bitterly, "There's nothing
in Winston. But he's got some of the cleverest women in England at his
back. That's the real secret of his success."[12]

Ever since Randolph's death, Jennie had eagerly employed her influence
on Winston's behalf. With her charm and intimate knowledge of society,
she had eased his adventures abroad and his political ambitions at home

by putting in the right word at the right time to the most useful newspaper editor, general, or statesman. "She left no wire unpulled, no stone unturned, no cutlet uncooked," joked Churchill in middle age. When he had wanted desperately in 1898 to secure a position with Lord Kitchener's army in the Sudan, it was Jennie to whom he turned for help in lobbying everyone from the Prince of Wales on down. "Your wit & tact & beauty," he wrote her, "should overcome all obstacles."[13]

Though tact wasn't usually her strong point, wit and beauty were hers in abundance. The daughter of a merchant and Wall Street speculator who lost fortunes almost as fast as he made them, she grew up in New York and Paris, and at twenty married Randolph—much to the disappointment of his family who had been hoping for a richer bride. Almost from the start the marriage was a troubled one, with much clashing of wills between a proud, erratic husband and a quick-tempered, passionate young wife. But everywhere she went she turned heads, and found admirers. One of those infatuated with her early on, Lord Rossmore, wistfully remarked of her in his old age, "Many Society beauties have come and gone, but I think that few, if any, have ever equaled her."

One of Queen Victoria's granddaughters described Jennie in her prime as a "flashing beauty. . . . Her eyes were large and dark, her mouth mobile with delicious, almost mischievous curves, her hair blue-black and glossy." Margot Asquith recalled being struck with wonder at her first sight of Lady Randolph: "She had a forehead like a panther's and great wild eyes that looked through you; she was so arresting that I followed her about till I found someone who could tell me who she was." Men and women were bewitched by this exotic quality in her appearance—one admirer called her "tropically handsome"—and she accentuated this effect by wearing shiny bracelets and a diamond star in her hair that sparkled whenever she tossed her head.[14]

On one wrist she had a "dainty tattoo" in the form of a serpent. It was the work of Tom Riley, the finest tattoo artist of the time, and occasionally drew stares of shocked disbelief. But it wasn't easy to spot. As the *New York Times* said of Jennie on September 30, 1906, "An elaborate tattoo mark on her left wrist is concealed by a broad bracelet that she always wears when in evening dress, and few know of its presence."[15]

She liked to shock and knew that some people had come to expect her to do and say unconventional things. As an American, she felt entitled to take certain liberties with old-world customs and to speak her mind when the proper thing might have been to hold her tongue. British prejudices against her foreign upbringing annoyed her at first, but she learned to make light of them and, occasionally, to turn them to her advantage. Of her early married life, she recalled, "In England, as on the Continent, the American woman was looked upon as a strange and abnormal creature, with habits and manners something between a Red Indian and a Gaiety Girl. Anything of an outlandish nature might be expected of her. If she talked, dressed, and conducted herself as any well-bred woman would, much astonishment was invariably evinced, and she was usually saluted with the tactful remark, 'I should never have thought *you* were an American.'"

She was not easily intimidated. Once, when she tried to improve her acquaintance with George Bernard Shaw by asking him to lunch, he sent an intemperate response, vaguely referring to his unwillingness as a vegetarian to eat with what he called elsewhere "carnivorous people." His telegram began bluntly, "Certainly not!" and then demanded, "What have I done to provoke such an attack on my well-known habit?" Jennie quickly put him in his place, replying, "Know nothing of your habits; hope they are not as bad as your manners."[16]

The abstemious Shaw was less to her liking than his notoriously self-indulgent rival in the theatrical world—Oscar Wilde. She had a favorite line from one of his plays, and once argued with some male friends when she quoted it and couldn't persuade them that Wilde was the source. She bet them she was right and promptly sent the playwright a note asking him to confirm it. He replied, "How dull men are! They should listen to brilliant women, and look at beautiful ones, and when, as in the present case, a woman is both brilliant and beautiful, they might have the ordinary common sense to admit that she is verbally inspired." And yes, he wrote, she had quoted him correctly when she had told her friends, "The only difference between the saint and the sinner is that every saint has a past, and every sinner has a future!"[17]

Though in her early years her social life kept her too busy to be an attentive mother to Winston and her second son, Jack (an unassuming, but dutiful Churchill), she was such an affectionate and exuberant character that her sons couldn't help but admire her. As boys, they were frustrated by her impulsive ways, never knowing when or where she might turn up. She missed birthdays and left letters unanswered, and breezed in and out of their lives so quickly that she seemed at times more a passing vision than a real person. Winston resented the neglect but tried consoling himself with the idea that she was "a fairy princess"—elusive and ethereal.

Little boys didn't interest her, but young men did, and when Winston came of age, he suddenly found in her an ardent ally on whom he could depend. He came to appreciate her passion for society life—as he discovered its immense usefulness to him—and to admire her willingness on occasion to defy its conventions. He liked her boldness, her loyalty, her impish smile, and easy laughter. The independent streak in her character he attributed to her freewheeling father, whose adventures in the cutthroat world of Wall Street finance always fascinated him. While examining late in life a photograph of his New York grandfather, Leonard Jerome, Churchill remarked, "Very fierce. I'm the only tame one they've produced."[18]

Forty-seven at the time of her son's maiden speech, Jennie was the envy of her close women friends not only because she retained so much of her youthful good looks, but because—five years after Lord Randolph died—she had married one of the handsomest bachelors in England, who was a good twenty years her junior. An avid sportsman and debonair man about town, George Cornwallis-West was none too bright, but Jennie found his athletic figure, military mustache, strong jaw, and bright eyes irresistible. He looked more mature than his years—he was only two weeks older than Winston—and when he fell in love with the widowed Jennie in the late 1890s, he thought "she did not look a day more than thirty, and her charm and vivacity were on a par with her youthful appearance."

He came from a good family but had no fortune to call his own, and his parents were livid that he wanted to throw away his chance at a lucrative match in order to marry a pretty widow of limited means who was almost twice his age. They made such a fuss that, according to one press report, "a social war" nearly broke out between Lady Randolph and George's mother. Most of Jennie's friends and family loyally attended the wedding in July 1900, but the pews reserved for the bridegroom's relations were empty. Normally, a marriage of this kind would have caused a scandal so great that Jennie would have found herself ostracized from much of society. Even the Prince of Wales warned her against marrying young George. But it is a measure of her extraordinary standing in the highest circles that the prince and many others eventually accepted her decision and either attended the ceremony or sent elaborate gifts.

She knew that she was taking a great risk, and that her second marriage might turn out to be a short one. But she was determined to have her romance while she could. As handsome George later said of her, "If something of beauty attracted her, she just had to have it; it never entered her head to stop and think how she was going to pay for it." He didn't seem to realize that he was also one of those things of beauty she craved, and that neither of them ever gave much thought to how they would make their marriage work. "Of course, the glamour won't last forever," she told a friend, "but why not take what you can, and not make yourself or anyone else unhappy when the next stage arrives?"[19]

American papers reported that the wedding ceremony at St. Paul's in Knightsbridge was dignified but "depressing." At the altar George "seemed somewhat nervous," while "Lady Randolph was perfectly self-possessed and looked pleased with herself." In fact, Jennie "appeared to be the only cheery person." Sunny gave the bride away, and Winston did his best to show his support by greeting his mother in the vestry with "a tremendous hug." He wasn't enthusiastic about the marriage, but he didn't want to disappoint her and had declared earlier that he wouldn't try to influence her decision. It was only necessary, he wrote her, "for you to consult your own happiness."[20]

As Winston and others feared, Jennie would come to regret her decision. But in the first year or two of the marriage she was happy, proudly accepting her new identity as plain "Mrs. George Cornwallis-West" instead of "Lady Randolph Churchill." In the short term the only cost of her decision may have been to Winston. Her sensational wedding of

July was followed less than three months later by his proposal to Pamela Plowden. There were many reasons for Pamela to say no, but Jennie's marriage was sure to give any young woman doubts about becoming the daughter-in-law of such an audacious and controversial figure. Agreeing to be Winston's wife meant accepting many burdens—not merely those of his ambitious career and demanding personality, but also those that came with joining a family that included such imposing women as Jennie and Consuelo, and the other grand Churchill ladies who sat in the dark gallery in February and watched their young relation shine for the first time in the House of Commons.

So Winston can't have been surprised when he saw Pamela in London a few weeks later and found that her view of their relationship remained unchanged. She was happy to regard him as a friend, but nothing more. There was only one thing that had changed since he had seen her last. She was, he wrote forlornly to his mother, "more lovely than ever."[21]

III

BORN FOR OPPOSITION

A few years before he won election to Parliament, Churchill was invited to lunch with an old Victorian statesman whose career was nearing its end. A "Falstaffian figure" nicknamed Jumbo, Sir William Vernon Harcourt loved to peer over his gold-rimmed glasses and "whisper the secrets of Parliament" to impressionable young men courting his favor. Every bit of his huge frame—he stood six feet, three inches tall—would shake as he chuckled over his own jokes, most of which he had been telling for years. But young Churchill was in an earnest mood and wanted to know what the future held. What big events might happen next? he asked the old man.

"My dear Winston," answered Sir William, "the experiences of a long life have convinced me that nothing ever happens."

He was only partly teasing. Having enjoyed a long and prosperous life in a century dominated by British economic and military power, Sir William inhabited in his twilight years a comfortable world not unlike that of Sir Leicester Dedlock in Dickens's *Bleak House*—"a world wrapped up in too much jeweller's cotton and fine wool, [which] cannot hear the rushing of the larger worlds, and cannot see them as they circle round the sun." More than most young men of his generation, Churchill had his eye on those larger worlds rushing toward the well-ordered one in which he had been brought up, and he was already bracing himself for the inevitable collisions.

When, in the 1920s, he recalled Harcourt's remark, Churchill observed, "Since that moment, as it seems to me, nothing has ever ceased happening. . . . The smooth river with its eddies and ripples along which we then sailed, seems inconceivably remote from the cataract down which we have been hurled and the rapids in whose turbulence we are now struggling."[1]

To the impatient young Winston of 1901, the future was clouded by the fact that far too many old Victorians were still running the country. The upper ranks of his own party were filled with graybeards, beginning with the Olympian figure of the prime minister, Lord Salisbury, whose family—the legendary Cecils of Hatfield House—had been part of the ruling establishment since Elizabethan times. A shrewd statesman in his best years, Salisbury had grown so ponderous and decrepit that he had become increasingly detached from the daily business of governing. He found breathing difficult, which forced him to sleep sitting up in a chair. (After his death in 1903 it was said that he had fallen from the chair and developed "blood poisoning from an ulcerated leg.") For years the only exercise he had taken was to ride a large "prehistoric tricycle" slowly on an asphalt path around his estate, with a servant trailing behind to push him up hills.

"He thoroughly enjoys his exercise," a visitor to Hatfield had noted of the prime minister, but "is always in terror lest he be ambushed by some of the numerous grandchildren who all think him fair game." (Two had recently been spotted by their mother on a wall near the path awaiting Salisbury's arrival with "huge jugs of water.")[2]

Failing eyesight and forgetfulness plagued the prime minister's last years. He had a habit of dozing off in the House of Lords, his massive beard covering his chest. A *Punch* satire suggested that the only public event guaranteed to keep him awake was "a Brass-band Competition." During one long official ceremony he was drowsily surveying the room with his dark, hooded eyes when he dimly perceived that a man standing nearby was smiling at him. He turned to another man and whispered, "Who is my young friend?" The answer came back, "Your eldest son."

Salisbury's ambitious former private secretary, Lord Curzon, couldn't understand why the old statesman refused to retire, and privately criticized him as "that strange, powerful, inscrutable, brilliant, obstructive deadweight at the top." One evening early in his parliamentary career, Churchill dined with Salisbury in the company of some other young politicians and recalled afterward that, on the way home, one of them had wondered aloud how it must feel to occupy such a high office, "and to be just about to die."[3]

It was widely assumed that whenever Salisbury left office, his place would be filled by Arthur Balfour, his dutiful but haughty nephew. (Told on a visit to New York that a big new skyscraper was fireproof, Balfour regarded it disdainfully and said, "What a pity.") To make sure that the Cecil clan continued to influence public affairs long after his death, the prime minister had filled his administration with so many of his relatives—including a son-in-law as First Lord of the Admiralty—that the political press started calling the government the "Hotel Cecil, Unlimited." Balfour was one of three nephews in important positions, which prompted a critic to remark acidly, "The Spartan woman gave all her sons to her country. The Marquis of Salisbury, not to be outdone in patriotism, adds his nephews."[4]

Even before he won his seat in Parliament, Churchill took pains to cultivate Salisbury's goodwill. He sent him respectful notes and dedicated *The River War* to him, praising the leader as one "under whose wise direction the Conservative Party have long enjoyed power and the nation prosperity." More important, in his first year in the House of Commons, he wasted no time establishing a close friendship with Salisbury's youngest son, Lord Hugh Cecil. Given the family's hold on the party, it was reasonable for Winston to seek a strong bond with Hugh before the next reorganization of the "Hotel Cecil," positioning himself as a kind of honorary member of the family.

Unfortunately, he was slow to realize that Linky—as Hugh was nicknamed—had no desire to follow in his father's footsteps. He was too self-absorbed to become an effective ally for anyone, spending much of his time studying obscure scholarly matters in the palatial comfort of Hatfield House, where the large family library with its priceless collection of old books and manuscripts served as a perfect postgraduate retreat after he completed his formal studies at Oxford. Though he shared Winston's love of drama and fascination with history, he lacked ambition and wasn't interested in the political plums his father liked to hand out to the family. A devout Anglican, he had been tempted to join the clergy but had settled instead for a seat in the House of Commons and a chance to sermonize from time to time on any issue that stirred his eccentric mind.

He was wary of Churchill at first, finding him too impulsive and "rather sentimental, addicted to the sort of sentiment that hangs on a phrase and is not very profound." He liked hard facts, not flights of fancy. Once, when his attention was drawn to a pretty sunset, he glanced at it, and then turned away with the dry comment, "Yes, extremely tasteful."

Yet it was partly Winston's fondness for romantic sentiment that made him think an alliance with Salisbury's son was worth having. The pedantic Linky—whom one contemporary described as having "a little puckered-up youthful old-face perched on the top of a long, thin rickety figure"—was transformed by Winston's overactive imagination into a more exciting companion trailing clouds of aristocratic glory. He saw him as a stalwart Cavalier reborn—"a real Tory, a being out of the seventeenth century," as he later put it, who would join him in a battle to rejuvenate the Conservative Party. (Others, less sympathetic, thought Hugh more closely resembled "an ascetic of the fourteenth century." His own brothers nicknamed him Linky because they so often joked that he looked like the missing evolutionary link.)[5]

In time Churchill's enthusiasm and flattery won over young Cecil. Together with a handful of other MPs—including the handsome society figure Ian Malcolm, who was shortly to become engaged to actress Lillie Langtry's daughter, and a few sons of the aristocracy such as Lord Percy and the Honorable Arthur Stanley—they formed a coterie of independent-minded Tories willing to entertain new ideas and fresh approaches. Winston was eager to stir up trouble, proudly spreading the word that the new group wanted to be known as the "Hooligans." He confided to his circle that he wanted "to develop that invaluable political quality—a desire for mischief." In part his inspiration was the Fourth Party of the early 1880s—his father's small band of political "skirmishers," which Arthur Balfour had briefly joined in an outburst of youthful indiscretion.

Mischief-making wasn't uppermost in his friends' minds. They seemed more interested in having endless discussions over late-night dinners. The general impression among other MPs was that the Hooligans "were really largely a supper club, and it was said in the lobbies that Mr. Malcolm's special function was to pay for the suppers." Usually the group gathered on Thursday nights in one of the dining rooms of the House, but they also traveled to Blenheim and other aristocratic citadels for weekend meetings. Consuelo recalled one of these Hooligan dinners at Blenheim when everyone "lingered until midnight, carried away by Winston's eloquence." (Unlike Churchill, Hugh Cecil was a good and patient listener. "Am I boring you, Lord Hugh?" a garrulous friend once asked. "Not yet," he answered politely.)[6]

For a time the statuesque Duchess of Sutherland—who was only a few years older than Winston—became a muse of sorts to the group. They were invited to her Scottish castle and to the lavish parties she gave at her London mansion, Stafford House. In her ballroom, with "a thousand candles sparkling in their chandeliers," she was always the center of attention and seemed to float effortlessly across the polished floors as she moved among her guests. One recalled that she looked as "slender as a reed, golden hair simply knotted, a skin translucent as the heart of an ocean shell." But some of her glamorous guests wondered what she saw in Winston. After one party at Stafford House, a society gossip complained that Churchill "trampled on the trains of three duchesses" and spilled champagne "into the lap of Lady Helen Stewart, a large blond heiress to whom he devoted himself the entire evening." (Lady Helen— or "Birdie," as she was known in her family—was Winston's second cousin, and a friend since childhood.)[7]

Innocent devotion seems to have been what the duchess wanted from her admirers, and in Churchill she had such a follower. From the start, his unconventional character intrigued her. Much as she enjoyed her parties, she wanted to be known for much more than her social skills and good looks. She saw herself as a social reformer and in recent years had been striving to help working-class families obtain better housing, medical care, and employment. One of her pet projects was reviving the cottage industry of spinners in Scotland who produced the Harris tweed. For her pains, the duchess, whose first name was Millicent, was ridiculed in the popular press as "Meddlesome Millie." She shrugged off the criticism and continued her good work, encouraged in no small part by her stout defenders in the mainstream press. One of the more persuasive was Winston Churchill, who wrote a letter to the *Times* praising her activism and damning an anonymous critic's "sneers about 'versatile duchesses.'"

She liked to challenge the views of the more reactionary members of her upper-class set and was curious to see if the Hooligans could do anything to shake up the Tory party. "As far as a miserable duchess could be an agitator," she said several years later, "I strove to be one." Her much older husband—whom she had married when she was only seventeen—didn't share her curiosity about Churchill's group. He thought they were up to no good, and in a fit of temper told his wife to cancel party invitations she had sent to Hugh and Winston. The old duke soon softened his resistance, however, and Millicent was fond of recalling the incident in later years because she was so amused by the different responses from her two young friends. She told a confidante:

> I still have in my possession the letters they wrote to me in reply. I kept them because they were so characteristic of these two contrasting temperaments. Hugh Cecil wrote: "My dear Millie, I understand and I am sorry. Will you do me a great favour and tell me what day next week you will be free to have lunch with me?" As to Winston, who was entirely lacking in the proverbial urbanity of the Cecils, he wrote such an angry letter that it made me laugh, declaring roundly that he would not set foot in my house as long as the duke lived.[8]

As a show of their political independence, the Hooligans met several times with the former Liberal prime minister Lord Rosebery, sometimes spending weekends at his country homes in Surrey and Buckinghamshire. Churchill turned these weekend visits into real adventures by driving to his destination in a recently acquired automobile. He was so inexperienced behind the wheel, and the vehicle was so noisy, that none of the other Hooligans would ride with him. "I am afraid I disturbed your horses with my motor-car," he wrote Lord Rosebery after one visit. "I am learning to drive at present, so this is rather a dangerous period."

Rosebery wined and dined the group and took delight in the knowledge that the youngest son of old Salisbury—his longtime rival and his successor as prime minister in 1895—was coming to him for political wisdom. Hugh Cecil, however, was embarrassed by his fellow Hooligans' free-spirited enjoyment of the Liberal statesman's hospitality. Churchill said that his friend suffered "from the inconvenience of high moral principles in social matters." Indeed, fastidious Hugh felt compelled to apologize for the Hooligans. "My colleagues behave very badly I am sorry to say," he wrote their host.[9]

But Churchill found these visits reinvigorating, not least because his father had been a close friend of Lord Rosebery. He liked hearing stories about his father's career and was welcomed as a proud son eager to honor Randolph's memory. At a party where many guests besides the Hooligans were present, Rosebery often interrupted the discussions to point affectionately at Winston and announce to everyone: "Pray do not let us come to any conclusion until we have asked the Boy." Few men could have addressed him this way and escaped his anger, but Rosebery could get away with it because of who he was, and because he so clearly admired Winston's precocious intelligence. He and his circle agreed that Randolph's son had "a very old head on young shoulders."

In Rosebery's presence Winston felt in close touch with not only his father's past, but also the grand sweep of historical forces dating back to ancient times. "The Past stood ever at his elbow," he later wrote of the former prime minister, "and was the counsellor upon whom he most relied. He seemed to be attended by Learning and History, and to carry into current events an air of ancient majesty. His voice was melodious and deep, and often, when listening, one felt in living contact with the centuries which are gone, and perceived the long continuity of our island tale."[10]

Winston was dazzled by Rosebery's elegant homes and priceless possessions. One large painting in particular caught his eye. "I carried away quite a queer sensation from the Napoleon picture yesterday," he wrote Rosebery. "It seems pervaded with his personality; and I felt as if I had looked furtively into the very room where he was working, and only just got out of the way in time to avoid being seen."

Because his image of Napoleon had been shaped mostly by his reading, Churchill was dumbstruck when he suddenly encountered the lifelike image of his hero staring at him from the canvas of Jacques-Louis David's *The Emperor Napoleon in His Study at the Tuileries*. Painted only three years before Waterloo and standing about seven feet high, the painting was acquired in the 1880s by Rosebery, whose marriage to a Rothschild heiress had given him the means to buy almost any treasure he wanted. He was known on occasion to rehearse his speeches standing in front of this picture and another one—even larger and just as striking—of George Washington, by Gilbert Stuart (the so-called Lansdowne portrait). "He would use them as the chorus," a family member recalled. Winston's expression of wonder at the magical effect of the Napoleon picture prompted Rosebery to offer him an uncharacteristically candid admission. "I find it," he said of the vivid image, "sometimes coming out of the canvas."[11]

Churchill may have been hoping that the visits to Rosebery's homes and Blenheim would inspire the Hooligans. But his friends regarded these expeditions as larks and weren't looking to cultivate a sense of destiny. They didn't share his particular passion for great men and great monuments. And they lacked his urgent desire to mount a sharp attack on the complacency of the Tory leaders.

In any case Lord Salisbury wasn't worried about the group. He never thought the Hooligans would amount to much, perhaps because he knew his son too well. According to Ian Malcolm, it was the prime minister himself who came up with a clever way to make light of their activities. He jested that they should be rechristened "the Hughligans after his youngest son." The name stuck, and led many Tories to regard the group as merely an object of derision.[12]

Churchill tried to maintain a good relationship with the quirky Hugh long after the Hooligans went their separate ways. But during the year or so when the group was most active, Winston was often frustrated by his friend's tendency to waste time on minor issues. A political dabbler, Hugh was happiest when confronting tangled questions involving fine points only he seemed to understand. With the grave resolve that others brought to questions of war and peace, he opposed a much-debated measure allowing widowers to marry a sister-in-law. Thirty years afterward, Churchill was still shaking his head in amazement over Hugh's "vehement resistance" to the awkwardly titled "Marriage with a Deceased Wife's Sister's Bill." (The issue had been debated for so many years that Gilbert and Sullivan found time to create a mocking rhyme for it: "He shall prick that annual blister/Marriage with deceased wife's sister.")[13]

* * *

In the spring of 1901, while bachelor Hugh was busy warning the House of Commons that allowing a man to marry his dead wife's sister would bring the ways of "the stud farm" to a sacred institution, Winston was preparing to launch an assault on one of his party's most important legislative items. "I was born for opposition," Lord Byron famously declared, and now Churchill was ready for some Byronic drama of his own. He wanted to show Salisbury and the rest of the Hotel Cecil that he was no ordinary backbencher they could take for granted.[14]

The matter at hand was the government's plan for reforming the army, whose reputation had suffered from numerous failures in the Boer War. Everyone knew that a reorganization was needed to weed out incompetent officers and eliminate outdated practices. As H. G. Wells later remarked, "Our Empire was nearly beaten by a handful of farmers amidst the jeering contempt of the whole world—and we felt it acutely for several years. We began to question ourselves." By the time a peace agreement was reached in May 1902, what had begun as a "tea-time war" against a "trumpery little state" had cost the lives of twenty-two thousand British soldiers.

Military and political misjudgments at every level had caused the war to drag on much too long. The problems undermined Churchill's confidence in the army, prompting him to complain privately that the war was "inglorious in its course, cruel and hideous in its conclusion." Commanders who had won fame decades earlier in Queen Victoria's "little wars" had shown themselves ill-prepared to deal with the new weapons and unconventional tactics used by the Boers. General Sir Redvers Buller made so many mistakes in the early period of the war that he came to represent the incompetence of the top brass and was ridiculed as "Sir Reverse Buller." During a dry parliamentary discussion of the number of horses and mules sent to the troops in South Africa, the Irish MP Tim Healy expressed the disillusion of many when he stood up and asked a government minister, "Will the rt. Hon. Gentleman state how many asses were sent to South Africa?"[15]

Churchill thought the government's plan for reforming the army was a costly expansion masquerading as a reform, and on the first night of the Commons debate he spent an hour tearing it apart. This was one of the best speeches of his career—forceful, practical, and prescient. He sounded like a veteran of the House instead of someone in his first year. The plan involved creating a new expeditionary force to deal with potential threats from a European foe. He thought the proposed force was far too small to be effective. Yet the government seemed to think that the troops could strike selective blows against an enemy and return home triumphant in a few days.

"A European war cannot be anything but a cruel, heartrending struggle," he warned, "which, if we are ever to enjoy the bitter fruits of victory, must demand, perhaps for several years, the whole manhood of the nation, the entire suspension of peaceful industries, and the concentrating to one end of every vital energy in the community."

As a result of his experiences under fire, he understood far better than most of his colleagues the dreadful consequences of modern combat. The fighting in South Africa, he told the House, had provided only "a glimpse" of the slaughter awaiting future armies. A real conflict would swallow up the proposed expeditionary force in no time. It would be wiser to spend the money on the navy, he suggested, insisting that sea power was the safest way to defend the British Isles and the empire.

He conjured a picture of a grim new reality, making it clear that the days when kings could spend years toying with their armies like pieces on a chessboard were gone forever. "Now, when mighty populations are impelled on each other . . . when the resources of science and civilisation sweep away everything that might mitigate their fury, a European war can only end in the ruin of the vanquished and the scarcely less fatal commercial dislocation and exhaustion of the conquerors. . . . The wars of peoples will be more terrible than those of kings."

These were powerful words, and though many in the chamber chose to shrug them off as mere rhetoric, others gave them serious thought. Even the sleepy old Victorian statesman Sir William Harcourt was moved to shed his usual complacency and marvel at the young man's stark description of total war. He wasn't sure of all the implications, but he did understand one thing clearly—Churchill would be a forceful voice in the House for years to come. The next day he dashed off a note congratulating him for "the brilliant success of your speech which has established your future in the H of C on a foundation which cannot be shaken."[16]

Arthur Balfour was not impressed. As leader of the House, his job was to win approval for the plan as it stood, yet every word of criticism from Churchill cast doubt on the soundness of the reform. A comfortable majority supported Balfour on the issue, but that didn't prevent him from being angry at his wayward colleague. He told a friend that Winston's "amazing conceit quite staggered him," and that this show of opposition was no more than a stunt "because it was without conviction or argument, and was mere self-advertisement." For much of the speech he directed "a glare of wrath" at the young troublemaker. But Churchill had made his point. He wouldn't be ignored.

"A new personality [has] arisen to enliven a moribund House," the weekly magazine *Black & White* announced a few days later. A veteran political observer called him a "party prodigy" and vowed he would never forget the sight of "this boy lecturing his elders." It was true that Churchill had important things to say, and wasn't afraid to say them; but, more to the point, he wanted important work to do. "The earnest party man becomes a silent drudge," he would soon conclude, "tramping at intervals through lobbies to record his vote and wondering why he came to Westminster at all. Ambitious youth diverges into criticism and even hostility, or seeks an outlet for its energies elsewhere."[17]

The question now for the Tory leadership was what to do with him. Should he be given some minor position to keep him quiet for a while? Or should the party be patient and slowly try to isolate him until he realized the error of his ways? For the time being Balfour decided that the best course was to do nothing.

But expecting Churchill to bide his time wasn't a good idea. Left on his own, he would not limit his criticism of the government to military affairs. In fact, he soon made the whole question of efficiency and economy his special subject. But it was obvious that he had larger plans, as *Punch* noted in a comic sketch that listed his interests as "the House of Commons—and its reform. The British Army—and its reform. The British Navy—and its reform. The Universe—and its reform."[18]

IV

THE DUKE'S SMILE

As a growing object of curiosity in society, Churchill began receiving so many letters and invitations that he was overwhelmed and complained to his mother that he was "hunted to death," with at least a hundred letters unanswered. Yet he couldn't resist the attention, and his engagement diary overflowed in 1901 with various social events he had agreed to attend. Several nights a week there were dinners at homes or clubs, and the rest of each month was crowded with banquets, luncheons, speeches, bazaars, and other festivities.[1]

One afternoon in May, at a lunch hosted by a newspaper editor, he found himself seated between the creator of Sherlock Holmes and the vicereine of India. With Arthur Conan Doyle—who had served briefly in the Boer War—there was much to discuss, and the two men enjoyed each other's company. But Churchill was just as happy to try his luck at charming Mary, Lady Curzon, who was taking a long holiday in England while her husband—to whom she was devoted—remained in India performing his duties as viceroy.

A delicate beauty with a lively sense of humor, Mary liked to tease, and to be teased. Winston held a special fascination for her because of his mother. Like Jennie, she was an American who had married into the aristocracy at a young age. She was only twenty-eight when she became the youngest vicereine in the empire's history. Her letters to Lord Curzon during her long holiday often include playful references to Winston, whose egotism both amused and irritated her.

In trying to explain the Hooligans to her husband, she took delight in writing that the group's "object" was "to teach Winston not to talk too much." Typically, however, he did nothing but talk during their lunch together, telling her of "his great speech" on army reform, which he had given the night before. He was brimming with confidence, she wrote Curzon, so much so that "he seems to consider [the speech] a greater success than any one else does!"

Still, Winston had qualities that she admired enough to make her wonder what kind of wife he might be looking for. By the end of her holiday she had delved into the question and picked up a few hints. She loved romance, gossip, and scandalous tales, and shared everything with Curzon, who was eager to know the latest details of the social and political news back home. Her first discovery was that Winston had finally given up any hope of winning Pamela's love. In June, after spending an evening with Jennie and Winston, she wrote her husband that a new woman had entered the young man's life: "Now for a bit o'gossip. Ettie has appropriated Winston & he is now in her train—Pamela Plowden quite cut out."[2]

For temporary comfort after the unhappy end of a romance, more than a few Edwardian men found the generous attentions of Mrs. Ettie Grenfell to be just the right medicine. She was, in the words of one young friend, "the tenderest of all companions to a broken heart." Blessed with a magnetic pair of dark blue eyes, Ettie had little trouble snaring a man's heart when she lowered her gaze seductively, and then looked up at just the right moment to whisper some emotionally charged remark.

That she was happily married and a doting mother of several children did little to inhibit her desire to have many men in her life, though she seems to have carefully avoided a full-fledged affair with any of them. In a thinly veiled social satire the writer and artist Max Beerbohm portrayed Ettie as a collector of fine examples of manhood. Like a queen, he suggested, she "sat aloft and beckoned desirable specimens up." Her amiable husband, Willie Grenfell (later Lord Desborough), showed little interest in her relationships with other men. He was content to amuse himself in harmless pursuits. When weary of conversation at Ettie's parties, he would sometimes move his arms up and down rhythmically, happily pretending that he was punting on the Thames—one of his favorite activities.

When she began helping Winston to mend his broken heart, Ettie was in her early thirties, but her lithe figure was more like a twenty-year-old's ("the slenderest waist you've ever seen," said one of her social rivals). She was well experienced at creating powerful relationships on the basis of nothing more than kind words, warm embraces, and fleeting kisses. (In the 1890s she was a leading light of the Souls, the tight-knit group of upper-class aesthetes who cultivated intense friendships with artistic devotion.) "You escape me like one of your own graceful smiles," wrote a young admirer, unsettled by her flirtations. Others appreciated her restraint and were happy to bask in her smiles without demanding more. One wrote, "I am very, *very* fond of you, [but] I love my wife first & you second, both far too much to make serious love to you."[3]

What she gave to Winston was probably little more than a sympathetic ear and a soft shoulder where he could rest his head while he poured out his troubles. She seemed to regard him as a wide-eyed boy in need of comfort from someone who knew more of love than he did. And it must have been clear to her rather soon that the end of his relationship with Pamela had not been pretty. The emotional upheaval was so great that even many months later both Winston and Pamela were still flashing wounded looks at each other. He couldn't suppress a lingering resentment of her rejection, and she was hurt that he had complained of her to Ettie and others.

Two revealing glimpses of their tense encounters have survived. The first was at a ball when Winston strode up to her and demanded to know "if she had no pride, because he had heard she was going about saying that [he] had treated her badly." Pamela denied his accusation but confided to others that his words had hurt her deeply. The second incident occurred at a large party hosted by Winston's aunt Cornelia. Arriving late, he came into a room and saw Pamela standing by the fire with another woman. She was dressed in white satin and her diamonds sparkled in the firelight. He approached her but appeared to be so taken by her beauty that he could barely say a word and failed even to acknowledge the other woman. He offered his hand to Pamela, but she didn't take it and refused to speak to him. It was a humiliating moment, made even worse when his uncle came to escort her to dinner and she swept past Winston as though he didn't exist.[4]

In early 1902 the announcement came that Pamela would marry an earl—Lord Lytton, who lived in the great Gothic mansion of Kneb-worth House. "She now makes an alliance," said the *Daily Chronicle,* "that was well worth waiting for." The common view among Churchill's biographers is that Winston and Pamela simply drifted apart, largely because he let this "dream wife" get away through lack of effort. Sadly, the truth is that he had misjudged her character from the start, attributing qualities to her that she never had. She wasn't the ethereal creature he had idolized, but a young woman of ordinary desires who always found it hard to limit her interests to one man. What really undermined their relationship wasn't his supposed "inertia," or the lack of money and a title, but her inconstancy. She juggled several relationships at once until she finally accepted Lord Lytton's proposal, and even after marriage she would continue to see other men.

Jennie's sister Leonie recalled that Winston was devastated when he learned that Pamela had been misleading him. "Looking ill and distraught" one morning, he had come to Leonie for sympathy, telling her, "I've paced my room the whole night through—till dawn came—without lying down." Blinded by her beauty, Winston may have only guessed at how widely Pamela had spread her affections. But there had been warning signs during their relationship. His normally unassertive brother, Jack, claimed that she wasn't to be trusted, calling her an "awful humbug" who was "the same to three other men as she is to Winston." She was even rumored to have had a brief romance with no less a figure than the Liberal statesman Herbert Henry Asquith, twenty-two years her senior. In old age, when asked his opinion of Pamela Plowden, Asquith confided to his intimate circle that she was a stunning woman who had enjoyed "the greatest erotic success of her day."[5]

There were always too many men in Pamela's life, and that circumstance didn't end for many years. In fact, one of her most passionate affairs came in her late thirties when she fell in love with handsome Julian Grenfell, one of Ettie's sons. As a result of her seduction of the younger man, she became known in the Grenfell family as the "wicked countess."[6]

When Pamela's engagement to Lytton was announced, Churchill gave no hint of bitterness or cynicism. Instead he sent the couple a gracious note wishing them happiness and promising to remain a devoted friend. All the same, the end of his long attachment to Pamela was a sobering experience he wouldn't soon forget. Ettie's attentions helped to take his mind off his troubles, but she was also the sort of person who could restore some of his faith in the enchanted future he had imagined for himself. After his stormy parting from Pamela, he welcomed Ettie's style of warm friendship, which wasn't encumbered by talk of marriage or any serious risk of scandal.

She shared his Romantic view of life as a heroic endeavor full of grand sentiments. She was fond of reading poetry, and in later years used to end letters with a favorite line from Tennyson in which Ulysses describes the aim of "heroic hearts": "To strive, to seek, to find, and not to yield." On a table in her room she kept a copy of an address by her American friend Oliver Wendell Holmes articulating a creed to which Churchill could easily have subscribed. "In our youth," Holmes said in his address to a gathering of Civil War veterans, "our hearts were touched with fire. It was given to us to learn at the outset that life is a profound and passionate thing. . . . Whether a man accepts from Fortune her spade, and will look downward and dig, or from Aspiration her axe and cord, and will scale the ice, the one and only success which it is his to command is to bring to his work a mighty heart."[7]

Spoken in Ettie's bewitching fashion, such words worked their magic on Winston, and over the next few years he kept returning again and again to her for encouragement and inspiration. As a friend observed of Ettie, "Sidonie the sorceress she is, the charming of Winston is a large sprig of laurel for her wreath." Churchill's friends soon realized that he and Ettie were so close that they were constantly confiding in each other. Soon she was showing off her new friend to the public at large. On July 20, 1901, an illustrated weekly featured a large photograph of "Mr. Winston Churchill, M.P." in Hyde Park as he sat contentedly in a carriage with Ettie and her husband, Willie.

Hugh Cecil worried that Churchill was sharing confidences too freely, particularly since Ettie's friends included politicians on both sides of the House. "Let me repeat again the desirability of great reserve in conversation," he lectured Winston, fearing that Hooligan confidences were being shared. "I tremble as to what you may have said to Mrs. Grenfell!" [8]

For Churchill, the air of enchantment surrounding Ettie had much to do with the way she lived and entertained at Taplow Court, a redbrick mansion above the Thames, with high gables and a corner tower with a tall spire and "a view that stretches the soul." On summer weekends the house would fill up with guests who were treated to massive breakfasts and dinners, boating parties on the river, long walks in the woods, tennis matches, tea-table conversations on the lawn, and late-night charades. "No one entertained more delightfully," Consuelo Marlborough recalled of Ettie. "There was the Thames, lovely in summer . . . shady walks in the woods and always an agreeable cavalier as escort." It was on such walks that Winston and Ettie forged their friendship, discussing politics and life as they strolled together, with romantic glimpses of Windsor Castle a few miles away.

Sometimes the parties were rowdy, and on one occasion Churchill was unceremoniously thrown into the river when he arrived from London wearing his top hat and frock coat. He took it well, and was generally a good sport, though he tended to monopolize the after-dinner discussions. "Winston leads general conversation on the hearth-rug," an amused Ettie wrote after one evening at Taplow, "solely addressing himself in the looking-glass—a sympathetic & enthusiastic audience." When the talk turned to nicknames, Winston was asked if he had ever acquired one, and he shot back, "No, except 'that young beast Churchill.'"

Churchill biographies rarely mention her, but Ettie was to remain his friend and supporter for the rest of her life, and she had the satisfaction in old age of knowing that her early faith in him had been vindicated. In 1947, after the Second World War had been won, she was approaching eighty and the glamour of her time as a society figure had long since faded. But she had not forgotten the intimacy that she and Churchill had shared in earlier times. To her "beloved Winston," she sent a few words of appreciation, telling him: "I think of you so often, & of all the old days, & of all you meant to me & mine." [9]

For Churchill, one feature of Taplow Court with special importance was that it belonged originally to a general who served with the Duke of

Marlborough at the Battle of Blenheim. A ten-year veteran of the European fighting in the opening years of the eighteenth century, the Earl of Orkney was a fearless leader of infantry who is described as the "gallant Orkney" in Winston's 1930s biography of Marlborough. After his retirement from the army, the earl acquired both the Taplow estate and the neighboring one of Cliveden, and divided his time between them for the remaining twenty-five years of his life. For most of Ettie's guests, the woods and the river were simply a playground, but to borrow the phrase that Churchill applied to Rosebery, the Past stood ever at Winston's elbow, and each visit to Taplow was enriched by its association with his illustrious ancestor.

Of course, this legacy was best appreciated about forty miles away, at Blenheim Palace, where Churchill delighted in studying the family history and in gathering inspiration from its countless reminders of Marlborough's glory. But the significance of Blenheim was not merely historical. As the family demonstrated in the summer of 1901, the triumphs of the past still had their uses in the present.

An enormous political rally on the grounds of the estate was planned for August. Its main purpose was to promote Conservative Party unity, but no one stood to benefit from the event more than Blenheim's native star, Winston Spencer Churchill. It was the kind of vast celebration that only a few families in the land could stage. And thus it was a reminder to the party that, however young and troublesome Winston appeared, his family was still a force to be reckoned with, and he had as much reason to expect preferment as any member of the Hotel Cecil.

Designed by a dramatist turned architect, Sir John Vanbrugh, Blenheim was always meant to have a theatrical quality. It is a baroque fortress with a great courtyard in which arriving visitors can't help but be overwhelmed by the towering colonnades on either side and the Corinthian portico looming straight ahead, with its statue of the goddess Minerva standing like a sentinel at the top. Carved emblems of Marlborough's military triumphs decorate the façade, including suits of armor, spears, swords, drums, and battle flags. As symbols of the duke's victories over Britain's enemies, two bound captives sit in stark isolation behind Minerva. Everything is meant to inspire awe for the conquering hero whose palace was intended as a grand tribute from the nation—his last trophy.

Blessed with such a monument, the great duke had gone to his grave without bothering to explain his deeds to posterity. "About his achievements he preserved a complete silence," Churchill noted of his ancestor. "His answer was to be this great house." [10]

Winston was in no danger of remaining quiet about his own achievements, but the house could still speak volumes on his behalf as a testament to the fighting spirit and boundless ambition of his breed. Like the duke, he had won fame on battlefields; like his father, he wanted to be the dominant political figure of the time. It was easy for his critics in London to scoff at his pretensions and to ridicule his youthful impudence. It was much harder to mock him at Blenheim amid the grandeur of the surroundings. The romance of epic endeavor speaks from every stone, and the vast solidity of the structure gives an air of permanence to the successes of the Churchill family.

Now the great question hovering over both the house and its latest champion was whether the old heroics had much significance in the twentieth century. At the dawn of an age of steady improvement through commerce, technology, and social reform, where was the need for another Marlborough subduing foes with, as Churchill once put it, "island blades"? Heroes still had their part to play in a limited military action like that of the Boer War, but why would anyone want another conquering goliath like Marlborough? The Continent didn't appear to be in any danger from the rise of a new political tyrant. The next battlefront seemed to lie at home in the growing discontent over questions of economic justice and basic human rights. Though the values enshrined at Blenheim had not lost their power to impress, they were now in danger of becoming merely quaint remnants of an irrelevant age. For much of his life Winston would have the uneasy task of trying to straddle the old world of smoke-and-thunder heroics and the new world with its expectations of a quieter valor. [11]

On the Saturday morning of the August rally, workmen were busy arranging long rows of chairs in Blenheim's great courtyard to seat an expected crowd of 120 MPs and three thousand of their supporters from around the country. At the base of the portico a stage had been built over the steps and a large sounding board was positioned in the middle for projecting the speakers' voices to the last rows. To provide a luncheon for such a big assembly, a small army of servants had been working since dawn under a large tent on the lawn, where the guests would soon be able to enjoy a feast of roast chicken and Yorkshire ham, followed by cheesecakes and French pastries. More than a thousand bottles of champagne were on hand to wash it all down.

Winston's cousin was paying for much of this hospitality. Sunny seems to have believed that the rally would enhance his influence among the Tories and their Unionist allies (independent-minded Liberals who opposed Irish Home Rule). But few had a high opinion of his political skills. It seems more likely that Jennie—who was to play a large part in the day's festivities—had used her charm to make Sunny think he was serving his own interests when he was really serving Winston's. His tasks for the day were merely to play the gracious host and to give a short speech welcoming his guests. The main event was reserved for speeches by Arthur Balfour and the powerful Colonial Secretary, Joseph Chamberlain ("Minister for Empire," as some called him).

But a third speaker was also invited to deliver a few brief concluding remarks. In the normal arrangement of such events that third slot would have been filled by another senior member of the government. Instead, to no one's surprise, it was given to Winston. The other MPs—including fellow Hooligans Hugh Cecil and Ian Malcolm—had to be content with sitting and cheering, but they were treated so hospitably that there was little cause for resentment. They were entertained in the main dining hall instead of the tent. A musical concert was given in the long library, and this was followed by special tours of the state rooms. Moving among them the whole time were three glamorous women doing their best to keep the politicians happy—Jennie, Consuelo Marlborough, and Millicent Sutherland.

Jennie was well versed in the history of the house and liked to play tour guide. In earlier years—for simple fun—she and her friends would sometimes dress in old cloaks and hats and join one of the groups of tourists who were led around the house by volunteer guides on certain days of the month. They enjoyed eavesdropping on the groups to discover what outsiders really thought of the place. One day she nearly gave herself away by bursting into laughter when she overheard an American visitor's reaction to one of the family portraits. "My," exclaimed the tourist, "what poppy eyes these Churchills have got!" [12]

When the courtyard began to fill up shortly after two o'clock, the sun was shining brightly, and everyone agreed the weather was ideal. Well fed and "clad in coolest country attire," the party faithful talked and sang patriotic tunes while they waited for their leaders to appear on the platform. As soon as the grounds were opened to the general public, the crowd swelled to more than seven thousand. To keep order, a few mounted policemen patrolled the grounds. A snobbish critic complained afterward that too many of the wrong sort of people had been allowed in, noting icily, "One thought one detected several publicans." [13]

A great roar greeted the entry of Chamberlain—accompanied by his American wife—and Balfour, who took a seat in the center of the stage with Millicent on one side and Jennie on the other. The usual group of news photographers was nearby, but there was a relatively recent addition to their ranks—a "motion picture man" furiously turning the handle of his machine to capture all the action for the new cinema halls opening up in London and other big towns. As if for the benefit of the movie camera, a few lazy clouds drifted by and were reflected in the tall windows of the palace.

Having given their foes two thumping defeats in the general elections of 1895 and 1900, the alliance between Balfour's Conservatives and Chamberlain's Unionists looked invincible to many, and the leaders were happy to encourage that view on this fine summer day. They characterized their Liberal opponents as "Little Englanders," petty critics of the South African conflict who were incapable of appreciating Britain's glowing future as an imperial power. Balfour claimed that the public no longer had confidence in the "hopelessly divided" Liberals, and Chamberlain boasted—to great cheering—that the Tory-Unionist alliance was the only "truly national party."

When the time came for Winston to speak, he had the opportunity simply to affirm all the talk of unity and to show appropriate gratitude to his leaders for addressing the rally. He started off well, thanking the crowd for attending the event, and explaining in a lighthearted way that he was chosen to speak "partly because he was a relative of the Duke, and had first seen the light at Blenheim." Then he decided to do something risky. He said little of Balfour but heaped praise on Chamberlain.

In the bad old days of Liberal rule, he said, the Colonial Office was a dull place whose ministers were often "lame ducks" sent there to mark time. Joe Chamberlain, he declared, had revolutionized the department, and he wanted everyone to know his delight in sharing "the same platform with a man whose administration at the Colonial Office . . . would be regarded in future days as perhaps the most remarkable page in English history for the last 50 years."[14]

As Churchill was well aware, the surface image of unity at the rally hid an intense rivalry between Balfour and Chamberlain, both of whom wanted to direct the alliance. Churchill decided to exploit that tension. By putting aside any concerns about the lessons of the Boer War, and shamelessly flattering Chamberlain—whom many blamed for mismanaging the conflict from the start—Churchill was playing one leader against the other. If Balfour wouldn't show him favor, perhaps Chamberlain would. Better yet, both men might decide it was in their interests to find him a useful position, and soon.

This sort of ploy could easily backfire, but Churchill was so anxious to get ahead, and so willing to do the unexpected, that he seemed to relish the dangers. It was the kind of attitude that had served his famous ancestor well on the battlefields of Europe.

Indeed, as Consuelo sat on the platform listening to all the speechmaking, she let her gaze drift above the heads of the crowd to the tall column on a grassy slope in the distance where a twenty-five-foot statue of the warrior duke stood majestically. "I could almost detect," she later wrote, "a satisfied smile on [the] Duke's countenance." She thought the old nobleman would have been pleased by Sunny's success with the rally. But if the spirit of the first Duke of Marlborough was smiling down on anyone that day, it was on the young firebrand who was such a keen admirer, and who was now eagerly employing his own maneuvers in the great game of politics.[15]

V

Empire Dreams

Joseph Chamberlain didn't need family connections or an inherited income to sustain his political career. He had an entire city devoted to him. In Birmingham he could do no wrong. He was a Victorian success story—a self-made man who amassed a tidy fortune as an industrialist, mass-producing the humble screw so cheaply that he dominated the market. He became one of Birmingham's largest employers, then moved into politics and transformed the city as its reforming mayor, and later as its constant champion in Parliament. Slums were cleared, the water supply was improved, and impressive civic buildings were erected. For more than thirty years he dominated the political life of the city. He was its uncrowned municipal king. But to the common man he was always just "good old Joe."

During the 1900 election he campaigned for Churchill, using his popularity in the industrial regions to boost the young man's chances of winning votes among the workingmen of Oldham. They had arrived together at a public hall in an open carriage and were surprised at the entrance by a large crowd opposed to the Boer War. Suddenly surrounded by angry demonstrators "booing at the tops of their voices," the pair had difficulty getting inside, but Churchill was impressed at how calmly Chamberlain—who was in his sixties—worked his way through the crowd. When they were greeted on the platform by the raucous cheers of their supporters, Chamberlain glowed with satisfaction. Turning to Churchill, he said with unself-conscious pride, "The first time I came here was to sell them screws."

After the election was won, Chamberlain invited his new colleague to spend a couple of days at Highbury, his mansion in Birmingham.

Though he liked to portray himself as a devoted friend of the ordinary workingman, Joe had developed expensive tastes over the years and seemed to enjoy showing off when he entertained this son of Blenheim. "He received me at supper in his most gleaming mood with a bottle of '34 port," Winston recalled. Far more impressive than his sixty-six-year-old liquor were his twelve greenhouses full of orchids, and twelve more full of less exotic flowers. A staff of twenty-five tended to the plants, and thus Chamberlain always had fresh orchids to adorn his buttonhole, an affectation that became one of his trademarks, along with his ever-present monocle, which a journalist once described as "a round glass in a frame of gold, thin as a grandmother's wedding ring."[1]

In parliamentary debates he would use that monocle to great effect, peering through it like a scientist with a microscope to fix an opponent with a cold stare or removing it to polish the glass with his handkerchief while he held the House in suspense with a dramatic pause. "When he was interrupted," an MP recalled, "he fixed his monocle very deliberately in his eye, leaned forward intently with finger outstretched in the direction of his opponent, purred out his pungent repartee, then sprang back to the upright." Even in repose on the green leather benches he looked intimidating as he surveyed opponents through his gold eyeglass while fingering his lapel with its bright orchid as big as a fist. He was always immaculately dressed and—unlike many men of his generation—he kept his face clean-shaven.

But orchids, monocles, and expensive port were not enough to make Lord Salisbury and Arthur Balfour forget that Joe was still a middle-class manufacturer whose career owed everything to screws. It was useful to have him as a political ally and an able Cabinet minister, but the Cecils and their circle never accepted him as their social equal. In his best condescending manner Balfour wrote a friend, "Joe, though we all love him, does not absolutely and completely mix, does not form a chemical combination with us. Why? I cannot tell, but so I think it is." Other aristocrats were less circumspect in expressing their reservations. "Chamberlain's faults all come from his upbringing," said the influential courtier Lord Esher. "Clever as he is, he has never learnt the self-restraint which everyone learns at a great public school or at a university. I mean everyone with his immense capacity."[2]

Churchill didn't share these snobbish doubts. He admired Joe's "sparkling, insurgent" energy and knew that even though Balfour led the House, Chamberlain "was the one who made the weather. He was the man the masses knew." The problem, as one political commentator put it, was that with Chamberlain, "the barometer . . . always stood at stormy." Like Churchill, he was impulsive and full of large ambitions. He had begun his parliamentary career on the Radical left of the Liberal Party and was once considered so extreme politically that Queen Victoria had urged Gladstone to exert more control over his "wild colleague." Now that he was allied with the Conservatives, there was always the worry that he would alter his course again. For the time being, Churchill sought to stay in Joe's favor in case a change at the top created opportunities for advancement.

He was friendly toward him in the same way that he was to Lord Rosebery, treating him like a father figure and engaging him in late-night talks, one of which lasted until 2 A.M. Looking back on this period many years later, he confessed, "I must have had a great many more real talks with him than I ever had with my own father." Chamberlain enjoyed giving him advice and encouragement and might have taken more of a fatherly interest in him if he had wanted to assume that part. But he already had two grown sons to keep him busy. The older son, Austen, was such a great admirer of his father that he seemed determined to turn himself into a carbon copy, wearing a monocle and orchid to match Joe's and pursuing a political career.[3]

In those days neither Austen nor his younger sibling Neville seemed headed for distinction. One day in 1902, when Winston and Austen were staying as guests of Millicent Sutherland at her home in Scotland, they fell into conversation about their political ambitions. "What do you want to become?" Winston asked bluntly. With great care Austen replied that he "had always thought the Admiralty one of the pleasantest offices and the post of First Lord one of the proudest positions that any Englishman could occupy." Winston was openly disdainful. For him there was only one goal in politics—the top—and everything else, no matter how pleasant, was just a stepping-stone. Austen never forgot his reaction. "Winston," he recalled, "pooh-poohed it as 'poor ambition.'"

As for Neville, in 1902 he was struggling to prove that he could duplicate his father's success in business. He wasn't making much progress. Sent by his father in the 1890s to manage a sisal plantation in the Bahamas, he worked conscientiously to turn a profit, but experienced one setback after another and was forced after several years of failure to admit defeat. The losses were spectacular, amounting to £50,000 of his father's capital. Joe did his best to absorb the blow, but it hampered the family for years. Neville's inheritance was substantially reduced in order to meet commitments to other family members. He would receive only £3,000 from his father's estate.[4]

Chamberlain's early success as an industrialist owed a great deal to ruthless cost-cutting and a sharp focus on the bottom line, but now this hard, competitive streak was mostly hidden under the carefully constructed exterior of the well-mannered statesman. On occasion Churchill caught a glimpse in him of the old cutthroat "King of the Screw Trade," and he was always unsettled to find "how deadly were the hatreds" lurking inside "my agreeable, courteous, vivacious companion." A harrowing incident at the end of 1901 vividly brought home how deep those hatreds went, and how rough were Joe's Birmingham roots.[5]

For much of the Boer War, one of its fiercest critics was a Liberal MP from Wales with a bushy mustache and a sharp, impudent stare—David Lloyd George. He had launched a series of increasingly personal attacks on Chamberlain, claiming that the sale of arms and other war supplies manufactured in Birmingham benefited Joe and his friends. Aiming straight for the heart of his adversary, he portrayed him as an aloof dandy who "strolled among his orchids" while "six thousand miles away" soldiers were slaughtered in his cause. "Few care to 'stand up to Joe,'" wrote a political reporter in 1901. "Only one man does so, and does it persistently. That is Mr. Lloyd George, an excitable, gleaming-eyed little Welshman, who finds joy in baiting Mr. Chamberlain."[6]

Lloyd George's passionate oratory helped to establish him as a national figure. But it also nearly caused his violent death on a cold December night in Birmingham, when he addressed a Liberal gathering at the Town Hall and a mob estimated in the tens of thousands surrounded the building.

While Lloyd George was speaking inside the hall, the crowd attacked the doors with a battering ram and broke in. The handsome neoclassical building was turned into a battlefield as the rival camps fought. Stones and bottles were thrown, windows were shattered, and glass rained down on everyone. When an angry wave of protestors surged toward the stage crying "traitor," the small army of policemen guarding it retreated with Lloyd George to another part of the hall and tried to fight back.

Fearing that the mob had the upper hand, the chief constable—the resourceful Charles Rafter, a local legend—disguised Lloyd George in a policeman's uniform and managed to escort him from the building using a back way. The politician made a clean escape, but not before dozens of rioters and constables suffered serious injuries. One young man was killed. "A good many broken heads were reported," said the *Times*. To their dismay, the local Liberal Association was ordered to pay for all the damages to the hall.[7]

When the news reached Churchill in London, he shook his head in disbelief and took up his pen right away to express his feelings to a prominent Tory acquaintance in Birmingham. "I am disgusted to read today's papers upon the riots," he wrote. "I hope the Conservative Party have kept their hands clean." The whole thing, he said, reminded him of "a much older story." He was referring to a time in 1884 when some of Chamberlain's supporters had rioted at one of Lord Randolph Churchill's rallies in Birmingham. Joe had loudly denied playing any part in that affair, though he and Randolph were then at odds and routinely hurling insults at each other. Winston now worried that Chamberlain was up to his old tricks again, but with a nastier twist that seemed uncharacteristically extreme.[8]

Chamberlain didn't help matters when he said afterward that although he "deplored the damage," he "could not blame the Birmingham citizens for protesting against Mr. Lloyd George's presence." Asked by an MP why the crowd had allowed Lloyd George to escape, Chamberlain dismissed the question, saying merely, "What's everybody's business is nobody's business." But the city had made its point. Criticizing Joe could be deadly. In a "good party fight," Chamberlain said a few weeks later, "when I am struck, I try to strike back again."[9]

It was an unsettling business, and Churchill was troubled by the idea that Chamberlain's agents might have planned the whole thing. The *Times* suggested such a sinister connection when it published a telegram sent to Joe at Highbury by one of his supporters, a prominent local politician named Joseph Pentland, who was vice chairman of the school board. It was sent shortly after the Liberal MP's narrow escape. "Lloyd George, the traitor, was not allowed to say a word," Pentland announced proudly. "Two hundred thousand citizens and others passed a unanimous vote of confidence in the Government and admiration for your unique and fearless services for King and country." [10]

The more Churchill thought about the riot, the more it bothered him. He was not well acquainted with Lloyd George at the time, but he didn't have a good opinion of him, privately describing him as "a vulgar, chattering little cad." He was outraged, however, to think that the game of politics could disintegrate so easily into mob violence. Though he enjoyed comparing it to war, politics in a democracy was fought with words and ideas, not weapons. ("Quit murdering and start arguing" was his advice for the leaders of the Irish Republican party, Sinn Fein, in 1920.) To get things done, he understood that hard choices had to be made, and that the process was often unattractive. He was happy to trade insults with his opponents, to plot and scheme against them for political advantage, and to shift allegiances when necessary; but there were limits, and Chamberlain had crossed the line. It was another sobering moment in Winston's education, another glimpse into Edwardian darkness.

The methods used against Lloyd George were not only "disgraceful," he told his Tory contact in Birmingham, but also self-destructive. "I shudder to think of the harm that would have been done to the Imperial cause in South Africa if Mr. Lloyd George had been mauled or massacred by the mob." [11]

After the Birmingham riot, Churchill took care to distance himself from Chamberlain. At a Conservative meeting in early January 1902 he made no excuses for Joe and his supporters. Yes, he admitted, Lloyd George had made inflammatory remarks, but there was no need for either side to overreact. "It ought to be possible," he said, "to shed the fullest light on political questions without breaking the windows."

The episode had opened his eyes to a growing discontent among party regulars, whose general attitude seemed to have turned in recent months from smug satisfaction to bitter resentment of their Liberal critics. The mistakes and losses of the war effort had revealed too many weaknesses in the government, and all the stinging criticisms from Lloyd George and others had undermined the party's confidence in its own powers. Churchill could feel the mood turning sour up and down the ranks. A few weeks after the riot, he told Lord Rosebery, "The Tory Party are in a very brutal and bloody frame of mind."[12]

Suddenly Churchill's political prospects looked grim. He had given Balfour too much trouble and now recognized that in Chamberlain's camp there was more trouble than he wanted. His little band of Hooligans looked more isolated than ever. They had not found a big issue to make their own, and their independent spirit was increasingly at odds with a party that was feeling embattled. Frustrated, Churchill worried that he had painted himself into a corner. In March, when he was well into his second year as an MP, he joked halfheartedly that he was "a politician who has the malady of youth and who has been wickedly independent."[13]

The very next month Chamberlain scolded Churchill and the Hooligans for persisting in their ineffective—and, to him, juvenile—displays of independence. It happened on a Thursday evening near the end of April, and the Hooligans had just voted against the government on an issue involving a newspaper editor in South Africa recently released from jail. Albert Cartwright had been convicted of libel for claiming that Lord Kitchener had ordered his troops to shoot prisoners. Now Cartwright wanted to come home to Britain so that he could tell his story, but the British authorities in South Africa were preventing his return. They had no right, Churchill thundered in the debates, "to proceed against a man who has already served all that the law has a right to require of him. If there is no right, there is no reason. What reason has the Government to be afraid of Mr. Cartwright?"[14]

The issue was resolved in the government's favor, but passions were still running high when the Hooligans left the chamber at about eight o'clock and soon found themselves joined at dinner by Chamberlain himself.

"That was a fine skirmish of yours in the House this afternoon," Chamberlain said when he arrived. "I hope you enjoyed it."

Churchill remembered Joe's first words as "I am dining in very bad company."

As was his habit when he was angry, Chamberlain spoke softly. The effect could be unnerving. "Smooth and sibilant," a journalist once remarked of Joe's voice, "it is . . . most silky when its matter is most deadly." [15]

"What is the use of supporting your own government only when it is right?" Chamberlain asked. "It is just when it is in this sort of pickle that you ought to have come to our aid."

The young men tried to explain their actions, but it wasn't the Cartwright case that mattered to Joe. He wanted to know whether the Hooligans were going to continue to be a thorn in the government's side. Was there any way to keep them in order?

"Has your little gang any principles at all?" he asked. "And, if so, what are they?"

This blunt demand left the Hooligans flustered. It was Earl Percy—the highest-ranking aristocrat among them—who finally offered the boss of Birmingham an answer. Trying to sound clever, he came up with three terms to describe Hugh Cecil's obsession with moral and spiritual issues, Winston's desire to cut government waste, and his own interest in the Middle East. The Hooligan principles, he told Chamberlain, were "Purity, Parsimony, and the Persian Gulf."

"I see," replied Joe, eyeing them critically through his monocle. "I thought they might be Pushfulness, Personalities, and the Press."

Having put the Hooligans in their place, Joe relaxed, enjoyed his dinner, and returned to his old genial manner. He lingered afterward, making easy conversation over cigars and his favorite late-night drink, a "mixture of stout and champagne."

By the end of the evening he had mellowed sufficiently to offer the group a few words of wisdom to ponder in the coming months. "You young gentlemen have entertained me royally, and in return I will give you a priceless secret."

In his best whisper, no doubt, he confided the magic word: "Tariffs!"

As the young Hooligan Ian Malcolm remembered it, Chamberlain went on to explain, "Why don't you young men take up some cause really worth fighting for, such as the protection of our markets against world-competition, and a closer economic union with the Colonies?" The group listened politely, but made no commitments. When the time came to go home, they all parted in good spirits. [16]

The "secret" that sly Joe had shared would indeed provide Churchill and his friends a cause "worth fighting for." But it would not be what Joe had in mind. They would use it against him, and it would prove his undoing. The stage was being set for the greatest battle of his career, and Winston would soon emerge as one of his most implacable foes.

What Chamberlain thought he had discovered in tariffs was the golden key to the British Empire. He was intent on unlocking its potential by allowing it to develop into a strong, unified market protected from foreign competition by a high wall of tariffs. This economic union would soon turn into a political one, and then become the basis of a grand, inseparable "Federation of the Empire," as he called it—something like a United States of Britain, governed by an imperial parliament representing England, Scotland, Wales, Ireland, Canada, Australia, and other major states. "The sons of Britain throughout the world," he told a Chamber of Commerce meeting in Liverpool, "shall stand shoulder to shoulder to defend our mutual interests and common rights."[17]

His dream was to become the George Washington of this federation, the father of an empire that would last for centuries, and that might even begin with Joe at the head of its imperial parliament. But getting the vast empire to unite behind a specific policy wasn't an easy undertaking. Voters usually think first of what they want for their own part of the world, and too many of those in the parts represented by the House of Commons didn't want what Joe was offering. They preferred free trade and cheap imported food to protection. The economic policy of the last half century had been guided by these principles, yet Chamberlain was ready to undo them. Misled by his popularity in Birmingham, and his power in the House, he failed to anticipate how fierce the opposition would be to his plans.

Not even a close call with death could make him reevaluate his ambitious project. Less than three months after confiding his "secret" to the Hooligans, he was riding along Whitehall in a hansom cab when the horse lost its footing, and he was thrown violently against the glass pane in the front, slashing open his forehead. The cut left a three-inch gash that exposed the bone. He lost a pint of blood before doctors at Charing Cross Hospital were able to tend to the wound. It was Monday, July 7, 1902, the day before his sixty-sixth birthday. The shock to his system was so great that the doctors kept him in bed for two weeks, first at the hospital and then at his London home. The enforced rest gave him lots of time to consider his future, but when he returned in August to his usual busy schedule, he had lost none of his enthusiasm for his imperial dreams. It was just a matter of choosing the right time and place for announcing his grand plan to the public.

But while Chamberlain was still recovering from his accident, and his supporters were nervously waiting for updates on his health, Lord Salisbury and his nephew Balfour decided the time was right for making big changes. In recent weeks Salisbury's health had grown worse, and rumors had been flying that he would soon relinquish his office. Even King Edward was worried that his prime minister couldn't last in the job much longer. He had recently given a new photograph of himself to Salisbury, who had gazed at it for a while with a confused look before mistaking it for someone else and putting it aside. "Poor old Buller," he remarked to the king, whose large, round face only slightly resembled that of the inept General "Reverse" Buller.[18]

Within a week of Chamberlain's accident, Salisbury had resigned, and Balfour was prime minister. Joe was consulted and accepted the change, but he had signaled beforehand that he was happy to stay at the Colonial Office. All the same, the move appeared to be made in haste, as if the various members of the Hotel Cecil were worried that Joe might change his mind when he felt better. They didn't understand yet that he was already looking beyond the prime minister's job to a future in which he would be the grand statesman of the empire.

To make sure that Joe's family was given honorary standing in the Hotel Cecil, Balfour handed Austen Chamberlain a minor plum—postmaster general. Other changes included a new Chancellor of the Exchequer, and a ministerial position for one of the Hooligans—Earl Percy. But there was nothing for Churchill. He had to stand by and watch as Balfour demonstrated how easily he could lure away a member of Winston's small group. By the end of the summer the new prime minister seemed to have a solid grip on power, and Churchill was left in a position where he had nothing to lose and every reason to continue his rearguard attacks.

One of these began on a trip to Egypt. Churchill decided to return to the Nile, which he had described so vividly only a few years earlier in

The River War. This time his destination was the Aswan Dam, the latest wonder of the empire, which had just been completed at an enormous cost after almost four years of construction. It was more than a mile long, but as magnificent as it was, the dam didn't interest Churchill as much as the company he would be keeping on the trip.

He was traveling with a distinguished party led by Sir Ernest Cassel, the brilliant German-born financier who had arranged the loan of £2.5 million to build the dam. Cassel had invited him to come as his guest to the opening of the dam on December 10. They left England on November 18 and were gone for six weeks. Among the others in their party was Sir Michael Hicks Beach, who had resigned from the Cabinet in the summer after serving for seven years as Chancellor of the Exchequer. His resignation had come in the wake of disagreements with Chamberlain in early discussions on the tariff issue, though this wasn't publicized at the time. For Churchill, however, what mattered was that he now had the opportunity to spend several weeks in close company with two of the leading experts on finance in the kingdom. In fact, Cassel was King Edward's closest financial advisor.

Churchill turned the trip into a crash course on the very subjects that Chamberlain would be raising in the coming year—budgets, tariffs, and economic growth. He was able not only to absorb great masses of information quickly, but also to ask the right questions and get to the heart of a problem immediately. Not many young men would have given so much of their holiday to such study while cruising the Mediterranean and the Nile, but it was pure joy for Winston.

He was preparing for a long struggle with a formidable opponent twice his age who was worshipped by many. The challenge was irresistible. And the line of attack seemed clear. It made no sense, he wrote in November, "to shut the British Empire up in a ringed fence. . . . Why should we deny ourselves the good and varied merchandise which the traffic of the world offers[?]"

From Cairo, shortly after his twenty-eighth birthday, Churchill sent his mother the good news that Sir Michael Hicks Beach had been immensely helpful. "I rejoiced in my talks with him," he wrote. "He is such a good and true friend; & we agree in almost everything political. . . . I foresee many possibilities of cooperation."[19]

For good measure, when he came home, he also consulted at length with Sir Francis Mowatt, the permanent secretary at the Treasury who had been around for so long that he had advised both Disraeli and Gladstone on financial matters. "He was one of the friends I inherited from my father," Churchill later said of Sir Francis. Indeed, all three of the older men who helped prepare him for combating Chamberlain's protectionism had been friends of Lord Randolph. Each seemed to relish the prospect of watching the son rise to prominence in a great public campaign fought over issues they knew so well. It was bracing to watch the son throw himself into a whirlwind of study. Long afterward Churchill would claim, "I had to learn economics in eight weeks."

Tutoring Winston stirred the emotions of old Sir Francis, who was nearing retirement and feeling nostalgic for the brief but exciting period in the 1880s when Randolph was Chancellor of the Exchequer. "He loved to talk to me about Lord Randolph," Winston recalled of their discussions: "How quick [Randolph] had been to learn the sound principles of public finance. . . . How resolutely he had fought for public economy and reduction of armaments! What fun he was to work with and serve!"[20]

So prodigious was Winston's energy at this time that he was preparing not only to make history in the inevitable clash with Chamberlain, but also to write it. For many months he had been collecting information for a biography of his father, and he had already started working on it when he went to Aswan. Both Ernest Cassel and Michael Hicks Beach were happy to share their memories of Randolph, filling gaps in the historical record.

On the journey Winston brought along a large tin case with compartments to hold pens and paper, various notes, and a few books. Whenever he had a spare moment he would turn his attention to the biography, getting up early to work on it every morning. "The book is making progress," he assured his mother in a letter written while he was sitting on the deck of Cassel's steamer at Aswan.[21]

He was alone that day. The rest of the party had gone to see the dam. But he was content to work at a peaceful spot on the river, thinking of the future, writing about the past, and looking up occasionally to stare at the Egyptian landscape with its reminders of other civilizations that had risen and fallen long ago.

VI

THE GREAT RIFT

O ne of Churchill's early champions in the press was Herbert Vivian, a handsome Cambridge-educated writer who hoped to launch his own political career someday. In the early 1900s he often sought out Churchill when he wanted advice or the latest parliamentary gossip, and usually found him in good humor. But when he called at Winston's London flat one morning in May 1903, he was surprised to find him looking preoccupied. "His eyebrows were knitted in deep thought" as he paced the room, slowly twisting the watch chain at his waist.[1]

Herbert had not yet seen the daily papers, but their pages held the clue to his friend's brooding appearance. They were full of news about a major speech Joseph Chamberlain had given the night before in Birmingham.

The powerful Colonial Secretary had at last made his big announcement, openly calling for protectionist legislation that would unify the economic forces of the empire and enable it to withstand competition from all rivals. Welcomed to the Town Hall on the night of May 15 by an organ playing "See, the Conquering Hero Comes," Chamberlain had conjured for his audience a vision of peace and prosperity within a tight imperial circle, "self-sustaining and self-sufficient." This new age would start, he assured the crowd, once the magical power of tariffs began nurturing trade within that privileged haven. As Joe explained it, this system of imperial preference was long overdue, and his followers warmly agreed, cheering him at great length.[2]

Churchill had been reflecting on the speech all morning. Turning to Herbert Vivian, he said with a serious look, "Well, politics are becoming exciting at last."

When his friend asked whether Chamberlain's plan had any chance of working, Winston was quick to dismiss the possibility.

"He has committed an irreparable blunder," he declared. "He cannot have realised all the consequences of his action. I believe it will be the death-warrant of his career. . . . The country will never stand a tax upon food, and without a tax upon food Protection is impossible."

"Then what will you do?" Herbert asked.

"Do?" Winston shot back. "The accursed thing must be fought." His blood was up, and he suddenly began sounding like a campaigner addressing a large crowd. "It must be denounced from every platform, it must be resisted as we would resist the advent of some loathsome pestilence. . . . We are confronted by a perilous crisis in the history of our party, in the history of our country."[3]

Churchill had been looking for a big issue to drive his career forward, and now Chamberlain had given it to him. He didn't need to make halfhearted trouble with his Hooligans on minor issues when free trade offered him a theme large enough to encompass both domestic and foreign concerns. As far as he was concerned, the lines were sharply drawn. At home, imperial preference threatened to increase the cost of living for ordinary people. In the international community, it increased the possibility of economic conflicts that could easily escalate into war.

In the week following Chamberlain's speech, Churchill publicly warned of the domestic threat, saying that while he valued the empire, "we must not disregard or think of small consequence the very urgent needs of our immense working-class population and the real sources of our national wealth." Among his political associates, he emphasized the dangers from abroad. "I do not want a self-contained Empire," he wrote on May 20. "It is very much better that the great nations of the world should be interdependent one upon the other than that they should be independent of each other. That makes powerfully for peace." (This echoed the old Liberal tenet, "If goods do not cross frontiers, armies will.")[4]

An outsider might have assumed that Joe held the winning hand in this game. After all, his political base in Birmingham was large and vocal, and Winston's supporters were relatively few. Joe's official position gave him power and influence, and in a political climate that placed a high value on age and experience, he enjoyed a clear advantage over a young man whose time as a backbencher was now just over two years. Yet Winston was right about Joe. The older man had blundered. Churchill understood, as Chamberlain did not, that protectionism would eventually undermine the government from within and energize the Liberal opposition.

In fact, the response to the Birmingham speech among some Liberal leaders was almost joyous. After Herbert Asquith read the report of it in the *Times*, he was no less convinced than Churchill that the shift away from free trade would be a disaster for the Colonial Secretary. He thought it was certain to bring down the government. Waving the *Times* triumphantly, he told his wife, Margot, "Wonderful news today . . . it is only a question of time when we shall sweep this country." Likewise, David Lloyd George sensed that victory was near. "The day of Mr. Chamberlain's ascendency in British politics is drawing to a close," he said, "and a fitting termination it is for such a career."[5]

Though Churchill was ready for a great crusade against protectionism, Chamberlain was an elusive target for several months while he worked behind the scenes to gather the necessary backing from the Cabinet. He didn't have much luck. Having made the basic mistake of announcing his plans without first obtaining the Cabinet's full support, Chamberlain realized too late that many of his colleagues were determined either to remain on the fence or to fight him to the bitter end. He seems to have assumed that the country as a whole would rally to him with such enthusiasm that the Cabinet would soon fall in line. When no overwhelming show of support was forthcoming, he needed Balfour to step up and back him without reservation.

But no politician of the time was more adept at equivocation than Balfour, whom Churchill once described as so slippery that he avoided entanglements "like a powerful graceful cat walking delicately and unsoiled across a rather muddy street." In a series of agonizingly convoluted statements Balfour successfully managed to make his position on protection almost indecipherable. When Churchill tried in late May to get a straight answer from him on the subject, Balfour brazenly argued that tariffs were merely incidental to Chamberlain's plan of a "fiscal union with the Colonies." He defined the issue in such a technical way that he was able to tell Churchill with a straight face, "I have never understood that Chamberlain advocated protection."[6]

Churchill's frustration with such evasiveness came into the open during the hot days of July and August. First, he rose in the House of Commons to criticize Chamberlain for launching "a very deliberate and insidious attack" on free trade while refusing to engage in a real debate on the question. Then, several days later, he tore into Balfour for not dealing straightforwardly with supporters on either side of the issue. Cleverly planting his barbs in a series of speculations, he suggested that the prime minister was employing a "disingenuous" and "undignified" stalling tactic. He warned that Balfour would have to take a stand or would soon "find himself in a difficult position." At that point, the prime minister interrupted Churchill to dismiss any concern about his future. "I shall be all right," he told the House with his usual air of urbanity.[7]

But the barbs hit home. Chamberlain felt betrayed. In view of the friendly relationship they had enjoyed earlier, he thought Churchill's personal attacks were especially unfair. Loyalty meant everything to Joe, and he made his disappointment clear. Meeting Winston in a corridor on his way to the debating chamber of the House, Joe paused long enough to give his erstwhile friend a look he would never forget. Writing afterward to Jennie, Winston described it as "an extraordinary look of reproach as much as to say 'how could you desert me.'"[8]

As he confessed to his mother, Churchill was sorry that he and Chamberlain had parted ways. He still found much to admire in the older man, but he didn't doubt what the future held. Joe was on a downward path. All the same, Churchill wrote a note to him saying he regretted that political differences had come between them, and he made a point of questioning the look Joe had given him.

A reply came almost immediately. It was full of excuses and veiled recriminations. It began with an unconvincing explanation of that look in the corridor. "I am afraid my shortsightedness is in fault," Chamberlain said. "I bear no malice for political opposition."

He went on to argue that he never expected absolute loyalty, but he seemed convinced now that Winston had gone too far in attacking the party's leadership. He suspected that the young man would soon "drift" to the Liberal side. He gave no sign that he would regret losing him, but only that he hated to be on the receiving end of Winston's stinging rhetoric.

"Is it really necessary," he wrote, "to be quite as personal in your speeches? You can attack a policy without imputing all sorts of crimes to its author."[9]

Winston might have taken this admonition more to heart if Chamberlain had not violated the spirit of it only a few days earlier by mocking him in the House. He had portrayed him as a shallow youth who was incapable of keeping to a steady course, and whose words couldn't be trusted. He cautioned his fellow Cabinet ministers "not to place too much faith in the valued and continued confidence of my hon. friend," and he recalled his own bitter lesson as one whose hand of friendship Churchill had rejected. "I remember my hon. friend at the time he came into Parliament, and I did the best I could then to secure his entrance into this Assembly—I remember how, in the heyday of his enthusiasm, he was going to give his ready and cordial support to his own Party, and to his own Government."

Chamberlain was just about to land his heaviest blow against Churchill as a political opportunist when a member of the opposition shouted, "What about yourself? Who has changed most?" This was a reminder that Joe, having years ago abandoned the Liberals over Irish Home Rule, was guilty of a similar charge. It set off a shouting match, sending the House into an uproar that ended only after repeated cries for order.

When Chamberlain was able to resume his attack, he dared Churchill to take his campaign against imperial preference into the industrial towns that favored it. A friendly backbencher suggested that Birmingham be included on the tour. "Oh! Birmingham," Joe said, as if the idea of Winston speaking there had just occurred to him. It was Chamberlain's favorite challenge. Criticizing him in the House was easy, but would one of his opponents have the courage to try it in Birmingham? Whether Chamberlain meant it as a dare or not, Churchill seems to have taken it that way. If Lloyd George was willing to risk speaking there, so could he. From that moment, it was inevitable that Birmingham would appear on his autumn itinerary.[10]

* * *

In the middle of his heated disagreements over protection Churchill had a curious encounter with a woman who had once been romantically involved with Joe Chamberlain. On July 8 Winston dined in London with the prominent Fabian thinkers and activists Sidney and Beatrice Webb. To advance their plans for social reform, the Webbs were seeking allies wherever they could find them, and they wanted to know if Churchill might be useful to their work. Beatrice was then in middle age, but in her twenties she had been desperately in love with Joe, who was two decades her senior.

They met in the 1880s, when he was still in his Radical phase, and she fell deeply in love with his forceful personality until she discovered just how forceful it was. Twice widowed (his wives died in childbirth), he was taking his time looking for another wife and had a few requirements in mind. One of them, as he informed Beatrice, was absolute adherence to his views. "It pains me to hear my views controverted," he explained.

Unwilling to bend to his will, she ended their relationship. She had looked closely into his personality and didn't like what she found. "By temperament," she concluded, "he is an enthusiast and a despot. . . . Running alongside this genuine enthusiasm is a passionate desire to crush opposition to his will, a longing to feel his foot on the neck of others." [11]

Her dinner conversation with Churchill included some discussion of his ongoing battle with Chamberlain, but it is doubtful that she made any mention of her old romance with his adversary. It had ended too painfully for her, and she had married Sidney Webb on the rebound, apparently attracted to him as Joe's opposite—a small, unkempt intellectual with "a tiny tadpole body," as she described him. When Sidney gave her his portrait during their courtship, she responded, "No, dear, I do not even look at your photograph. It is too hideous . . . it is the head only that I am marrying." [12]

Life with Sidney had turned her into such a detached, cerebral character that she scrutinized Winston at dinner as though he represented some new specimen for dissection. He emerged from her analysis much better than Chamberlain, but the pen portrait of him in her diary is generally negative. From her dry, middle-aged perspective, he was too emotional, too full of himself, and too immature. She also thought there was too much of the "American speculator" in his character, overshadowing that of the English aristocrat. But successful Americans often annoyed her. (Instead of Beatrice, Joe had chosen as his third wife the daughter of the secretary of war in President Grover Cleveland's administration. She was Mary Endicott of Salem, Massachusetts, and Joe liked to call her his "Puritan maiden." Beatrice wasn't impressed but admitted that Mary was "warm-hearted within the limits of her somewhat narrow nature.")

A few days after their dinner, Mrs. Webb wrote Churchill a friendly letter and recommended some reading material on the free trade question. She gave no hint of her private feeling that he lacked the mental focus to benefit from the worthy books she was suggesting, including one of her own with an appendix she urged him to study on "The Bearing of Industrial Parasitism and the Policy of a National Minimum on the Free Trade Controversy." Devoted to statistics and abstract theories, she was willing to tolerate Churchill if he could promote one of her favorite welfare schemes, but she was dubious of his intellectual potential except in a few of his unquantifiable personal characteristics.

"First impression," she wrote of him in her diary: "Restless, almost intolerably so, without capacity for sustained and unexcited labour, egotistical, bumptious, shallow-minded and reactionary, but with a certain personal magnetism, great pluck and some originality, not of intellect but of character. . . . Talked exclusively about himself. . . . No notion of scientific research. . . . But his pluck, courage, resourcefulness and great tradition may carry him far."[13]

In September, Churchill felt that the tide had turned against Chamberlain. There were rumors at the beginning of the month that the Cabinet was hopelessly divided and that some upheaval was imminent. In the party leadership few shared Joe's zeal for imperial preference, but even fewer wanted to criticize him publicly. Wherever he looked, Joe saw party leaders sitting on their hands. "The time is very close when we must all take sides," he pleaded. "I want to know on whom I can depend." But, try as he might, he couldn't win the full support of the Cabinet, and his options were running out.

On September 11 Winston wrote his mother that "JC is plainly beaten." Exactly one week later, Chamberlain resigned from the Cabinet, ending his eight years of service as secretary of state for the colonies. The announcement was all the more unsettling because it followed so closely the news in August that Lord Salisbury had died, only a year after stepping down as prime minister. Both Salisbury and Chamberlain had been fixtures in government for so long that it was difficult for many to accept that one was now dead and the other had stepped down.

Joe had been plotting his move for several days and didn't see it as the act of a beaten politician. In fact, he thought it would be the beginning of a great comeback through the realization of his dream of an imperial union, and he believed he could rally support for it more effectively "from outside" the government.[14]

Churchill was convinced from the start that Joe's one-man crusade would fail, but he was ready to fight it at every turn until it collapsed. To hasten the end, he knew that he had to take the fight to Chamberlain's home territory. Bravely, one of the Hooligans agreed to accompany him to Birmingham in November. It was Lord Hugh Cecil, who loved lost causes and seems to have assumed that opposing Joe in Birmingham was sure to go wrong. Winston understood that his friend found "a melancholy satisfaction" in defeat. Still, he couldn't resist making light of it, employing a touch of gallows humor with Hugh's brother. "You had better bid Linky farewell before Birmingham," wrote Winston. "You may never see him again."[15]

The local sponsors of the talk expected trouble. Their spokesman told the press, "We are anticipating a disturbance, and it is quite possible the meeting will be broken up." On the day before the talk a number of paid thugs suddenly appeared in the streets wearing sandwich boards that called for workingmen to turn out "in thousands" to show Churchill what they thought of anyone who dared "to oppose our Joe." Hoping to avoid a repeat of the riot over Lloyd George's speech, the chief constable made sure that hundreds of policemen were on hand to keep order.

Churchill asked one of Chamberlain's oldest friends, John Morley, whether another mob assault was being planned. The reply was not reassuring. Though Morley thought that such a disturbance was "most unlikely," he "was perfectly sure nothing would be done unless [Joe] wished it to be done."

The political world held its breath, wondering how Joe's followers would respond. It was one thing to rough up Lloyd George, who was still a relatively minor politician. But what would be the consequences if any harm came to Churchill, the hero of the Boer War, or to Lord Hugh, the son of the recently deceased prime minister? The stakes were raised even higher when a last-minute guest joined the two parliamentary Hooligans. Unwilling to let her son face the crowds without her, Jennie came to Birmingham to take the stage with Winston and Hugh. It is little wonder that one national newspaper remarked on the day of the event, "Exciting times are expected tonight."[16]

At seven on the evening of November 11 the expected crowd of protestors surrounded the Town Hall. Estimates of their number were as high as forty thousand. Policemen were lined up behind heavy barricades to prevent anyone entering without a ticket. The crowd made repeated attempts to break through but were held back. Frustrated, some threw stones and broke a few panes. Most, however, seemed content to stand back and make as much noise as possible, chanting slogans and singing patriotic songs.

A largely sympathetic audience of four thousand packed the hall, and when Winston, Hugh, and Jennie were ushered to the stage, the great majority responded jubilantly, roaring their approval as they waved hats and handkerchiefs. In the early part of his speech, Winston was often interrupted by a scattering of hecklers—"ironical gentlemen," the press called them—but he made a point of speaking respectfully of Chamberlain, and his moderate tone had a calming effect on the audience. Though the noise of the crowd outside was a constant reminder of the danger presented by Joe's supporters, Churchill showed no sign of unease.[17]

"I have not come here tonight to say anything bitter or unkind about anybody," he told the audience. "I have come to uphold, as far as I can, two great causes, in both of which Birmingham is most profoundly interested, the cause of Free Trade, and a greater cause than that, the cause of free speech."

Instead of encouraging discontent with Joe's specific plans for protectionism, Winston looked beyond the technical points of the dispute to sketch for his audience a broader vision of an empire held together by a strong moral bond rather than by merely economic or military interests. He gave this view a personal slant, recalling his own experiences as both soldier and correspondent in far-flung parts of the world, and taking a romantic view of imperialism as a force for uniting people in the service of a common good. Whatever the reality was, Churchill preferred this exalted notion of the empire to the more calculating plans of Chamberlain, and he expressed it in a sonorous conclusion that thrilled his audience.

"I have seen enough in peace and war [on] the frontiers of our Empire," he said, "to know that the British dominion all over the world could not endure for a year, perhaps not for a month, if it was founded upon a material basis. The strength and splendour of our authority is derived not from physical forces, but from moral ascendency, liberty, justice, English tolerance, and English honesty. . . . It is by these alone that [in] the future, as in the past, we shall remain, under an inviolable circle, the proud possessions of the King."[18]

David Lloyd George had received rough treatment in Birmingham not only for opposing Chamberlain but also for opposing the Boer War in a way that was seen as unpatriotic. By contrast, Churchill—as his speech made clear—wasn't suffering from a deficiency of patriotism. And for that reason alone it was harder for Joe's supporters to demonize him. To be sure, the crowd outside remained restless and angry to the end of the night, but by the time he finished speaking, Winston had effectively silenced those in the hall who had come to protest his visit. The press reported that the applause was "deafening" when he sat down.

It was also noted that there were tears in Jennie's eyes. Her son had done a brave thing, and had done it well, and she was proud to share the moment with him. His exploits on real battlefields had been experiences she could only read about, but the political battlefield allowed her to be a spectator, and to show, by her mere presence on the stage, that courage did indeed run in the family. Moreover, thanks to the superior force of the police and the relative restraint of the protestors, Jennie, Winston, and Hugh were able to leave the hall safely and return to London without having to don any police disguises. It was a humbling moment for

Chamberlain, but Winston had outmaneuvered him and survived this incursion into the heart of Joe's personal empire.[19]

Not known for his bravery, Hugh was later singled out in one newspaper as showing remarkable composure in the face of danger. He had spoken at the Town Hall immediately after Winston, and the *Daily Mirror* marveled at his show of "political valour." The paper didn't doubt that the risks to his safety were real. "He cannot have forgotten the perilous adventures of Mr. Lloyd George in the capital of the Midlands," the *Mirror* noted. "But he had something to say in Birmingham, and no consideration of personal discomfort deterred him."[20]

Churchill was keenly aware that he was at war with Joe. He had been thinking of their clash in that way for some months. Earlier in the summer, while sitting on the terrace of the House of Commons one sunny day, he had given a revealing glimpse of his thinking on this question in an interview with the journalist and social reformer Harold Begbie.

"Politics are everything to you?" asked Begbie.

"Politics," Churchill replied, "are almost as exciting as war, and—quite as dangerous."

Thinking the point was overstated in a time of deadly new weapons that could pick off unsuspecting soldiers at a great distance, Begbie asked, "Even with the new rifle?"

"Well, in war," answered Churchill, "you can only be killed once. But in politics many times."[21]

In the course of their interview, Begbie soon realized that Churchill was fashioning his career to endure the heat of many deadly battles, and to risk losing certain fights that might seem catastrophic defeats to others, since he was confident he would rise again. In fact, Winston was already willing to admit that if he stayed in the Tory party—and he was then insisting that he would not leave it—the free trade cause would prevail, but at a terrible cost to the party. He predicted "a collapse . . . worse than anything since 1832."

Then why stay in a party that wouldn't heed such a dire warning? asked Begbie.

This question stirred the young MP's fighting spirit and revealed that he saw his struggle with Chamberlain as not merely a contest over economic or imperial policy, but also as a war for the future of the party.

"I am a Tory," said Winston, "and I have as much right in the party as anybody else, certainly as much right as certain people from Birmingham. They can't turn me out of the party."

Sounding very much like the prime minister he would become in his sixties, Winston vowed to fight his adversaries to the last defensive position in the field. "I shall stick to the party, and fight the reactionaries to the last hedge. There is no doubt about that—not a shadow."

Churchill was so convincing in his arguments that Begbie came away from their interview believing that he had just spoken to one of the most promising young men in Europe. "It seems to me that, given health, it is safe to prophesy that he may become one of the great figures in political history. As one of his friends remarked to me on this subject, 'If you measure his future by his past, you find yourself on the steps of the throne.'"

The one obstacle that Begbie could see blocking Winston's path was the growing number of enemies he was making in his short life. A habit of picking fights with powerful people had left him vulnerable to attack from all directions. "It must be admitted," wrote Begbie, "that Mr. Churchill is a very well-hated man in certain circles of Society." [22]

At the same time that his political life was heating up, Winston had fallen deeply in love again. This time the woman in question was even more glamorous and unobtainable than Pamela. She was Ethel Barrymore, then a Broadway sensation in her early twenties, and a frequent visitor to Britain. For several years she had been spending her summer holidays with friends in London and at various country retreats, and had become especially close to Millicent Sutherland, who had ambitions to produce a play with Ethel in the starring role.

It was thanks to an introduction from Millicent that Winston came to know the young woman in 1902, when, as the *New York Times* reported, Ethel was "being made much of in London." He had seen her on-stage in town the previous summer in a one-night-only performance of her Broadway comedy hit, *Captain Jinks of the Horse Marines*. As he told her later, he fell in love with her the moment she made her entrance. [23]

She had that effect on men. She was known for her low-cut costumes with pretty flowers pinned to her bodice and other shimmering frills. After seeing her for the first time, the veteran explorer Arnold Landor wrote of her as though he had discovered some new exotic breed of woman, calling her "a pretty creature, with dangerously expressive eyes, luxuriant dark hair, and highly captivating manner." For Winston, it was not only Ethel's appearance that attracted him. It was also her voice, which he is said to have described as "soft, alluring, persuasive, magnetic."[24]

She visited Blenheim in 1902 and became friends with both Consuelo and Jennie. The next summer she spent part of her holiday as Consuelo's guest at the palace and saw Winston frequently, but, like Pamela before her, she was elusive, darting from one engagement to the next in a busy social whirl. Everyone wanted to meet her. She went to Warwick Castle to see the countess, visited the Asquiths at their rented summer home in Scotland, dined with Lord Rosebery, played bridge with Arthur Balfour, and was introduced to Max Beerbohm in London.

One summer day in 1903 Millicent invited her to lunch. The only other guests were Churchill, Millicent's brother Lord Rosslyn, and the American novelist Henry James. "Millie made the mistake," Ethel recalled, "of saying to Henry James, 'Did you have a pleasant walk this morning.' And he said, 'Yes,' in two and a half pages, with hardly a semicolon and never a period—a superb performance." Winston never had a chance to get Ethel's attention.[25]

What seemed to interest Ethel most, when she did focus on Winston, was his political career. She was fascinated by the Hooligans and their tactics, which she described with amusement as "unruly." The theatrics of British politics appealed to her, but she didn't appear to understand what all the sound and fury signified in a fight such as the one Churchill was waging against Chamberlain. Writing to Winston from New York in the autumn of 1903, she seemed to think he would be pleased to hear that she was following the political news from Britain. But she heaped praise on the wrong man.

"I have been so awfully interested in all the wonderful doings in England," she wrote excitedly. "I can't help thinking Joe the most brilliant living creature. I thought the Glasgow speech too wonderful—Is it true that he is succeeding?"

For a young American, it was easy to assume that because Winston and Joe sat on the same side in the House of Commons, they must be working toward the same end. Chamberlain's argument in favor of "tariff reform" at Glasgow on October 6, 1903, was so long and complex that Ethel may have supposed it was safe to call him "brilliant." But it was a mistake that Winston could easily shrug off. He would have been more than happy to spend time elucidating for her the correct view. In fact, he was anxiously awaiting her next visit in the summer.

And, in her cheerful manner, she led him to believe that it would be a visit worth waiting for. She was busy now acting in a new play on Broadway, but she expressed in her letter the hope that she was missed in Britain. There was even a chance that she might be starring in a play that would open in London in the late spring. Meanwhile, she encouraged him to keep her in his thoughts. "Do write often dear Winston," she gently commanded. His end of the correspondence has not survived, but it must have been lengthy and passionate, because by the time he saw her again in London he was ready to propose.[26]

VII

DEPARTURES

C hurchill's internecine war with Chamberlain reached its climax early in 1904. It was on a Tuesday in the House of Commons at the end of March, and the government was being pummeled by the opposition for not calling a general election to let the country decide the free trade issue. Lloyd George was leading the attack, arguing that other pressing problems were being neglected, and that the nation had been left adrift, while Conservatives tried to decide how to make protectionism acceptable to the electorate.

Staring at Balfour, he mocked the leader's coy refusal to take a clear stand and fight openly for it. The prime minister, Lloyd George claimed, wanted to pretend that the country shared his complacent attitude.

Churchill rose from the benches behind Balfour. The prime minister could easily guess what was coming—more pointed criticisms from a man who was supposed to be one of his followers. In the words of an excited parliamentary commentator, "A nasty look came into [Balfour's] face which transfigured it in the same way that the claws do a cat's paw." At that instant the prime minister apparently decided that he had put up with enough from Winston. With uncharacteristic haste, he strode out of the chamber and didn't look back.

Then something even more extraordinary happened. One by one the other ministers of the Crown got up and followed their chief, as did most of the backbenchers. The Tory dandy William Burdett-Coutts paused on his way out to regard the scene with "a look of studied insolence" until the opposition benches began shouting angrily at him, and he left. In a few minutes the long rows of benches on the government side were empty except for a dozen or so Tory free traders and Winston, who was still standing and trying to carry on with his speech in the wake of this shocking rebuke from his party.

Though taken aback, he finished speaking and didn't spare Balfour for failing to lead. If anything, he was harder on the prime minister than Lloyd George had been. "The time had come," he told the delighted members who stayed to listen, "when the country ought to be relieved from this shifty policy of equivocal evasion; they had a right to know what public men thought on public questions, and what political chiefs believed on great political principles."[1]

In walking out Balfour had broken with the traditions of the House, and he was widely condemned for it. In typical fashion he wouldn't even take responsibility for walking out, claiming that his absence was necessary because of "an engagement with the Chancellor of the Exchequer," and that he had not intentionally snubbed Churchill. Few accepted his excuse. One paper referred to his "running away" as a "schoolboy antic and a sign of weakness." The *Spectator* was convinced that the protest was "an organized attempt to slight Mr. Churchill" and scolded his party for refusing to play fair with a man "who shows courage as well as vivacity."[2]

Instead of blaming Chamberlain for dividing the party over an unrealistic imperial scheme, Balfour and others found it easier to turn on Churchill and the handful of determined free traders in their ranks. Of course, Winston was headstrong and overbearing, but so was Joe. Yet little effort was made to accommodate Winston's views or to give him any incentive to stick with the party. The Tories were in need of an energetic young fighter willing to question its elders, but Balfour was so indecisive and Chamberlain so intolerant that neither had much use for Winston. And he, in turn, slowly came to the conclusion that he couldn't stay in a party dominated by these two men. They had created an impossible situation. Joe was too strong to be ignored but not strong enough to win the argument for his cause. Balfour had the power to lead but had chosen instead to prevaricate.

Churchill had been thinking about leaving for several months. In the autumn he had revealed his inclination in a letter to Hugh Cecil, saying that he was sick of "feigning friendship to a party where no friendship exists, & loyalty to leaders whose downfall is desired." He even went so far as to say, "I hate the Tory party." Knowing that this blunt talk would offend Hugh, whose Conservative roots ran deep, he didn't send the letter. But by the end of 1903 he had said enough in public to make Hugh fear that he might soon abandon the party.[3]

His friend tried to talk him back from the edge, urging him "to go on fighting the battle within the party" and to win over those "who are in doubt, who hesitate not much liking Joe & his plan but strong in their devotion to the party." He wanted him "to fight JC hard but at the same time to use the language of Conservatism." Hugh didn't yet understand that Winston wasn't inclined to speak the language of conservatism. Whatever else it might be, what he spoke was always first and foremost the language of Winston. "He is a party all by himself," the *Scotsman* newspaper correctly concluded in March 1904.[4]

The question was whether any party would ever be willing to offer him a leash long enough to make him happy. He would spend the rest of his career testing that proposition. Meanwhile, he had inspired in Hugh—his best follower to date—such a strong sense of outrage against Joe's methods that it couldn't be contained. It boiled over in the spring. Having survived his foray to Birmingham, Cecil felt emboldened to confront the great Joe face-to-face and tell him what he thought of him. It took place during an evening session of the House and left many members stunned at the vehemence of the attack.

Since leaving office, Chamberlain had tried to avoid parliamentary debates on protection, preferring to discuss it in public speeches so that Balfour and other ministers wouldn't have to be drawn even deeper into the controversy. But what Hugh Cecil dared to do in the House was to point his finger at Joe and call him a coward for not debating the issue in its proper forum. Members could hardly believe that anyone—least of all Lord Hugh—would hurl such an insult at mighty Joe. But then the bookish aristocrat made the charge even more inflammatory by saying that Chamberlain reminded him of the buffoonish Bob Acres in Sheridan's eighteenth-century play *The Rivals*.

"I should . . . compare my right hon. friend," said Hugh, "to Bob Acres in the comedy, who exhibited courage elsewhere than on the field of battle, because my right hon. friend shrinks, like that character, from facing his opponents on the field of combat which is the House of

Commons. When Bob Acres found himself in that situation his courage oozed out through the ends of his fingers."

The comparison was witty but humiliating, and was greeted with laughter from the Liberals and indignant howls of protest from Joe's friends. At first, Chamberlain pretended not to care. "It was a sight to see Mr. Joseph Chamberlain whilst Lord Hugh was speaking," remarked a member of the press gallery. "His face wreathed itself into a great giant of a smile, and he did his utmost to appear like one who looked on the whole matter as a debating society joke." But when Joe's time came to respond he struck back with all his verbal skill, scornfully dismissing the notion that Hugh should lecture him on courage. If it came to a physical fight, there would be no contest, Joe suggested in a bullying way.

Partly as a result of his association with Winston, Hugh had emerged from the shadows of the Cecil family to tackle the biggest issue of the day and to put one of the most important politicians on the defensive. Even his cousin the prime minister was caught off guard by his audacity. At the end of the evening he felt obligated to defend his former Cabinet member and to disassociate himself from Hugh's criticisms. Of Chamberlain he said, "The utmost ingenuity of hostility, which sometimes, I grieve to say, has risen to malignity, has been used to vilify him, and yet, in all the vocabulary of attack which I have ever heard levelled against him, I have never until this evening heard it even whispered that the quality that he was lacking in was courage."[5]

Hugh innocently assumed that he could now get away with his attacks on a weakened foe, but Joe was not finished yet and never forgot the indignities of this night. He vowed revenge and began a campaign to discredit Hugh in his Greenwich constituency. Winston tried to warn his friend of the danger, telling him that Joe would retaliate whenever possible. "Have no sort of illusions as to any surrender," he wrote him.

It would take time, but Joe worked methodically over the next year and a half to ruin Cecil's political career, making it clear to his associates that he would rather see the party "lose 20 seats than allow [Lord Hugh] to be returned to Parliament." Too late, Hugh realized that Joe had targeted him for defeat in the next election and would at one point be "spending £50 a day" to unseat him. Hugh lost badly in 1906 and would angrily blame Chamberlain for it, casting him in extravagant language as a Machiavellian monster who "engaged in a system of Renaissance style assassination of opponents by parliamentary bravos." Wisely, Churchill would avoid such a fate by planning far ahead and placing himself in a position where Joe was powerless to reach him.[6]

From the time he entered Parliament, Churchill had been looking for ways to lead without having to bend to party discipline. He had hoped that by the sheer force of his personality he could win acceptance as an independent-minded Tory whom others would follow because of who he was and what he did, and not because of what he was owed in the party hierarchy. As early as 1901 he had told a learned society in Liverpool, "Nothing would be worse than that independent men should be snuffed out, and that there should be only two opinions in England— the Government opinion and the Opposition opinion. The perpetually unanimous Cabinet disquiets me. I believe in personality."

It wasn't a practical stand for a young man with only a few "unruly" Hooligans trailing in his wake. Though some in his party saw promise, many others saw only conceit. And the more trouble he caused the less he was liked. A burly backbencher's response to him during an especially rowdy debate is not untypical. James L. Wanklyn, a railway speculator who had made a lot of money in South America, was one of many calling for order one afternoon when Churchill turned on him and told him to stop "shouting people down." Wanklyn, a Chamberlain supporter, was not pleased. "Permit me to warn you," he wrote Winston the next day, "that if I have any more impertinence from a young man like yourself, I shall know how to deal with it."[7]

For several months Churchill had flirted with the idea of pushing for a "Government of the Middle," as he called it, which would be led by Lord Rosebery and other powerful figures from the center of both major parties. He tried repeatedly to get Rosebery excited about the idea, but the pampered aristocrat was too attached to the easy life on his grand estates and was reluctant to throw himself into a new political movement with many hurdles facing it. As this idea faded, and life in the Tory ranks became increasingly difficult for him, Winston had little choice but to contemplate a fresh start as a Liberal.[8]

He had several friends among their number and felt especially at home in the company of the old Victorian statesman John Morley, who was so gracious and tolerant that he maintained close relationships with politicians of every kind, including even Joe Chamberlain. An accomplished man of letters, Gladstone's official biographer, and an ardent free trader, Morley was an old-fashioned liberal who championed individual freedom against the reactionaries in the landed classes and the established church. Quietly, he had spent his life trying to keep the ship of state from racing into foreign entanglements or sinking under the weight of domestic burdens. He was happy to become one of Winston's intellectual and political mentors, recommending books to him and occasionally offering advice in his modest, polite way. At Morley's suggestion, Winston had made a close study of Seebohm Rowntree's groundbreaking work *Poverty: A Study of Town Life,* which started him thinking seriously for the first time about ways of alleviating the suffering in Britain's worst slums. "I see little glory," Churchill wrote after reading the book, "in an Empire which can rule the waves and is unable to flush its sewers."

A steady, undemonstrative man, Morley tried to soften Winston's bellicose manner and teach him the value of moderation and a slow, contemplative approach to formulating and carrying out policies. He didn't have much success. In later years he would quietly lament Winston's tendency to rush headlong into complex matters and to misjudge "a frothy bubble for a great wave," as he put it. When he was told one day that Winston was caught up in reading yet another book on Napoleon, he shook his head in disappointment and said, "He would do better to study the drab heroes of life. Framing oneself upon Napoleon has proved a danger to many a man before him."[9]

By and large, the Liberals were willing to accept Churchill into the fold, warts and all. As they had watched him travel the country denouncing Chamberlain, they could not help but be impressed by his passion and his way with words. None of their rising stars came close to him except Lloyd George, who seemed to like the idea of working in tandem with Winston against Chamberlain. It was this common foe that drew them together at this stage, and not much else. But it was enough. As even some of Joe's friends were willing to admit, the two men would make a formidable team. The irascible Wanklyn thought of them as a couple of racehorses who would pull the Liberal cart at a breakneck speed. "You will make a perfect match-pair, you two," he wrote Lloyd George in a taunting letter, "but I should be devilish sorry to try and drive you."[10]

The prospects for advancement in the Liberal Party looked good for Winston. Its leader in the Commons, Sir Henry Campbell-Bannerman, was a portly, amiable man with an open mind who wasn't likely to stand in his way, and whose grip on the party machinery was weak. When he had become the party's leader, no one thought of him as a powerhouse with grand ambitions. His talents were so modest that the *Times* called him "a leader who will serve adequately enough as a warming pan until a more commanding figure emerges."[11]

In later years the charge would often be made that Churchill finally left the Tories because he saw a better chance of advancement on the other side. That was certainly one reason, but it is important not to underestimate just how hostile the atmosphere had become for him, thanks to Chamberlain. And it is worth keeping in mind that before he walked over to the other side, his party—led by his prime minister—had walked out on him, leaving him conspicuously isolated in the House on that dramatic day at the end of March. From that moment, he knew he had to go.

But he suffered under the strain of having to decide when and how to part not merely with Balfour and company but also with his friend Lord Hugh, who would rather die than leave the Tories. Just as Hugh had tried to persuade him to stay in the party, so he tried to coax his friend into leaving with him. But Hugh wouldn't hear of it. Winston would have to do it on his own.

The strain showed on April 22 as Churchill was speaking in the House. He was discussing the history of the Tory party's relationship with the working classes and had just finished pointing out that the two groups were on better terms twenty-five years ago, when the party "was not the sham it was now." He knew that he was pushing his luck to say such a thing and that members might start walking out again. But no one moved, and something seemed to snap in his brain. He faltered and suddenly lost the train of his thought. He tried to continue but couldn't find the words, and was forced to sit down without finishing his remarks. For a few moments he held his head in his hands; finally he stood up and left the chamber. It was so unlike him to be at a loss for words that many in the House showed genuine sympathy for his plight and wondered if he had fallen ill.

MOVING INCIDENT IN THE HOUSE, said one headline the next day. "Mr. Winston Churchill Unable to Continue His Speech." Later reports raised the question of whether the young man had suffered a nervous collapse: "Mr. Winston Churchill's dramatic breakdown in the House of Commons has naturally caused a considerable amount of anxiety among his friends. Mr. Churchill may not be universally popular as a politician, but everybody recognises that he is a power to be reckoned with in the future."

He recovered quickly and insisted that nothing was wrong, saying that it was merely an unfortunate lapse. But it was obvious that the walkout in March had unsettled him. In fact, he had begun his remarks on April 22 by self-consciously expressing "the hope that the House would not resent his taking part in this discussion."[12]

But, in addition to the political turmoil surrounding him, there was a personal matter weighing on his mind, one with which few people were familiar. In just six days he was expecting a reunion with the woman he wanted to marry. On April 28 Ethel Barrymore would be arriving from New York to begin rehearsals for a play that her backers expected to be a big hit. It was set to open in mid-May, and Winston was hoping for a long run, by the end of which—if he happened to be lucky—the Broadway star might agree to stay on as his wife.[13]

Charles Frohman, the Broadway producer who had launched Ethel's career in America, was counting on her to bring him success in London playing the title character in *Cynthia*, a new comedy by the young English playwright Hubert Henry Davies. This was her first chance to shine in a major British theatrical production. Opening night was already the subject of much discussion, largely because Millicent Sutherland—Ethel's host for the summer—planned on bringing all her literary and society friends to give the star a warm reception. For the first two weeks of her stay Ethel had little time to herself as she tried to meet her social obligations with Millie and also complete her rehearsals at Wyndham's

Theatre. But Winston was anxious to see her alone and didn't waste time arranging to dine with her. His engagement diary lists the dinner date as May 3, with her name discreetly given as "EB."

This meeting seems to have marked merely the opening salvo of Winston's campaign to woo Ethel. Many years later one of his daughters would say of the romance, "Papa besieged her with flowers and notes, and every night he used to go to Claridge's for supper where she always went after her performance." In old age Ethel herself confirmed that Winston had proposed, and she admitted that "she had been much attracted to him." Preoccupied with her play, she didn't give him a firm answer right away. And, then, while he was settling in for a long romantic siege, something went wrong. It wasn't through any fault of his own, but it caused Ethel to make a hasty departure from London and to put aside any thought of marrying him.[14]

The trouble began on May 16, the opening night of the play. Despite the friendly audience, the comedy fell flat, and the critics showed no mercy for the author, though they did praise Barrymore's performance. The review in the *Times* was typical. The play was so slight, observed the critic, "that it can hardly be said to have been written at all. It can hardly be said to exist. It is not a play but a part, and the part is not a part but Miss Ethel Barrymore." The verdict was that the star's performance alone had made the comedy worth watching, but that even her charm couldn't compensate for the weak plot and bad dialogue.

Winston brought flowers to Ethel's dressing room, but she knew the play was in trouble, and so did he. "Oh, my poor darling," he said. The production limped along for two more weeks, but at the beginning of June, word came that it would close on the eleventh. It was a very short run for a play that had raised such high expectations. Embarrassed, Ethel announced that she would return home to America immediately after her last performance. The closing was regrettable, said the *Daily Express,* "because it unfortunately shortens the stay in London of the charming American actress, Miss Ethel Barrymore. It is a pity that Mr. Frohman is not able to 'present' Miss Barrymore in another and more attractive play."[15]

Ethel not only fled London at the first opportunity, but kept going all the way to San Francisco, where she spent July acting at a local theater, avoiding the spotlight in New York, where the short run of her London play had made news. Though she admitted to a San Francisco paper that her stay in England had been disappointing, she made it clear that she would go back soon. "London means so much to me," she said.[16]

But she wasn't referring to Winston. Whatever interest he had held for her quickly faded. By the time she showed up in London again, a year had gone by and she was already in love with another man. She didn't have any time for Churchill. "I was so in love with her," he recalled half a century later. "And she wouldn't pay any attention to me at all."[17]

It wasn't for lack of effort that he was failing to find a wife. For the second time in his quest he had aimed high and fallen short.

With her sketchy understanding of British politics, Ethel may not have realized, however, that while she was struggling with *Cynthia*, Winston had staged a brief dramatic performance of his own. It was lightly attended, and its significance may not have been widely appreciated at the time, but for those who understood its importance, it was unforgettable.

On May 31, 1904, when the House was almost empty on a rainy afternoon, Churchill entered and, in the words of the *Manchester Guardian*, "glanced at his accustomed place . . . made a rapid survey of the corresponding bench on the Opposition side, marched a few paces up the floor, bowed to the Chair, swerved suddenly to the right, and took his seat among the Liberals."

And the man he sat next to wasn't an ordinary Liberal. He was David Lloyd George—already Lucifer incarnate to Joe and his followers. Churchill's break with his party could not have been sharper. All the Hooligans had drifted away from him except for Hugh, who nonetheless was so offended by Lloyd George's criticisms of the landed classes and the Anglican Church that he vowed not to "touch such . . . propaganda with a punt pole." So, at twenty-nine, Winston was restarting his political career with a new set of allies and aiming high again.[18]

VIII

THE BACHELOR AND THE HEIRESS

At the end of June 1904 the journalist Herbert Vivian visited Churchill at the House of Commons and was impressed by the attention the young MP was receiving. Much had changed since their meeting at Winston's rooms the year before, when Chamberlain had launched his ill-fated campaign for protection. Now Winston had become much more of a national figure, and it showed. Making their way to the terrace for tea, the two men passed several other members with guests—including a number of well-dressed ladies—and Winston created a little stir of excitement among these visitors. "I marked the general interest which he aroused," Herbert Vivian recalled. "All turned to observe him, the greater part with a smile of approval. He seemed little concerned with the attention which he aroused, but led the way with many a merry quip."

On the terrace all the tables were occupied except for a few in the area reserved for the House of Lords. For Churchill, this was no inconvenience. He simply strode across the invisible line separating the two groups and sat down with his friend at one of the empty tables. The servants, however, were aghast at this breach of decorum and refused to bring them tea. Smiling, Winston got up and walked back to his proper side, where he pointed and said, "Very well. Put the tea down there, and I will carry it across myself."

After that, no one troubled Churchill and his guest for the rest of the afternoon. They talked politics, and as far as Winston was concerned, it was the only subject for the terrace. "If I had my way," he said, casting a severe gaze at the many tables of visitors who were laughing and enjoying their tea, "I would abolish all this nonsense. The House of

Commons should be a place of business, not a place of entertainment."[1]

Even on the terrace, he couldn't resist looking for something to reform. Now that he was a Liberal, he was eager to throw out the Tories and get his hands on the machinery of government, tinkering here and there, or overhauling parts that no longer worked, and making the whole thing run much better. No longer a Hooligan taunting his elders from the wings, he was a political star preparing to occupy the limelight when—as he felt was sure to happen—the Liberals swept into power on a wave of antiprotectionist feeling.

Already political cartoonists were portraying him more often in their work, though one complained that his features weren't distinctive enough for a good caricature and suggested, tongue in cheek, that he should wear a monocle. To satisfy the growing curiosity about him, Madame Tussaud's added Winston to its waxworks, which caused no small amount of resentment among critics who considered his prominence undeserved. "He has won the blue ribbon of advertisement," said a satirical article in a weekly magazine. "His struggles after notoriety have raised him to the level in popularity of murderers and card-sharpers, millionaires and crowned heads. Everything comes to the man who knows how to advertise."

Many others, however, didn't think his reputation was inflated at all. The old bearded veteran of Victorian journalism, W. T. Stead, wrote in July, "Today Winston Churchill is the centre of the political arena. He is the most conspicuous, and in many respects the ablest, of our rising statesmen." And in August a journalist sympathetic to the Liberals cheered the party for now having in Churchill and Lloyd George a one-two knockout punch. They embodied "the bull-dog spirit" that would put the Tories flat on their backs.[2]

The Liberals were pleased enough with their new recruit so that he wasn't questioned too closely about his overall political views. Whether he was now a real Liberal or simply a Tory dissident looking for respect was a question that everyone—including Churchill himself—seemed happy to put off until the next general election. For the time being, the main thing was to chip away at Balfour's authority until he saw the hopelessness of his position and stepped down, clearing the way for a new government.

Though the prime minister pretended in public not to be troubled by Churchill joining the Liberals, he knew the defection had set a bad example for others in the party, and he was always worried about further losses. For months it nagged at him, and a few Conservatives did slip through his grasp to join Winston on the other side. But when—out of the blue—Hugh Cecil began to waver one day, Balfour was so alarmed that he wrote to his cousin in a near panic, begging him "to remain in the party!! . . . Never talk of leaving the Party!"[3]

As it turned out, Hugh was only letting off steam after Joe had made some irritating remark. But Balfour didn't want to endure another embarrassing defection by a prominent member. It was bad enough having Churchill unleashed on the other side. There was no mistaking the danger he posed. In October Winston told a Welsh audience that his goal was "to harass, to embarrass, and ultimately to drive from power an Administration which has forfeited the confidence of the country."[4]

In his October visit to Wales, Churchill shared the platform with Lloyd George, who said that his new friend was trying "to strengthen his infant steps as a Liberal." What this meant in practice was that Winston now had Lloyd George as his guide to modern liberalism, whose aims were much more ambitious than those of the old Victorian party. The new Liberals wanted to use the power of government to transform society, making major improvements in the lives of the poor, the sick, and the elderly. In his Liberal "infancy" Winston was willing to loosen some of his aristocratic roots and give the new ideas close attention. All the same, what he really wanted now from Lloyd George wasn't social policies, but a war plan to topple Chamberlain and the Conservatives. As he told the audience in Wales, "Mr. Lloyd George is the best fighting general in the Liberal ranks." (Everyone liked to call Churchill by his first name, but in the political world it was unusual for Lloyd George to be called David, though in private Winston usually addressed him that way once their friendship began in earnest.)[5]

The prospect of a good fight against Balfour's government created one of the most unusual partnerships in British political history. Until now the only political partner Winston had known was Linky Cecil. In Lloyd George he had found someone who was Cecil's polar opposite. The ancestral mansion, the relatives in high places, the comfortable private income, and the noble title—all these were alien to the Welshman who had risen from modest beginnings to become a powerful figure in the Liberal Party. Just as alien was Lord Hugh's prim, ascetic character. Lloyd George was nearly twelve years Churchill's senior and in 1904 had already been married for sixteen years and fathered five children. He didn't care much for religion—except when it suited his political purposes—and his fondness for women kept him constantly involved in clandestine affairs.

Lacking the polish of the typical Edwardian gentleman, Lloyd George was a convenient figure for the Tories to ridicule, which is why Churchill had found it so easy at first to dismiss him as "a vulgar, chattering little cad." But after a few years of watching him stand up to Chamberlain, Winston didn't care whether the Liberal fighter was a proper gentleman or not. He was simply relieved to find in him the kind of Hooligan he had been looking for all along—a fearless sharpshooter to cover his advance. The only problem was that Winston would insist on viewing the relationship through a romantic prism, just as he had with Hugh Cecil. He innocently assumed that the partnership was essentially for his benefit, and that this faithful marksman wouldn't one day plug him in the back.

But even if Churchill had been more realistic about their relationship, he couldn't have guessed at this stage that Lloyd George had resolved long ago to allow almost nothing to stand in the way of his own ambition—including friendship. "My supreme idea is to get on," he had confessed in the 1880s in a remarkably candid letter to his wife, Margaret. "To this idea I shall sacrifice everything—except, I trust, honesty. I am prepared to thrust even love itself under the wheels of my Juggernaut if it obstructs the way."[6]

Among old admirers who had known Lloyd George from his early days in Wales, there was no doubt that his new partnership could easily erode into an intense rivalry. As his friend D. R. Daniel noted, it was inevitable that Churchill and Lloyd George would "meet face to face one day on that narrow path which leads to the highest pinnacle of honour." Winston probably assumed that if that day arrived, he would prevail. But what would happen if they weren't face-to-face? He didn't seem to give much thought to the risks of leaving his back turned to Lloyd George.

In one thing, however, the characters of the two men were perfectly attuned. Though he had no experience of real battlefields, and had never served as a soldier, Lloyd George saw himself as a warrior in the political realm. It was not just in Winston's imagination that the Liberal stalwart was like a general bravely preparing an assault on some political stronghold. Lloyd George had always looked on his opponents as soldiers who, as the need arose, could be mown down by relentless fire. Where he differed from Churchill was in his cold, bloodless manner of imagining the battlefield.

"I recollect," he once told an audience in Cardiff, "what an American soldier once said when he was asked: 'When you aim your rifle at the men on the other side, do you hate them?' . . . His reply was: 'No, I don't fire at anybody. I simply fire at the line of battle.' Really, that is what I have been doing all my life."[7]

For Churchill the next election would be fought in a new constituency. There was no place for him as a Liberal in Oldham, so he accepted an offer to contest a seat in nearby Manchester. Though he couldn't predict when the general election would occur, he knew the costs would force him to dig deeper into his dwindling supply of cash. He was quickly running through the money he had saved up three years ago, and was now counting on his biography of Lord Randolph to replenish his bank account. But it was far from being finished. The intense political activity of the last year and a half had delayed his work on the book. He would need at least another year to complete it.

He had lived well and spent his money freely. When he traveled, he stayed at the best hotels and ate well—he was fond of treating himself to oysters and champagne. He was also playing polo fairly often, on the excuse that it gave him good exercise, despite the expense.

Before Ethel Barrymore had fled London with little warning, he had been planning to make another trip to America. When it had become clear that her play would close in June, his first thought seems to have been to follow her home to New York. On May 31—the very same day that he sat for the first time with the Liberals—he accepted an invitation to attend the Democratic National Convention in July as the guest of his mother's old friend New York congressman W. Bourke Cockran.

Presumably, he would be able to combine business with pleasure, observing the American political system up close while reserving some time to continue his gentle siege of Ethel. Staying with Cockran, a strong free trader, would also give him the chance to talk strategy with a man he admired.

But in mid-June, about a week after Ethel had left London, Winston wrote Cockran to say that he couldn't come. His decision was abrupt, and he blamed it on the need to continue fighting "Chamberlain & his Merrie Men." What seems more likely is that between the end of May and the middle of June, he realized that it wasn't worth the time or money to chase reluctant Ethel, especially after her last-minute decision to go to San Francisco.[8]

Instead he did the sensible thing. His ever-generous friend Sir Ernest Cassel invited him to stay at the enormous gingerbread villa he owned high in the Swiss Alps, and Winston accepted. He spent a good part of August there, devoting his mornings to writing the biography of his father, spending the afternoons hiking, and reading in the evenings or playing bridge. The weather was perfect, he slept well at night with the windows wide open, and dinners were prepared by a French cook. As a holiday, it was much easier on him than pursuing Ethel across the American continent, and much more productive.

A shrewd judge of character, Cassel always believed that Winston had the talent and the will to succeed in British politics. As a man with great wealth to employ and protect, he was careful to cultivate the friendship of those in high places—even when, as in Winston's case, the heights had yet to be reached. But their close relationship was based on much more than money and influence. They genuinely liked each other and enjoyed spending time together. After Cassel's death in 1921 Winston would tell the banker's granddaughter, Edwina, Lady Mountbatten, "I had the knowledge that he was very fond of me & believed in me at all times—especially in bad times. I had a real & deep affection for him."[9]

He made such good progress on the biography that he was feeling unusually confident when he returned home. So confident, in fact, that he did something stunningly audacious, even for him. On September 22 he visited Joe Chamberlain at his Birmingham mansion and stayed overnight. Afterward, Churchill could hardly believe what he had done, and he told a few friends about it only after asking them to keep it a secret.

His excuse for the visit was that he wanted information from Joe about Lord Randolph. Bravely, he had written him asking for letters that might be useful for the biography. With even greater bravery, Joe had invited him to come to Highbury and spend the night. It is rare that such bitter foes would be able to meet in this way, especially since they were still very much at each other's throats in the political arena. But they couldn't resist the chance to size each other up before the final battles began. Despite all the bad blood that had flowed between them, they had a steely respect for each other.

As in earlier, friendlier days, Joe brought out the expensive port and they stayed up late into the night talking about the past, and a little about the future. It was almost as if nothing had happened over the past few years to change their relationship, for here they were again in the sprawling mansion that was still the same, with its rows of hothouses sheltering the treasured orchids. And here again was the young man closely observing while the older one looked back on life and dispensed wisdom with his stiff smile and dry laugh.

Joe conceded that Winston had done the right thing for his own career by joining the Liberals, but he warned that the Conservatives would never forgive his decision, and that he would have to endure abuse from them for a long time. Having switched parties himself almost twenty years ago, Chamberlain knew the cost of being labeled a turncoat. But he had learned a valuable lesson, and probably suspected that Winston had learned it too—the ordeal made you stronger. "If a man is sure of himself," he said in his soft voice, "it only sharpens him and makes him more effective."

When they parted the next day, they did so on polite terms, but each knew that in a year or so only one of them would stand triumphant. Joe tried to make light of the fact that the government could fall sooner rather than later. As he wished Churchill success with the biography of Lord Randolph, he expressed the hope that the book would appear before any major political change in the country. "The public cannot stand two sensations at the same time," he joked.

Despite all the smiles and pleasantries, Winston went away thinking that he had sensed vulnerability in his opponent. He concluded a little later that Joe and Balfour would, in the end, "cut their own throats and bring their party to utter destruction." He was so sure of this that he thought the Liberals would win the next election in a landslide. It was as if the meeting at Highbury had been Joe's way of tipping his hat to the victor before the blade fell.[10]

So, after a tumultuous spring and summer, Churchill was looking forward to enjoying the fruits of his hard work—money and more fame from the publication of the biography, and a place in the new government after the defeat of Joe.

Something was missing, however. As he approached his thirtieth birthday he was still searching for a wife. The press was beginning to speculate whether he would ever marry and settle down or simply drift into middle age as a "confirmed bachelor," which is the very phrase a society magazine applied to him at the end of the year. It was the last thing he wanted to be. But, after two failed proposals, he was beginning to have his doubts. Then, again, he wasn't the kind to give up.[11]

Perhaps because he didn't think he had anything to lose, he set his sights on another woman who seemed beyond his reach. She was Muriel Wilson, whom he had known for years. They were the same age and had always liked each other. Their names had been linked romantically once or twice when they were younger, but this had been mostly idle gossip. For much of their friendship, she had refused in a good-natured way to take him seriously as a potential mate. Other men always seemed to have a stronger claim on her attention. Yet they all went away disappointed. For the past ten years some of the handsomest and best-connected men in the kingdom had tried and failed to win her hand. Now, as she was nearing thirty herself, Winston dared to hope that she was ready to contemplate a future with him.

She loved her freedom and didn't need to rush into anything. She lived like a princess and never wanted for money. Her father, Arthur Wilson, ran the world's largest privately owned steamship company, with a fleet of almost a hundred ships. At his death in 1909, he was one of Britain's richest men, worth an estimated £4 million (an astounding sum at a time when the prime minister's pay was £5,000 a year). The family had a mansion near Buckingham Palace, a sprawling villa in the south of France, and a country house in Yorkshire—Tranby Croft (scene of a notorious incident in the early 1890s involving a guest who cheated the Prince of Wales at cards).

The family fortune was not Muriel's only attraction. She was a strikingly lovely woman. Ethel Barrymore's brother, Lionel, said Muriel was one of the "most beautiful women I ever saw in my life." In her early twenties the American press called her "Great Britain's most beautiful girl." She bore some resemblance to the young Jennie Churchill, with dark features, a small, delicate mouth, large eyes, and a rich mass of wavy hair. Her dresses were legendary, cut from the finest materials to accentuate her tall, willowy form. "Singularly handsome," said the *London Journal*, "she could nowhere pass unnoticed."

Fluent in French, possessed with a good sense of humor, and popular with both sexes, she seemed to do everything well. "She skates, cycles, and dances to perfection," one society magazine gushed. She even had a career of sorts, routinely acting in amateur theatricals. Not wanting a salary, she performed only for friends at country house parties or onstage in London and elsewhere for charity. She was celebrated for the memorable costumes she wore in historical pageants, where she would walk onstage like a goddess, personifying some epic moment. In a flimsy white gown she would appear as "Peace" or in a heavy Wagnerian robe as "War." She could not have failed to excite Winston's deepest passions when she played the "Muse of History," her eyes soulfully fixed on the heavens while waving a sword. Photographs of her posing in costume for these parts were reproduced in the Edwardian society magazines, where she was hailed as "the finest of our lady amateurs on the stage."[12]

How could Winston Churchill have resisted the chance to court the "Muse of History"? When Muriel gave him a photograph of her playing one of these allegorical figures, he was thrilled and vowed to keep it with him always. In this way and others, she gave him enough encouragement in the autumn of 1904 to make him think a proposal might be met with success. He believed their long friendship was suddenly ripening into something more serious. But he had misread the signals. When he asked the all-important question, she gave him such a firm rejection that he went away crushed.

He begged her to reconsider, and told her in a letter written in the heat of his distress that he was willing to wait for her to change her mind. "Perhaps I shall improve with waiting," he wrote, sounding desperate. "Why shouldn't you care about me someday?" Trying to think of something convincing to say, he offered her both a promise and a prophecy. If she would trust him to prove that he was worthy of her, she wouldn't be disappointed. No matter how long it took, he would make her proud. And then came the prophecy. "Time and circumstance," he said, "will work for me." Then he told her that he loved her and couldn't bear to go forward without her.

She seems to have been touched by the letter, but not enough to change her mind. For the rest of 1904, and well into the next year, he kept writing to her, and they continued to see each other. He recited poetry to her, then recommended that for an insight into his feelings she should read Robert Burns's lyric "Mary Morison," which includes the question, "Canst thou break that heart of his, / [Whose] only fault is loving thee?" He praised every hair on her head, told her he could be happy just to be near her, and kept reminding her that she had completely captured his heart. Every now and then, she allowed him to take her to a dance or to accompany her on a long walk at sunset. Yet there was a "key" to her own heart, he told her, that he couldn't seem to find. "You dwell apart," he wrote, "as lofty, as shining & alas as cold as a snow clad peak."[13]

She wasn't so cold to others, however, and Winston couldn't understand how she could spend time with his rivals, none of whom impressed him as having better claims to her affection than his own. The problem was that, for the time being, marriage simply wasn't in Muriel's plans. She was having far too much fun to settle down. Instead of devoting herself to Winston, she preferred the company of such easygoing playboys as Luis de Soveral, the Portuguese ambassador and one of King Edward's closest friends.

Referred to by one social historian as the "greatest ladies' man" of his time, Soveral may have earned his nickname—the "Blue Monkey"—as a result of some long-forgotten episode in a boudoir. Many decades after his death a flirtatious letter from Muriel was found among his papers— along with love notes from other Edwardian beauties—and it includes her provocative suggestion that he spend the afternoon at the family's

London mansion. "Are you too busy to lunch with me tomorrow?" she wrote. "I am quite alone, but the butler and the parrot are excellent chaperones."[14]

It was her casual willingness to share private afternoons with unscrupulous characters like Soveral that drove Winston to distraction. One of her few surviving letters to him is a note saying she would rather not meet him for lunch because "it is a meal I dislike intensely." Such rebuffs were difficult for Winston to accept. Her failure to settle down and marry was, he told her, "a sad pity & a scattering of treasure."[15]

Muriel was content to play with Winston's emotions for as long as he kept coming to her door. She didn't resent his attentions, for he always fascinated her. She just didn't want his life to become hers. Politics didn't interest her that much, and she didn't want to be stuck in London if she suddenly felt the urge to enjoy a few weeks of sunny warmth at the Villa Maryland, the family home on Cap Ferrat.

The fact that he refused to give up on her, and continued pressing his claims over the next year, became a subject of considerable gossip in London and even in America. Some assumed that he was interested in her only because she was rich. "Winston must marry money," an anonymous "friend" told a society magazine. No one could ignore the Wilson fortune, but Winston had fallen in love with Muriel after a long friendship and wasn't suddenly drawn to her simply because she came from a wealthy family. He was working hard to make money from his pen and would always want to earn his living. He would have been happy to marry Ethel if she had said yes, even though she lived from one play to the next, and had no fortune to speak of.[16]

In Muriel he found many of the same qualities he admired in Ethel Barrymore. In his romantic concept of his life it was easy for him to think that the kind of woman who belonged at his side was a glamorous, theatrical personality with an air of mystery and remoteness. There were predictions in the press that Winston would prevail this time, and that Muriel would marry him in the end. He was teased in one American newspaper for having three consuming ambitions: to achieve a great success with his biography of Lord Randolph, to marry Muriel Wilson, and "to grow a moustache." But, the reporter deadpanned, "The last is generally regarded as the most difficult achievement of the three."[17]

IX

FORTUNATE SON

In his imagination Churchill had no trouble staging the perfect courtship. Around the time that he was so desperate to marry Muriel Wilson, he wrote a novelistic scene in which a couple become engaged. The man is a handsome aristocrat in his twenties, the woman "a singular beauty" of nineteen. They meet at a ball in an old seaside resort and fall madly in love in the course of just three days.

Churchill wrote, "That night—the third of their acquaintance—was a beautiful night, warm and still, with the lights of the yachts shining on the water and the sky bright with stars. After dinner they found themselves alone together in the garden, and—brief courtship notwithstanding—he proposed and was accepted."[1]

In fiction love could seem so easy. Except this wasn't fiction, though it sounds like it. This was simply Winston the biographer describing the night his parents were engaged. His mother had told him the story, and he cast it in romantic prose that enhanced the past and reflected his own current frustrations. If Lord Randolph could meet and win Jennie so effortlessly in three days, why couldn't Winston—after three *years*—find the right woman to marry him?

The biography was meant to honor Randolph's memory, but writing it was also a way for Winston to understand his own life. He had never established a close connection with Randolph, though he had yearned for one. His father was a tragic figure—an ambitious and outspoken politician, but a failure as a statesman; a restless man always searching for attention, but never getting enough to please him; the proud son of a great family, but a difficult husband and father. Living in Randolph's shadow for much of his life, Winston couldn't help wondering if his father's legacy was a blessing or a curse.

It was too early in his life to answer the question, but he could craft a plausible answer in his book. He tried to enhance Randolph's story by turning his father into a version of himself. They had much in common, but the Winston-Randolph composite in the biography comes across as nobler and steadier, and much more determined and farseeing, than the real Randolph. In several passages Winston could easily have been describing himself rather than his father. "He seemed an intruder, an upstart," he wrote of Lord Randolph, "a mutineer who flouted venerable leaders and mocked at constituted authority with a mixture of aristocratic insolence and democratic brutality."[2]

The Randolph who emerges from Winston's book is a misunderstood hero who tries to inspire his party and his country to achieve great things, but who is defeated by the forces of reaction and selfish interests. Too soon, his wings are clipped and he slowly falls to earth; another aristocratic dreamer like Lord Byron, he lives large and dies young, scorned by the unimaginative but mourned by all those with understanding hearts. A thousand pages long, the biography is a towering, gleaming monument that was meant to be a kind of manifesto, with the son gathering up the disordered pieces of his father's life to construct a romantic vision that might guide his own career.

One day, while Winston was working on the biography, he was visited at home by the poet Wilfrid Scawen Blunt, an old friend of Randolph. Tall, eccentric, and outspoken, Blunt had been drawn to the unconventional side of Lord Randolph's character and had always taken an indulgent view of his friend's faults. Like Winston, he was inclined to see a touch of the Byronic hero in the charming, erratic Randolph. But, in truth, Blunt was obsessed with Lord Byron, so much so that he married the poet's granddaughter—Lady Annabella Noel—and liked to think of "himself as Byron reborn."[3]

Listening to Winston discuss the biography, Blunt was struck by how much of the father he could see in the son. The physical resemblance wasn't strong, but he thought Winston embodied in an uncanny way some essential element of his father's spirit. "He is astonishingly like his father in manners and ways, and the whole attitude of his mind," Blunt wrote in his journal in August 1904. "He has just come in from playing polo, a short, sturdy little man with a twinkle in his eye, reminding me especially of the Randolph of twenty years ago. He took out his father's letters which I had left with him six weeks ago, from a tin box, and read them to me aloud while I explained the allusions in them, and gave him a short account of the political adventures of the early eighties in which Randolph and I had been connected. There is something touching about the fidelity with which he continues to espouse his father's cause and his father's quarrels."[4]

At his best, Lord Randolph was witty, urbane, eloquent, and passionate. At his worst, he was so impulsive and reckless that some of his contemporaries thought he was deranged. Lord Derby wrote of him in 1885, "With all his remarkable cleverness, [he] is thoroughly untrustworthy: scarcely a gentleman, and probably more or less mad." Even his good friend Lord Rosebery wrote that Randolph always suffered from a certain "waywardness," which grew worse in his last years when his mind seemed "unbalanced and almost unhinged."[5]

What Winston knew, and what some of his father's contemporaries must have assumed, was that Randolph suffered for years from the debilitating effects of the syphilis that killed him. Though recent efforts have been made to suggest that a brain tumor may have been the cause of his troubles, this is mostly speculation. The subject of venereal disease was such a taboo in Victorian and Edwardian societies that Winston was forced in the biography to explain his father's death in the most awkward euphemisms, saying that Randolph was the victim of a mysterious "ghastly disease" that caused those "who loved him [to be] consumed with embarrassment and grief."[6]

In a much shorter book on Randolph, Lord Rosebery used language that was more conclusive. Writing that his friend "died by inches in public," he described the malady as a "cruel disease which was to paralyse and kill him." More telling, he wrote that Randolph grew steadily worse from "the stealthy poison of his illness." Randolph's best modern biographer, Roy Foster, has written that the specialist in the case, Dr. Roose, believed that his patient had syphilis and "ministered to him accordingly."[7]

In the last year of his life Lord Randolph was closely attended by Dr.

George E. Keith, a fellow of the British Gynecological Society, whose expertise in venereal cases apparently led him to treat both sexes. He was Jennie's doctor, and in the weeks leading up to Randolph's death one of her great fears was that the nature of her husband's illness would become widely known. She wrote her sister Leonie, "The General Public and even Society does not know the real truth . . . it would be hard if it got out. It would do incalculable harm to his political reputation & memory & be a dreadful thing for all of us." (How and when Randolph was infected is unknown, but for a long period his relations with Jennie had been distant, and she was immersed in love affairs of her own, seemingly unharmed by her husband's disease.)[8]

Winston discovered the truth while his father was still alive. Even at twenty he was good at getting what he wanted from his elders, and had talked Dr. Roose into showing him the medical reports and telling him "everything." Afterward, he explained to his mother what he had done. "I have told no one," he wrote her. "I need not tell you how anxious I am."[9]

Winston was always haunted by his father's death. It had been disturbing to observe Randolph's deterioration; and for his family, the whole experience was—as Winston says in the biography—an "embarrassment." It was also heartrending to a son who wanted to idolize his father. He never forgot the snowy morning that Lord Randolph died. More than half a century later, when he was prime minister for the second time, he surprised his doctor by suddenly remarking, "My poor papa died on January 24, 1895. It is a long time ago." The date was seared into his memory.[10]

Strangely, his own death would fall on the same day. In a future that would have seemed light-years away to the Edwardians, Winston Churchill took his last breath at the age of ninety on the morning of January 24, 1965, the seventieth anniversary of Randolph's death.

Churchill finished the biography as the summer of 1905 was coming to an end. Writing it was an emotionally and physically draining experience, and at times he had been so overworked that his haggard appearance shocked those who happened to see him at a bad moment. Exaggerating the effect, one journalist seemed eager to write young Churchill's obituary: "There is nothing of 'the Boy' left in the white, nervous, washed-out face . . . It is a tired face . . . worn, harassed. He talks as a man of fifty talks—a little cruelly, slowly, measuring his words, the hand for ever tilting the hat backwards and forwards or brushing itself roughly across the tired eyes."

Such was Winston's physical resiliency, however, that he could look completely exhausted one day, and the next have all the necessary energy for playing polo or giving a couple of speeches two hundred miles from home. It was this deep well of strength that often left his contemporaries in wonder, and that set him apart from so many other sons of the aristocracy who thought it vulgar to appear too energetic. It also distinguished him from his father, who liked to play hard but wasn't known for his dedication to hard work. "Mr. Churchill is superior to his father," wrote A. G. Gardiner, the editor of the London *Daily News*. "For to Lord Randolph's flair and courage and instinct for the game he adds a knowledge and industry his father did not possess. He works with the same fury that he plays, attacks a subject with the intrepidity with which he attacks an opponent in the house."[11]

It helped him at one point to find what he called "an American rubber"—or in modern terms a "massage therapist," who also happened to be an older American woman. She was a miracle worker, he told all his friends. Recommending her to Hugh Cecil, he assured him that the woman was thoroughly respectable—a "venerable God-fearing old lady"—who could do wonders to cure Linky's chronic "debility." After just "four rubbings," by which he meant four sessions, Winston boasted that his circulation was better than ever and his heart was beating strongly. Teasing his friend, he told Hugh that she would "compel you to circulate and digest properly. You would then be certain of surviving Joe."[12]

Despite all the time and energy invested in the biography, Churchill wasn't sentimental about letting go of it. He was glad to be done with such an enormous task, and to have on paper at last the story that had been simmering in his head for years. Now he was eager to see what publishers were willing to pay for it. At a time when many established writers were happy to make several hundred pounds from a new book, Winston was expecting several thousand. One publisher had already offered £4,000 but he was sure he could get more.

To help him negotiate the best deal, he turned to a man he barely knew who wasn't a proper literary agent, and who had a reputation for mismanaging money, both his own and other people's. He had boundless enthusiasm, however. "Properly worked," the author and editor Frank Harris wrote Winston, "this book shd bring you in £10,000, or I'm a Dutchman." [13]

Frank Harris was a controversial figure in literary London whose career was on the decline in the early 1900s after he had taken a break from editing magazines to open a hotel in Monaco. He had gone bankrupt in that venture and was back in London, struggling to earn his living by his pen, when Winston entered his life. Almost fifty, he was said to resemble a superior kind of bartender, with his handlebar mustache, his dark hair parted in the middle, and his worldly air. He had not yet written the erotic memoir that would win him his greatest notoriety—*My Life and Loves*. That book was a product of the 1920s, when he was near the end of his life and desperate for money.

Like Wilfrid Scawen Blunt, Harris was an old friend of Lord Randolph. He had been one of his seedier companions, living by his own rules and reveling in the pleasures afforded by the usual trilogy of wine, women, and song. Harris was never respectable, but now that his days were over as a prominent editor of the Victorian era, he was increasingly seen in literary circles as a dissolute has-been. George Bernard Shaw described him as "neither first-rate, nor second-rate, nor tenth rate . . . just his horrible unique self."

But there was an all-important reason that Winston was willing to risk using Harris as a literary agent. In better days, when he was editing the *Saturday Review*, Harris had written a glowing tribute to Lord Randolph, which had appeared on January 26, 1895. It was in this article that he had made the impassioned argument for Randolph as the Lord Byron of the late-Victorian political world. That comparison had been resonating in Winston's imagination for a decade, and now he wanted Harris to play a part in this new biographical tribute to Randolph. [14]

Of their brief work together Harris recalled, "He knew me, it appeared, chiefly through the article I had written in the *Saturday Review* on the occasion of his father's death. He was kind enough to call it 'the best article which had appeared anywhere,' and added that the Duchess of Marlborough, Randolph's mother, always showed it about as establishing her estimate of her favorite son's genius."

Whatever anyone else may have thought of Harris, Winston trusted that his father's old friend would understand the point of the biography and would be able to sell others on it. And, as it happened, his faith wasn't misplaced. Harris was surprisingly successful at representing the book to publishers. He played all the right cards, emphasizing Winston's celebrity; the great potential for publicity; the book's intimate understanding of political life; the son's sympathetic treatment of his famous father's tumultuous and tragic career; and the many quotations from letters by a host of famous Victorians, including the queen herself. Harris didn't get an offer of ten thousand, but he came close. At the end of October the prestigious firm of Macmillan agreed to buy the rights for £8,000.

Winston was overjoyed and told Harris, "That'll make me independent; you've no idea what it means to me; it guarantees success; I am extremely obliged to you."

He paid Harris £400, in keeping with an agreement they had made at the outset. (His "agent" was to receive 10 percent of any money that topped the earlier offer of £4,000.) Their business done, the two went their separate ways, and thus Winston became one of the few who ever escaped without a scratch from a financial arrangement with Frank Harris. Improvident all his life, Harris died virtually penniless, so perhaps it isn't surprising that he recalled listening scornfully one day to Churchill lecture him on the virtue of planning ahead. "Get enough to live on, without asking anybody for anything," Winston had advised him. "That's the first condition of success, or indeed, of decent living; that's the prime necessity of life. Every man of us should think of nothing but that till it's achieved. Afterwards one can do what one likes—please keep that in front of you as *the* object of your life!"[15]

Such words were wasted on Harris, but as Winston proved with his prodigious labors as a paid speaker and author, he was practicing what he preached, "getting enough to live on, without asking anybody for anything." In the end, Lord Randolph, the father who died without providing much for his family, left Winston a gift more valuable than mere money. He left the example of his own life. It gave the son a story worth telling—financially and otherwise—and one worth reshaping to suit his own views and his own aims.

* * *

While he was taking the biography through its final stages in 1905, Winston did not fail in his promise to bedevil the government at every opportunity. In March he had made a lively indictment of Balfour and company as undemocratic obstructionists afraid "to face the verdict of the country" in a new election. The prime minister held office only because his uncle had handed him the job "as a private inheritance," Churchill said. But that title would soon be taken away after the electorate—"the high court of appeal"—rejected him. In this taunting way, Churchill cast Balfour as a man with power but no true authority.

By the middle of the summer, Balfour had been castigated so often by Churchill that he seemed impervious to further attacks. Winston suggested that the prime minister and his allies had fallen into a trance and were behaving like a half-dead character in Edgar Allan Poe's "The Facts in the Case of M. Valdemar," making "certain feeble and erratic motions" but leaving everyone guessing "whether death had or had not supervened." [16]

Churchill's ridicule was so stinging that some of his new Liberal friends pleaded with him to ease up. "I like the fighting portion of your speeches," a well-meaning Liberal member told him, but then advised that others on their side with "more tender susceptibilities" were becoming uncomfortable with the way Winston "scourged" the Tory leaders. As the year drew to a close, even the king himself felt obliged to give Winston a warning.

They dined together at the end of October, and Edward spent half the time castigating Churchill for the virulence of his attacks on Balfour. It was a painful experience, and Winston came away feeling like a disgraced schoolboy leaving the headmaster's study after a heavy reprimand. "I accepted it all with meekness," he wrote afterward. To make sure that Winston behaved himself, the king later sent him a newspaper article containing an ordinary journalist's admonitions and rebukes. His majesty seemed to think that Winston still needed more instruction in civility. "It might be worthwhile," said the journalist, "to suggest to [Churchill] that hysterical violence of language is not usually regarded as evidence of statesmanlike qualities, and that the country expects those who aspire to govern it to show some signs, at least, of their ability to govern themselves." [17]

It was doubtful, however, whether Churchill would be able to restrain himself if Balfour managed to cling to power much longer. But the pace of events suddenly picked up at the end of the year, and the prime minister finally found himself cornered. Support in his own ranks was beginning to crumble, and Chamberlain—weary of Balfour's prevarications—wanted him to take decisive action. Dissolve Parliament, he told him. "You will wreck the Party if you go on." [18]

But the prime minister preferred to resign rather than call an election. He wasn't eager to face that "high court of appeal" and wanted to force the Liberals to go into the next general election as a caretaker government. So he went to the king on the first Monday in December to submit his resignation. Word having leaked that he was contemplating this step, the country wasn't taken by surprise. When he arrived at Buckingham Palace, there were no crowds. The king had just returned from visiting a cattle show, and the moment lacked a sense of grandeur. It took only twenty minutes for Edward to accept the resignation, and for Balfour to slip away quietly.

His resignation didn't cause much rejoicing nor much sorrow. Having failed to unite his party and to save his old partnership with Chamberlain, he was forced to confront his failure and make his overdue exit. To his critics, it was a dismal end to a do-nothing administration. The *Manchester Guardian* saw his departure as an occasion that deserved a damning verdict borrowed from Shakespeare's *Julius Caesar*: "When beggars die, there are no comets seen."

The king sent for the Liberal leader Sir Henry Campbell-Bannerman to form a new government. All the newspapers were full of speculation about the various leaders who might be included in the new Liberal Cabinet. One name missing from most lists was Churchill's. The *Daily Mirror* was an exception, suggesting his name for postmaster general. After all his efforts to topple Balfour, such a dull office wasn't what he had in mind. But he seemed content to wait patiently for a worthy offer, confident that one would be forthcoming. "I await with composure," he wrote his mother in early December, "the best or worst that Fortune has in hand."

Jennie wasn't as composed. Whitelaw Reid, the American ambassador, heard that she was telling her friends, "The next Government will have to put Winston in the Cabinet. If it doesn't, God help them!" [19]

PART II

1906—1910

X

WINNERS AND LOSERS

To some in his party, the man who sailed straight to the premiership was a plodding, unremarkable old man with a sunny but shallow personality. They made fun of Sir Henry Campbell-Bannerman behind his back and called him "Aunt Jane." One of his strongest critics—the cerebral Richard Haldane, an MP with a habit of quoting German philosophers—later complained in his memoirs that Sir Henry "was not identified in the public mind with any fresh ideas, for indeed he had none."

In the end, C.B.—as he was often called—gave some of the top jobs to his strongest critics. Asquith became Chancellor of the Exchequer, Sir Edward Grey the head of the Foreign Office, and Haldane the head of the War Office. Lloyd George was also brought into the Cabinet as president of the Board of Trade.[1]

Though many in the party didn't think Churchill was ready for office, C.B. understood what Balfour had not—that it would be a mistake to ignore Winston. He needed a reward, and the new prime minister saw a way to bestow it without appointing him to the Cabinet. What C.B. offered was the position of Financial Secretary of the Treasury, a prestigious job with a handsome salary of £2,000. It meant that Winston would be serving as Asquith's deputy and would have immense responsibilities. This was a magnificent offer to a young man who had just turned thirty-one, and who had been a Liberal for only a year and a half.

Yet Churchill turned it down, and asked instead for a slightly less impressive job that paid only £1,500. It was a risky move, but it made sense. He had little experience of dealing with the Treasury and didn't think his ambitions would be served by laboring in Asquith's shadow. What he wanted, he told C.B., was the position of undersecretary to the Colonial Office, a department he understood far better than the Treasury. The old man thought it over and said yes.

There was a certain satisfaction in taking the number-two job at a department that Chamberlain had run for eight years as his own fiefdom. If the Liberals could finally deal a crushing blow to Joe's imperial dreams, Winston wanted to do his part from within the Colonial Office. There was also the added advantage that the new man appointed to head the department was in the House of Lords, which meant that Churchill would be its spokesman in the House of Commons. In effect, he would be doing much of what Chamberlain had once done.

The new secretary of state for the colonies was the ninth Earl of Elgin, whose grandfather had been responsible for the controversial removal of the marble sculptures from the Parthenon in the early nineteenth century. ("Curst be the hour when from their isle they roved," wrote Lord Byron, who denounced the seventh earl as a vandal.) Winston didn't think he would have much trouble from his aristocratic chief, who was a capable administrator but had little interest in politics. Lord Elgin disliked giving speeches or taking part in Cabinet debates. Churchill thought he could run circles around him and get his way more often than not.

At first, his decision to go to the Colonial Office may have mystified many in the party, but a few sharp-eyed observers were quick to understand his scheme. In fact, *Punch* gave the game away not long after Churchill joined the department. One of its brilliant cartoonists decided to portray Winston as a young Greek warrior charging into action on a galloping steed labeled "Colonial Office." Behind him in robe and sandals stands a bearded Lord Elgin with staff in hand, trying to rein in Winston by grasping at his flowing cape. The whole thing is designed to look like a Parthenon frieze and was published over the caption "An Elgin Marble," with a note jokingly attributing the design to Winston himself.

Only Churchill could work for an earl and act as if he were the boss. As one popular journal said of him, "If he were only a deputy-assistant coatpeg, he would be the most prominent hook in the row."[2]

* * *

The news that Churchill had succeeded in becoming part of the government brought congratulatory notes from many friends, including Hugh Cecil, who gave him a well-intentioned warning to avoid "gaseous" speechmaking and to focus on turning himself into a skilled administrator. Winston took the criticism in good humor and agreed to do his best as a junior minister.

There was no sign that his new job had made Muriel Wilson think any better of him as a potential husband, but another old flame did come back into his life. It was Pamela, now Lady Lytton. She had been gradually renewing her ties to him, clearing away old animosities and misunderstandings. They had met at parties now and then, and she and her husband had entertained him at Knebworth House. Impressed by Winston's accomplishments, she had a new appreciation for him and wanted his friendship. She was affectionate and kind, and—grateful for that—he reciprocated. They started writing to each other again, with Pamela addressing him warmly as "Winston Mine." However much she may have disappointed him, he still had powerful memories of their earlier times together and wanted once again to know that she had a place in his life.[3]

A few days after Churchill accepted the offer to serve in the Colonial Office, Pamela's great friend Lady Granby gave a party in London to which Churchill was invited. Pamela was among the guests, and so was a young friend of hers—Edward Marsh—who had been an assistant private secretary to Chamberlain at the Colonial Office. Marsh was still employed by the department as a clerk in the West African section. It was Pamela's idea that Lady Granby should invite him to the party. He was two years older than Winston, and so much in awe of him that he stumbled over his words when they met at the party, and treated him with great deference.

Having met him once or twice before, Churchill was startled by his "exaggerated courtesy" and asked why he was being treated with such respect. "Because," Marsh replied nervously, "you are coming to rule over me at the Colonial Office."

He had not been intimidated by Joe Chamberlain, but Winston was another matter. "I was a little afraid of him," Marsh later acknowledged. High-strung and extraordinarily sensitive, Marsh looked as if he might run from his own shadow. He was a couple of inches taller than Winston, very slim, and darkly handsome, but curiously inattentive to his bushy eyebrows, which tended to twirl up at either end of his broad forehead. His voice was squeaky, his manner skittish. On a first encounter, it was easy to be underwhelmed by him.[4]

The next day at the office, however, Marsh was surprised to hear that Churchill wanted him as his new private secretary. He didn't believe it was true, and then when he realized the offer was serious, he began to panic. Having followed the stories in the press of Winston's relentless attacks on Chamberlain, he worried that he would be the next victim— a mild-mannered civil servant browbeaten and worked to death by a merciless taskmaster. After leaving the office, he went immediately to seek advice from a trusted old friend—Edith, the Dowager Countess of Lytton, who was Pamela's mother-in-law.

Eddie, as all his friends called him, was almost an adopted member of the Lytton family. The only son of a distinguished doctor, he had become a close friend of Victor, Lord Lytton, when they were both students at Cambridge University. Later he shared a flat with Victor's bohemian brother, Neville, who was a painter and had married Wilfrid Scawen Blunt's pretty daughter, Judith. When Pamela became part of the Lytton family, she also became Eddie's friend. As he later wrote, Knebworth became "a second home to me." Pamela thought that he should work for Winston. But she didn't tell Eddie that until much later.[5]

Desperate, Marsh begged the dowager countess for guidance. She had known Winston and Jennie for many years—not intimately, but socially. She had also been acquainted with Lord Randolph. So she understood Marsh's concerns, but she gave him some good advice while they sat and discussed his future. "The first time you meet Winston, you see all his faults," she said, "and the rest of your life you spend in discovering his virtues."[6]

Encouraged, Marsh agreed to dine that evening with Churchill, who was not only charming but also reassuring, making the demands of the job sound reasonable. At the end of the evening Eddie accepted the offer. It must have pleased Winston to know that he would enter the new year ruling over Joe's old fiefdom with one of the former assistants now serving him. At the end of the night Eddie wrote Pamela of his decision.

"I expect I've told you how much I admire [Winston], so I shall do my best. Do pray for me."[7]

Within a few days he was working at Winston's side, where he would remain a fixture for much of the next twenty-five years, following Churchill from office to office as his trusted assistant, confidant, and friend. He didn't always find him easy to work for, but he soon learned how to weather Winston's stormy outbursts of temper. "I myself never much minded having my head bitten off," he wrote in his autobiography, "because I knew that instead of throwing it into the wastepaper basket, he would very soon be fitting it back on my neck with care and even with ceremony."[8]

Winston and Eddie would always seem an incongruous pair; but, like his boss, Marsh's best qualities took time to discover. He loved poetry and art in general, and always lived modestly so that he could spend every spare penny on buying paintings or supporting writers whose work he admired. He was an early collector of the Bloomsbury artist Duncan Grant.

He would become a great friend and champion of the poet Rupert Brooke and would serve as his literary executor after Brooke died in 1915. He would also help to write a popular song in partnership with his friend Ivor Novello. The melody of "The Land of Might Have Been" (1920) is Novello's, but the lyrics are Eddie's. The words give an idea of why Pamela thought her old suitor would like Marsh, for the song reveals the deep romantic heart beating inside the starchy breast of the timid civil servant. Dreaming of the "land of might have been," Marsh wrote of a better world as a fleeting vision that haunts the common life below: "Sometimes on the rarest nights comes the vision calm and clear, / Gleaming with unearthly lights on our path of doubt and fear."

On a more practical level, Eddie was an avid student of English grammar, and loved nothing better than tracking down mistakes and correcting them in any text he was asked to check. His bosses—including Churchill—valued this talent, but so did friends, some of whom were successful authors seemingly beyond his help. Somerset Maugham was one friend and writer who, in later years, routinely submitted manuscripts to Eddie for close reading. They would argue over whether it was acceptable in formal English to shorten *luncheon* to the more common *lunch*.

Eddie insisted that only *luncheon* would do. Maugham didn't always agree with his advice, but wrote him, "I think you must know grammar better than anyone in England."[9]

Eddie also had discovered a secret to surviving the long working days of a tireless bureaucratic life. He was the original master of the power nap. When he was very young, he had taught himself to sleep "without jerks," so that he could nap in church without drawing attention to his slumber. As a civil servant, he used this talent to take a nap every afternoon sitting straight up and seemingly deep in thought instead of sleep. If anyone interrupted him, he could promptly stir into action and appear fully alert until he was left alone again, at which time he would close his eyes again. He taught Winston this technique and called it the afternoon "coma."[10]

In the busy days ahead, however, the new junior minister and his assistant would get little sleep. As soon as the Cabinet was in place, Campbell-Bannerman sought the country's approval by calling a general election for January. Winston had little time to become acquainted with his new duties. On January 3, 1906, he arrived in Manchester to do what Lord Elgin as a member of the upper chamber wasn't required to do—stand for election.

To help him, Eddie sprang into action and came along on the train ride to Manchester, where they took rooms near the central station at the Midland Hotel—"a brand-new mammoth" establishment, as Winston would recall it, "vaunting the wealth and power of the Lancashire of those days." Balfour, whose constituency was also in the city, was staying nearby at the Queen's Hotel. The hectic campaign would last only ten days, so the candidates were girding themselves for an intense fight in the damp gloom of winter.[11]

Churchill's opponent was William Joynson-Hicks, a Tory lawyer with a special interest in religious and temperance issues, and also in efforts to stamp out vice, and to put more motor cars on the road. He was the author of a mind-numbing reference volume titled *The Law of Heavy and Light Mechanical Traction on Highways of the United Kingdom*. Joynson-Hicks had been defeated when he stood for election in 1900 and though some Liberals may have been tempted to dismiss him as a minor candidate, Churchill took him very seriously.

Shortly after Winston arrived in Manchester, huge posters began appearing with the slogan "Vote for Winston Churchill and Free Trade." His name was in letters five feet high, and the slogan was well suited to Manchester, the birthplace in the 1840s of the old free trade movement of Richard Cobden and John Bright. Not to be outdone, Joynson-Hicks ordered his own posters with his name five feet high, but the slogan was not quite as direct nor as euphonious: "Support Joynson-Hicks and Consistency." It left many people scratching their heads. Churchill interpreted it as a veiled claim by his opponent "that he has not changed his opinions so much as I have done." With self-deprecating wit, he turned the charge upside down. "I said a lot of stupid things when I worked with the Conservative Party," he told a campaign gathering, "and I left it because I did not want to go on saying stupid things."[12]

The line produced both laughter and cheers. Winston was in high spirits during the campaign, and it showed. He never seemed to run out of energy. He was up early each day, and was still talking to supporters late at night. In between he would give as many as four speeches, addressing overflow crowds at halls and theaters, or standing on the edge of rickety platforms in the open air with banners waving overhead. At night, he planned out the next day and kept Eddie busy for two or three hours answering letters and telegrams. Wherever he went, he was mobbed by admirers who treated him the same way later generations would treat pop stars. On one occasion the crush of the crowd following him was so great that several people were trampled, and four were sent to the Royal Infirmary, including one man whose head was "pushed through a glass window."

When word spread that Churchill was staying at the Midland Hotel, crowds gathered in the lobby and in the surrounding streets to wait for a glimpse of him. "In passing through the hotel corridors," wrote one reporter, "he is . . . beset by autograph-hunters and all sorts of hero-worshippers." They hailed him affectionately as "Winston" and pressed his hand as if he were an old friend. As for Joynson-Hicks, he appeared with Balfour at a big rally, and was usually able to attract large crowds on his own, though he did have to dodge a few stones thrown at his carriage after one meeting. The newspapers said that no one could remember a time when an election "was so charged with electrical excitement."[13]

Everything seemed to break Churchill's way. Besides the normal press coverage of his campaign, he was also receiving considerable attention for his biography of Lord Randolph, which appeared with great fanfare in the middle of the election battle. The reviews were mostly full of praise, and not a small amount of wonder that a politician so young could write so well. Some reviewers even understood and enjoyed the romance of the story without accepting the biographer's exaggerated claims for Randolph's political importance. The critic in the *Spectator* was especially evenhanded, pointing out that Randolph had been able "to dazzle but not to lead," yet acknowledging that the political world had rarely "seen a more romantic career than that of the statesman who was famous at thirty, the virtual leader of his party at thirty-seven, and a broken and dying man at forty."[14]

Winston was taking a great risk bringing out his biography in the middle of a hard-fought campaign, with the possibility he might compare unfavorably to his father. But reviewers failed to see how cleverly the author had embedded his own views in the story of his father, and—with the big election still undecided—they didn't dare speculate on the parallels between Winston and Randolph at the age of thirty. In many ways the dramatic rise of the son's career was more striking than the father's similar rise because Winston was doing a lot more with a lot less. He didn't have the magical title, a beautiful wife, or a father with a ducal purse; but he was a braver, brighter, and stronger man than Lord Randolph. Yet all that wouldn't have mattered much if he had gone down to an ignominious defeat in Manchester.

On polling day—Saturday, January 13—Churchill seemed confident of victory. His cause was popular, and he had been a dynamic campaigner, whereas the Tories were still struggling to explain their mistakes of the past few years and were still searching to find a strong message for the future. When the results were announced that night, Balfour lost his own seat, suffering a stunning rejection by the voters. Winston, on the other hand, won with a comfortable majority, as did six other Liberals in the Manchester area. It was a complete disaster for the Conservatives and a runaway triumph for the Liberals. A radiant Churchill was carried away by his supporters to enjoy a late-night victory supper at the Midland Hotel. The streets, he recalled, "were one solid mass of humanity."[15]

Overall, the Liberals won 377 seats, while the Tory Opposition was reduced to slightly more than a hundred and fifty MPs. It was every bit the disaster that Churchill and others had been predicting that Chamberlain and Balfour would create for their party.

In his Birmingham constituency Chamberlain was safe from the electoral tide that devastated so many others of his party, but he wasn't protected from the toll that the long battle for his imperial ambitions had taken on his body and mind. He couldn't ignore the verdict of the voters and must have understood that his career was all but over. Yet he was determined to press ahead.

He wouldn't make it very far. His health was failing. For years he had boasted that he never took any exercise, and that the cigars he smoked incessantly had no effect on his health. But, six months after the general election, he collapsed in his bedroom one evening, having just attended a party for his seventieth birthday. His wife found him trying to drag himself across the floor. He had suffered a massive stroke, and his right side was paralyzed.

He would make a partial recovery but would never see his full powers of speech or movement restored. Though his family pretended for months that he might still be able to return to an active life, he appeared infrequently in public, and then only as a shriveled figure in a wheelchair, his face twisted and pale. He lingered as a shadow of his former self until 1914, when he died just days before his seventy-eighth birthday. Balfour would win another seat and revive his political fortunes, but for Joseph Chamberlain the election of 1906 was the last hurrah. Churchill's own view of Joe would mellow over the years and lead him to discount the ferocity of their old rivalry. Gradually, the bad memories faded, and what he preferred to keep in mind were their moments of shared pleasure in the political game.

Before they left Manchester, Winston and Eddie went for a long walk and wandered by mistake into a slum area. They made a short tour, peering silently into dark lanes, and then suddenly Winston had a thought he couldn't suppress. "Fancy," he said, "living in one of these streets—never seeing anything beautiful—never eating anything savoury—never saying anything clever!" Many years later Marsh would quote these words in his autobiography, and afterward they would sometimes be used against Churchill as evidence of snobbery. But when such charges are made, what is often left out is Eddie's remark just prior to the quotation. He wrote, "Winston looked about him, and his sympathetic imagination was stirred."[16]

Churchill wasn't trying to look down on anyone. He was trying to understand what a life of such poverty would mean to him. Men like Balfour wouldn't have paused long enough to wonder, if they had bothered to look in the first place. Winston couldn't stop being Winston. He knew what he loved, and what made him happy. But he could be roused from his usual preoccupation with his own affairs to look around and grasp other points of view, and to ask questions. He had been doing a lot of that since switching from one party to another, and would do even more of it in the coming years as he experimented with new ideas in an age overflowing with them.

XI

THE WORLD AT HIS FEET

F lora Lugard, crusading journalist and former colonial editor of the *Times*, was prepared for a fight. On a morning early in February 1906 she was headed to Whitehall to talk some sense into Winston Churchill. As an ardent imperialist who had traveled widely in Africa, and whose husband was the high commissioner of Northern Nigeria, she had been dismayed to hear that the young adversary of the great imperial champion Joseph Chamberlain was now the number-two man at the Colonial Office. She had ambitious plans for herself and her husband, Sir Frederick Lugard—who was toiling faithfully at his post thousands of miles away. But she was afraid that Churchill might stand in their way.

She intended to show him that she wasn't to be trifled with. Serious and uncompromising, she had enjoyed a career in journalism that was rare for a woman of her time. When she wanted something, she worked hard to get it, and had managed to become the first woman appointed to the permanent staff of the *Times*. The writer and African explorer Mary Kingsley described her as "a fine handsome, bright upstanding woman . . . [but] hard as nails."[1]

When she arrived at the Colonial Office in Downing Street, she asked to see the new undersecretary and was taken through the long corridors to Churchill's room. She didn't have an appointment, but with her accustomed air of confidence she handed Marsh her card, requested a meeting, and sat down to wait for a response. She wasn't expecting a warm welcome. The Conservative government had tentatively agreed to her husband's request to administer Nigerian affairs from London for half the year. She had heard that Churchill was opposed to this arrangement. If her information proved correct, she intended to change his mind, arguing that the job didn't really require Sir Frederick to be in Africa full-time, and that his imperial expertise was needed in the Colonial Office, where he could direct operations over the whole of West Africa.

To insist on such an arrangement was breathtakingly audacious. It would have allowed the Lugards—who were middle-aged newly-weds—to treat West Africa like their own kingdom from which they could come and go as they pleased. As they saw it, the idea wasn't so unreasonable. It was simply a way to improve the system and provide a well-deserved reward for exemplary service.

But there was a problem. The high commissioner had a stained record that even his outspoken new wife couldn't explain away. During his time in Africa he had shown a tendency to slaughter local tribes when they didn't bend to his will. A heavily armed force under his command had recently killed twelve hundred men when shellfire and bullets blasted away a primitive fortress of mud walls and cowhide gates. Another expedition wiped out two thousand, including women and children.

The best solution for the people of West Africa would have been to keep him home all year long. But the Lugards believed that the empire was destined to improve the lives of everyone who embraced British rule, and they were prepared to see a lot of blood spilled in the service of that greater good.

Instead of being sent away, Flora Lugard was invited into Churchill's office and received politely. She was shocked by Winston's youthful appearance, later telling her husband it was "ridiculous that a boy of his age and experience should have the power and influence that he has." He had been hard at work, and his desk was covered with documents and books. They stared at each other for a moment, and then she began with flattery, saying that she had heard some good reports of him. "But amongst the good things," she said, "this bad thing has reached me."

Was it true that he was opposed to Sir Frederick's plan? Yes, he informed her, and that wasn't all. There were going to be some major changes in the way Nigeria was governed.

"There are many things this new House of Commons won't stand," he told her bluntly, "and they will have to be reformed."[2]

What she couldn't have known—but might have guessed from all the paper on his desk—was that Churchill had so immersed himself in the work of the Colonial Office that he already knew not only the details of Lugard's proposal, but also the brutal nature of his military expeditions. Only a week earlier Lord Elgin had ordered Lugard to refrain from launching any more raids against the tribes, and Churchill had agreed, noting sarcastically to his chief: "The chronic bloodshed which stains the West African seasons is odious and disquieting. Moreover the whole enterprise is liable to be misrepresented by persons unacquainted with imperial terminology as the murdering of natives and stealing of their lands."

As for Sir Frederick himself, Churchill soon concluded that, based on the evidence in the files, the high commissioner's real ambition was to be another imperial czar, with Nigeria serving as his "sultry Russia."[3]

The Lugards represented the dark underside of Chamberlain's empire dreams. It was Joe who had authorized Sir Frederick to raise what amounted to a private army—the West African Frontier Force—and then to arm it with modern weapons to enforce British rule in the region. Flora Lugard didn't know it yet, but Elgin and Churchill were hoping to put an end to her husband's activities in Africa.

In the meantime, the "boy" listened patiently to her ideas and never once let on that he thought any privileged arrangement for her husband was absurd. He had already told Elgin, "We shall not simplify the labour of the Colonial Office by converting it into a pantheon of proconsuls on leave." Flora Lugard left his office thinking she had impressed Churchill with her knowledge and reason, but when, a month later, Elgin officially rejected the proposal to give her husband equal periods of duty in London and Nigeria, she knew who to blame. In a letter to her husband, she tried to be upbeat, telling him to keep up his spirits and not to take the rejection too hard. It was only a spiteful blow delivered by an upstart.[4]

"Men like you . . . do their work, and the Empire is gradually well built," she wrote. "And then an ignorant boy like Winston Churchill at the [Colonial Office] can at a critical moment dash in and seize your arm just when a sharp blow is essential."[5]

It did not take long for the new masters of the Colonial Office to bring Lugard home from Nigeria and persuade him that returning wasn't a good idea. The next year he would be shipped off to serve as governor of Hong Kong, where he did no harm. But after Churchill and Elgin had left the Colonial Office, he would manage to win another tour in Nigeria and shed more blood, ordering the public hanging of captured rebels as a warning to others and putting down disorders by sending in large numbers of troops to fire on protestors. In 1918, at Abeokuta, his men killed a thousand people.[6]

"All civilization rests on force as a background," Flora told Winston. "I assure you that there is nobody in the world less military than my husband. His government is essentially a government of peace, but he has made it so by knowing how to repress disorder."

Winston seemed to respect her tenacity and was always cordial, even acknowledging that Sir Frederick had done some good things and made personal sacrifices for the empire. But Churchill refused to endorse his repressive tactics. Flora mocked his scruples when they met one day at Blenheim, where she was Sunny's guest. She told him that "the Manchester mob which governs your party vote" didn't understand Africa. He told her the way forward was simple: "Give up the greater part of Nigeria, which is much too big for us to hold! Put an end to the whole system of punitive expeditions and be content with the peaceful administration of a small part of the whole."

She stared at him in disbelief and asked, "How can you expect an Empire to prosper if these are to be your methods?"[7]

Churchill was looking for new ways to make the imperial system work without resorting to the crude methods of violence and coercion. It is true that he suffered from many of the prejudices of his time, and in a long life he would make many mistakes of his own. But by and large, his work at the Colonial Office was enlightened and farsighted.

It was also relatively free of humbug—except perhaps on the occasion in the House when he was trying to defend the government and called a dubious statement a "terminological inexactitude."[8]

With several years of experience behind him as an author, he delighted in bringing the tricks of one trade to another—spicing up the ordinarily dull pronouncements of government officials with language that was both playful and pertinent. Jonathan Swift couldn't have improved on some of Churchill's satiric criticisms of the bureaucratic mentality in departments like the Colonial Office.

The best of these is his long comment on a recommendation for getting rid of an African chief in Bechuanaland, a large but obscure protectorate. The tribe wanted their chief out of the way, so the Colonial Office was proposing to imprison Chief Sekgoma on a distant island. Half in righteous anger and half in jest, Churchill asked, "Why stop there?" If the government could justify deporting and imprisoning a man without trial, why not go ahead and kill him and get it over with.

"Why not poison Sekgoma by some painless drug?" he asked. "If we are to employ medieval processes, at least let us show medieval courage and thoroughness. Think of the expense that would be saved. A dose of laudanum, costing at the outside five shillings, is all that is required."

Lord Elgin was not amused. He had spent much of his life solemnly dealing with the complex machinery of British bureaucracy, and didn't see in Sekgoma's case that a principle of law was at stake. In this instance, he believed that deportation and imprisonment were necessary administrative expedients. When Winston refused to agree, Elgin lost his temper—which was not common for him—and refused to admit that Sekgoma had any rights. "This man is a savage," he insisted, "and is said to be contemplating proceedings in defiance of all law to disturb the peace."[9]

When passions cooled, Elgin appeased his junior minister by throwing out the deportation and making the prison sentence a short one. Just as important, he admitted that these actions were being undertaken as extralegal precautions to preserve the peace. Elgin may not have realized it, but Churchill was using these disagreements not only to get his way, but also to wear the older man down and make him more accommodating the next time.

To his credit, Elgin put up a strong fight. One day Winston wrote of a certain proposal, "I cannot take responsibility for this." Elgin responded simply, "I can." On another occasion Winston ended a memo with the words, "These are my views," to which Elgin responded, "But not mine."

Back and forth it went, even to the point of Churchill rashly taking his pen and crossing out objectionable lines in certain documents, daring the Colonial Secretary to restore the change. Quietly, Elgin would solve the problem by using the proofreader's symbol for "let it stand," firmly writing in the margin "stet." [10]

For all their disagreements, however, they did share a determination to put the brakes on the engine of imperialism. In Africa, for example, Churchill couldn't see the point of continuing to claim authority over areas that were too remote to control. His advice to Elgin was consistent with what he had told Flora Lugard: "We should withdraw from a very large portion of the territory which we now occupy nominally, but really disturb without governing, and that we should concentrate our resources upon the railway and economic development of the more settled . . . regions."

Elgin agreed and lamented the fact that, pushed on by Chamberlain and others, Britain had "engaged in the game of grab in the African continent" and now "cannot escape the consequences." [11]

Churchill was a child of the imperial age and wanted the empire to prosper, but not if it meant neglecting or undermining what was best for Britain. It was a waste of resources and lives to fly the flag over lands that created more burdens than benefits, and that made life worse for the inhabitants than it was before. Instead of an empire held together by tariffs, Churchill wanted one governed by goodwill and a shared commitment to justice and security. Perhaps it was an unrealistic goal from the start, but in the days when the empire still had an air of romance attached to it, Winston believed in the goal wholeheartedly.

Meanwhile, he could at least try to keep the empire from extending the blessings of civilization at the point of a gun. As he soon discovered, Frederick Lugard was not the only administrator willing to crush any opposition with heavy force. When he learned that troops had killed 160 people in East Africa, he denounced the "butchery" and said with exasperation—and a touch of sarcasm—"Surely it cannot be necessary to go on killing these defenceless people on such an enormous scale." [12]

Much of Churchill's job at the Colonial Office involved the typical bureaucratic drudgery, but he was always aware of his power to affect the lives of ordinary people in far-flung places that, in most cases, he knew only as bits of color on the map. He tried to keep in mind that each colony—however remote—was populated by individuals with real concerns worthy of London's attention. It was said of an earlier head of the office that when he arrived his first words to the staff were "Let us come upstairs and look at the maps and see where these places are."

Churchill didn't have many people to help him. The regular staff of civil servants was surprisingly small. There were only thirty-five clerks of various grades, and twelve assistant, private, or permanent secretaries, all of whom were supported by a good number of office messengers and "lady type-writers." They had enough work to keep them busy, but Winston often burdened them with matters that the old hands considered beneath their dignity. When a letter from a minor English figure in British Guiana went unanswered, Churchill reprimanded his staff, telling them not to be "too stiff and proud in answering this man's loyal and civil letter. By snubbing a would-be supporter you can nearly always make a bitter enemy." [13]

Between his work at the office and his duties in the House of Commons, he didn't have much time for himself. In January he had left his rooms in Mount Street and moved into a house of his own at 12 Bolton Street, near Green Park and the Ritz Hotel. It was an easy walk from there to the office, and he could often be seen hurrying to Whitehall early in the morning and returning home late at night. The leasehold cost him £1,000, and he spent another £200 fixing it up. A narrow house built partly of red brick, it would have been cramped for a family but was spacious and comfortable for a bachelor. [14]

With his money from the biography and his new salary, he could afford to live well on his own, though not in any great luxury. He didn't often entertain at home, because he was working so hard, but he wanted a convenient base that he could call his own and where he could unwind at the end of a long day.

Perhaps predictably, his most important work at the office involved South Africa. Campbell-Bannerman wanted to enhance the peace settlement with the Boers by granting self-government to their Transvaal stronghold. He saw it as their reward for ending the fighting and as a chance to win their allegiance by a conspicuous act of generosity after an ugly war. The Conservatives saw it as a national betrayal and an insult to all who had fought to subdue the Boers in defense of the empire.

Churchill, who had encouraged his prime minister to undertake this bold action, was given the job of working out the details and neutralizing the opposition.

The Boers—his former enemies—proved easy to work with. The Tories—his former friends—attacked him ferociously. Anything he said or did in relation to South Africa drew the ire of his opponents. In March, when he was discussing in the House the career of Lord Milner—the former high commissioner in South Africa, an empire builder in the Chamberlain tradition, and a Tory hero—the opposition exploded with anger. They thought he was disparaging the recently retired official when he said, "Lord Milner has gone from South Africa, probably for ever. The public service knows him no more. Having exercised great authority he now exerts no authority. Having held high employment he now has no employment. Having disposed of events which have shaped the course of history, he is now unable to deflect in the smallest degree the policy of the day."

This was one occasion when Churchill's lofty rhetoric backfired. A motion had been introduced earlier to censure Milner for official misconduct during his time in South Africa, and Churchill was trying—too slowly and too grandly—to say it was unnecessary in this case to censure someone who no longer exercised any authority. He had already conceded that Milner was guilty of misconduct, but he was now arguing that it would be a mistake "to pursue a private person" for old wrongs that were better left "wholly in the past." [15]

But the wrongs in question were serious. Mine owners in South Africa had been mistreating their Chinese laborers, using them like slaves, and Milner's administration had been accused of tolerating this abuse, allowing floggings and other unjust punishments. Milner, now in the House of Lords, was questioned about this and had confessed that he sanctioned the floggings in the interests of maintaining order, but that he regretted it, and acknowledged he was wrong.

Churchill and other Liberal leaders wanted to prevent further abuses and not be dragged into a long fight with the Tories over the past, especially when it involved a long-serving imperial leader who was also popular in the country as a whole. But in his eagerness to move on and bury the past, Churchill sounded as if he also wanted to bury Lord

Milner. The Tories certainly jumped to that conclusion and began shouting him down, crying out, "Shame!" It didn't matter to them that Milner was guilty of misconduct. They thought that Churchill—now on "the winning side"—was trying to humiliate both the former official and the defeated government, writing them off as relics who weren't even worth the trouble of a slap on the wrist.

The more eloquent Churchill was on the subject, the more the opposition hated him. They heard arrogance and contempt in the rolling cadences; the sound hurt them more than the sense. In defeat, they didn't want any show of generosity from him, so they seemed to revel in misconstruing his words, hearing what they wanted to hear, and believing that his message of reconciliation was actually a smug insult from a young turncoat.

Whether Churchill laid it on too thick or not, many of the Tories left the House that day boiling with anger. They had wanted his scalp badly enough before; now they couldn't wait to get it and would be watching him closely for a good opportunity to take it. The first time that he stumbled badly, the first time he seemed vulnerable, they would remember this day and pounce on him.

In the end Winston did exactly what he said he would do, ruling out any action against Milner and moving instead to condemn the flogging, but "in the interests of peace and conciliation in South Africa, to refrain from passing censure upon individuals." This motion received overwhelming support from the Liberals and smaller parties, though not from the Conservatives.[16]

The opposition members could complain all they wanted, but Winston's composure in the face of their attacks gave the prime minister greater confidence in him. When, in the early summer, Campbell-Bannerman needed to attend to his ailing wife, he sent for Winston and asked him to lead the final debate on self-government for the Transvaal. As expected, the Liberals easily prevailed on the question, but what especially pleased the prime minister was the calm, patient way that Churchill handled the debate. Even the king was impressed. He thought that Winston was finally showing some maturity and commended him for it. "His Majesty," Winston was informed, "is glad to see that you are becoming a *reliable* Minister and above all a *serious* politician."[17]

* * *

While he was busy at work on South African matters, Churchill received a letter from an American war correspondent who had spent time with him during the Boer War. Actually, Richard Harding Davis wasn't just a war correspondent. He was one of the most celebrated journalists in America, a ruggedly handsome, square-jawed man who had covered the Spanish-American War, the Russo-Japanese War, several sensational crimes, the Johnstown Flood, and dozens of other major stories. He wrote fiction and travel books and had interviewed Walt Whitman, and was an honorary member of Roosevelt's Rough Riders.

In his youth—before cynicism had fastened its grip—H. L. Mencken was such an admirer of Davis that he considered him "the hero of our dreams." [18]

In 1906, however, Davis wanted to make Winston Churchill one of the heroes in a new book. "I am writing a book called 'Real Soldiers of Fortune,'" he explained in a letter from his farm in Mount Kisco, New York. "Of the six soldiers I want to include you. A boy who has been in four wars . . . is a child of fortune, and a soldier of fortune, and ought to make most picturesque reading."

A year or two earlier, Winston might have been delighted by this idea, but now he was doing his best to be taken seriously as a statesman, and as an advocate of peace and understanding in the empire. It wasn't the best moment to revive the image of the swashbuckling Winston, especially under the title of "soldier of fortune." There were already many critics who thought he was a reckless opportunist who didn't belong in office.

There wasn't much Churchill could do to stop the project. The chapter about him was "half written" already, Davis told him, and he boasted that he had most of the information he needed after digging through all the available newspaper files in New York. "I wager," he wrote, "that I know more about your young life than you do yourself."

Such a statement would normally make any politician nervous, but as Winston was aware, Davis also knew very personal details of his life, and not simply because of their encounters in South Africa, and later in London. Davis had been a friend of Ethel Barrymore since her youth and was like a brother to her. In his letter of May 4 he told Winston,

"Miss Barrymore has been very ill. She is just recovering from an operation for appendicitis, and has been up at our farm here getting strong."

So here was a famous American journalist at his desk writing the story of Churchill's life while one of the loves of it was recuperating a few steps away. Winston could only hope that both Ethel and his surprise biographer would say nice things about him. He could at least take some comfort from Davis's comment "Don't forget me when you are Prime Minister."[19]

XII

PRIVATE LIVES

After a few months of trying to behave himself and ignore the taunts of his Tory foes, Churchill took a long holiday at the beginning of August 1906 and misbehaved a little. At the invitation of an old childhood friend, he spent the first week of his holiday at the fashionable resort of Deauville on the Normandy coast. Baron de Forest, his friend, had a beautiful wife, a large fortune, and a steam yacht said to be one of the largest afloat. Winston went sailing and played polo, but in the evenings he headed to the Grand Casino, "gambling every night till 5 in the morning." He was lucky, ending his stay with £260, essentially the same as two months' salary at the Colonial Office.

With his winnings in hand, he went straight to Paris for a few days to enjoy the nightlife and buy some expensive French books. Then he was off to Sir Ernest Cassel's retreat in the Swiss Alps, where he worked off some of the rich food he had eaten in France by climbing the Eggishorn, a peak almost ten thousand feet high. "A very long pull," he wrote Jennie, "& I should never have got home without the aid of a mule."[1]

By the middle of September he was in Venice soaking up the sunshine and meeting up with Muriel Wilson, who had kindly consented to spend a week with the undersecretary for the colonies. They joined another couple for a drive that took them by an indirect route to Tuscany, sailing through the countryside in a motorcar at the dizzying speed of forty miles an hour. All was peace and good cheer in his relations with Muriel, but that was the problem. Their trip was full of romantic ingredients—bright vistas and sleepy villages, wine and sunsets—but no actual romance. She was as beautiful and as charming as ever, but still as remote. Winston felt they were doomed to be just friends.

He couldn't complain too much, however. He was living like a prince and enjoying his much-deserved holiday. But it wasn't all play. In the middle of it he spent a week in Silesia observing the annual maneuvers of the German army. It was a chance to take a close look at the military machine that posed the biggest threat to peace in Europe, though Kaiser Wilhelm insisted he didn't want a war with anyone—especially not with Britain, where his uncle Edward was king. "We are a military people, but not a warlike people," one of Wilhelm's diplomats explained to a British newspaper editor. "It is you who are warlike without being military."[2]

The idea of attending the army exercises was Winston's, but the Germans welcomed his interest, and their embassy in London arranged all the details. The Kaiser himself issued the official invitation, asking Winston to be his personal guest for the week. The embassy also advised that, at each event, Churchill should dress in a British Army uniform, complete with sword.

So for a week in the fields and woods of Silesia (then on Germany's southeast frontier), Major Winston Churchill rode a borrowed horse as he followed the mock battles of fifty thousand men in the German infantry, artillery, and cavalry. For several years he had kept up his military connection through the yeomanry reserves, training in the summers for short periods with the Queen's Own Oxfordshire Hussars at Blenheim and at other camps nearby. It was good fun, but the regiment was a proud one and took itself seriously as a fighting force, as did Winston. He made an impressive representative of it as he stepped off the train at Breslau on September 6 wearing his cavalry boots, sword, dark trousers and tunic, and a white cap with a black visor.

Winston's visit troubled King Edward, who asked the prime minister to give the undersecretary a word of caution. "The K told me you were going to the maneuvers," Campbell-Bannerman wrote Churchill, "and asked me to warn you against being too communicative and frank with his nephew." It was good advice, because the Kaiser wanted very much to gain Churchill's confidence. In fact, one of the more interesting tactical exercises on view in Silesia was the charm offensive directed toward Winston.[3]

At Wilhelm's command, Churchill was given a good room at "a comfortable old-world" hotel in Breslau. An army captain was assigned as his special escort, and every night he was entertained lavishly at the officer banquets. The Kaiser gave him a special pass to inspect the latest German artillery weapons and invited him to a field conference with his generals. Dressed in his full regalia, Wilhelm made a point of drawing Churchill to his side at the conference. Then he pointed authoritatively with his sword to some distant object, which is when a conveniently placed news photographer snapped a picture of them together as though they were in the middle of planning a big battle.

With his commanding stare and long, bristling mustache, Wilhelm looked forbidding, but his manner with Winston was warm and almost fatherly. "What do you think of this beautiful Silesia?" he asked in his fluent English, and then began showing off his knowledge of all the great battles fought in the area over time. His history lesson had a serious point. He was clearly suggesting that blood would be spilled again if any army was unwise enough to attack Germans here. "Well worth fighting for," he said of the surrounding land, "and well fought over." The fields, he told Churchill melodramatically, were "ankle-deep in blood." Though delivered in a friendly tone, the words reinforced the message of the maneuvers: Germany was ready and willing to make war if pushed.[4]

It was an extraordinary conversation, though Winston didn't have the chance to say much. The Kaiser cut him off in the middle of what sounded like a speech and told him "not to make phrases," but to speak plainly. So Winston smiled and stood straight and made agreeable sounds as Wilhelm monopolized the conversation.[5]

The photograph of the two together was widely published around the world. The *Daily Mirror* printed it across the top half of the front page. The Kaiser was fond of posing with his British royal cousins, but in this case the dramatic scene featured merely a part-time major on holiday. Like many others, Wilhelm sensed that Winston was heading quickly to positions of greater importance, and that the young major of today might be Germany's fiercest opponent tomorrow. Before that day arrived, it was prudent to impress on Winston the determined spirit of the German military.

In some quarters of Britain, however, the photograph was cause for laughter. Here was the upstart at work again, now pretending that he was the equal of mighty monarchs, and completely unaware of how insignificant he looked standing next to the Kaiser with his polished helmet, long cape, and imperial sword. It presented an opportunity that *Punch* couldn't pass up. A week or so later the inevitable cartoon appeared with boyish Winston pointing his finger at Wilhelm and offering him instruction in military tactics. "Now mind, your majesty," says "Our Winston" in the caption, "if any point should arise during the maneuvers that you don't quite understand—that you can't get the hang of—don't hesitate to ask me!"[6]

If Churchill had dared to speak his mind to the Kaiser, he wouldn't have made him happy. The colorful troops playing at war were impressive in a theatrical way, but not militarily. All the cavalry squadrons charging at full speed with their lances flashing in the sun was a spectacular show, but Churchill knew from experience that modern weapons could mow them down in quick order. His participation in the charge at Omdurman had taught him that such assaults were obsolete. "There will never be such fools in the world again," he had wanted to believe after leaving the battlefield in the Sudan. Yet here were the Germans grandly displaying tactics from the 1870s, as if they would work just as well in the twentieth century.

He had heard grumblings among some German officers that their methods were outdated, and indeed they would soon be modernized. For the time being, however, nothing he had seen was enough to alarm him. And though he had liked all the attention given him by the Germans, he came away from the exercises more exhausted than charmed. He had been worn out by Prussian efficiency and diligence. He never had a free moment and was hurried from one event to the next, starting early in the morning and ending late at night. "I have hardly ever been so short of sleep," he said afterward.[7]

In his report to Lord Elgin he noted the Kaiser's weakness for theatrical displays and his apparent disregard for the effects of modern firepower. But he gave the Germans credit for superiority in "numbers, quality, discipline & organization." Those alone, he emphasized, were "four good roads to victory."

* * *

Winston's travels on the Continent kept him away from home for almost two months, and when he returned he was dismayed to learn that his family was threatened by scandal. The Duke and Duchess of Marlborough were in trouble. After eleven years of marriage, they couldn't stand each other, and they weren't bothering to hide it. Sunny had a reputation for losing his temper and making cruel remarks, and Consuelo—a proud American heiress—was willing to take only so much abuse before hurling it back in his face. Each accused the other of being unfaithful, and apparently they were both right, though Sunny's jealousy made him exaggerate the problem and imagine that Consuelo had lovers hiding under every bed.

There were stormy scenes at Blenheim. After enduring a tense weekend as a guest at the house, the author Pearl Craigie—one of Jennie's friends—thought its atmosphere was more like that of a prison than a palace. "I could not lead the life of these houses," she wrote. "I'd sooner die in an attic with an ideal. There is no affection in the atmosphere: the poor Duke looks ill and heartbroken." In October the couple separated, with Consuelo taking refuge at their London home and with her father in Paris. News of the trouble quickly spread in society. Soon it was a topic in the American press—where Sunny was gleefully attacked as the wicked English duke who married the innocent American for her money.[8]

Sunny could survive these kinds of attacks, but it was bad for the family in general, and for Winston in particular. There was the possibility that the feuding couple would end up in court—Consuelo's father, William Vanderbilt, was threatening legal action—and in that event a wave of nasty publicity wouldn't do Winston's political career any good. So Winston tried to arrange a truce.

Jennie wasn't much help. Tough and honest, she said things that Consuelo took the wrong way, and then they started fighting. Jennie wrote her a sharp note after a heated argument, saying, "I have left your house deeply wounded & hurt at your inexplicable conduct—I make every allowance for the frame of mind you must be in during such a terrible crisis in your life—but that you should turn on *me* who have not only been a true friend to you, but had you been a sister could not have shown you more loyalty & affection, is indeed an unexpected blow."[9]

Jennie had her own troubles at this time and wasn't in a good position to be advising Sunny's wife. Her own marriage to the much younger George Cornwallis-West was beginning its slow decline. George was spending more and more time away from her, supposedly on business or on long fishing trips and other country excursions. He was also losing a great deal of money in poor investments and bad management of his finances. "During all the years we lived together," he would later say of their marriage, "the only serious misunderstandings which ever took place between us were over money matters." He blamed Jennie, saying "extravagance was her only fault," but in 1906 he managed to lose £8,000 entirely on his own, and a rich relation had to rescue him from ruin at the last minute.

Her marriage troubles made Jennie short of temper and moody. She even blew up at Winston and was miserable about it. After quarreling with him one night, she couldn't go to bed without sending an apology. "Dearest Winston," she wrote, "I cannot sleep without telling you once more I grieve that any disagreeable words shd have passed between us tonight—I was tired & hasty—You have always been a darling to me—& I love you very dearly."[10]

In her current state Jennie just made things worse with Consuelo. But Winston was far more understanding of the young woman's position and easily gained her confidence. She listened to his advice, and later told him how much she appreciated his help. "Everything you said was so sensible," she wrote after one of their discussions.

But no one found Sunny easy to deal with, and in desperation Winston asked Hugh Cecil to advise him on the best way to handle the duke's marital troubles. Though Linky seems to have enjoyed being asked his opinion, he didn't see much hope for Sunny ever reconciling with his wife, and thought he would end up causing "harm" to Consuelo's reputation and his own.

Winston didn't give up on the couple, however, and by the early months of 1907 an uneasy peace prevailed. Sunny and Consuelo agreed to stay out of court and to maintain their separate lives in a quiet, understated way. Custody of the children was shared, and in 1921—after the two boys were grown—the duke and duchess finally divorced. Each would remarry. Rumors swirled around the couple during their long separation, and though at the end of 1906 Winston had expected the breakup to end in "catastrophe," everyone was spared the kind of public ordeal he had feared.[11]

When she wrote her autobiography in the 1950s, Consuelo had the advantage of looking back at Winston and seeing him as the future prime minister, but what she remembered most about him wasn't any sign of the budding statesman. It was the striking contrast between his personality and Sunny's. The duke had so many of the material things that Winston was always having to work for, yet it was Sunny who seemed stunted and bitter, the very opposite of the character suggested by his nickname. In Consuelo's admittedly biased view, she saw in her husband the flagging spirit of an old aristocratic line, and in Winston its revitalization.

"Whether it was his American blood," the duchess wrote, "or his boyish enthusiasm and spontaneity, qualities sadly lacking in my husband, I delighted in his companionship. . . . To me he represented the democratic spirit so foreign to my environment, and which I deeply missed."[12]

Just when Churchill looked to be in the clear where scandal was concerned, Richard Harding Davis published his collection of short biographical tales, *Real Soldiers of Fortune*. At first glance his account of Winston's youthful adventures looked harmless. He gave straightforward descriptions of the young warrior in battle, and summarized at length Churchill's own comments on his escape from the Boers. But as a colorful example of Churchill's adventures off the battlefield, Davis chose an old, half-forgotten incident that was sure to raise eyebrows now.

He played up the story of nineteen-year-old Winston creating a disorder at the Empire Theatre in London while valiantly defending the music hall girls against anti-vice campaigners. Davis's version of the event appears to be based on what Churchill must have told him in an indiscreet moment, or more likely on stories repeated by Ethel Barrymore, who probably thought the whole episode was a charming example of Winston's free spirits. But Davis made it seem too much like a night of debauchery, and Winston was mortified when he read it. In Davis's account, Winston does everything but swing from the chandeliers and sip champagne from a slipper.[13]

Now, as a government official and young leader of the Liberal Party, the last thing Churchill needed was a lurid scene in a new book portraying him as the ringleader of a riotous celebration on behalf of music hall beauties. At first, he hoped that no one in Britain would pay any attention to the book, but the press soon discovered the sensational passage and appeared at his door to question him. He refused to make any comment and then waited to see what would happen next. Meanwhile, he contemplated suing Richard Harding Davis, and wrote him a stern note saying that he considered the passage "defamatory & injurious."

But because the incident had taken place more than ten years ago, there wasn't much to report beyond what was in *Real Soldiers of Fortune*. As a result, the story received little attention except as the subject of a few throwaway jokes about the undersecretary and the empire. "Mr. Davis is very frank in some of the things he says about Mr. Churchill," remarked a reviewer in *Black & White*. "It scarcely seems tactful at this time of day to repeat that story about the Empire—the music-hall, not the other thing."[14]

Winston was perhaps overly sensitive on the subject of music hall girls. They had a reputation as friendly hostesses of easy virtue, and many decades later Lord Rosebery's son Harry recalled that Churchill didn't lose interest in them after that one night in his late teens. Harry liked to tell the story of a time when Winston was several years older and the two of them had taken out a pair of "Gaiety girls." At the end of the night, he claimed, they each went home with one of the women. Meeting Winston's date a short time afterward, he asked how the rest of the night had gone. Her reply didn't surprise him. She said that he had done nothing but talk "into the small hours on the subject of himself."[15]

If Winston was worrying too much about his reputation at the beginning of 1907, it may have been because the first vacancy in the Cabinet had opened up and he had failed to win the spot. He pretended not to mind, but some in the press had been speculating that he would be the next to enter the Cabinet, and when he wasn't, it looked like a setback. He was receiving so much attention in print that one writer complained,

"It is all part of the most skillful game of puffery ever played, the sole object being to set going a Winston Churchill craze."

The prime minister had seen the newspaper stories and hastened to assure Winston that he wasn't losing favor with him. "We want your help at the [Colonial Office]," Campbell-Bannerman wrote on January 22. "I am sure therefore that you gain by your continuance at the CO whatever might be the charms of change." That wasn't the whole story, however. The prime minister had given serious consideration to promoting him but then had decided against it partly on the recommendation of John Morley. The opening was for president of the Board of Education—not a job that Winston would have enjoyed, and not one that would have done much to enhance his reputation. But it came with a seat in the Cabinet, and that was where he wanted to be.[16]

Morley was doing what he thought was best for Winston and the country when he wrote the prime minister that his young friend was "unfit and even unthinkable" for the Board of Education. The older Liberals were developing more confidence and respect for Winston's abilities but were still wary of giving him too much responsibility, and so were happy to see him flapping his wings under Elgin's watchful eye at the Colonial Office. But, to Winston, their caution was a sign that he might have to wait a long time for a better position. It couldn't have pleased him when he heard that the Education job was going to a safe, conventional choice—Reginald McKenna, who was more than ten years his senior and a sober, respectable figure. Reggie, as he was known, was an earnest Liberal with plain features who lived with his sister and kept a low profile. If McKenna was the kind of man the Cabinet wanted, Winston's future as a Liberal might not be as bright as he had hoped.[17]

It's a good thing that he didn't know the prime minister's reason for promoting McKenna. It would have made him worry even more about his reputation. Writing to Asquith, C.B. explained that McKenna "had nearly all the qualities" for the job, "all save notoriety, and that is better absent." Of course, by contrast, Winston had more "notoriety" than the rest of the Cabinet put together.

To another colleague, C.B. explained that a promotion for Winston "would be what the public might expect, and what the Press is already booming; he has done his job brilliantly where he is, and is full of go and ebullient ambition. But he is only a Liberal of yesterday, his tomorrow being a little doubtful." No matter how well Churchill performed today, there was always the fear that he might crash and burn tomorrow. "The P.M. won't hear of Winston being in the Cabinet at present," the well-informed courtier Lord Esher noted in January. "He is, like [Gladstone], old fashioned and disapproves of young men in a hurry." [18]

Yet there was one Cabinet member who thought C.B. had made a mistake and that Churchill should have been offered the job. It was Asquith, who was not yet on close terms with Winston but whose admiration for his work in the House of Commons was growing. He considered McKenna's claim to the job "inferior" to Churchill's and questioned whether it was wise to make this safe choice rather than the more unconventional one. McKenna had worked for him at the Treasury, so Asquith was in a good position to judge the relative merits of the two men. [19]

Winston didn't know that he had a new admirer in Asquith, but he would soon discover it, though not from the man himself. Instead he would learn it from his daughter, who shared her father's admiration for Winston, and who wanted to know him much better.

XIII

THE POLITICAL MAIDEN

I t was in the spring that Winston Churchill and Violet Asquith became close friends. She had just turned twenty and was enjoying life in the spotlight as the only grown daughter of the Chancellor of the Exchequer. Several handsome young men seemed interested in her, but she wasn't ready for marriage and found most men her age a little dull and predictable. Devoted to her father, she loved nothing better than talking politics with him and following the latest events in the news. Her stepmother, Margot, worried that Violet was so intelligent and serious that she would never find a suitable mate.

Violet needed to be less demanding, insisted Margot, telling a friend, "You must give gold for gold to find [the right man] and Violet has always given copper. She is brilliant, alas too brilliant!"[1]

She was also pretty in a way that set her apart from the average Edwardian beauty. Her figure wasn't statuesque or busty; her nose was a little too long, her fine wavy hair a little unruly. But her features were attractive in an unaffected way, fresh and natural. She had a bright, curious gaze, a full mouth, strong chin, and a slender waist. Ettie Grenfell thought Violet was heartbreakingly pretty and encouraged her to fall in love as often and as madly as she desired. "There are tracts before you to ravage darling," Ettie would tell her, "crowds I wish to see in the dust at your feet."

Perhaps it was no coincidence that Violet and Winston began their friendship in earnest one April weekend in 1907 at Taplow Court as Ettie's guests. (Willie Grenfell was now in the House of Lords, so Ettie had become Lady Desborough.) As Violet mentioned afterward in a letter to a friend, the house party was memorable chiefly because it was her first chance to have long talks with Winston. They had met socially in the past year, but had merely exchanged pleasantries. Now, after a weekend of the usual fun and games at Taplow—charades, bridge, tennis, walks along the Thames, water fights—she concluded that there were few things more stimulating than conversations with Winston. His humor and political shop talk were unlike anything she had heard from other men—except, of course, from her father. Getting to know him, she said, filled her with a sense of "new excitement."

To Ettie, she sent a note of thanks full of ebullience. "Being with you always means happiness for me," she told Ettie, "with or without waterfights."[2]

Over the next few months her delight in Winston's presence grew. They met at balls and dinner parties, or at her home when Winston came to see her father, or at the House of Commons before a big debate. At the balls, as soon as he arrived, she would throw "all engagements to the winds" and steer him to a corner where they would talk for hours while others danced.

"Was he, as people said, inebriated by his own words?" she asked herself. "I did not care, I only knew that I was."

Finally, at thirty-two, Winston had found a young woman who took him at his own estimation. She didn't doubt his talents or resent his air of confidence or laugh at his moments of complete self-absorption. She saw from the start that he lived so deeply in his thoughts that he often seemed cut off from everything else, submerged in his own world "like a diver in his bell," as Violet put it. Over the summer a special bond began to form between them—an unbreakable one, she thought. It was as if she had found the key to his heart. "By a blessed fluke," she would later write, "I found my way into the bell and never lost it."[3]

Those last words were written when she was in her seventies. She loved language, and knew how to turn a phrase, but never published anything substantial until 1965, when the memoir of her friendship with Churchill appeared shortly after his death. (It was published in Britain as *Winston Churchill as I Knew Him,* and in America as *Winston Churchill: An Intimate Portrait.*) For the most part, it was respectfully received as a revealing look at Winston the private man. (The *New York Times* described Violet as "an affectionate admirer.") But because the image of the public man was then so omnipresent, and because most people thought of him only as the famous old man with his cigars and impish smiles, Violet's portrait of Churchill in the Edwardian period—when she was closest to him—didn't make much of an impression and was soon pushed aside by bigger books on the great statesman of later years.[4]

It would have helped if she had not pretended—partly for decorum's sake—that Winston had been merely a friend. Her memoir is clearly a story of unrequited love, and it shows in countless passages. She writes glowingly about being "transfixed" and "spellbound" in Winston's company, and of "seeing stars" as she sat next to him, and of feeling "a great void" whenever he was absent for any length of time. There is certainly something deeper than friendship in her declaration near the end of the book that he was "the searchlight" that "illumined" her course in life. "For ten years," she wrote, "my first impulse in any crisis had been to find out [Winston's] attitude to what was happening. Next to my father's his was the mind whose reaction to events I awaited most eagerly."

She began the book with a scene from a dinner conversation between them that took place almost a year before their important weekend at Ettie's. The surviving evidence of her letters and diaries suggests that she confused this dinner with the ones at Taplow, but her scene captured the essence of their first talks, which involved poetry and politics, history and gossip. Many of her pretty contemporaries might have fled in tears of boredom or alarm as Winston discoursed on the brevity of human life and his determination to accomplish great things in the short time available. Without the slightest trace of modesty, he told her, "We are all worms. But I do believe that I am a glowworm."[5]

Winston liked to talk, and Violet liked to listen. More important, she perfectly understood the nature of his talk—that it was essentially Winston thinking aloud, but in a form that seemed perfectly shaped, with polished sentences and witty epigrams. It was a performance, but full of unexpected twists and turns, and making no concessions to the ordinary conventions of polite conversation. The trick for his sympathetic listener who wanted to be part of the conversation was to leap nimbly in and out of the flow of his talk without impeding it. Violet seems to have mastered that trick early on.

In many ways they were a lot alike—both were highly opinionated, strong-willed, idealistic, romantic, intense. She could be overwhelming and demanding, just as he could be. And she could be just as pugnacious. But they weren't often at odds with each other, simply because their views were so similar. At times Violet seems to have found in Winston's mind a mirror image of her own. Margot—who thought Winston and Violet were two of the brightest young people she knew—once said that her stepdaughter, "though intensely feminine, could have made a remarkable man."[6]

But, as much as he enjoyed her companionship and admired her intelligence, Winston never seems to have felt that spark of passion that so animated her attachment to him. He wasn't looking for a female Winston. He was searching for the same thing that he thought his father had found in Jennie—a great beauty with an air of mystery about her, a glittering star to guide and inspire him, a muse who was also a companion. Violet understood the romantic in him, but she wasn't romantic enough for him. She was a little too young, too awkward, and too much in awe of him to be his guiding star.

In 1907, however, there was no one else on the horizon. Violet was it—the one young woman in whom he could confide, the one who didn't laugh when he called himself a "glowworm."

If Churchill had wanted a serious relationship with Violet, he would have needed to consider carefully the attitudes and expectations of her father and stepmother—especially the latter. Capricious and passionate in her likes and dislikes, Margot was a walking stick of dynamite, and no one could predict when and where she might explode. She was perfectly capable of thinking one day that Winston belonged to the devil ("a little treacherous gutter genius," she called him), and then deciding the next day that he was harmless and could stay in limbo ("Winston is a child. . . . It is the side of him I am really *fond* of").

For the most part, she disapproved of his relationship with her stepdaughter because she thought he planted unrealistic notions in her head. She was also convinced that Violet behaved differently after spending too much time in his company. She thought her stepdaughter was always insufferably full of herself after talking to Winston. "His attention," Margot scoffed, "is vain-making."[7]

Winston did his best to please Asquith's high-strung wife, but she was hard to satisfy. Consuelo Marlborough, who remembered her as "small and phenomenally thin" with "hawk-like nose and shrewd eyes," found her overbearing and waspish. Margot had a habit of talking over other people or abruptly insulting them. "[She] found it difficult to listen," said Consuelo. "She would shoot forth exclamations that soared like rockets, and loved to throw in pointed criticisms or to scold satirically."

In later years Winston would offer a much more generous assessment of her, saying she was "a great woman, impudent, audacious, a flaming creature." From his mother, he knew of Margot's early life as a proud young figure in society who spoke her mind freely, captivated older men with her frank manner, and rode a horse with the wild abandon of a "featherweight daredevil," to use Churchill's phrase.[8]

As she grew older, she grew more difficult. Her marriage to Asquith was both exhilarating and exhausting. His first wife had died in 1891, leaving behind five young children—four boys and Violet. Three years later Asquith married thirty-year-old Margot, who struggled to be a good mother to another woman's children, and often failed. She had five children of her own with Asquith, but she lost three in childbirth, and these deaths did much to cloud her view of life, and to weaken her health.

Asquith—whom she always called Henry—made things worse by his philandering. He had a weakness for younger women like Winston's Pamela, but he always came home to Margot, and she usually chose to turn a blind eye to his short spells of infatuation.

Margot liked to believe that she had the greatest influence on Asquith's thinking. Henry was careful to humor her in this regard, nodding in apparent agreement with her views, but he paid as much attention to Violet's opinions as he did to Margot's, and this was often a source of conflict in the family. The two women were frequently at odds. Margot's shifting moods and sharp tongue were hard for Violet to bear. There were moments when the two would almost come to blows. After one of their tense standoffs, Margot was so incensed by Violet's "strong will" that she scrawled in her diary, "I could hit her with my fists."[9]

Society tended to put up with Margot because she was Henry's wife.

In later years, she would find much less deference. When Margot's autobiography appeared in the 1920s, Dorothy Parker quipped, "The affair between Margot Asquith and Margot Asquith will live as one of the prettiest love stories in all literature." Privately, an American diplomat complained that she was "perhaps the most irritating personality in the world."

But some of her best insults were gems and will live on. What can't be recaptured is the way they were delivered in her deep, thick voice, which her grandson said was as "low as a man's." The most infamous of her insults was unleashed on a visit to America in the early 1930s. There she met Jean Harlow, who mispronounced her name as "Mar-gott," prompting her to explain, "My dear, the *t* is silent, as in *Harlow*." [10]

Herbert Henry Asquith was distinguished looking in his late middle age, with silver hair and a large, well-shaped head. It was easy to imagine him as a senator in ancient Rome, and many cartoonists were fond of depicting him in a toga. He was a little stout, though solidly built. Except for golf, he rarely exercised. Once, when a frantic Margot told him they would miss their train unless they ran, he replied calmly, "I don't run much."

Reserved in public, he seemed a reliable, even-tempered statesman, but in private he was quick to let down his guard and indulge his weaknesses for strong drink, good food, a relaxing game of bridge, an easy round of golf, or a stolen moment with a pretty girl.

Winston had little trouble getting along with Asquith in purely social settings, but he always found the older man hard to read when the talk turned to the business of state. Henry was wary of confiding in him, but—unlike Margot—he was delighted when Violet began to grow close to Winston. He would listen patiently to her enraptured accounts of his latest comments or activities. On the first occasion when she told him that Churchill was a "genius," he laughed and said, "Well, Winston would certainly agree with you there." [11]

Yet he understood her enthusiasm and was affected by it. There was something in Churchill's boundless drive that reminded him of his own youthful ambitions. As a young lawyer he had spent many years waiting for the chance to move up in his profession, and he still could recall the painful frustration of those years. To a friend he confided, "No one who has not been through it can know the chilling, paralysing, deadening, depression of hope deferred and energy wasted and vitality run to seed." The press and many of his colleagues would always have their fun ridiculing Churchill's impatience, but Asquith had reason to be more sympathetic.[12]

Given Violet's devotion, Churchill was well aware of the advantage she gave him where her father was concerned. Henry might even have been agreeable to the idea of Violet marrying her new hero. But from Winston's point of view, it was debatable whether the advantages of being Asquith's son-in-law would outweigh its disadvantages. The Liberals weren't likely to start their own version of the Hotel Cecil and hand out political plums to relatives, so Churchill could easily imagine that marrying Violet might hamper his career instead of help it. If he attached his star to Asquith's, he might rise by it; but he could also fall with it.

In the Liberal ranks, however, Asquith was generally recognized as the favorite to be the next prime minister. And by June 1907 Churchill and others in the party had good reason to believe that a change at the top wasn't far off. In that month Campbell-Bannerman suffered a heart attack, his second in nine months. There were attempts to play down the seriousness of his condition, and he was soon able to resume work, though his doctors tried to make him slow down. But the decline in his health couldn't be disguised, and many worried that he couldn't last much longer in the job. If C.B. suddenly resigned or died, Churchill fully expected the successor to be Asquith. As he remarked to a colleague later in the year, "Asquith must be the heir: and I am sure no better workman will have been installed since the days of Sir Robert Peel."[13]

The question for Churchill was whether the inevitable Cabinet reshuffle would bring him into that body. His chances looked good, for he already had the high opinion of the future prime minister and the warm approval of his daughter. At this point it made sense for him to remain unmarried and to see where he stood when the next government was formed.

Of all the great Liberal families in the land, Winston had both the good fortune and the misfortune to attract the support of the Asquiths.

They would play a crucial part in his rise to power and would often treat him like one of their own. But their help would come at a considerable emotional and professional cost. It would draw him into a complex drama full of high expectations and hidden dangers. In their rich and troubled complexity the Asquiths resembled a family in an Elizabethan tragicomedy where bright surfaces slowly dissolve into dark undercurrents.

Violet provided an opening for Winston to enter the family's intimate circle, but once inside he needed to tread carefully.

In the spring of 1907 a rumor did emerge linking Churchill romantically to a young woman, but it wasn't to Violet. On April 27 the editors of the *Daily Mail* and the *Manchester Chronicle* wrote Churchill asking him to confirm or deny a story that he was going to become engaged to Miss Helen Botha. He denied it, but the story was picked up by other papers, and for a few days it provided a good laugh to his enemies, who probably started the rumor in the first place. To all those Conservative critics who had condemned Churchill for supposedly belittling Lord Milner's service in South Africa, there was nothing more comic than the idea that he would marry the daughter of the once-feared commander of the Boer resistance, General Louis Botha.

The Bothas—father, daughter, and other relatives—were in London for a conference of prime ministers from the empire. Thanks to the self-government act for the Transvaal, elections had been held and General Botha was the new prime minister. He was now enjoying the respect shown to him by an imperial power that had wanted to kill him not that long ago. The newspapers seemed surprised that his daughter was not only attractive but well-dressed and reasonably sophisticated for a girl brought up in a remote colony. They praised her pretty hair and her "coral pink dress" and her excellent English as though such things were wonders to behold in a Boer maiden. Churchill seems to have met her during the conference, which he helped to organize, but he knew very little of her.

For many of the embittered Tories the spectacle of Churchill and the Liberals giving Botha and his family a warm reception was like rubbing salt in their wounds. They looked on Botha and Winston as traitors who deserved each other, and thus for them it was mordantly amusing to think of Churchill marrying what they would have considered the half-civilized daughter of a man who had shed so much British blood. It was what Churchill deserved for his treachery, they would have said, snickering over the prospect of Winston fathering a lot of little Bothas. (These critics seem to have been unaware that the force that captured young Winston in South Africa was led by the general.)

It was embarrassing enough for Churchill to see himself portrayed as a hapless bachelor reduced to begging engagements from colonial women passing through London, but then the rumor reached the one woman he did want to marry, and she couldn't resist teasing him about it. Muriel Wilson knew the story was false and that Winston wasn't going to run away with a provincial girl he hardly knew. But she liked to toy with his emotions.

From her villa on Cap Ferrat, where spring was already in its full glory, she wrote Winston to wish him well with Helen Botha, joking that she could already imagine the day when he would come to the villa and pay her a call with his new family. She couldn't wait for him and "Miss Botha & all the little Bothas" to "come & see me & my garden." He was used to her teasing, and may have smiled when he read her letter, but no doubt it also hurt.[14]

Helen Botha returned to obscurity in South Africa, but her father offered the king a spectacular gift that Churchill saw as a tribute to all who had urged a full reconciliation between the Boers and the British. With the approval of his parliament, Botha proposed giving the king on his sixty-sixth birthday the uncut Cullinan diamond—considered the largest in the world, weighing just over three thousand carats. It had been discovered in a South African mine in 1905 and was estimated to be worth at least £500,000. The Tories disparaged the gift, suspecting some darker motive behind it. Churchill described their objections as "sneers & snarls of disappointed spite." But many Liberals also had doubts, questioning the propriety of accepting such a valuable stone. Churchill dismissed this lukewarm response and was the most vocal advocate in favor of its acceptance.

In the House of Commons he praised the announcement of the gift as "a wonderful event" and declared, "It will probably be remembered for hundreds of years after a great deal of the legislation on which we are engaged has been forgotten."

Still, the government wavered. "Believe me," Churchill urged in his official advice to the king, "it is a genuine & disinterested expression of loyalty & comes from the heart of this strange & formidable people."

The king agreed, the Cabinet slowly arrived at the same decision, and on November 9, 1907—the monarch's birthday—the Colonial Office sent an official under heavy guard to deliver the diamond to Edward. It was later cut, and two extraordinary stones were among those added to the royal jewels: the First Star of Africa—which was mounted on the scepter, and is still the largest cut diamond in the world; and the Second Star of Africa, which was mounted in the Imperial State Crown. As a keepsake, Churchill received a glass model of the uncut diamond.

Years later, during a long lunch at his home, he wanted to show off the model and asked for it to be brought to the table. When, after a long search, it arrived on a tray, one of his guests looked down at the white lump, and—thinking it was some sort of hardened jelly—said, "No, thank you." [15]

XIV

A Place in the Sun

The autumn of 1907 found Churchill taking another break from politics, touring once again in France and Italy to see friends and relax. One of his stops was Venice, where Muriel Wilson happened to be staying with her wealthy friend Helen Vincent, who owned the magnificent Palazzo Giustinian on the Grand Canal. In 1904 John Singer Sargent had painted Helen in Venice leaning seductively against a wall near one of her balconies. Revealing her white shoulders in a black silk dress with gold and white trim, she looks in this portrait every inch the Edwardian goddess of Churchill's dreams, and with the same remote air that he found in Muriel.

He was in heaven on a warm day in late September when Helen Vincent invited him to lunch, and then Muriel joined him in a gondola for a tour of the canals.

"Such a dream of fair women," he wrote Pamela, who belonged in the same class. "You will think me a pasha. I wish I were."[1]

It would have tormented him to stay and watch the spell dissolve as Muriel and Helen turned their attention to other interests, but on this autumn break he had business as well as pleasure to occupy him. In two weeks he was due in Malta, where he would start a long voyage taking him to British colonies in the Mediterranean and East Africa. The trip didn't start out as anything official, because he led Lord Elgin to believe it was merely "a private expedition." But behind his back, Winston turned it into a fact-finding mission that had all the appearances of an official tour. It was a kind of "royal progress," to use Jennie's lighthearted description of it, with her son playing the part of a minor prince inspecting various outposts of the empire.

Before Elgin realized what was going on, Winston had arranged for Eddie Marsh to accompany him, and for a navy cruiser to take them everywhere they wanted to go. Almost four hundred feet long and armed with eleven six-inch guns, HMS *Venus* looked like the kind of ship a prince would have at his command. Two cabins were reserved for Churchill's personal use, and he was allowed to observe all the ship's operations from the bridge. As he sailed into the Red Sea in late October, he boasted to Jennie that he was "becoming quite a mariner." (After it was reported in Britain that the Admiralty was "lending" Churchill the use of the cruiser, an old Tory supposedly joked, "I hope the Admiralty will get her back.")

Lord Elgin never did understand how Churchill pulled all this off. He was still confused many months later, when he wrote of the tour, "I really don't know how it drifted into so essentially an official progress."[2]

As always, Churchill had big ideas and wanted to act on them without delay. At every opportunity he dutifully sent reports to London on colonial affairs, explaining the latest thing he had learned about Cyprus or the Somaliland Protectorate, and proposing administrative reforms. But the civil servants in his office dreaded receiving each new report because it added significantly to their paperwork. "8 letters from Winston on Saturday!" cried one senior official, who complained to Elgin that Churchill was "most tiresome to deal with."[3]

Unlike the colonial officials in the old days who might have needed a few minutes to find "these places" on a map, Winston actually wanted to visit them and talk to the people who lived there. If, as he expected, there was a Cabinet reshuffle next year, his first choice was Elgin's job, and this trip was meant to strengthen his qualifications. There were lots of Liberals who knew the older, well-established colonies, but the ultimate object of Churchill's trip was to explore vast, unfamiliar reaches of Kenya and Uganda, and to do it partly on horseback and on foot.

After his navy cruiser landed him in Kenya at Mombasa, he and Eddie—with a small band of guides, servants, and various local officials—spent all of November and most of December traveling across East Africa to reach the Nile at the northern end of Lake Victoria, and then to the Murchison Falls, where they continued on to Khartoum and Cairo. They dressed in khaki and wore sun helmets, and when they were on foot, they had as many as 350 porters trailing behind with their gear and supplies. Eddie was worried about lions, and before leaving England had asked Mrs. Patrick Campbell, the darling of the London stage, what she would do if she heard that a lion had eaten him. "I should laugh first," she said, "and then be very, very sorry."[4]

The highlight of the trip for Churchill was Uganda, which he described as "one beautiful garden" from end to end. He loved the people, whom he called a "polite and intelligent race," and was delighted to meet the eleven-year-old king, who later sent his portrait to Winston with a beautifully handwritten note saying, "The words on the fortographs mean I am your friend." The place would be perfect, Winston believed, except for an entrenched enemy that posed an especially dangerous threat to Europeans. "Uganda," he wrote succinctly, "is defended by its insects."[5]

Churchill was troubled by Kenya, where he saw trouble brewing. He feared that inevitably the "fierce self-interest" of the white settlers would create conflicts with the native Africans, and that Britain would be caught in the middle trying to keep the peace. What impressed him in Uganda was the progress that education and self-government had made among the population, but he didn't see the same sort of progress in Kenya, and took a patronizing view of the Kikuyu and other tribes of that land as "willing to learn" but in need "of being led forward."

He ended his trip with one major piece of advice for the empire: "Concentrate upon Uganda." He saw this part of Africa as a model for the future development of all colonies. It showed how a light helping hand from the British authorities could accomplish much more than the heavy fist used so wantonly by Frederick Lugard. At this idealistic period of his life, Churchill still believed that the cultural and racial differences within the empire could be bridged. But he thought it all depended on the mutual pursuit of three goals: "Just and honourable discipline, careful education, sympathetic comprehension."[6]

These were the noble aims listed in his book *My African Journey*, a short volume published at the end of 1908. But colonial concerns interested his readers much less than his stories of hunting big game, escaping from crocodiles, and sightseeing from the cowcatcher of a locomotive. Purely as a travel writer, he was a hit, for his narrative and his prose sparkled. The latent poet in him almost ran away with the book, filling it with memorable images—Malta "glistening on a steel-blue Mediterranean"; the dry hills of Cyprus before the autumn rains; the "long red furrow of the Suez Canal"; the "vast snow dome of Kilimanjaro"; and the "rainbow spray" and "thunderous concussions" at the Murchison Falls.[7]

To Churchill's amazement, Eddie Marsh loved the trip and held up well from start to finish. Because he was taller and was thought by the natives to have the fiercest look, Eddie was sometimes mistaken as the leader of the expedition. This amused Churchill to no end because Eddie was so hopeless as a big-game hunter that his rifle was more of a danger to his companions than to the wild animals. During one hunt he was told to put his weapon away after Churchill saw him waving it around as he marched along quoting passages from *Paradise Lost*. Winston later joked that Eddie was so happy in Africa that he stripped naked and "retired to the Bush, from which he could only be lured three times a day by promises of food."[8]

By the end of the trip Churchill was amazed at how much territory he had covered in a relatively short time. He was back in London by the middle of January 1908, having traveled more than nine thousand miles through a variety of warm climates in the past four months. He was a little surprised that he had survived the journey in one piece. It had not been without its dangers. Malaria and sleeping sickness were constant threats in East Africa, and he had feared that he might come down with one or the other. But he suffered no problems until he reached Khartoum, where his servant on the trip, George Scrivings, who had worked for him in London, fell ill and died of cholera the next day.

He was devastated by the death, and as he walked to the grave for the service, he couldn't help thinking that the disease might have struck him instead. He was also reminded that earlier in his life he had attended another burial in this part of the Sudan. "The day after the Battle of Omdurman," he recalled, "it fell to my lot to bury those soldiers of the 21st Lancers who had died of their wounds during the night. Now after nine years . . . I had come back to this grim place where so much blood had been shed, and again I found myself standing at an open grave, while the yellow glare of the departed sun still lingered over the desert, and the sound of funeral volleys broke its silence."[9]

* * *

The wealth of the empire and the potential of its enormous resources had started Churchill thinking once more about that slum in Manchester he had visited with Eddie. Again, he wondered why Britain was building an empire overseas when so much rebuilding was needed at home. Pursuing the imperial dream, of course, was more exciting than struggling with the intractable problem of poverty, but his feuds with the Conservatives had opened his eyes about a lot of things. The Tories had pushed him so far from their camp that he was now thinking along more radical lines—at least by Tory standards.

The time for action was getting closer. Campbell-Bannerman had missed the opening of Parliament on January 29, 1908, and his heart disease was entering its final stages. Many assumed that he would be gone by the spring. As Asquith began planning a new administration, he discussed various possibilities with Churchill. In a letter of March 14, Winston explained that his own job preference was to head the Colonial Office. But, he added, he was increasingly concerned about social issues at home and was eager to share his ideas with the rest of the government. "Dimly across gulfs of ignorance," he wrote, "I see the outline of a policy which I call the Minimum Standard."

Churchill had in mind something like the reforms Beatrice Webb and her friends had been pushing for years. Winston called it a "network of State intervention & regulation," which he hoped would give everyone in Britain a minimum standard of security in such areas as employment, housing, and old age pensions. This was heretical thinking for a politician who had left the Tories only three and a half years earlier. But it was the result of a natural progression, beginning with his experience in imperial methods of "intervention and regulation." The more he contemplated reforming the empire, the more he was tempted to start by reforming Britain.[10]

But the difference between Winston's position and that of many other radical reformers was his focus on the individual rather than the state. He had little sympathy for elaborate theories and intricate, coercive bureaucratic plans. The problem was to balance rights and responsibilities, and to find the acceptable "minimum" for government intervention. "There were some things," he had said in 1904, "which a government must do, not because the government would do them well, but because nobody else would do them at all."[11]

Some of Winston's Liberal friends thought it strange that a former Conservative and son of Blenheim would suddenly take so much interest in making life better for the underprivileged. Charles Masterman—an MP who was Winston's age and had already written a book about slum life, *From the Abyss*—was amused by Churchill's passion for the subject. Joining him for a weekend in the country, he wrote afterward of watching Winston march "about the room gesticulating and impetuous, pouring out all his hopes and plans and ambitions. He is full of the poor whom he has just discovered." Later, as they were talking at night, Churchill said without any apparent self-consciousness, "Sometimes I feel as if I could lift the whole world on my shoulders."[12]

Violet Asquith yearned to discuss Winston's latest ideas with him, but she was out of the country. She had become ill at the end of January with a bad cough and general fatigue, and Margot thought she needed a long rest to regain her health. So off Violet went to spend several quiet weeks at hotels in Switzerland and Italy. This separation was probably for Margot's benefit as much as Violet's. The strain on both was considerable as they waited anxiously for the moment when Asquith would become prime minister. Violet had begged to stay in London, where she could follow the latest news of old C.B.'s health. But Margot insisted that she go abroad, and Violet lost the argument.

To keep peace in the family, Asquith went along with the decision, but didn't like it. He wrote Violet of his regret that she was "away in these trying & exciting times" and recalled fondly, "You & I have been through so many adventures together." They kept in close touch through letters and telegrams, and Violet made a point of urging him not to forget the importance of bringing Churchill into the Cabinet. "Make the most of Winston," she wrote.

"You need have no fear on W's account," he hastened to assure her. "He will be well looked after and provided for in your absence."[13]

Winston knew how to provide for himself, and this time he took a step that would mean more to his life than joining the Cabinet. One day in the middle of March he went to a dinner party at 52 Portland Place, the

London home of Lady St. Helier—a society hostess so determined to keep a steady flow of guests coming to her house that the novelist Edith Wharton called her "a sort of automatic entertaining machine." She was an effusive character who loved bringing an eclectic mix of guests to her table, with the very famous seated among others who were simply very promising or very amusing.

She loved to watch as politicians talked to novelists, or explorers listened to art critics. Hundreds of guests trooped in and out of her house every year, and some may have chuckled afterward over a famous story told about their hostess. It was said, Edith Wharton recalled, that one day a cannibal chief was about to boil a captive explorer but changed his mind after looking closer at the man and exclaiming, "But I think I've met you at Lady St. Helier's!"[14]

In Churchill's official biography, the party that Winston attended in March is said to have been in honor of Frederick and Flora Lugard, and Winston is described as having been rude to Flora. Though Lady St. Helier was usually quick to defuse such situations, she didn't need to intervene on this occasion because the Lugards weren't there. They were six thousand miles away, in Hong Kong, where Frederick had been sent to keep him out of trouble. Flora didn't come back to England until May and isn't mentioned in the one written account of the dinner that has survived—a diary entry by Ruth Lee, the wealthy American who, with her British husband Arthur, owned the country house Chequers, which they later donated to the nation.

On March 15, 1908, Ruth Lee wrote, "We dined with Lady St. Helier and, amongst others, Winston Churchill was there. He arrived late, after we had gone in to dinner, and took the vacant place on his hostess's left. He paid no attention to her, however, as he became suddenly and entirely absorbed in Miss Clementine Hozier, who sat on his other side, and paid her such marked and exclusive attention the whole evening that everyone was talking about it."[15]

The twenty-two-year-old woman who captured his attention that night wasn't rich and theatrical like Muriel, or political like Violet, or famous like Ethel. But she did have that air of mystery that Winston liked, and there was a touch of the exotic in her beauty. One admirer called her a "sweet almond-eyed gazelle," and the rakish old poet

Wilfrid Scawen Blunt was mesmerized by her when she appeared at a fancy-dress party wearing "a kind of Mermaid's dress which looked as if she had no clothes at all underneath her outer sheath of crimped silk. . . . She is certainly a lovely woman with no small share of knowledge of the fact." [16]

Clementine—or Clemmie, as she would always be known to Winston—was the granddaughter of the Earl of Airlie, but was one of his relations who had fallen on difficult times. Her mother, Lady Blanche, was—like Jennie Churchill—a spendthrift and a free-spirited woman with a long romantic history. She had four children, but it wasn't clear whether her husband—Sir William Hozier—had fathered any of them. Suspicion later fell on a cavalry officer named William "Bay" Middleton as Clemmie's father. In any case Sir William lost patience with his wayward wife, and the couple separated when Clemmie was only six.

Thereafter, Blanche and her young family lived a frugal but often colorful life in England and France. They frequently stayed in Dieppe and Paris, where Blanche enjoyed the company of writers and artists. James McNeill Whistler and Walter Sickert were two of the more important painters in her life, and both were impressed early on by the beauty of Clemmie and her older sister, Kitty. For a time Clemmie had a schoolgirl infatuation for Sickert, who once spent a day giving her a tour of his favorite museums and galleries in Paris. Her French was excellent, and by her early twenties she was earning a little extra money giving French lessons to English pupils.

Winston liked her unconventional background and her knowledge of France and its culture. They added to her romantic charm. He had met her briefly in 1904 but had been too much under the spell of Ethel and Muriel in those days to give her much thought. But now, in the candlelight of Lady St. Helier's dining room, he suddenly discovered a radiance about her that he had failed to see before. She, too, saw something new in him. When they had met earlier, his immaturity and arrogance had stood out and left a poor impression. Now he seemed less a boy and more a man.

Like Winston, she had also experienced disappointments in love. She was attracted to older men and had been engaged to two of them. The first was a lawyer and banker fifteen years her senior; the second was a civil servant almost twice her age. She seemed to be looking for a father figure, for there had never been an older male relative in her family capable of giving her the love and security she craved. Her only real parent was a restless and improvident mother. But her engagements didn't work out. She had second thoughts about each man and abruptly ended the relationships.

Now one of her aunts was trying to get her back on track, and to bring her the renewed attention she deserved from society. This was her "Aunt Mary"—otherwise known as Lady St. Helier, who just happened to know everyone, and who specialized in surprising her guests with unexpected companions for dinner. Thanks to Lady St. Helier's legendary hospitality, Winston found an empty seat waiting for him at Clemmie's side, and he didn't have to worry if he spent the rest of the evening ignoring the aunt in order to give all his attention to the niece.

On April 3, 1908, the prime minister lay in his bed at 10 Downing Street unable to go downstairs or to hold up a newspaper long enough to read it. His face was as white as his snowy thatch of hair, and his voice was weak. But he gathered enough strength that day to dictate a brief note to the king. It read, "Sir Henry Campbell-Bannerman with his humble duty to Your Majesty submits his resignation of the appointments of Prime Minister and First Lord of the Treasury." With difficulty, he leaned forward to sign it, and then said wearily, "That's the last kick. . . . I don't mind. I've been Prime Minister for longer than I deserve."

Five days later, Herbert Henry Asquith—now, as expected, the new prime minister—asked Churchill to join the Cabinet as president of the Board of Trade, the department that dealt with industry, transportation, and labor. Though it wasn't his first choice, and the ponderous title came with unglamorous responsibilities, Winston quickly accepted, and he thanked Asquith for showing confidence in him. At thirty-three he was finally taking his place in the Cabinet, and was the youngest to do so in almost half a century. John Morley—always cautious—advised his young friend not to overestimate the importance of his achievement. "At this stage," Morley wrote him, "the department is not all; it matters less than the acquisition and accumulation of influence, authority and power in the Cabinet."[17]

Margot took advantage of Violet's absence to discover whether Winston could be useful to her. One of her jobs, as she saw it, was to protect her Henry from being stabbed in the back by his colleagues. She was worried that Lloyd George, who had been promoted to Chancellor of the Exchequer, would one day become the Brutus to Henry's Caesar. She intended to watch him closely, but first she wanted to test Winston's loyalty, and his potential as an informant.

Out of the blue she asked Churchill to go with her for a drive to Richmond Park. The list of Cabinet appointments had yet to be released, but somehow the *Daily Chronicle* had learned the details and published them. Margot suspected the culprit was Lloyd George. She wondered if Winston knew anything about it?

Wisely, he professed ignorance, but he defended Lloyd George when Margot named him as the most likely source of the leak. That evening she sent a messenger to Churchill with a note explaining that she had done a little investigating and now had a strong case against Lloyd George. She said that Henry was "furious." Would Winston help her, she wanted to know, by confronting Lloyd George with the evidence?

"Dearest Winston," she wrote, "I am told Lloyd George dines with you tonight. I wish you wd speak to him & tell him quite plainly that the staff of the *Daily Chronicle* have given him away to 3 independent people. . . . Lloyd George's best chance if he is a good fellow, wh I take yr word for, is not to lie about it. . . . I think you might [help Henry] & the Cabinet if you do this courageously."

To emphasize the importance of his mission, and the confidence she was placing in him, Margot wrote melodramatically, "Burn this," at the end of her note. (He didn't.)

With such a request Churchill couldn't win. If he played the part of her enforcer, he would offend Lloyd George. If he kept silent, he would offend her. At midnight he responded with a note, but sent it to Asquith instead of Margot, explaining that he had "broached the matter" with Lloyd George, who had denied any responsibility. To remove himself from the cross fire, he gently suggested that the prime minister solve the problem by talking directly to his new Chancellor of the Exchequer.

Not for the first time, Asquith was put in a difficult position by Margot's fondness for intrigue. Lloyd George—though apparently guilty—was offended by her meddling, and angry that he had been exposed as the prime suspect. This was no way to start a new administration, and Asquith realized it was better to back away gracefully than to sink deeper into the muck of suspicion. "I accept without reserve your disclaimer," the prime minister wrote his colleague, and deftly shifted the blame to journalists and their clever snooping. "The press in these days is ubiquitous, difficult to baffle, and ingenious in drawing inferences from silence as well as from speech."[18]

Margot was proud of having given Henry a chance to admonish Lloyd George, and thereby to put him on notice that he was being watched. But then both Henry and Winston let her down by not taking a harder line against their colleague. It was a humiliating setback for her. She didn't care that they were merely trying to avoid a nasty fight at an inopportune time. So she took to her bed—supposedly ill from "nausea and weight loss"—and stayed there for a few days, nursing grievances.[19]

In the circumstances Churchill was fortunate to have an excuse for spending the next two weeks away from London. As a new minister entering the Cabinet, he was required in those days to stand again for election. Given his great victory in 1906, he was optimistic that he would win the contest. He shared his feeling with Clementine Hozier, whom he had recently seen again. They had met at his mother's home, and had enjoyed another long talk.

"I must say," he wrote her on April 16, "I feel confident of a substantial success." He was referring to the election, but he might just as well have been describing his feelings about her. He was hopeful, he said, that they would soon "lay the foundations of a frank & clear-eyed friendship."[20]

XV

BEST-LAID PLANS

N o one had ever seen anything like it before. Politicians often stood and waved from their open motorcars, but giving speeches from the top of a limousine was unheard-of. Most politicians would have considered it beneath their dignity—not to mention a risk to their safety—to clamber over the chauffeur's compartment and stand on the roof as if on a giant soapbox. But there, in the middle of a Manchester street, was Winston Churchill addressing a crowd from his limousine perch, pounding the air with his fist just as he did in the House of Commons.

A crowd quickly gathered and soon filled the street from end to end, giving the appearance from above that Churchill's car was anchored in a sea of hats. His words were difficult to hear, but the real object of this stunt was to project a certain image instead of his voice. He was the embodiment of spontaneity and originality, and was showing it by seizing the chance to turn a fancy piece of modern machinery into a stage for himself.

His critics weren't surprised. To them, it was just another example of Winston's reckless determination to make a spectacle of his life. And what was worse, claimed a hostile journal, he was polluting British politics with vulgar "American methods of electioneering." But, in fact, even Americans were stunned when they saw the photographs of Churchill campaigning from the roof of his car. "Occasionally the motor car has been utilized as a platform from which to address gatherings," observed a New York automotive magazine, "but it remained for Winston Churchill to discover the top of a limousine as a point of vantage from which to appeal to his hearers for support."[1]

During the April by-election Winston often seemed to be the same height as the lampposts as he went aloft to plead his case at street corners. On one occasion his driver stopped in a neighborhood at midnight, and Churchill drew a surprisingly large crowd as he hovered in the misty glow of the lampposts denouncing the Conservatives and promising better days under the Liberals. His opponent once again was William Joynson-Hicks, whose campaign style was just as dull as before. While Churchill commanded the heights in the election battle, the Conservative candidate made speeches in front of posters with another bland slogan, "Joynson-Hicks This Time."

But even though Winston was by far the more exciting candidate, he soon noticed that his rival was drawing crowds as large as his. The mood of the voters had shifted since 1906. Some had been disappointed by the cautious leadership of Campbell-Bannerman and weren't sure that Asquith would do any better. Others were no longer concerned about protectionism, for Chamberlain—crippled by his stroke—had now been silent for almost two years, and the cause had lost its urgency. But the Tories were as eager as ever to revenge their defeat in the last election, and they were united in their desire to humble Winston.

He also faced a new foe whose campaign tactics were more unusual than his. Hoping to compel the Liberals to give women the vote, the militant suffragettes targeted Winston for defeat. They wanted to demonstrate their power to influence elections, and in this by-election involving a Cabinet minister, they saw an ideal opportunity. It didn't seem to matter that Churchill was in favor of their cause. He had voted for enfranchisement in 1904 and was ready to do so again. Asked directly during the by-election whether he favored women's suffrage, he declared flatly, "The claim of women to exercise the Parliamentary franchise cannot be disputed on any ground of logic or justice. . . . I have said that I may be counted on as a friend of the movement, and I expect that I shall be taken on my word when I say that I will do what I can to help when and as opportunities occur."[2]

Churchill could have become a useful ally to the suffrage cause, but its militant wing showed little interest in working with him. Because older leaders of the Liberal Party—especially Asquith—were unsympathetic to the cause, the suffragettes decided to send a message to the leadership by making an example of Winston. And they did it in a way that cut him to the quick—they ruined his speeches. They would wait until he was on the verge of delivering one of his cherished phrases and then shout out, "Votes for women!" or would create a racket by swinging a hand bell.

Based in Manchester, Emmeline Pankhurst, the preeminent leader of the suffragettes, cheerfully admitted that Churchill was harassed simply because he made a convenient target. He had been the subject of sporadic protests in the 1906 election, but in 1908 the demonstrations were relentless. "Not that we had any animus against Mr. Churchill," Pankhurst would recall. "We chose him simply because he was the only important candidate standing for constituencies within reach of our headquarters. We attended every meeting addressed by Mr. Churchill. We heckled him unmercifully; we spoiled his best points by flinging back such obvious retorts that the crowds roared with laughter."[3]

It was the ringing of bells in the middle of his meetings that nearly drove him over the edge. It rattled his nerves and undermined his confidence just when he needed it most. He would rise to one of his well-rehearsed rhetorical heights, and then somewhere in the crowd a bell would sound, laughter would erupt, and Churchill would stamp his foot in frustration. In a rare understatement he later wrote of the disruptions, "It became extremely difficult to pursue connected arguments." As Lloyd George later joked, "Winston is bitter against the suffragettes because they spoil his perorations."[4]

These annoying tactics would take a violent turn in the coming years, and with each assault Churchill would become less willing to back a movement that he initially favored. The worst came in 1909 when, without warning, a woman at the train station in Bristol struck Winston over the head with a dog whip. A second blow slashed his face. A detective sergeant who witnessed the attack testified that if the whip had hit Churchill in the eye "it might have blinded him." More alarming at the time was his dangerous position on the platform. The woman drove him so far backward that he nearly fell under a train waiting to depart.

"The two struggled on the edge of the platform just in front of the space between two carriages," said a contemporary report. "It was a very exciting half minute. The woman was shouting frantically, being evidently beside herself with fury. She made another vigorous attempt at assault, but Mr. Churchill had her by the wrist, and this time the lash did no more than touch his face. She was shouting, 'Take that, you brute, you brute!'"

The two were saved from a fall at the last second when policemen grabbed the woman and hustled her away. After her conviction, she demanded the return of her whip, saying that it now had "historical interest" and promising not to use it again to "assault Cabinet ministers." The demand was refused.[5]

A short time later a woman threw a heavy iron bolt at Churchill's car and almost hit him. The next year three women rushed him and tried to strike him in the face but managed merely to knock his hat off. A few years after that, a male supporter of the movement did succeed in punching him in the mouth after lunging at him in a crowd and knocking him to the ground. Countless threats were made against Churchill and his family. Though the windows of his house were smashed, he was spared the kind of deadly attack directed at Lloyd George, whose weekend retreat was bombed. The explosion tore apart an upper floor and rattled windows hundreds of yards away. Fortunately, Lloyd George wasn't there at the time.[6]

In the brief by-election campaign Churchill worked feverishly to overcome the tactics of his foes. Jennie showed up to help, but her remarks on the platform were less than electrifying. She tried out a slogan of her own making, with a bad pun about the high cost of sugar and beer, and it didn't go over well. "They talk a lot about dear sugar and dear beer in this election," she said, "but all I can say is 'Vote for dear Winston.'"

The Churchill name seemed to have lost some of its magic. When the results were announced on the evening of April 24 Winston went down to defeat by 429 votes. The Conservatives were overjoyed and sang "Goodbye, Winston" as he left the Manchester Town Hall looking dejected. He told his supporters that the defeat was a terrible blow, "heavy, bitter and crushing." It was difficult to accept that the people of Manchester who had treated him like a hero only two years earlier were now casting him aside in favor of the mediocre Joynson-Hicks, whom H. G. Wells—a Churchill booster in the election—called "an obscure and ineffectual nobody."[7]

Emmeline Pankhurst was sure that she and her followers were responsible for Winston's fall, later claiming that all the newspapers said "it was the Suffragettes who defeated Mr. Churchill." Her claim was exaggerated, but great damage had been done, and she was determined to inflict more. On election night he was offered the chance to stand for a supposedly safe Liberal seat in the Scottish city of Dundee, where the previous MP had stepped down after being given a peerage. Already exhausted from one campaign, he had no choice but to throw himself into another by-election in May. Pankhurst vowed to follow him to Dundee and take "personal charge of the [suffragette] campaign" against him. She wanted to prove that no Liberal was safe if she could drive out of office a Cabinet minister as famous as Churchill.[8]

For many weeks after his defeat Churchill was ridiculed for it. Whitelaw Reid, the American ambassador, spread the story later in the spring that Winston was humbled by a joke made at his expense involving Manchester. Churchill was often accused of ignoring one of his dinner companions while he talked to another, and on this occasion Reid said that he ignored Maud Allan, the provocative Canadian-born entertainer known for her "Dance of the Seven Veils," and for revealing costumes that caused some cities to ban her performances.

"Well, Mr. Churchill," said Maud Allan as she and the other dinner guests left the table, "we don't seem to have had much in common tonight. In fact, I think there is in the whole world but one thing we do have in common. We were both kicked out of Manchester."[9]

A week after his election defeat Churchill was busy touring the streets of Dundee in search of votes when his car stopped at the gates of a large factory. It was the lunch hour and the workers came pouring out to greet him. He stood up in the back of his open car and started to make a short speech. His voice was slightly hoarse as he braved the damp air on this cool spring afternoon in Scotland. He didn't bother to wear his hat, and he was just getting fired up when he saw a carriage appear with two strong horses, a driver in livery, and a smiling young woman in a flowery hat standing up with a very large brass bell in her hand. A placard across the front of the carriage said, "Votes for Women."

The Irish suffragette Mary Maloney wasn't associated with Emmeline

Pankhurst, but as a one-woman army she posed the greatest challenge to Churchill in Dundee. With her hired carriage she followed him everywhere for a week, and the railway bell she carried was deafening. On this occasion at the factory entrance she didn't wait for any particular moment to interrupt him. Every time he spoke she set the bell going, drowning him out. As the newspapers reported, Maloney's bell was one of the most effective weapons Churchill had ever faced.

"When, to avoid the horrible clangour, he moved away," observed a reporter, "she followed him up. He could not make himself heard; he could not speak or think with that dreadful bell ringing in his ears. . . . The worst of it was that the crowd of workmen laughed at his discomfiture more than they resented Miss Maloney's interference with their hearing. Eventually the President of the Board of Trade had to give up the contest. He drove away amid laughter and jeers."

Churchill showed extraordinary patience in the face of this ordeal, even tipping his hat to Maloney on one occasion as he walked past her to speak at a meeting that he knew she would disrupt. As soon as her bell sounded, he would shout, "If this lady thinks these are good arguments to use in Dundee let her use them. I wish you, 'Good afternoon.'" With that he would raise his hat and drive away, hoping that she wouldn't catch up before he finished the next event.[10]

By the end of the campaign the bell-ringing began to get on everyone's nerves and the tide of public sympathy shifted to Churchill. Mary Maloney may have inadvertently done him more good than harm. But he was worried right up to the last moment. On May 9, while the votes were being counted, he was seen standing by himself in a corner of the Court House seemingly lost in thought while nervously "twisting little rubber bands around his fingers." In the final count he received less than half the votes, but because he was competing against three other candidates, he came out on top and was well ahead of his rivals.[11]

He made a victory speech from the balcony of the Court House, but when he emerged to get into his car, the jubilant crowd surrounding it was so large—at least ten thousand—that scores of police had to make a path for the vehicle while other policemen pushed it at a walking pace all the way to Churchill's hotel. He stood up in the back and waved, immensely relieved to be the winner this time. In his victory speech his gratitude showed in his new enthusiasm for everything Scottish. "Dundee for ever, Scotland to the fore," he shouted to loud cheers.[12]

What had caused him the greatest concern in the election wasn't his Conservative opponent, but the candidate standing for the Labour Party, which was then beginning its rise to prominence in the House of Commons. The party's leader—Scottish socialist Keir Hardie—campaigned vigorously for the Labour candidate, George Stuart, whose share of the votes was almost the same as the Tory candidate's. The challenge for Winston was to explain to his working-class voters why they shouldn't be tempted to abandon liberalism for socialism.

Blissfully bell-free, his campaign speech in Dundee on May 4 was one of his better efforts to set forth a general political philosophy. He spoke at night to a packed crowd of twenty-five hundred at Kinnaird Hall. It was a long and detailed speech composed at short notice in the heat of the campaign, but Churchill had been trying for the last year to formulate his objections to socialism. In the autumn, when he had been packing for his trip to Africa, a friendly journalist had noticed that he was taking along some serious reading material. "What are all those books on Socialism?" asked the journalist. "They are going to be my reading on the voyage," Churchill had replied. "I am going to see what the Socialist case really is."[13]

Because Winston cared more about results than theory, he concentrated in his speech at Kinnaird Hall on the flaws in socialism. The basic problem, he argued, was that socialism sounded coherent in theory, but was a mass of contradictions when applied to reality. Its followers, he said, "tell us that we should dwell together in unity and comradeship. They are themselves split into twenty obscure factions, who hate and abuse each other more than they hate and abuse us. They wish to reconstruct the world. They begin by leaving out human nature. . . . I have never been able to imagine the mechanical heart in the Socialist world which is to replace the ordinary human heart that palpitates in our breasts. What motive is to induce the men, not for a day, or an hour, or a year, but for all their lives, to make a supreme sacrifice of their individuality?"

The choice between serving society or the individual was a false one, he said, because it was possible to do both. "For certain of our affairs we must have our arrangements in common. Others we must have sacredly individual and to ourselves. We have many good things in common. You have the police, the army, the navy, and officials—why, a President of the Board of Trade you have in common. But we don't eat in common; we eat individually. And we don't ask the ladies to marry us in common."

Instead of rigid rules, he wanted adaptable guides. Instead of adherence to the dictates of theory, he advised allegiance to common sense, the lessons of history, and the examples of tradition. "You will find the truth lies in these matters," he said, "as it always lies in difficult matters, midway between extreme formulae."

In liberalism he believed that he had found "a house of many mansions" large enough to hold even the oversized individuality of Winston Churchill, giving him the chance to belong to a party that he could define as he chose. His thinking was benevolent, broad-minded, individualistic, uplifting, practical, progressive, and therefore impossible to contain within the limits of any strict theory. But complex arguments and elaborate rules weren't necessary if the great aims of government were as simple as those he gave his audience—"to encourage the weak, to fortify the strong, to uplift the generous, to correct the proud."[14]

If Churchill had lost his second by-election in a row, Asquith might have had second thoughts about risking his prestige and the party's by giving his new minister a third chance. In April, when he had offered Winston a place in the Cabinet, he had reminded him of a remark attributed to Gladstone, "The first essential for a Prime Minister is to be a good butcher." As Churchill stood twisting those rubber bands in Dundee, he must have been imagining his own head on the chopping block.

He knew that Asquith had a ruthless side. His old chief at the Colonial Office could testify to that. When Churchill had been promoted, Lord Elgin had been let go abruptly and resented it. "Even a housemaid gets a better warning," complained Elgin. It is little wonder, then, that Violet was worried as she followed news of Winston's contest. Writing on May 5 to Eddie Marsh, who was in Dundee helping Winston, Violet said that a second defeat "would be beyond bearing," and ended her letter with a plaintive, "*Oh do* win."[15]

Finally allowed to return home from the Continent, Violet was still upset at missing out on the exciting change of administration, but she wasn't looking forward to moving into 10 Downing Street. She disliked the look of the place and felt that an air of death still hovered over it. Campbell-Bannerman had died in his bed there on April 22, and just two weeks later the Asquiths moved in. Margot wasn't impressed by the place, either. She called it "an inconvenient house with three poor staircases," and described the exterior as "liver-coloured and squalid."

One thing that Violet did enjoy about her new home was its proximity to Winston at the Board of Trade. As soon as he returned from Dundee, she came at his invitation to see his new office in Whitehall Gardens and to have tea. For the next two months they saw each other often. As Violet would recall decades later, whenever he conferred with the prime minister at Number 10 he would come down "to talk to me in my little sitting room in the garden on his way out." [16]

There was speculation in the press that spring on the subject of Winston and marriage. The only reason that he remained unmarried, suggested the society magazines, was that his mother had supposedly decreed, "Winston must marry money." This was nonsense, of course, but the pressure was mounting for Churchill to crown his political success with a big wedding. One of his fellow Cabinet ministers, Reginald McKenna, had recently announced that he would marry in June, which was a great surprise because Reggie was unusually homely and, at forty-four, not the most appealing bachelor. Yet his bride was a pretty young woman who had just turned nineteen, Pamela Jekyll, and Violet was one of her friends.

"What [Pamela] was waiting and longing for," Violet learned from a mutual friend, "was someone to write and say she was the only person he wanted to marry." It didn't seem important to the new bride that Reggie was so much older and, in Violet's estimation, repulsive—with his "spots, spats, speckles & tricot tights." [17]

After Winston and Violet attended the McKenna wedding on June 2, Violet must have wondered why her great friend and hero couldn't manage to follow Reggie's lead and ask someone to marry him. She had done enough to make it clear that she was available, and he knew she adored him and would do anything for him. Though she wasn't rich, she was, after all, the prime minister's daughter.

She didn't know at this point, however, that Winston was interested in Clementine Hozier. Violet did have other young men to turn to, but there was no one like Winston. Everyone else was second best in her estimation. As she later wrote of him, "He generated his own light—intense, direct and concentrated as a beam." [18]

Margot planned for the whole family to spend much of August and September at a remote castle they had rented on the Scottish coast above Aberdeen. There was a golf course nearby to keep the prime minister busy during the day, and friends were asked to come and stay. Violet invited Winston, among others, perhaps hoping that the romantic location would stir him to action. He agreed to come on August 17 and to remain for a few days.

By the end of July, Winston seems to have given Violet encouraging signals. All his hopes and passion were aroused by Clemmie, but he was still unsure of their future together, and was wary of having another proposal rejected. On the other hand, he knew that he could count on Violet to say yes. She became his alternative in case Clemmie let him down. It wasn't fair to lead one woman on while secretly hoping to win another, and he knew it. "I behaved badly to Violet," he later admitted to his friend Harry Primrose, Lord Rosebery's heir, "because I was practically engaged to her." [19]

XVI

THE CASTLE

At the beginning of August 1908, as his date with the Asquiths in Scotland grew closer, Churchill was beginning to worry that Clemmie's interest in him was fading. She was enjoying a holiday on the Isle of Wight, and he had not heard from her for a while. But then something happened to him that brought a quick response from her. He was almost killed in a house fire.

It happened while he was staying with cousins at a large rented mansion—Burley-on-the-Hill, in Rutland. At one in the morning on August 6 a fire broke out in the kitchen and spread quickly. Guests and servants escaped without delay, wearing only their nightclothes and carrying a few valuables with them to the lawn, where they watched the blaze in horror. Eddie was one of the guests and lost everything, including Cabinet papers he was carrying for Winston. Everyone except Churchill remained on the lawn out of harm's way. He insisted on dashing back into the burning house to retrieve some of its valuable artworks and rare books.

As the *Times* reported the next day, "By the time the fire brigades began to arrive the house was almost destroyed, and just as Mr. Churchill left one part of the mansion carrying two marble busts, the roof, which had been blazing furiously, fell in with a crash, Mr. Churchill being just in time to escape injury."

Churchill's eyes were still smarting from the smoke when the newspaper reports reached Clemmie, and she promptly telegraphed to find out if he had been hurt. In his reply he boasted that the fire had been a great adventure and gave a lively description of the moment when the roof collapsed behind him in "a molten shower." He teased her that it was a pleasant surprise to get her telegram "& to find you had not forgotten me."[1]

In fact, they had planned to meet before the middle of the month, and now—perhaps realizing that he must seize this chance—he suddenly suggested that she come to Blenheim on August 10 to visit him and spend a couple of days as Sunny's guest. She hesitated at first, nervous about being thrust into what she imagined was a glamorous life at Blenheim. But Winston calmed her fears, telling her that only his mother and a few friends would be there, and that he would make sure she enjoyed her stay.

She agreed and arrived on time at Blenheim, but she felt that she was walking in a dream. Then it was Churchill who hesitated. He failed to meet her on time for a morning walk on the eleventh, and the longer he made her wait, the more she was tempted to race back home to her mother in London. Finally, later in the afternoon, while they were making a tour of the grounds, a sudden shower sent them running for cover to an ornamental Greek temple. He decided to get it over with and risk having a fourth woman turn down his proposal of marriage. But, to his joy, Clemmie said yes.

Lord Randolph had presented Jennie with three rings when they were married, and she had given Winston one to place on Clemmie's finger. It was a large ruby with two diamonds. Clemmie loved it and was soon writing various relatives to tell them her life was now "heavenly."[2]

Her grandmother was pleased. Knowing that Winston was close to Jennie, she declared confidently, "A good son is a good husband."

Blanche Hozier later said of her daughter and Churchill, "I do not know which of the two is the more in love."

A few days after he proposed, Clemmie wrote Winston, "I wonder how I have lived 23 years without you."[3]

He could hardly believe his good fortune. The engagement—which was announced on August 15—was to be a short one. Winston didn't want to take any chances that a long delay might cause problems. In any case he needed to be in London in October to do his work at the Board of Trade. There was just enough time to get married in mid-September and to spend the rest of the month on their honeymoon.

Churchill wrote notes to dozens of friends telling them the good news, including Pamela Lytton and Muriel Wilson. Pamela's response has not survived, but Muriel wrote a cheerful reply full of warmth, and seemed more appreciative of him than ever. Perhaps she was relieved to know he would no longer be pining for her. After telling him how lucky Clemmie was to have him, she said that they must always remain friends. "I shall always count you as such," she wrote. "Bless you dear Winston."

The king offered his congratulations, Lord Rosebery wrote a kind note, and Joe Chamberlain—with his wife's help—dictated a gracious letter from Highbury "in my enforced retirement." Even the Hooligans emerged from the far reaches of his past to wish him well. Ian Malcolm sent his good wishes "in kindly remembrance" of an old friend, and Hugh Cecil volunteered to be best man. Winston gladly accepted the offer. (When he was a little late in replying to a later question about the wedding from Winston, Hugh responded with an apology and an explanation—"Frailty thy name is Linky.")

The cleverest response to the engagement came from one of Jennie's friends, who wrote her a note mentioning Churchill's escape from the house fire, and then added, "I'm glad Winston is fulfilling the Scriptures—& realising that it is better to marry than to burn."[4]

The wedding was set for Saturday, September 12, at St. Margaret's Church in Westminster. The couple had less than a month to prepare for the big event.

But what about Violet? She seems to have had little warning of the engagement until Winston sent her the news a day before the public announcement. She made a great effort to pretend to her friends and family that she was pleased for him, and that she didn't envy the task of trying to manage Winston for a lifetime. But the news stunned her, and she felt the loss deeply. She didn't know Clemmie well, yet she knew enough to conclude that Winston deserved someone better.

Her standards were high. She was an avid reader of serious literature, a fluent writer, and a highly informed observer of the political scene, with an intimate knowledge of Winston's world. She recognized that Clemmie was beautiful and charming but thought her appeal was superficial. She wondered, bitterly, "whether he will ultimately mind her being as stupid as an *owl*."[5]

Time would soften her view of the woman who had captured Winston's heart, but for now she was jealous and in a state of shock. With a hint of self-satisfaction, Clemmie revealed in old age, "When Violet heard that Winston was going to marry me, she fainted."[6]

In fact, in that eventful summer of 1908, each woman had reason to be jealous of the other. On Monday, August 24—with the wedding less than three weeks away—Winston left Clemmie in London and boarded a train at King's Cross for the fourteen-hour journey to the little Scottish village of Cruden Bay, where the Asquiths were spending the summer holidays at their rented fortress. It had an ominous name—Slains Castle—and was built at the edge of a dangerous stretch of high cliffs on the North Sea. It was owned by the Earl of Erroll, and had belonged to the family for more than three hundred years.

Visiting the castle in August 1773, Samuel Johnson stood at the large windows overlooking the coast and marveled at the tumult of the waves and the vast stretch of sea that ran uninterrupted to Norway. "I would not for my amusement wish for a storm," said Johnson, "but as storms, whether wished or not, will sometimes happen, I may say, without violation of humanity, that I should willingly look out upon them from Slains Castle."

On August 25, 1908, there was a brief, innocuous announcement in the London papers: "The President of the Board of Trade . . . left last night for Aberdeenshire, where he will be the guest of the Prime Minister at Slains Castle." It was a round-trip of eleven hundred miles, and Churchill wouldn't return to London until the end of the week. He didn't have any pressing business of state to discuss. The prime minister himself had just come and gone from London a few days earlier.[7]

Clemmie was furious. She threatened to break off the engagement. Her brother Bill had to talk her out of it, telling her that it would be disastrous for all concerned to "humiliate" a public figure of Winston's stature. There was also the problem that wedding gifts were already arriving daily from dozens of distinguished friends in high places. By the day of the wedding, the gifts would number in the hundreds and fill a large room.

Unaware of Winston's trip to see Violet at Slains, Churchill's previous biographers have suggested that Clemmie was just suffering from an ordinary case of nerves, or that she was worried about the burdens of becoming a politician's wife. "Maybe she even wondered if Winston truly loved her," her own daughter has speculated. The most that Clemmie ever revealed in later years was that she had been upset because Winston didn't pay her "sufficient attention."[8]

He had made it clear that he loved her, but he also had a debt to pay to Violet. Nothing could stop him from making this last-minute dash to see her in Scotland, where he could explain his decision face-to-face. Instead of allowing a heartfelt letter to make his case, he knew that Violet would want to hear it from his own lips. One of the things she loved most about him was the sound of his words, and it would have deepened her disappointment if he had not come to Scotland to break the silence.

But none of that would have been easy to explain to Clemmie, who had already broken two previous engagements and was under great stress as she prepared for her wedding day. While Winston was away, journalists followed her around London, reporting on her trips to dressmakers and various shopkeepers. Photographs of her were everywhere in the newspapers.

At the end of the week, when Winston was on his way home, the *Daily Mail* reported: "One of the busiest women in London yesterday was Miss Clementine Hozier, whose marriage with Mr. Winston Churchill . . . takes place a fortnight tomorrow. In company with Lady Blanche Hozier, her mother, she was shopping and in the hands of her dressmaker from before noon until nearly six o'clock. Both arrived home fatigued with the day's round."[9]

In her memoir of Churchill, Violet briefly mentioned his visit to Slains Castle that summer, but she was vague about when and why he came. She recalled that they discussed the subject of marriage, but only "in the abstract." Because they rarely spoke in abstracts, this would have been a first for them. No doubt what they said to each other was, as usual, highly specific and very spirited. Violet's best friend, Venetia Stanley, certainly expected fireworks. On August 26 she wrote to ask if Winston had arrived at Slains. "Have you yet thought it was your duty to tell him exactly what you think of her?" she asked, referring to Violet's low opinion of Clemmie.[10]

There were ample opportunities for discussion. The days were long at that time of year, and there were miles and miles of footpaths and lanes stretching out from the castle on the coast to the rolling hills west of it. There couldn't have been a more romantic setting. The green meadows were lush, the sky enormous and full of racing clouds, and the top of each hill revealed a sweeping view of the sea and the lonely coast. At the castle—which was a rambling collection of old and new wings framed by high stone walls and the occasional turret—they were never far from a door that led directly to the cliffs. They could sit in the sun on the soft grass high above the shore and watch as the occasional fishing boat sailed by.

They spent hours walking, discussing their lives as they explored the countryside. One day they visited the Cruden Bay links while the prime minister played golf. In the evenings they dined with the rest of the family and other guests, and then sat by one of the big fireplaces and played cards. To cheer up Violet, Winston invented amusing word games to play. One that made her laugh involved attaching funny, alliterative adjectives to the various stations on his rail trip from London to Aberdeen, the challenge being to find the most outlandish phrase for such places as Doncaster, York, or Edinburgh. To such activities, Violet recalled, he brought "the excitement of a child."

On the serious subject of his marriage he seems to have persuaded her that he had done the right thing, at least for himself. He also tried to make it clear that there was nothing to stop them being friends, no matter what else happened in their lives. He was eager to humor her.

As it happened, she loved exploring the coastline, and he readily agreed when she invited him to go on a rock-climbing expedition that would take them from one precipitous cliff to another. It was a perilous course interrupted by deep gorges where the sea crashed against the rocks.

He began by following her but soon took the lead. She liked his fondness for taking risks and later wrote of how much he enjoyed their adventurous outings at Slains. She remembered him "reveling in the scramble up crags and cliffs, the precarious transition from ledge to ledge, with slippery seaweed underfoot and roaring seas below." There was no beach, just a few large rock formations strung along the coast—jagged islets thick with seagulls. In a few cases it was possible to jump from one to the next, but it was difficult to find a secure foothold in the crevices, and in every leap there was the danger of plunging into the foamy waves.[11]

There was a manic quality to all this hiking and rock climbing, as though neither Winston nor Violet wanted to pause long enough to reflect carefully on the future before them. Any outsider watching the two clinging to the rocks as the North Sea churned below might have assumed they were a couple of young thrill-seekers with nothing to lose, or who were too madly in love to mind the danger. Few would have believed they were watching the prime minister's twenty-one-year-old daughter and the thirty-three-year old president of the Board of Trade. Even more surprising was the fact that the Cabinet minister was marrying someone else in two weeks.

Their adventures on the red-granite cliffs and the rugged shore didn't end well. Violet slipped on a wet rock and hit her face, opening a nasty cut. "I scratched my face rather badly rock-climbing with Winston," she wrote Venetia Stanley. She was lucky the injury wasn't worse. A fall from one of the islets would have thrown her into a current so strong she might easily have drowned. Or—on the way back up—one false step on the cliffs, and she could have fallen fifty or sixty feet to her death.[12]

The cut to her face made Violet self-conscious about her looks, and she was overwrought with emotion when the time came for Winston to leave at the end of the week. He had no choice but to go, and dutifully said his good-byes, leaving Violet behind at the castle. She refused to attend the wedding, even though Venetia—who was Clemmie's cousin—was one of the bridesmaids. It would have been a simple matter to travel to London for a few days, stay at Downing Street, and attend the wedding with Winston's many other friends and admirers. But Violet didn't feel up to it, and the ceremony took place on September 12 without her.

She was able to read about it, however, in nearly every major paper. The *Times* treated it as something akin to a state event, noting the large crowds that lined the streets, the impressive guest list, the church packed "to its utmost capacity," and the dozens of policemen—mounted and on foot—who were needed to keep order when cheering broke out as the bride and bridegroom emerged from the ceremony. "Undoubtedly," said the *Times*, the wedding "captured the public imagination." The *Scotsman* article began, "Not for many years has a marriage excited such widespread interest as that which took place on Saturday afternoon at St. Margaret's Church." In a front-page headline the *Daily Mirror* called it "The Wedding of the Year."[13]

Pamela, Lady Lytton, attended the ceremony, looking "damnably pretty," as Ettie Desborough observed. Ettie approved of Clemmie and enjoyed watching Winston bask in the limelight. "He was delighted with everything," she wrote afterward, "counted every head in the crowd, & showed me all his presents one by one." The weather was perfect, the bride's white satin gown "showed off the rather majestic lines of her figure," and David Lloyd George talked politics with Winston in the vestry. Blanche Hozier sat near the front with three of her former lovers sharing the pew. George Cornwallis-West cried, the victor of Manchester— William Joynson-Hicks—paid his respects, and when Wilfrid Scawen Blunt came in late, people stared at his long white hair and flowing beard and whispered, "Who is that tall, beautiful man?" For Ettie, there was no question that "the beauty of the day" was "Linky as best man, in a waistcoat of duck's egg green."[14]

The newlyweds spent the night at Blenheim, where they had the enormous house more or less to themselves. (The usual servants were there, but Sunny had gone to Paris.) After a second night, they rushed off to Italy to enjoy the rest of their honeymoon. Everything was going smoothly, and the trouble over Violet seemed behind them. But exactly one week after the wedding something happened at Slains Castle that showed Violet wasn't holding up well.

Late on Saturday afternoon, September 19, the prime minister's daughter left the castle with a book in her hand and wandered along the same path above the cliffs where she and Winston had been rock climbing. Asquith and Margot were hosting a dinner at the castle and didn't notice her absence.

When darkness fell, Venetia Stanley, who had just come from London after doing her duty as Clemmie's bridesmaid, burst into the dining room and announced that no one could find Violet. Everyone rushed out to look for her, with servants carrying lanterns and the dinner guests following them. They scanned the rugged slopes and ledges for any sign of movement, and tried to avoid the black gorges. Lord Crewe, Elgin's replacement at the Colonial Office, was one of the guests who joined in the search. The night was starless, with a heavy mist hanging in the air. It was difficult to see anything, and the shouts of "Vi-o-let!" had to compete with the constant roar of the sea.

After an hour of looking, the prime minister began to grow desperate and called for help from the nearby village. Dozens of people soon joined the search, including several fishermen, who knew the coast well and had powerful searchlights on their boats.

As midnight neared and there was still no sign of her, Asquith collapsed in Margot's arms, fearing that his daughter had fallen and been swept away by the heavy waves that beat along the coast. Margot heard the voices of the searchers coming from all directions and saw men and women risking their own safety to crawl over the rocks in the mist and search every crevice. Desperate, Margot went down on her knees and began to pray in the darkness.

A few minutes later she heard the fishermen cheering, and then she fainted. Her stepdaughter had been found and was apparently unhurt. Violet claimed that she had slipped and landed on a ledge where she hit her head. But when she was found, she was lying in the soft, spongy grass along the coastal path and showed no signs of injury.

The episode produced sensational headlines—MISS ASQUITH'S PERIL, PREMIER'S DAUGHTER MISSING, HOUSE PARTY'S THRILLING SEARCH— and reporters besieged the castle with requests for interviews and photographs. It was more attention than Violet had ever received in her life, and Margot began to suspect that the "accident" was staged for the sake of the attention. A closer look showed no evidence of a blow to her head, and Violet couldn't explain why she had remained unaware for so long of the efforts to find her. The more Margot considered the evidence, the angrier she became over "this unfortunate foolish & most dangerous escapade," as she called it in her diary.[15]

Lives had been endangered in the search, so the family tried to downplay the story, anxious that the press not discover that Violet's supposed "peril" was simply an unhappy young woman's cry for attention. She had wanted sympathy after Winston left but didn't get it because she had tried so hard to pretend that his marriage didn't matter to her. There were other young men now whose sympathy she may have wanted, and in letters to them after the event she exaggerated the danger, telling one young man in October, "I'm drearily normal again. . . . I escaped death narrowly in about 5 different ways—such as drowning, smashing into smithereens, brain fever, 'exposure'(!) etc etc." [16]

Margot tried to persuade her to keep quiet about the event. As she noted in her diary, "I wanted her just to thank the fishermen & poor people who found her & to say nothing more about it: poor Violet! Nothing was further from her ideas & she felt hurt I cd see by my attitude." In an effort to put the whole episode behind them, Margot decided that the family should spend the rest of their holiday somewhere less isolated, so she moved the family from Slains to a house near Edinburgh owned by her brother. It was a timely decision, for the stark beauty of the castle had a dark appeal that wasn't helpful to someone in Violet's frame of mind. Indeed, there was such a mysterious, forbidding air to the place that in the 1890s it had become an object of great fascination to Bram Stoker, who visited it often, staying at the Kilmarnock Arms Hotel in Cruden Bay. Many believe that Slains was the inspiration for the castle in Stoker's novel of 1897, *Dracula*. He wrote the last pages of the book at the village hotel. [17]

A close watch was kept on Violet, who seems to have suffered a nervous breakdown after what she called her "rock-affair." She continued to show signs of manic behavior, especially in any matter connected to Winston. In October the prime minister himself had to intervene when she wanted to race off to meet Winston after he returned from his honeymoon. Hearing that he was in Dundee for the annual Scottish Liberal Congress, and was giving speeches, she suddenly decided that she needed to appear on the same platform with him and speak on his behalf. A wire from her father instructed her to say nothing.

"I was sorry," she wrote Venetia afterward, "as I had thought of one or two things I quite wanted to say!" Her father told her that she needed to stay silent for "political" reasons, but both he and Margot must have dreaded that she would attract more publicity—and generate more gossip—if she said anything about Winston in public. [18]

This manic phase soon faded, especially when Margot began to speak of sending her troubled stepdaughter to Switzerland for her health. Margot didn't know all the details behind Violet's emotional upheaval, but she was sure of one thing. "This summer," she wrote, "it seemed as if she changed suddenly." Another long winter abroad was the last thing Violet wanted. Desperate to immerse herself in the political scene, she was willing to do anything to avoid being sent away again. Over the next few months she would settle into a less intense friendship with Winston, though it would take time for her to accept Clemmie as his wife. As it happened, she did accompany Margot to the Continent for six weeks at the end of the winter, but she endured it well and came home feeling grateful at having escaped a longer exile.[19]

Churchill wanted Violet and Clemmie to like each other and tried to smooth away any hurt feelings. Two months after his wedding, he arranged for the three of them to have lunch in London. Violet behaved herself but still wasn't impressed with Clemmie. When she was alone with Winston, he told her that his wife "had more in her than met the eye." Violet wanted to say something cutting. Yet it is a measure of her new effort at self-restraint that she simply smiled and gave him a double-edged response: "But so much meets the eye."[20]

Though Violet's mood was still bitter, it was in everyone's interest to forget about the troubles of the summer, and so the subject was hushed up. Violet would remain Churchill's strongest advocate in Downing Street, yet it seems that both took precautions in later years to obscure the depth of their involvement with each other. Very little correspondence between them has survived, which is unusual since both were avid letter writers. Churchill said almost nothing in public about Violet. There are just a few scattered references in his published comments, the best of which was his memorable description of her devotion to her father. He called her Asquith's "champion redoubtable."[21]

Trying not to hurt Violet, and to keep Clemmie happy, was a struggle for Winston. But his efforts were sincere. He didn't want to lose the friendship of one or the love of the other. In their first year or two together his wife did have fears that he was having second thoughts about the marriage. There was no one else, he hastened to assure her. She was the only one he loved. "You ought to trust me," he told her, "for I do not love & will never love any woman in the world but you."[22]

He meant every word of it, unusual though that was for a politician of his age and ambition.

XVII

EMINENT EDWARDIAN

It was a remarkable rise. In little more than seven years Churchill had gone from the Conservative backbenches to a prominent place in the Liberal Cabinet, with commentators on all sides predicting that he would one day be prime minister. When his engagement was announced, the *Daily Mirror* made the case that the glowing expectations for his political future were perfectly reasonable. With a tongue-in-cheek reference to his narrow escape from the burning mansion in Rutland, the newspaper declared, "If prophecy were ever safe, it would be safe to predict that Mr. Winston Churchill—soldier, war correspondent, traveller, biographer—and in view of quite recent events one may add, fireman—will one day, and that not far hence, attain to the Premiership."

A. G. Gardiner, of the *Daily News,* portrayed him as a kind of premier-in-waiting: "He stands before the country the most interesting figure in politics, his life a crowded drama of action, his courage high, his vision unclouded, his boats burned." James Douglas, an editor at the *Star,* was so excited by the young statesman's prospects that he didn't see much point in following any other politician's career. "There are many clever men in the House of Commons," wrote Douglas, "but not one of them stings you with the romantic excitement of adventurous ambition. . . . Mr. Churchill alone tingles with a dramatic future."[1]

It was time now for the promising politician to prove that he could meet some of the high expectations for his career. Could he establish himself as the capable head of a major department, a powerful force in the Cabinet, and a parliamentary figure with impressive legislative skills? Over the next year, in fact, he would demonstrate convincingly that he could do all three. Though he is not usually given credit for it, Churchill, as president of the Board of Trade, was largely responsible for three major legislative achievements of the Edwardian age.

Two became law in 1909. The first was the Labour Exchanges Act, which created a national job placement system. It was a bold but practical initiative to help the unemployed in one region find work in another. The second was the Trade Boards Act, which helped to alleviate the unhealthy working conditions and miserable pay among so-called sweated laborers—mostly women in small workshops. It was the first important legislation to establish the principle of a minimum wage. After it became law, a grateful Mary Macarthur—secretary of the Women's Trade Union League—said of the reform in an address to an American audience, "I don't think England quite realizes what has been done. It is simply a revolution. It means revolution in our industrial conditions."[2]

The third achievement took more time, but it was Churchill who began work in 1908 to develop what would become the scheme for unemployment insurance in the National Insurance Act of 1911. Lloyd George would claim credit for it, but it was Churchill who did the spadework with his staff at the Board of Trade. He first suggested the idea to Asquith in early 1908, then proposed a detailed plan at the end of the year, and circulated a memo to the Cabinet with specific costs a few months later. But, at Lloyd George's specific request, he delayed bringing a bill to the House of Commons. The two men had decided that unemployment and health insurance needed to be coupled as one bill, and Lloyd George wanted more time to prepare the health provisions. The Chancellor of the Exchequer wasn't even sure he could create a viable plan, but he wanted to try, and Churchill agreed to wait.[3]

Almost two and a half years later Lloyd George would insist that the whole plan originated with him, and that Winston had simply "walked off"—as he put it—with the unemployment scheme. There was no truth to this. In fact, Lloyd George was so caught up in preparing his budget of 1909 that he could do little more than listen to Winston's ambitious plans for reform. But, in 1911, he would pretend that his colleague's contributions to the insurance bill had never been significant. As Winston would later point out, in a letter to Clemmie, "Lloyd George has practically taken Unemployment Insurance to his own bosom, & I am I think effectively elbowed out of this large field in which I consumed so much thought and effort."[4]

As one way to put these matters in a broader context, it is worth looking back at Lloyd George's own tenure as president of the Board of Trade. He was there from the end of 1905 to April 1908, when Churchill took over. In all that time he did little to formulate plans for social reform. His major legislative accomplishments were the Merchant Shipping Act, the Patents and Design Act, and the Port of London Act. His was not exactly a record of radical innovation.

One of his biographers has wondered why Lloyd George's long period at the Board of Trade was nothing like what came "afterward" for the "radical" politician. The answer, in part, is that his greatest Cabinet colleague and rival—Winston Churchill—came afterward, stirring Lloyd George to do more than simply sound radical. Once Churchill joined the Cabinet everything changed. As a pair of powerful personalities with high ambitions—a colleague called them "the two Romeos"—Winston and Lloyd George came to dominate the Liberal government, both as partners and as rivals, with each trying to reinforce or undermine the other, depending on their shifting self-interests.[5]

But Winston was the spark that ignited the change from the old liberalism of the Campbell-Bannerman administration to the more radical agenda of the Asquith years, and what was sometimes called the New Liberalism. The Cabinet noticed the change right away. Winston made it clear that he was not there to do business as usual. "I intend to make myself damned disagreeable!" he was heard to say before heading off to a Cabinet meeting in 1908. He succeeded. In a diary entry from the same period Charles Hobhouse—the new Financial Secretary of the Treasury—wrote, "Winston Churchill's introduction to the Cabinet has been followed by the disappearance of that harmony which its members all tell me has been its marked feature."

Hobhouse put the blame on Winston for provoking Lloyd George into becoming a more demanding colleague. He so disliked Churchill's abrasive manner and unconventional ideas that he thought it was all part of a ploy to lead Lloyd George over a cliff. "I cannot help suspecting that Winston Churchill is deliberately urging Lloyd George to ride for a fall."[6]

More than one minister thought that Churchill was causing trouble just to get others in trouble and clear the path for himself. Hearing the grumbling from the Cabinet, Lord Esher observed, "My idea is that Winston wanted to push to the front of the Cabinet. He thinks himself Napoleon."[7]

Like everyone else, Lloyd George had read the stories in the press about Churchill "the future Prime Minister" and knew that he had to work fast to stay ahead of his colleague. From his new home at the official residence of the Chancellor of the Exchequer—11 Downing Street—he was in a good position to keep track of what was happening at Number 10. No doubt he was aware of Winston's close relationship with the prime minister's daughter. And he could not have mistaken Violet's contempt for him. She thought he was a shallow schemer, and she wasn't good at hiding her opinions.

Violet liked to tell the story of the time she asked John Maynard Keynes, "What do you think happens to Mr. Lloyd George when he is alone in the room?" Smiling, Keynes had replied, "When he is alone in the room there is nobody there."[8]

For a short period in late 1908, Beatrice Webb was so encouraged by Churchill's work at the Board of Trade that she began to think he had eclipsed Lloyd George as the most impressive Liberal figure. Winston was proving to be "brilliantly able," she noted in her diary. She now liked him better than Lloyd George, whom she called "a clever fellow" with "less intellect than Winston, and not such an attractive personality—more of the preacher, less of the statesman."[9]

But while Winston may have seemed merely personally ambitious to some, he was also doing the hard work of reform. He worked so hard that by the end of 1908 he was able to outline for Asquith a comprehensive plan. No one else in the Cabinet—including Lloyd George—moved so far ahead in mapping out real changes to British society through Liberal legislation. With his usual confidence, he more or less dictated the way forward to the prime minister, writing him that the government had two years to get the job done.

"The need is urgent & the moment ripe," he wrote Asquith. "Germany with a harder climate and far less accumulated wealth has managed to establish tolerable basic conditions for her people. She is organised not only for war, but for peace. We are organised for nothing but party politics."

His list of necessary reforms included his plans for labor exchanges, unemployment insurance, a system of "National Infirmity Insurance," a general overhaul of poor relief, improvements in education and transportation, and a more aggressive industrial policy to promote better relations between employers and workers. It was just the beginning of his initiatives. But these first steps constituted a bold plan for the times, and in Churchill's estimation they were practical and affordable. More important, he thought that the legislation could be crafted in ways that would win wide acceptance, even in the House of Lords.

If they were successful, he told Asquith, they would make the nation and the Liberal Party stronger. Even if they failed, he said, it would be better "to fail in such noble efforts, than to perish by slow paralysis or windy agitation."

Asquith welcomed Winston's agenda, encouraging him to "push on" with his efforts to promote new legislation. In effect, Churchill was proposing to do for the nation what he had been doing for himself—to achieve quick success by thinking big, taking risks, and making the most of opportunities while they lasted.[10]

Criticized so often for being erratic and unreasonable, Churchill showed a steady nerve as he methodically put forward groundbreaking measures that passed into law with relative ease. As he noted proudly after the Trade Boards legislation was introduced, it was "beautifully received" in the House, with even "friendly" nods of agreement from Balfour and other leading Conservatives. As a government minister determined to amass legislative victories, he so tempered his language and manner in the House of Commons that for a while he was able to get what he wanted without resorting to invective. Now he was happy to speak kindly of Balfour, thanking him for the "extremely fair" treatment he had received from the opposition and declaring that it was his "object in the conduct of the Bill to endeavour to carry at all stages the greatest measure of support."[11]

At the beginning of 1909 Churchill was brimming with confidence. He told a friendly journalist that the coming year would be full of exciting progress. "Very large plans," he confided, "are being industriously and laboriously shaped." In two years, he believed, if all went well the country would have in place a rational and efficient system to help those who couldn't help themselves and to create better opportunities for those who could. As he had argued a few months earlier—in October, when he had returned from his honeymoon to speak in Dundee—his great purpose now was to meet "the need of this nation for a more complete or elaborate social organisation."

It was in this speech at Kinnaird Hall in Dundee on a Friday night with more than two thousand of his constituents in the audience, and with his new bride beside him, that he had made his stirring claim: "We are marching towards better days. Humanity will not be cast down. We are going on—swinging bravely forward along the grand high road—and already behind the distant mountains is the promise of the sun."[12]

Just when Churchill was relishing his new part as the great Liberal prophet—a young, clean-shaven Moses pointing the way to the promised land—two powerful forces rose up to throw huge obstacles across his "grand high road." One was Germany, the other Lloyd George.

While the Kaiser's generals had been playing war games as if they were knights training for chivalric tournaments, his admirals had been busy planning a modern fleet to rival that of Britain's. In 1906 they had been forced to modify their plans when the Royal Navy launched HMS *Dreadnought,* a monster battleship with such impressive firepower that it could sink any ship afloat. It might have been wise not to trumpet the superiority of its long-range guns, but the British couldn't resist. As a proud officer told the press, "On the day that the battleship *Dreadnought* hoists the pennant, all the navies of the world will be rendered obsolete." By the end of 1908 a dozen of these British warships had been built or were in the works.

The German admirals were undeterred. They saw the new ship as a challenge that must be met and surpassed. They didn't waste much time getting started. In 1908 they launched four battleships with capabilities similar to those of the *Dreadnought,* and they were reportedly on course to create a fleet of twenty-one by 1912. Fears grew in Britain that the nation's long reign of naval supremacy might be endangered. The earlier claims that the new British warship was superior to all others had helped to create an arms race. "If we were about to make foreign fleets obsolete," said the *Edinburgh Review,* "we had shown foreigners the way to do the same to ours."[13]

Shrouded in secrecy, the naval preparations in Germany created so much uncertainty that British authorities couldn't say how lethal the new ships were nor exactly how many were in production. One day in December 1908 a member of the opposition, John Lonsdale, asked Reginald McKenna, now head of the Admiralty, if he could provide "the number and description of the big guns to be carried by the new German battleship *Posen.*" McKenna responded, "I am unable to give the information desired."

Incredulous, Lonsdale asked, "Does not the right hon. Gentleman think it desirable to take steps to make himself acquainted with these facts?" McKenna tried to turn the question on the questioner. "If the hon. Gentleman," he said, "can help me to discover the armament of the *Posen,* I shall be extremely glad." Lonsdale shot back, "It is not my job."[14]

McKenna may have been in the dark about the specifics of certain battleships, but he knew more than he was willing to admit. The problem was that he didn't want to say anything to start a panic. As he confided to Asquith two weeks later, "German capacity to build dreadnoughts is at this moment equal to ours." If this "alarming" information became known, he warned, it "would give the public a rude awakening." McKenna was so worried by the latest reports that he gave his backing to a plan for adding six—and perhaps as many as eight—British dreadnoughts to the fleet at a staggering cost of at least £9 million. The Cabinet took up the question in January 1909, and for the next two months its members argued over what to do.[15]

Immersed in his plans for social reforms, and caught up in the excitement of courtship and marriage, Churchill had been paying less attention to foreign affairs than usual. The prospect of war wasn't on his mind. The young man who had once been so eager to go into battle and risk his life had become accustomed to the less harrowing adventures of political combat, and he was slow to see the dangers in the growing naval rivalry between Britain and Germany. Reform, retrenchment, and peace were the great Liberal watchwords, and Churchill had been stirred by these noble aims. They seemed now to offer him a better path to glory than the old-fashioned one of war.

Far from being a warmonger, which later critics would assume was an intrinsic part of his character, Churchill wanted to believe that no reason for war existed between two nations as highly advanced as Germany and Britain. "I think it is greatly to be deprecated," he told an audience in Wales, "that persons should try to spread the belief that war between Great Britain and Germany is inevitable. It is all nonsense. . . . No, these two great peoples have nothing to fight about, no prize to fight for, and no place to fight in. . . . I have a high and prevailing faith in the essential goodness of great peoples."[16]

While Winston dreamed of peace and prosperity, it fell to mild-mannered Reggie McKenna to push for a massive expansion of the British war machine. The amount of money required was so large that Winston couldn't help but question it. After months of carefully searching for affordable ways to improve society, he wasn't in any mood to see millions spent to meet what seemed a dubious threat. So he decided that it was more important now to do battle with McKenna than to step up preparations for some future conflict with Germany.

His comrade in the effort was Lloyd George. They argued that building four new dreadnoughts would be sufficient for the coming year. Together they fought their colleague so tenaciously that Reggie was driven to the edge of a nervous breakdown. "I hate my colleagues," he told his wife after months of turmoil over the naval issue.[17]

His adversaries questioned everything he did. McKenna would submit a written statement of his plans to the Cabinet, and Churchill would resubmit it with copious criticisms in the margins. Reggie became so angry and frustrated that he started coming to Cabinet meetings with a letter of resignation in his pocket, just waiting for the moment when Winston would push him too far. Lloyd George was delighted by the conflict. He urged Winston on in warlike language, telling him how much he enjoyed the verbal firepower "raking McK's squadron."[18]

Because his own modest power with words was no match for Churchill's, McKenna kept hoping that Asquith would intervene to stop the pummeling. But the prime minister was inclined to sit back and let the battle rage until one side surrendered or a good compromise could be found. As First Lord of the Admiralty, McKenna naturally expected more support from Asquith when the subject concerned the Royal Navy, and the chief critic was the president of the Board of Trade. Instead he often fought alone, and was sometimes reduced to silence as Churchill stormed the heights and took over the meetings. "Today's cabinet gave the usual opportunity for an exhibition of Winston's rhetoric," Reggie complained to his wife. "Cabinet rule is impossible unless the driver holds the reins with an iron wrist. . . . My work is a trial." [19]

Part of his problem was that neither Churchill nor Lloyd George respected him, and so they tended to dismiss what he said out of hand. When he insisted that the Germans were on a path to war and would soon threaten Britain's control of the seas, they simply refused to believe him. In their view he was a weak First Lord who was being used by his admirals to get more ships. When Lloyd George first heard that "we may have to lay down 8 Dreadnoughts," he told Winston, "I believe the Admirals are procuring false information to frighten us." [20]

As the dispute dragged on and attitudes began to harden, Asquith finally stepped in to offer a compromise. Instead of building eight new dreadnoughts right away, he suggested starting with four and adding the rest later if the Admiralty's suspicions of German naval advances were confirmed. No one seems to have been happy with this compromise, but McKenna was allowed to present it to the House of Commons on March 16.

To a hushed chamber, he gave his view of the crisis facing the navy. General reports of dissension within the Cabinet had leaked out, but the public wasn't aware of how grave McKenna considered the situation to be. He didn't hold back now because of any fear of starting a panic. He was blunt.

"There will come a day," he said, "when by an almost automatic process, all ships of an earlier type than the *Dreadnought* will be relegated to the scrap heap. The maintenance of our superiority then will depend upon our superiority in Dreadnoughts alone. We could not be sure of our supremacy at sea if we fall behind in this class of ship." Though his words were carefully measured, they hit the Commons and the nation like a thunderbolt.

For most of the British public it was almost unimaginable that a First Lord of the Admiralty would ever have any doubts about Britannia ruling the waves. It was the equivalent of suggesting that one day the sun might fail to rise. But the sentence in his speech that caused the greatest sensation was this unusually frank statement on the German navy's shipbuilding plans: "The difficulty in which the Government find themselves placed at this moment is that we do not know—as we thought we did—the rate at which German construction is taking place."[21]

If even the First Lord didn't know how fast the Germans were turning out dreadnoughts, it was easy for fears to escalate in the general population. Suddenly there was a widespread sense of urgency that Britain must speed up its own production of the mightiest warships. Otherwise, it was said, the island nation might wake up one day to find itself surrounded by the German navy. "It is impossible to open a newspaper," noted a retired naval officer who was also a member of the opposition, "without seeing nearly a page devoted to the alarm felt throughout the country."

It took less than two weeks for the public to find a rallying cry in a slogan first used on March 27 by the handsome Tory George Wyndham: "We want eight and we won't wait." From that moment—and whether all the politicians realized it or not—there was no escaping the great Edwardian arms race. The anxious public would soon get their eight new dreadnoughts, and many more. Convinced that a war with Germany would break out "in a few years," Wyndham told Wilfrid Blunt, "The only thing we can do is to go on building ships."[22]

Lloyd George desperately wanted to save the cost of those four extra battleships and use the money instead for the social agenda that he and Winston were promoting. He told the House that he considered it "an act of criminal insanity to throw away" millions on "gigantic flotillas to encounter mythical Armadas." Yet as Chancellor of the Exchequer he was obliged to find the money to support the Cabinet's decision while also creating more revenue to supply the domestic side. Accordingly, he filled his "People's Budget" of 1909 with tax increases. He spread them over a wide variety of sources—everything from motorcars and mineral royalties to land values and incomes. But a primary target was the rich, whose incomes would be subject to greater taxes to support a 10 percent increase in government expenditure.[23]

Churchill was so eager to have the extra revenue that he altered his view of retrenchment to make an exception for worthy social plans. After the budget was introduced in April, he wrote his wife that he was looking forward to having "ample funds for great reforms next year." Carried away by this prospect, he conveniently put aside many of his old notions about government—notions that he would return to in time, but which, in this heady period, when his eye was so fixed on the "grand high road" to a better future, he chose to modify.[24]

One old notion went back to the days of his fight against protectionism, when he was still a Conservative. He had argued then against using tariffs to raise revenue because so much money went into the pockets of government that it merely encouraged spending for its own sake. "Governments create nothing and have nothing to give but what they have first taken away," he had said. "You may put money in the pocket of one set of Englishmen, but it will be money taken from the pockets of another set of Englishmen, and the greater part will be spilled on the way."

Now, in 1909, one difference for him was that government no longer carried the taint of corruption and incompetence that it did in the days of the Hotel Cecil. He wanted to believe that he and Asquith and Lloyd George could put the increased revenues to good use. They were noble stewards, he hoped, who would spend wisely and well for the benefit of society, and not for their own selfish interests. "I am not going to pretend that taxes are good things in themselves," he told a London audience in 1909. "They are not. All taxes are bad." He hastened to add, however, that they were needed to supply such vital things as national security—and, in his estimation, "social security" was as important as military security. Lloyd George's budget, he told his audience, would provide the "necessary" money "for the country to embark upon the great field of social organisation."[25]

But neither Churchill nor the other Liberal leaders would have the chance to do much more than "embark upon" this endeavor. They would be held back by not only the increasing cost of naval security, but also the disastrous way in which Lloyd George handled his "People's Budget" after presenting it to the House of Commons. Instead of at least trying to guide its passage into law in the usual way, he picked a fight with the House of Lords from the start, daring them to reject it. A 10 percent increase was considerable but hardly revolutionary, and not at all impossible to pass with careful management. The Liberal journalist and political insider J. A. Spender believed that if the budget had "been in Asquith's hands, it would almost certainly have been let pass," with just a modest protest from the opposition. After all, much of the budget increase was necessitated by the very naval expenditures that the Tories themselves wanted to boost to even higher levels.

But Lloyd George insisted on turning his budget into a fight over political power instead of pounds and pence. He wanted a fight more than he wanted a budget, and he was certain he would win. He saw himself leading the Liberals triumphantly into the next general election to crush the Tories and humiliate the House of Lords. In fact, what he did was plunge the country into a two-year constitutional crisis, which delayed social reforms, and which would—before he was finished—cost his party its overall majority, and allow the Tories to pick up more than one hundred seats in the Commons. Lloyd George's decision to wage class warfare would, in Spender's words, drive "the Tory party off its mental balance. It saw red and acted accordingly."[26]

Lloyd George inflamed passions by referring in the House of Commons to his "War Budget." He was going to take money from the rich "to wage implacable warfare against poverty and squalidness," as he put it. But this was mostly rhetoric. More than two-thirds of the increase in his budget went to pay for just two things—new dreadnoughts and old-age pensions. (Devised and advanced by Asquith, the new pension scheme covered only those over seventy, but it was proving more costly than expected.) Lloyd George fully expected that he would have to put even more money into the Royal Navy. If the four extra dreadnoughts were ordered, he admitted, "the Naval bill for the year will attain very serious and grave dimensions indeed, at which the taxpayer may well shudder." Understanding that the new arms race would dishearten Liberal supporters, he cleverly promoted the budget as being more progressive than it was.

The Liberals may have wanted to wage a general war on poverty, but preparations for an expected naval showdown with Germany would consume an increasingly large amount of the available revenue. In just the next two years naval expenditure would grow by 20 percent. Meanwhile, the few major weapons against poverty that emerged from this period owed much to Churchill's ideas on national insurance. [27]

In his reform efforts Winston would make the mistake of deferring too much to Lloyd George. For a time he seemed to forget how crucial his independence had been to his success. Knowing how much Churchill enjoyed a fight, Lloyd George chose the battle, and then persuaded him to join it. It was a brilliant way to steal the lead from his upstart colleague. In middle age Churchill would offer one explanation for why he had allowed himself to fall under his rival's influence. "At his best he could almost talk a bird out of a tree," he wrote. "I have seen him turn a Cabinet round in less than ten minutes, and yet when the process was complete, no one could remember any particular argument to which to attribute their change of view." [28]

Everyone who worked closely with Lloyd George was aware of how easily he could lay on the charm when it suited him. "When you entered the room," recalled the diplomat and author Harold Nicolson, "he would come bounding up to you, lead you in, throw his arms about you as he spoke, give a great impression of friendliness, exuberance and simplicity. His voice was very attractive, very warm and intense. He was a good listener, too, and when he was listening, or pretending to—half the time he wasn't—he used to look at you as though you were the only intelligent person he ever met." [29]

It was difficult to break the spell of the man who would come to be known as the "Welsh Wizard." Winston liked to think that they were equals and would later say, "Together we were a power." But Lloyd George didn't see their relationship in that way. Watching the pair in Cabinet meetings, Charles Hobhouse noted in his diary that Lloyd George had a "wonderful power of managing men for a short time. He knows no meaning in the words *truth* or *gratitude*. Asquith is afraid of him, he knows it, but likes and respects Asquith. He . . . treats Winston Churchill like he would a favourite and spoilt naughty boy."

Now and then, Winston would rebel and tell Lloyd George, "You can go to Hell your own way. I won't interfere. I'll have nothing to do with your [damned] policy." Or, as a mutual friend remembered him saying once, "No, no, no, I *won't* follow [Lloyd] George." [30]

But, time and again, he would come back and take his place at the other's side. It was an odd show of weakness in a young man whose lack of deference toward his leaders had been a hallmark of his rise to power. Somehow he had convinced himself that Lloyd George was a necessary partner—in part, perhaps, because of a dispassionate quality that made him valuable in a fight. But that same quality also made him more cynical, though Winston was slow to see that. "You are much stronger than I," he once remarked to Lloyd George. "I have noticed that you go about things quietly and calmly, you do not excite yourself, but what you wish happens as you desire it. I am too excitable. I tear about and make too much noise."[31]

XVIII

SOUND AND FURY

T he tall, creamy stucco house at one end of Eccleston Square—
Number 33—was in a quiet part of London in those days, a
leafy enclave tucked between the river and exclusive Belgravia.
The area was home to many large, prosperous families headed by established professionals or successful businessmen, who lived well but not
luxuriously. They were proud of the long, elegant gardens that graced
both Eccleston Square and nearby Warwick Square, each neatly tended
behind high railings. Yet just up the road—only half a mile away—was
busy Victoria Station, where great waves of London commuters came
and went all week long. Peaceful, but close to the heart of Westminster,
Eccleston Square was an ideal place for Winston Churchill to settle
with his young wife and start a family.

They moved into Number 33 in May 1909, with "a perpetual stream
of vans" unloading furniture and carpets—both old and new—on a
Friday and Saturday. Jennie had picked out wallpaper for some of the
rooms, Winston had supervised the installation of bookshelves to
hold his growing library, and Clemmie had ordered an attractive blue
carpet for the dining room. She was also busy looking for new things
to brighten a room for the baby she was expecting in the summer. At
thirty-four Winston's next big adventure was fatherhood.[1]

With mischievous glee, Lloyd George spread the false story that the
child exemption in the income tax (or the "Brat," as he called it) was the
only thing Churchill liked in the financial overhaul. "Winston," he told
friends, "is opposed to pretty nearly every item in the budget except the
'Brat,' and that was because he was expecting soon to be a father himself."[2]

When Diana Churchill was born at Number 33 on July 11, her parents were overjoyed. Her hair was reddish like her father's, which amused him. He was fascinated by her and was encouraged to see how healthy and strong she was. "Her little hands shut like a vice on one's fingers," he wrote.[3]

But, like many young families, the Churchills were sometimes overwhelmed by the various burdens of taking care of a new baby while establishing themselves in a new house. Clemmie's pregnancy went well, but she was slow to recover her strength after giving birth, and spent many weeks recuperating in the countryside with her mother and family friends. When they were apart, husband and wife kept a steady stream of correspondence going, sharing news and endearments. They took a childish delight in calling each other by nicknames and in exchanging the private codes of affection, their relationship deepening into a comfortable intimacy with occasional flashes of a more intense passion.

Bachelor life had been lonelier than Winston had wanted to admit, and now he finally had a companion with whom he could share everything. They were a good match, and they were grateful for it. "I feel a vivid realisation of all you are to me," Winston wrote, "& of the good and comforting influence you have brought into my life. It is a much better life now."[4]

This happiness in marriage was noted by others. After lunching with the couple at his place in Sussex, Wilfrid Blunt was struck at how close the two had become after just a year together. "They are a very happy married pair," he wrote in his diary. As might be expected of a poet, he found meaning in small gestures—how Winston took pains to indulge Clemmie's wishes or spare her any discomfort. Sitting with them in his garden, he watched Winston's reaction when a wasp came near. "Clementine was afraid of wasps," he wrote, "and one settled on her sleeve." Before she could panic, her husband leaned over and silently eliminated the threat. "Winston gallantly took the wasp by the wings, and thrust it into the ashes of the fire."

Clemmie was fond of Blunt and often boasted to him of her pride in her husband. After watching Winston give a lively speech in the House of Commons, she wrote the poet, "I was very proud when I heard him from the gallery. I hope he will never catch the usual Official Mood."

Following a lunch at Eccleston Square—not long after Diana was born—Blunt wrote in his diary, "There is no more fortunate man than Winston at home."[5]

But such happiness wasn't cheap. The responsibilities of family life brought increased expenses. The new furnishings needed to be paid for, the doctor had sent his bill, and the new house, which was much larger than his previous house, required him to spend more on servants and general upkeep. Fortunately, he had recently made £225 from a new reprint of his novel *Savrola,* and his investments managed by Sir Ernest Cassel were continuing to produce good returns. Among his holdings were bonds in the Atchison, Topeka & Santa Fe Railroad, and United States Steel. His annual salary as president of the Board of Trade was £2,000. But he was stretching his resources, and no longer had the free time to turn out bestselling books.[6]

When Diana was born, a story was told about Churchill's great pride in his first child. Though it has the ring of truth, the story was probably embellished a bit for the purpose of gently mocking him in political circles. It was said that one day he was seated on the front bench in the House of Commons beside Lloyd George, who turned to him during a lull and asked, "Is she a pretty child?"

Winston supposedly beamed. "The prettiest child ever seen."

"Like her mother, I suppose?" asked Lloyd George.

"No," Winston replied with a serious look, "she is exactly like me."[7]

For Winston, an important reason for moving to Eccleston Square was that his friend F. E. Smith had a house there. With his wife and two young children, Smith lived at Number 70, and Winston thought the two families would make great neighbors. A brilliant barrister, Smith had entered the House of Commons as a Conservative in 1906, but for several months he had avoided getting to know Churchill, whose defection to the Liberals he was slow to forgive. Once they had a chance to talk, however, they became friends almost immediately.

On the surface, they didn't seem to have much in common. Frederick Edwin Smith had the dark good looks of a matinee idol, and dressed like one in expensive suits perfectly tailored to fit his muscular figure. A naturally gifted athlete, he was a strong swimmer and a hard-driving tennis player. In the early years of his relationship with Winston, he was one of the strongest and wittiest critics of the Liberals. All the government ministers, including the prime minister himself, tried to avoid tangling with him for fear of being stung by his rapid-fire barbs. Churchill was one of the few who could match wits with him, and it was their shared love of high-speed repartee that helped to forge a bond between them.

F.E.—as he was usually known—made a small fortune as a barrister and was often in the news because of his dazzling success in a string of sensational trials. He was even wittier in court than in the House of Commons, and judges were the victims of some of his best retorts. When one judge solemnly informed him, "Mr. Smith, having listened to your case, I am no wiser," F.E. fired back, "Possibly not, m'lud, but much better informed." A pompous county court judge named Willis was a favorite target. Offended by his impertinence, Judge Willis asked in desperation, "What do you suppose I am on the bench for, Mr. Smith?" Politely, F.E. answered, "It is not for me, Your Honour, to attempt to fathom the inscrutable workings of Providence."

Like Winston, he could set off sparks at dinner parties when seated next to the wrong guest. "I've got a silly sort of fancy to tell you the story of my life," a society matron once whispered in his ear, to which he replied, "My dear lady, if you do not mind I would rather postpone that pleasure." Fond of strong liquor, he could sound a little less debonair if he had been drinking too much. When a dinner companion introduced herself as "Mrs. Porter-Porter with a hyphen," he gave her a boozy stare and snarled that he was "Mr. Whisky-Whisky with a syphon."[8]

If anyone could help Churchill polish his own verbal skills, it was F.E. They would spend hours trading quips and laughing, enjoying the kind of verbal games that Winston liked to play with Violet Asquith, but raised to dizzier heights. In fact, it was Violet who later said that of all Churchill's friends it was F.E. with whom he had the greatest fun. But because F.E. was often wickedly funny at the expense of Liberals, he wasn't much welcome in their circles, and Margot Asquith regarded him as a vulgar reactionary. She admitted he was "very clever," but added in her inimitable way that "his brains have gone to his head."[9]

Clemmie didn't care for him. She disapproved of his hard drinking and thought he was a bad influence on Winston, encouraging him to drink too much and to stay out too late. But once both families were in Eccleston Square it was hard to keep the two men apart. Whether at home or in the House of Commons or on field exercises with the Queen's Own Oxfordshire Hussars (F.E. was one of Winston's fellow officers in the reserve force), the friends were quick to find excuses for separating from others and entertaining themselves. After spending time with F.E. at the summer camps for their regimental training, Winston would always come home exhausted, partly from the physical exertion but mostly from staying up all night with his friend.

There were memorable nights when Sunny Marlborough, Winston, F.E., and a few other friends would gather in a field tent and sit "on up-turned barrels, by the light of tallow candles, playing cards till the flush of dawn." One evening, when everyone was a little drunk, Sunny asked, "What shall we play for, F.E.?" Perhaps only half kidding, he looked at the duke and answered, "Your bloody palace if you like." Wisely, Sunny passed.

It was a good thing that Winston and F.E. were so determined not to let their political differences affect their private lives. When the battle over Lloyd George's budget became increasingly nasty in the summer of 1909, the political divide between Liberal Winston Churchill and Tory F. E. Smith (who called the budget "that bladder of imposture") would grow ever wider.[10]

It was a warm night on July 30, 1909, when Lloyd George arrived at a large mission hall in the East End to give a speech on his budget. He had been waiting for a good opportunity to launch a public attack on his Tory opponents, and had decided to speak at a location that would in itself send a strong message to them. It was a grimy, rambling building called the Edinburgh Castle, which had a façade that gave it the look of a cut-rate medieval fortress. Surrounding it were the dark, forbidding streets of Limehouse, one of the roughest districts in London. Part of it had been used in years past to house an enormous pub notorious as a vice-ridden "gin palace." But then Thomas Barnardo—a reformer known for his charitable work with poor children—had come along and turned it into a center for an evangelical ministry to the poor, with a "Coffee Palace" to replace the pub, and the addition of a big hall for the "People's Mission Church."

It was an unusual place to find a Chancellor of the Exchequer defending his budgetary proposals. Normally, those who spoke from its platform were thumping Bibles as they addressed audiences that sometimes numbered well over three thousand, which was the stated capacity of the hall. As one of Barnardo's early biographers noted, "A great many of the best known and most influential evangelists and ministers in the country have taken mission services at the Edinburgh Castle, men of every degree and variety of gift, from Ned Wright, the converted prize-fighter, to University graduates and dignitaries of well-nigh all denominations of the Christian Church."[11]

Lloyd George didn't want an ordinary political hall. He wanted a pulpit from which he could launch a secular crusade, and he wanted to do it surrounded by the people he was claiming to help—the poor who lived in places like Limehouse. Dutifully, they came in great numbers and filled the hall to overflowing, with hundreds gathered outside listening near the windows, which had been thrown wide open to let in the breezes on this warm summer night. They cheered him when he arrived, sang "For He's a Jolly Good Fellow," and quickly hustled out the few suffragettes who came to heckle him.

Then they leaned forward and listened as Lloyd George ran his eyes over the crowded benches and began what would be one of his most important speeches. They were probably expecting him to do what Churchill had done in his "promise of the sun" speech at Dundee—give them a glimpse of the better things to come under Liberal reforms. But he barely mentioned what his budget would do for them. Instead he began almost immediately to pour his wrath on the devils of the Tory aristocracy who in his view were hoarding their wealth and anxiously plotting to block his tax proposals in the House of Lords. They were so stingy, he said, that they didn't even want to pay for the dreadnoughts they had demanded.

Like a good actor, he conjured a scene for his audience in which humble Liberals were going from one end of the country to the other collecting money for dreadnoughts. The poor workingman gladly paid his share, he said, but the rich in their fancy London mansions didn't want to pay a penny more than they had to. "We went round Belgravia," he told the Limehouse poor, "and there has been such a howl ever since that it has completely deafened us." Great wealth, he said, came with responsibilities, especially in the case of the landed aristocracy. If rich dukes on their vast estates refused to pay more to help the larger community, then, he warned darkly, "the time will come to reconsider the conditions under which land is owned in this country."

To this threat he added another. "No country, however rich, can permanently afford to have quartered upon the revenue a class which declines to do the duty which it was called upon to perform since the beginning."

The Limehouse audience delighted in this vision of dukes being stripped of their land and their power because they refused to bow to the small Welshman speaking in Barnardo's slum fortress dedicated to God and temperance. When Lloyd George roared to his conclusion by pledging to fight for the poor against the devil dukes, he cried out, "I am one of the children of the people." And the crowd answered exuberantly, "Bravo, David." [12]

It was a powerful performance, and it had its intended effect on the Tories, who threw down their newspapers after reading the speech and were seized with such fits of apoplexy that some didn't stop shaking for days. They couldn't believe that the head of the Treasury was stirring up thousands to join him in a crusade of class warfare, and they were dumbstruck by the frightening suggestion that the hallowed acres of grand estates might somehow be subject to confiscation. CABINET SOCIALISM, the headlines said. "THE CHANCELLOR'S THREATS AGAINST LANDLORDS." The *Fortnightly Review* called Lloyd George "the mob orator of Limehouse." (His threats against property were, in fact, bluster. His land taxes would never produce much revenue and would be repealed in 1920 under the premiership of—David Lloyd George.) [13]

If there had been any hope of passing the budget without a full-scale battle with the House of Lords, the Limehouse speech destroyed it. For the Tory peers, it was a call to arms they couldn't ignore. The opposition MP Sir Edward Carson immediately concluded that the real purpose of Lloyd George's budget wasn't to address financial questions but rather to force a confrontation between the two chambers of Parliament. Carson was a successful politician and barrister known for his unflinching resolve and stern speech. Like many others on his side, he was more than ready for a fight.

"The Chancellor of the Exchequer," he said, "has been posing as a Minister anxious to meet objections to the Finance Bill and as a responsible trustee for the public welfare and public peace. In his speech at Limehouse Mr. Lloyd George has taken off the mask and has preached openly a war of classes, insult to individuals, the satiation of greed, and the excitement of all the passions which render possible the momentary triumph of the unscrupulous demagogue. . . . He is attempting to legislate, not for a Budget, but for a revolution."[14]

The Limehouse speech changed everything for Lloyd George, making him unquestionably the most feared Liberal among the upper class and the most respected among the working class. Misled by his overheated rhetoric, both ends of the social spectrum exaggerated his potential for changing Britain. But image and word mattered more than deeds in the making of his public persona. Having successfully seized the initiative as the boldest defender of the people against the mightiest peers of the realm, he was now free to assail privilege and to wait until later to help the poor.

Churchill didn't want to wait. He admired Lloyd George's brazen tactics, had no sympathy for the House of Lords, and thought the fight over the budget was a winning campaign issue. But he also wanted to act on some of the things his colleague was only vaguely promising. While the Liberals marched toward an inevitable collision with the upper chamber, Winston was traveling the country trying to drum up support for what he called "a mighty system of national insurance."[15]

Only four days before the Limehouse speech, he outlined for an audience in Norwich his plan for creating unemployment insurance that would cover 24 million workers. He expected that Lloyd George's budget would provide the money to start this plan, and that both workers and employers would also contribute to the system. It represented a major social advance but received little attention. As long as the budget was stalled, the plan couldn't move ahead. In November, as the battle over finance dragged into its seventh month, an exasperated Churchill complained that the budget had "received a greater measure of Parliamentary time and attention" than any other bill he could recall.

From the start of the battle he had been torn between waging an uncompromising fight or allowing room for negotiation. In July he was still trying to sound moderate, reassuring the landed classes that property wasn't under threat. "If property is secure here," he told a Liberal club, "it is because we have over a long period of history been consistently laboring to force reactionaries to concede and revolutionaries to forbear." But the Limehouse speech encouraged him to abandon moderation, though not without an inner struggle. Right up to the last minute, as he prepared his own version of a Limehouse explosion, he was still debating with himself over which direction to take. On August 30 he wrote Clemmie, "To-day I have been working at my speech for Leicester again. . . . I cannot make up my mind whether to be provocative or conciliatory and am halting between the two. But on the whole I think it will be the former!"[16]

In fact, the speech he gave at Leicester on September 4 was mostly measured and mild except for the beginning and the end, where his language was even more provocative than Lloyd George's. At the beginning he ridiculed the reactionary dukes as "unfortunate individuals" and "ornamental creatures" who had no business meddling in politics and who ought to be content "to lead quiet, delicate sheltered lives." By the end he was using violent language to threaten their power, saying, "We will smash to pieces their veto." He damned all the peers as "a miserable minority of titled persons who represent nobody, who are responsible to nobody, and who only scurry up to London to vote in their party interests, in their class interests, and in their own interests." His pugnacious character came fully to the fore as he threatened not simply to defeat the House of Lords but to beat it into submission and demand unspecified forfeitures.

It should be understood, he said, that "the fight will be a fight to the finish, and that the fullest forfeits which are in accordance with the national interests shall be exacted from the defeated foe." Exactly what this meant wasn't clear, but it sounded like an ultimatum from a general whose troops had the enemy surrounded.[17]

Enraged Tories immediately condemned the speech for its "vulgar abuse" of the upper chamber, but if Churchill had been hoping to overtake Lloyd George as the "People's Champion," he failed. He was too late, for one thing. But, more important, his remarks lacked the theatrical effect of his rival's at Limehouse. Whereas the feisty Welshman had cleverly taken his stand in the slums at a dusty mission hall, Churchill came out swinging on the well-lit stage of a brand-new theater in a prosperous provincial town with a mostly middle-class audience seated in comfort in sweeping balconies and private boxes. Leicester's Palace Theatre even had a grand marble staircase with brass rails, and a pair of polished walnut doors at the main entrance.

Though largely sympathetic, his audience couldn't help but notice the incongruity of Winston damning the dukes from the stage of the well-appointed Palace Theatre. In fact, at his first mention of the noblemen, someone in the crowd shouted, "What about your grandfather?"

As much as Winston may have wanted to lead the Liberal charge on privilege, he couldn't escape his Blenheim background. He merely gave his enemies on both the right and the left an opportunity to ridicule him for trying. A Tory politician in Manchester asked how Churchill could presume to attack the aristocracy when he had a dozen titled relatives and came from "a family who had produced nine dukes." Instead of upstaging Lloyd George, Winston made himself look foolish. There was no effective way to answer the headline that appeared shortly after his speech: TWELVE TITLED RELATIVES. MR. CHURCHILL'S CLAIM TO ATTACK DUKES.[18]

The audience at Leicester was the same size as the crowd at Limehouse, but Churchill's impassioned speech fell flat, and Lloyd George's became a legend.

In the middle of this raucous period Winston stopped to chat with Violet Asquith at Number 10. After listening to him explain the latest political developments, she looked at him with something of an accusatory air and said, "You've been talking to Lloyd George." She knew him well enough to note a difference in his way of speaking.

"And why shouldn't I?" he asked.

"Of course there's no reason why you shouldn't," she said, "but he's 'come off' on you. You are talking like him instead of like yourself."[19]

He denied this, but the influence is unmistakable in his Leicester speech, and Violet was quick to note the change and to warn him that it showed. Perhaps it made a difference that Clemmie was encouraging him to sound more radical. She didn't care for Sunny Marlborough, and thought that Winston was too enamored of his old Tory friends, and too quick to forget and forgive the bitter disputes that had driven him out of the Conservative Party.

In one letter from these years Clemmie urged him not to be misled by the glamorous lives of his Tory friends. "They do not represent Toryism," she wrote; "they are just the cream on the top. Below, they are ignorant, vulgar, prejudiced." She signed the letter, "Your Radical Bristling."

Though Winston was careful to maintain good relations with Sunny, Clemmie would find it increasingly difficult to hide her disapproval of the duke's high Toryism and general arrogance. For the most part in this period she managed to treat him with polite reserve, but a few years later she would lose her temper in dramatic fashion when she stormed out of Blenheim Palace after a thoughtless remark from Sunny. Having noticed one day that she was writing to Lloyd George, he scolded her, "Please, Clemmie, would you mind not writing to that horrible little man on Blenheim writing-paper." Without another word Clemmie packed and left for the station, ignoring Sunny's apologies.[20]

It was wise not to mention Lloyd George's name in Tory mansions. One aristocratic landowner announced to his tenants that the day Lloyd George was thrown out of office he would, "in token of his joy, roast a live ox in his park." When informed of this, Lloyd George calmly replied that he "would strongly advise the noble lord not to get too near the fire on that day lest he should be mistaken for the ox."[21]

As often happens in politics, the fight over the budget descended into bitter name-calling and rhetorical blasts that had little or nothing to do with the facts of the case. Both sides exaggerated their virtues and their grievances until the sound and fury of it all drowned out the chance for a reasoned argument between them. At the end of October Charles Hobhouse bluntly asked Lloyd George about his reasons for waging such a heated battle over the budget. Was he hoping to go down in history as "the author" of a triumphant "financial scheme"? The chancellor agreed that he was "but added that he might be remembered even better as one who had upset the hereditary House of Lords."[22]

Whatever else he may have wanted from this fight, he was determined to score a victory over the old ruling class by goading the House of Lords into fighting an unwinnable battle. An hereditary chamber with a veto power was an anachronism that couldn't survive for long in the twentieth century, but reforming it didn't become a do-or-die issue for the Liberals until Lloyd George made it so, and then it overshadowed all other issues. It must have delighted him to have a duke's grandson fighting at his side.

As the day of reckoning grew near, he was gleefully rubbing his hands at the thought of how neatly he had manipulated the crisis. He wrote his brother in October, "They all realize—both sides—that they must fight now or eat humble pie. . . . I deliberately provoked them to fight. I fear me they will run away in spite of all my pains." He had done his work so well that it was too late for either side to retreat. When the House of Lords reacted as expected and rejected the budget on November 30 (Winston's thirty-fifth birthday), the stage was set for a constitutional showdown, and a general election was called for the beginning of 1910.[23]

Instead of being able to build on their large majority by pointing to solid legislative achievements, the Liberals went into the election to plead for the right to have a budget that increased taxes, spent millions on dreadnoughts, and frightened the establishment. It wasn't exactly a winning formula, yet only two months before the polling began, Lloyd George optimistically predicted that his party would emerge with a majority of ninety seats. He would be proven wrong.

In any case, not everyone shared his rosy view. Reggie McKenna's wife, Pamela, sat in the Ladies' Gallery on December 2 and thought the future looked grim as she watched the House of Commons finish its business. She was unhappy that the government didn't have more to show for its time in power. "Starting its work with such promise," she wrote in her diary, "and an almost unprecedented majority it seems cruel looking back on the four years of arduous toil that so little has been accomplished."[24]

It wasn't apparent to many at the time, and it has been obscured ever since, but the greatest—and most effective—Liberal figure in Britain in the crucial year of 1909 (the last year of the party's commanding majority in the House of Commons) was Winston Churchill. Brash and cunning, Lloyd George was the standout on style, which had usually been Winston's strong point. But after entering the Cabinet, Churchill had shown that he was also a political leader of real substance. He was the one with the most innovative ideas, the most detailed plans, and the most coherent explanations of New Liberalism's aims. Though not a theorist, he knew how to get results, and his views were practical and straightforward.

Just before the Lords rejected the budget, he published a collection of speeches that was, in effect, a manifesto for his party, but it arrived too late. Already the party was in dire trouble, and the details of social insurance were not as vital to candidates or voters as the more immediate question of the budget. Yet Churchill's *Liberalism and the Social Problem* was welcomed by some of the party faithful, and by a few radical reformers. They found it inspiring, and were holding out hope for a big election victory in 1910, when they could renew efforts to promote a progressive agenda. One of these admirers was the economist J. A. Hobson, who praised the book as "the clearest, most eloquent and most convincing exposition" of the New Liberalism.

Even prolific Liberal journalists were astonished at how swiftly Churchill had managed to lay out his vision of a Britain protected and liberated by what later generations would call a social safety net. H. W. Massingham—"the spiritual godfather of the New Liberalism," as one historian has called him—wrote the introduction to Winston's book. He praised its "directness and clearness of thought" and its author's "power to build up a political theory, and present it as an impressive and convincing argument." He stopped just short of declaring it the movement's bible. In its "force of rhetoric and the power of sympathy," he wrote, "readers of these addresses will find few examples of modern English speech-making to compare with them."[25]

In the relatively short period of Liberal ascendancy Churchill led the way in passing or proposing measures "designed to give," in his words, "a greater measure of security to all classes, but particularly to the labouring classes."[26] Besides helping to create such vital services as labor exchanges and unemployment insurance, he also had ambitious plans to use public works to provide employment in hard times, and to use education as a way of creating a better workforce. Unfortunately, the window of opportunity was closing for Churchill as the champion of comprehensive reform. Though he didn't know it yet, his new book—supposedly a blueprint for the future—was in fact his valediction as Liberalism's leading legislator.

XIX

LIFE AND DEATH

It was when he was desperately trying to escape a mob by scrambling over a brick wall that David Lloyd George may have realized his party wouldn't do well in the election of January 1910. He had wanted to start a fight, he had told his brother. He got one.

Conservative diehards in the northern seaport of Grimsby let him know he wasn't welcome from the time he arrived in the town late at night on Friday, January 14. Mounted policemen surrounded his motorcar when it left the railway station around midnight. Supporters had organized a torchlight parade to welcome him, but as they made their way to the house where he was spending the night, a rival crowd tried to block the way and struggled with police. Bottles and potatoes were hurled at the car, breaking one of its windows. The protestors shouted insults, including the cry "Traitor!"

The next day detectives escorted him to a local skating rink, where he was scheduled to address a modest gathering. Uniformed officers guarded the platform and the entrances. But soon the rink was surrounded by a few thousand angry opponents, and the police were faced with the same dilemma that had confronted the authorities in Birmingham when Lloyd George was cornered there by a mob in 1901: How could they get him out safely? Chief Constable Stirling decided it was best to make a run for it. He advised leaving by a back door, and then trying to race across a bridge over the rail line before anyone was the wiser.

They didn't make it. The mob spotted them and gave chase. The only hope was to climb over a brick wall next to the rails and seek safety inside a nearby fire station. And so the Chancellor of the Exchequer scaled the wall with the help of a few constables and disappeared inside the fire station, where he hid out until a fast car picked him up twenty minutes later and whisked him away to his next speaking engagement. A few days later a cartoon appeared in the national press showing a frantic Lloyd George getting a boost over the wall by a burly policeman. "Still running," said the caption.[1]

While the chancellor was busy trying to outwit the Grimsby mob, Winston was safely at work on his campaign in Dundee, where he was now a favorite of the townspeople and wasn't worried about losing his seat. The speeches he gave were generally mild, partly because Asquith wanted him to tone down his rhetoric for the election. But he experienced a few lapses. Attempting to account for early election losses in other parts of the country, he darkly hinted that the backwoods peers had intimidated their local people and pressured them into voting against the government. "No doubt," he said, "there has been, as we expected, a very sharp turn of the feudal screw."[2]

When the final results were announced, he won his seat easily. But the Liberal losses in the rest of the country were so large that they couldn't be dismissed as simply the result of Tory dirty tricks. The Conservatives and their Unionist partners saw their number of seats soar from 157 in 1906 to 272. The Liberals fell from 377 to 274. To survive in power, Asquith would now have to rely on the support of two minor parties—Labour and the Irish Nationalists—creating new tensions (especially over Irish Home Rule) that would make governing increasingly difficult. The Liberals wanted to treat this election disaster as a mild setback, but it emboldened the opposition and should have cast doubt on the wisdom of following Lloyd George's divisive approach.

In private, Margot Asquith told Churchill that the chancellor's inflammatory rhetoric alone had probably cost the party thirty seats. The electorate had given them a strong rebuke, she admitted, acknowledging that a lack of "moderation & self control has smashed our splendid majority." She congratulated Winston on behaving more responsibly in the campaign and urged him to continue being agreeable. "Why not turn over a completely new leaf and make everyone love you and respect you?" she asked in her demanding way. "You think it's dull, but it's much duller to talk to journalists and to be always bracketed with Lloyd George."[3]

Winston didn't make much of an effort to defend his colleague. He understood that the new alignment in the House of Commons would make the work of passing legislation more time-consuming and complicated. The Liberal losses undermined much of what he had been doing for the last two years. He could have stayed at the Board of Trade and continued to slog ahead, but he was always looking for quick results and was rightly worried that the Liberal reign might end abruptly. It was also important to raise his standing in the Cabinet so that he was on an equal footing with Lloyd George.

Conveniently, the prime minister agreed that he deserved promotion and offered him "one of our most delicate and difficult posts—the Irish Office." But Churchill had his eye on bigger things and wasn't interested in a "difficult" job that would become even more onerous because of fresh demands from the Irish Nationalist MPs. Knowing Asquith and his family as well as he did, he felt comfortable taking the risk of turning down the Irish Office and suggesting his own promotion. Two jobs appealed to him as offering both the scope of action he craved and the prestige he thought he had earned. He wrote the prime minister on February 5, "I should like to go either to the Admiralty (assuming that place to become vacant) or to the Home Office. It is fitting, if you will allow me to say so—that Ministers should occupy positions in the Government which correspond to some extent with their influence in the country."[4]

In other words, as he had shown in the last year, he was worthy to stand alongside any of his colleagues, and he wanted a position to prove it. Asquith didn't see any reason to argue and gave it to him. Within a few days the announcement was made that Churchill was the new Home Secretary. The promotion vaulted him into the first rank of the Cabinet. Not incidentally, it also gave a major boost to his own finances, more than doubling his salary at the Board of Trade to £5,000.

A few days after he took up his duties at the Home Office—where his responsibility for law and order involved him in the work of the police, the prisons, and the courts—he was at a dinner party and was so lost in one of his intense, thoughtful moods that he didn't say much until halfway through the meal. And then he suddenly turned to the handsome older woman seated beside him and said—as though thinking out loud—"After all we make too much of death." Jean Hamilton, the wife of Winston's friend General Ian Hamilton, knew him well enough to understand that he cared little for small talk and often made unusual, abrupt remarks for no apparent reason. So she took his comment in stride and responded politely, "Yes, I think we do—but why do you say so now?"

As it happened, Churchill had been brooding the whole day about his first experience with the most difficult part of his new job.

"I have had to sign a death warrant for the first time today," he said, "and it weighed on me."

"Whose?" she asked. "For what?"

Winston's answer revealed why he couldn't stop thinking about the case: "A man who took a little child up a side street and brutally cut her throat."

Jean Hamilton was shocked but didn't see any reason to lament the death of such a killer. "That would not weigh on my mind," she said.[5]

But it weighed heavily on Winston's mind because he couldn't understand how such a horrible crime could take place in a supposedly civilized society. Joseph Wren, an unemployed former sailor living in a Lancashire mill town, had murdered a child of three and a half in December and left the body near the railway. Convicted in January, he had been sentenced to death on February 14, the day Churchill was appointed to the Home Office. Wren had already survived a suicide attempt in his prison cell and had admitted his crime, saying that when he killed the child he had been "so depressed that he did not know what he was doing." On February 21 Churchill reviewed the case and found no reason to issue a reprieve. That night, while Jean Hamilton debated the wisdom of capital punishment with the new Home Secretary, Wren was sitting in his cell at Strangeways Prison in Manchester. The next day he was hanged.[6]

In his work as a Liberal legislator, Winston had been trying to create a better life for the millions struggling to survive in the hard conditions of industrial Britain. But in his job at the Home Office he was given a harrowing view of the crime and depravity in the nation's slums and was forced to confront how intractable these problems were. Details in case files brought the underside of the Edwardian world vividly—sometimes painfully—to life by putting before him the intimate, human stories of crime and punishment. He had not expected to be so affected by this work, nor to wrestle so much with his duty as the government official who, with a few strokes of his pen, could condemn a prisoner to the gallows or order a reprieve.

He kept near his desk a grim ledger with the words "Death Sentence" in black at the top of each page. Forty-two names were added to this book for the period in which he served as Home Secretary, all of them prisoners condemned to die by hanging. At the end of a row of information on each name was a column marked "Result." For twenty prisoners, Churchill decided to allow a reprieve, but for twenty-two the word written in the "Result" column was "Executed." This last group included the infamous murderer Dr. Hawley Harvey Crippen and more common killers like William Henry Palmer, who strangled an old woman after breaking into her house and robbing her.[7]

One case haunted Churchill for the rest of his life. It concerned a confessed murderer, Edward Woodcock, who was an obscure former soldier living in Leeds with a woman he never married. During a drunken fight he killed her with a knife, and he was devastated when he realized what he had done.

"After the crime," Churchill recalled, "he walked downstairs where a number of little children to whom he used to give sweets awaited him. He took all his money out of his pocket and gave it to them saying, 'I shall not want this any more.' He then walked to the police station and gave himself up. I was moved by the whole story, and by many features in the character of this unhappy man. The judge who tried the case advised that the sentence should be carried out. The officials at the Home Office, with their very great experience, suggested no interference with the course of the law. But I had my own view, and I was unfettered in action in this respect."

By Churchill's order—and to the consternation of his subordinates—the man was reprieved in early August 1910 and imprisoned for life. But at the beginning of the next month the Home Secretary was shocked to learn that the man had managed to hang himself and was found dead in his cell with a suicide letter addressed to his family.

Thirty-eight years later, when Winston Churchill was internationally famous as the defender of his country against the evil of Nazism, he still had a copy of Edward Woodcock's suicide note and brought it with him to the House of Commons, where he read it as evidence for capital punishment. The country had survived the carnage of two world wars, large parts of Europe were still in ruins, but Winston had not forgotten the man who had committed a crime of passion in 1910, and had given all his money to some street children as he walked off to surrender to the police. What had stuck in his mind was Woodcock's despair at a life sentence.

"I wonder myself," he told the House, "whether, in shrinking from the horror of inflicting a death sentence, hon. Members who are conscientiously in favour of abolition do not underrate the agony of a life sentence. To many temperaments—to some at least—this is a more terrible punishment."

Winston spoke, of course, as someone who had made his name in his twenties as a prisoner who had risked everything to escape confinement, hiding out and traveling by the stars to reach freedom. In Woodcock's dread of a long imprisonment he saw a desperation that he had felt himself in South Africa. Restless and reckless, Winston was never going to be anyone's prisoner for long, either figuratively or literally. He had thought he was doing Woodcock a favor to spare him the death sentence, but the man's suicide had come to serve for him as an important reminder—some things were worse than death.

Perhaps few in the House on July 15, 1948, understood that the man who had led them through the worst days of the war—who had fought so hard to avoid capitulation—was revealing to them in this debate something of his own personality. When he insisted on reading Edward Woodcock's suicide note to them, they must have thought it was just an old man revisiting the past for his own eccentric reasons. But he was sharing with them an image that filled him with a particularly intense dread—the hopeless man with nowhere to run.

It is the only reasonable explanation for why one of the most accomplished orators of the age, in the years of his greatest fame, would pause to read out loud to the House of Commons the rough prose of an Edwardian suicide. "I was pleased at the reprieve," Woodcock had written to his relatives, "for the sake of you; not for myself, because I knew it meant 'for life' in gaol, and there is no pleasure in that. I think I had rather be dead than be in gaol for life. I've been studying ever since how to do away with myself. . . . I think I will be a lot better off in my grave, because if I had to get out with 15 years I should be 61 years old. Where could I find work at that age? So I hope I manage alright, so goodnight and God bless you all. Your poor unfortunate brother, E. Woodcock."

Churchill put down the letter and looked at the House. "I mention this case," he said, "in order that those who shrink from the horror of inflicting the death penalty may not underrate the gravity and torment of the alternative."[8]

Edward Woodcock had been arrested at the end of May, but the murder of his victim, Elizabeth Ann Johnson, received little notice, and his quick conviction went almost unreported. The whole country was too absorbed in grief over the sad end of another Edward—the king—to care about the small, daily tragedies of the slums. It was on May 6, 1910, that Edward VII died at Buckingham Palace.

Even though his reign had been relatively short, the king had come to seem a towering figure to his subjects, a reassuring, avuncular character who did his duty but also lived on a grand scale—indulging his gargantuan appetite with all the gusto of a Tudor monarch. It was the good life that ruined his health, adding so much bulk to his modest frame that he could barely move at the end. As a German diplomat observed of the king in his last year, he was "so stout that he completely loses his breath when he has to climb upstairs."

Life had become one long feast, much of it served to him by a parade of society beauties who added their fond caresses to his many other comforts. Winston's mother was one of those women, and had managed to stay on good terms with the king even when her son was causing him distress. At his death she called him "a great King & a loveable man."[9]

Jennie had understood how to keep him happy. The right kind of pampering went a long way. Once she had advised Winston on the best method of handling him, saying of the king, he "only wants a little cosseting to be kept quite tame." No doubt her softer touch had helped to calm his temper on the many occasions when Winston upset him.[10]

The problem was that in his last year the king regarded her son as one of his most troublesome subjects. In September 1909 Edward had taken the extraordinary step of directing his private secretary to rebuke Winston publicly. After a Scottish paper reported that Churchill had ridiculed the Conservatives for having created peerages for their friends in the newspaper business, Lord Knollys fired back with a response on behalf of the king. Published in the *Times,* it was terse: "I beg to inform you that, notwithstanding Mr. Winston Churchill's statement, the creation of peers remains a Royal prerogative."

Thanks to the feud between the Liberals and the Lords, the protocol of creating peers had become a touchy subject. The king wanted to remind Churchill and the rest of the Cabinet that, strictly speaking, the decision to grant a peerage belonged to him and not to the politicians. Winston thought the king was being too sensitive. Everybody knew, he complained to Clemmie, that "the Royal prerogative is always exercised on the advice of Ministers, & Ministers & not the Crown are responsible." Revealing a little aristocratic disdain of his own, Winston dismissed the rebuke as beneath his consideration. "I shall take no notice of it," he told Clemmie.[11]

Though the royal lion was on a tight constitutional leash, he could still roar and snarl, and Edward did a little of each in his final months. Asquith wanted his agreement to create hundreds of Liberal peers if the House of Lords refused to limit its veto power over the Commons. The idea was that the mere threat of flooding the upper chamber with Liberals would be enough to make Conservative peers surrender their veto. But the king hated the idea, fearing that it would make a mockery of the royal prerogative and lead "to the destruction of the House of Lords." His strategy was to stall as long as possible and to hope that the struggle between the two chambers resolved itself without drawing the monarchy into the fight.

But Churchill insisted on dragging him into it and bringing the dispute to a prompt conclusion. Though Lloyd George had started the fight with the upper chamber, Winston thought he knew the fastest way to finish it. Buckingham Palace had warned him not to use "nebulous allusions to the Crown" in his speeches, saying that the king found them "most distasteful." Such a warning would have stopped most Cabinet ministers, but not Churchill. Only five weeks before the king's death he stood on the floor of the Commons and declared, "It has now become necessary that the Crown and the Commons, acting together, should restore the balance of the Constitution and restrict for ever the Veto of the House of Lords."

On his own authority Winston was claiming that Edward had already taken a stand and was ready to fight with the people against the peers. It was a daring affront to royalty.[12]

If he had not been so ill at the time, the king would surely have made Churchill pay for his impertinence. His courtiers were so outraged that some of them later said such antics had hastened Edward's death. By mid-May, when the nation was in deep mourning, rumors were spreading in London that the king had been pushed toward his grave by the Liberal troublemakers who had filled his last years with anxiety over threats of class warfare and assaults on the House of Lords.

On May 9 the Tory politician Lord Balcarres noted in his diary, "There is certainly a feeling widely prevalent in lower middle class circles in London, that the King's death was accelerated by anxiety caused by Asquith's announcement that the Cabinet intend to bring pressure on the Throne. That the King was upset we all know: he was for instance furious when Churchill indicated an alliance between the Throne and the Commons."

Poor health—not the supposedly poor manners of Liberals—killed Edward. But the rumors persisted all the same. Eddie Marsh complained to a friend, "The cock-and-bull stories that are going about as to the King having been killed by the Liberals are too amazing. The Queen . . . is supposed to have taken the P. M. and [Reginald] McKenna into the [king's] room and said, "Look at your work!"[13]

In fact, Edward's death was a blow to the Liberal cause. Churchill and others had been hoping that the threat of Crown and Commons in league against the Lords would be enough to settle the question of the veto power. It didn't matter that Edward had wanted to remain neutral. It was only important to make the Lords believe that their constitutional position was impossible and thereby force them to capitulate. Churchill was pursuing this goal when Edward surprised everyone by dying. Until that point the strategy appeared to be working. In April, Lloyd George's budget, which had started all the trouble, finally won approval in the House of Lords, a full year after it was introduced.

Now the larger question of whether their lordships might ever again kill any bill was going to have to wait. Such a momentous issue couldn't be considered in the immediate aftermath of Edward's death, and certainly not before politicians could take the measure of the new monarch—George V. No one knew his intentions. But all knew that the stakes were high. Receiving the news of Edward's death while on a Mediterranean cruise, Asquith stood on deck and stared at the night sky, wondering what the future would hold. There was a sign in the heavens, but there was no way to know whether it portended good or ill.

"I remember well," he recalled of that night in May, "that the first sight that met my eyes in the twilight before dawn was Halley's comet blazing in the sky." It was a moment that seemed ready-made for a scene in a history play, modeled on one of Shakespeare's. The fate of the nation swayed in the balance as one monarch died and another took his place.

"At a most anxious moment in the fortunes of the State," continued Asquith, "we had lost, without warning or preparation, the Sovereign whose ripe experience, trained sagacity, equitable judgement and unvarying consideration, counted for so much. . . . We were nearing the verge of a crisis almost without example in our constitutional history. What was the right thing to do?"[14]

It would cost Asquith many more sleepless nights before that question was resolved.

A few months before the prime minister found himself gazing up at the comet under the Mediterranean sky, a plain-looking woman in an old tweed hat and scruffy clothes was being arrested in Liverpool for leading a suffragette protest. The police found three rocks in her cloth coat and charged her with a breach of the peace. Brought before a magistrate with other suffragettes, she was quickly convicted and sentenced to fourteen days at hard labor. In her cell she was given meals of porridge and meat and potatoes, but she refused to eat. After four days on a hunger strike she was force-fed by a doctor and four women guards, but she resisted this treatment every day for a week. Then, abruptly, she was released after a surprising discovery was made about her identity.

She had given the authorities a false name, telling them she was "Jane Warton," a seamstress. But her family—worried by her disappearance—had tracked her down and rescued her. When she was released, she was still suffering from the violent methods of the force-feeding, and her mistreatment exploded into a major scandal. For the supposed seamstress was none other than Lady Constance Lytton, of Knebworth House, the forty-year-old sister of Victor, Earl of Lytton, and therefore sister-in-law to the former Pamela Plowden.

As fate would have it, Winston became Home Secretary three weeks after her release. For the next few months—while trying to keep up with all his other work—he was involved first in a brief investigation of Lady Constance's mistreatment, and then in a longer disagreement with Lord Lytton over the best way to handle the suffragette protests and to begin enfranchising women. Lady Constance suffered from a bad heart, and her brother was angry that she had not received proper medical attention in prison. He wanted heads to roll and accused Winston of failing to crack down on those responsible.

But it was difficult to charge anyone for abuse when, as Victor Lytton acknowledged, "my sister concealed her identity & refused to answer medical questions." Churchill was sympathetic to the family but couldn't do much to satisfy them, and Victor resented him for it. The whole unpleasant episode was especially hard on Eddie Marsh, who wrote Victor: "Nothing in my life has pained me so much as the hideous breach between you and Winston, two of my dearest friends."[15]

Part of Lord Lytton's anger toward Winston—which became exceptionally intense—may have been rooted in deeper frustrations. His sister's mistreatment came at a bad time. He was going through his own troubles at home with the woman whom Winston had once hoped to marry. Pamela had turned out to be not the best of wives and was now in the middle of one of her most passionate affairs. Ettie Desborough's twenty-two-year-old son Julian was constantly finding excuses to be with Pamela, and it would have been difficult for her husband not to notice the growing attachment. Certainly Ettie was aware of the relationship because her son couldn't hide anything from her, much to Pamela's dismay.

"Oh Mummie," Julian wrote his mother in 1910, "I had *such* a wonderful two days at Knebs [Knebworth House]. You will be sorry (or not sorry?) to hear that I love Pamela better every time I see her."[16]

Though Winston couldn't understand why Victor was now so difficult and intemperate, he tried to treat him well. When he gave directions to his staff for drafting a letter to him, he cautioned them: "Endeavour to couch it throughout in a manner which will safeguard our position while showing consideration to Lord Lytton."[17]

The government's lack of progress on the suffrage question was one of its greatest failures, and Lady Constance's experiences highlighted the absurdity of punishing women for demanding their rights. Though the violence of some militant suffragettes alienated the Cabinet, the issue wasn't going to disappear and needed to be resolved as urgently as the other pressing problems. Asquith, Churchill, and Lloyd George would have better served the Liberal cause if they had devoted as much attention to suffrage for women as they gave to the veto in the House of Lords.

But, as Winston made clear in a memo summarizing his differences with Lord Lytton, his view of the question had been so poisoned by personal attacks that he couldn't summon any enthusiasm for legislative action. Cast in the third person, his memo of July 19, 1910, reveals the depth of Churchill's bitterness toward the militant suffragettes: "They have opposed him with the whole strength of their organisations at four successive elections. . . . They have at all times treated him with the vilest discourtesy and unfairness. They have attacked him repeatedly in the most insulting terms. They have assaulted him physically."

Though not mentioned in the memo, the last straw was a threat made against his daughter, Diana. As the press later revealed, "For a long time . . . Mr. Winston Churchill's baby was carefully protected by police because of a suffragette plot to kidnap the little one." When Churchill met with a group of suffragettes at the end of 1910 to discuss their concerns, he emphasized that he had lost patience with their tactics. "Every step taken in friendship," he complained, "had only met grosser insults and more outrageous action."[18]

Writing to a supporter of the suffrage movement, Lloyd George warned that Winston had been humiliated too often by protestors. It was a mistake to target him, he said, and explained, "He is not the kind of man to overlook that."[19]

PART III

1910—1915

XX

VALIANT

A violent energy had been building in Edwardian society for years, the result of expectations raised too high and harsh realities neglected far too long. Change was wanted, but it was slow in coming. Perhaps the greatest measure of discontent was found not in the growing antagonisms between classes, political parties, the sexes, or the rich and the poor, but in the sheer numbers of people who were fleeing the country each year for better lives elsewhere. In the ten years following the death of Queen Victoria, when the population of the United Kingdom averaged 43 million, 7 percent—three million people— chose to emigrate. The exodus was so great in Glasgow, for example, that the number of vacant houses soared to twenty thousand in 1910.[1]

Churchill had assumed that his service at the Home Office would prove more rewarding and less complicated than a stormy spell at the Irish Office. But it placed him at the very heart of the growing domestic unrest and consumed his days with a steady flow of angry people complaining about prison conditions, police conduct, court sentences, industrial disputes, or threats from spies, revolutionaries, and anarchists. He liked the subject of prison reform and introduced many improvements to the system during his time in office, and he enjoyed helping the newly formed Secret Service Bureau root out foreigners suspected of espionage. But everything else was a trial to his spirit and wore him down. Near the end of his political career he would say of the job, "There is no post that I have occupied in Governments which I was more glad to leave."[2]

The episode that gave him the most trouble began one day in the autumn of 1910 when a chief constable in South Wales sent him an urgent telegram. It began with the news that striking miners were rioting in the area of Tonypandy—a compact town of thirty-four thousand surrounded by collieries and smokestacks. There were "many casualties," and troops were desperately needed to restore order, reported the police official. It ended with the words "Position grave. Will wire again. Lindsay, Chief Constable of Glamorgan."[3]

A former officer with the British Army in Egypt, Lionel Lindsay was an old-fashioned, tough-minded military man who had little tolerance for lawbreakers. To put down the riot, he had requested a force that included two hundred cavalrymen and two infantry companies. Churchill must have shuddered when he read the telegram because it indicated that the troops were already on their way to the mining district. The last thing the Liberal government needed was a battle between enraged Welsh miners and a large military contingent. Yet the riot was a threat to innocent civilians, with attacks on shops that resulted in broken windows and looting.

For decades afterward, however, Churchill's critics pointed to this incident as one of his worst moments, claiming that he broke up the strike by allowing troops to go into Tonypandy and attack the miners. In 1978 the Labour prime minister James Callaghan started a verbal brawl in the House of Commons when he said that Churchill had pursued a "vendetta . . . against the miners at Tonypandy." He was urged to withdraw the charge ("a cheap and totally unnecessary slur," one member called it), but he stuck to his words, claiming, "The actions of the late Sir Winston Churchill in Tonypandy are a matter of historical dispute. I take one side of the quarrel."[4]

But, in fact, the event is well documented, and the evidence shows that Churchill acted to keep the military from confronting the miners, and that only policemen armed with truncheons were used in the conflict. In the thick of the dispute the main criticism of Churchill came not from the miners, but from the owners of the coal mines and the advocates of law and order. On November 8, the second day of rioting, a reporter for the *Times* in Tonypandy was so frightened by the mobs in the streets that he couldn't believe the authorities in London weren't supplying Chief Constable Lindsay with the requested military reinforcements.

In his article "A State of Siege," the reporter complained, "The troops which have been detailed for duty here have not arrived, although they have been anxiously expected all day. Apparently orders were received which caused them to halt at Cardiff. The vacillation shown by those who are responsible for the absence of troops in the present crisis cannot easily be excused."[5]

It was at Churchill's request that the troops stopped at Cardiff. The military would not be available, he wired Chief Constable Lindsay, "unless it is clear that the police reinforcements are unable to cope with the situation."

No one in Tonypandy was shot or trampled by charging cavalry. The troops were kept in reserve by their commander, General Nevil Macready, who was placed under Churchill's command and worked tirelessly to make sure his men remained at a distance and didn't aggravate the conflict. Meanwhile, hundreds of police battled with the strikers in the November chill, with many bandaged heads on both sides.

Much to the distress of the colliery owners, Churchill sent a conciliatory message to the miners offering to do his best "to get them fair treatment" and informing them, "We are holding back the soldiers for the present and sending only police." The owners reacted to this message by condemning Churchill as hopelessly biased toward the miners. The managing director of the Cambrian Coal Trust told the *Times,* "Mr. Churchill has put himself entirely out of court as a mediator by his telegram to the workmen's representatives, in which he prejudged the questions at issue and implied that the Cambrian men were not receiving fair play."[6]

But Churchill soon found that he couldn't please either side. For reasons of his own, the leader of the Labour Party—the grizzled former miner Keir Hardie—decided that Churchill would make a better villain than hero. No doubt it was easier to rally support for more industrial unrest if the Home Secretary was portrayed not as a moderate, but as a strikebreaker conspiring with the army to repress the miners. Hardie issued a dark warning: "Troops are let loose upon the people to shoot down if need be whilst they are fighting for their legitimate rights." In the House of Commons on November 28, after the crisis had passed, Hardie told Churchill, "There is no love lost between us." He claimed that at Tonypandy "99 per cent of the people would have preserved order without either the constabulary or the military."[7]

His claim may have sounded brave to his supporters and heightened their resentment of Churchill. But the Labour leader was holding back an important fact. While he was stirring up fears about the army during the disturbances, he was also meeting with General Nevil Macready and being treated with the utmost courtesy.

As Home Office documents have revealed, Hardie agreed to help the general correct a popular misconception of the army's mission. On

November 13, Macready's report from Wales to the Home Office included the following information: "Mr. Keir Hardie lunched at the hotel
and I afterwards asked him to have a talk with me. We had a very friendly
conversation and he agreed to contradict the rumours which had been
spread about that the military were here for an ornament and would in no
case take any action."[8]

As Hardie was well aware, Macready was determined to avoid any
bloodshed and wanted to make sure the miners understood his position—that his troops would fight if provoked, but that "in no case should
soldiers come in direct contact with rioters unless and until action had
been taken by the police. In the event of the police being overpowered . . .
military force would come into play." The general had also made it clear
that his job was to be an impartial guardian of the peace, declaring that
his soldiers were not "the blind agents of the employer class," and forbidding the usual practice of billeting officers with colliery managers.[9]

But such efforts didn't stop Hardie and others from maligning
Churchill as the villain in the dispute. This treatment was especially dis-
heartening to Winston because only two years earlier he had received a
rapturous welcome from an annual gathering of miners in South Wales.
Thanks in no small part to his efforts, a bill giving the miners an eight-
hour day became law at the end of 1908, and he was welcomed as one
of their champions. He had passionately defended their demands for
shorter hours, dismissing complaints from other industries that the
measure would decrease coal production and increase prices. At their
meeting in Swansea in August 1908 he had received "thrice-prolonged
applause," as one of the miners quaintly put it.[10]

The man who had encouraged Winston to visit Wales during that
summer was David Lloyd George. But now, with the coalfields in turmoil, he was conspicuously absent from any of the dealings with the
miners in Tonypandy. Struggling to keep the riots from spreading, Winston pleaded for his help and emphasized the good he could do "with
your influence in Wales and your knowledge of the Welsh language." Yet
Lloyd George carefully kept his distance, avoiding any direct involvement in the affair. If things took a turn for the worse, he had everything
to lose. His whole career was built on his high standing in Wales, and
it was dangerous to risk making enemies there if he could avoid it.[11]

It was Winston's bad luck, however, to emerge from this crisis with a whole new set of enemies on the right and left blaming him for doing the wrong thing—one side saying he was too tough, the other that he wasn't tough enough. His idealism was taking a beating. Before he entered the Cabinet and began to exercise real power, he had imagined that his good intentions and high purpose would help him overcome most obstacles. But now he was learning that some political problems were merely deep pits of quicksand perfect for swallowing up the overeager Cabinet minister who failed to tread carefully.

It didn't cause him to lose faith in his own powers. But it hardened him, making him less willing to be conciliatory, less trusting in the good faith of others, and more interested in striking the first blow against opponents with raised fists. The boy wonder of British politics was maturing fast.

Like Lloyd George, Asquith was content to let the Home Secretary carry the burden of dealing with the Welsh miners. Many years earlier, in 1893, Asquith's own political career had been damaged when he mishandled a mining dispute, sending troops to restore order who overreacted and shot two civilians at the Featherstone colliery in Yorkshire. Ever since, he had been taunted by protestors who would disrupt his public appearances with cries of "murder" and "Featherstone." He didn't want to risk adding "Tonypandy" to those cries.

In any case, at the very same time that Winston was trying to avoid a disaster among the unhappy miners of South Wales, the prime minister was confronting an even greater crisis involving his relationship with the new king. It was time to bring the battle with the House of Lords to a conclusion, and Asquith needed the king's help. But the well-educated lawyer and politician didn't have much in common with George V, who had little interest in serious books or any kind of demanding intellectual activity. He didn't like to travel or entertain or vary his daily routine, which included faithfully checking a barometer twice a day for any change in the weather. If he could have avoided becoming king, he would have happily spent his life as a simple country gentleman.

Short and stiff, he wasn't an imposing figure. His best feature was his neatly trimmed beard, which—more than anything else—made him look regal. It helped to hide a poor complexion. He was a nervous, often irritable man with a wary, haunted gaze, but he liked uniforms and wearing fancy dress on court occasions and always tried to look his best. His great passions were stamp collecting, shooting, and smoking. "The King is a very jolly chap," said Lloyd George privately, "but thank God there's not much in his head."[12]

The Liberal leaders may have assumed that a monarch of limited intellect would be easier to manage. But Asquith found that it wasn't easy to explain a political plan to a man who couldn't easily understand the politics or the plan. Two long meetings in November 1910 were needed for the prime minister to secure a firm but confidential promise from the king to do what Edward VII had hesitated to do—create the necessary number of peers to reform the House of Lords. Asquith also wanted another general election, after which he planned to reveal the king's promise at an opportune time and use it to overwhelm the opposition.

None of this was too clear to King George, but he knew it didn't sound very sporting. Incredibly, he asked if he could discuss the plan with Balfour, the Tory leader, first. Asquith had to explain that such a discussion would rather spoil his political surprise.

Though he later complained to courtiers that Asquith had "bullied" him into making this secret deal, the new king wasn't in a position to refuse. When he asked the prime minister what would happen if didn't go along with the plan, Asquith answered, "I should immediately resign and at the next election should make the cry 'The King and the Peers against the people.'" Swallowing his pride, King George let Asquith have everything he wanted.

But the prime minister didn't have much of a choice in the matter himself. As Winston never tired of reminding him, "Until the Veto is out of the way there can be no peace between parties and no demonstration of national unity. The quicker & the more firmly this business is put through, the better for all." The Liberals now believed that only fast action could help them catch the Conservatives off guard. Two days after getting the king's promise, Asquith announced that Parliament would dissolve at the end of November 1910 and that the general election would be held in the first two weeks of December.[13]

Fighting two elections in one year was hard on everyone, but once again the Liberals thought they had the people on their side and would earn a great victory. And once again they were wrong. The result was no better than the previous one—in fact, it was worse. Liberals and Tories emerged from the election with exactly the same number of seats, 272. And once more Asquith was able to keep his government in power only because of the support of the Irish, with 84 seats, and to a lesser extent with the increasingly unreliable support of Labour, with 42 seats.

The result would certainly have been worse if Churchill had not skillfully managed to contain the violence in South Wales. Just one shot fired by mistake could have turned a regional fight into a national cause and given both the Conservatives and Labour a rallying cry. The strain of the crisis on Winston was considerable. He seemed to be juggling more than one man could handle, and not getting any rest. As soon as he had successfully defended his own seat in Dundee, he did take a brief break to enjoy a country house party in Yorkshire. But Clemmie had to warn him to go easier on himself.

"Dearest you work so hard," she wrote him, "& have so little fun in your life." Of course, she was only partly right. Hard work in exciting times *was* Winston's idea of fun.[14]

Perhaps at Clemmie's urging, Winston was spending a relaxing morning at home in Eccleston Square on January 3, 1911—soaking in his bath—when the Home Office telephoned with shocking news. A gun battle had broken out in the East End between police and a heavily armed Russian gang of anarchists. One constable had already been wounded and the rate of fire from the gang, who were barricaded on the upper floors of a run-down house in Sidney Street, was so intense that a policeman had rushed to the Tower of London seeking help, and had just returned with twenty riflemen of the Scots Guards.

Winston was asked to approve this use of the military. He gave his consent while he stood at the telephone wrapped in a towel. An hour later he was standing beside the police and soldiers, peering at the action from a side street as the shoot-out continued to rage. Bullets were flying everywhere, slamming into the surrounding brick buildings and whizzing past the heads of the many onlookers. For the most part, the hastily armed police—who normally didn't carry guns—were ineffectual. Their revolvers and shotguns couldn't match the firepower coming from the gang's hideout. As for the soldiers, they were hampered by the difficulty of getting a clear shot. The house was in the middle of the block, and the soldiers were pinned down at either end, shooting at an angle.

"Nothing of this sort had ever been seen within living memory in quiet, law-abiding, comfortable England," said Churchill afterward.[15]

As the police suspected, the gang had armed themselves with a rapid-firing weapon then known as the Mauser "magazine pistol." The handle could be attached to a stock and used like a rifle, making it easier for the shooter to fire in all directions from a concealed space, where he could quickly empty one magazine—usually holding ten cartridges—and replace it with another. Manufactured in Germany, it was a relatively new weapon and was almost unknown in Britain except among army officers. As it happened, there was one high-ranking official on the scene who knew the pistol well and had used it effectively in combat. That was Winston Churchill.

When the weapon was brand-new in 1898, he had purchased two and had used one in the cavalry charge at Omdurman, emptying his magazine as he killed several attackers, including one "at less than a yard" who was about to spear him. The semiautomatic Mauser was a pistol that had saved his life, and because he knew from experience how deadly it could be, he was able to save more lives at Sidney Street during the long shootout. When several armed constables wanted to rush the besieged building, it was Churchill who talked them out of it, knowing they would be cut to pieces. A reporter on the spot put it more politely: "The Home Secretary, fearing that this might endanger lives unnecessarily, prevented any such proceeding."[16]

Innocence of the danger was so great that Churchill also had to forbid the fire brigade from approaching the building as smoke began to rise from its upper windows. He was unable, however, to prevent an insanely dutiful postman from delivering letters to the house next to the hideout while shots rang out overhead. It was all he could do to restrain a fire brigade officer who insisted that his duty was to put out fires regardless of the risk. After a "heated" argument Churchill said that he would take full responsibility if the house burned down, and the officer reluctantly stood by and watched while the flames did indeed consume much of the structure.

The anarchists died in the blaze, but the "gang" apparently consisted of only two men, whose badly burned bodies were found in the rubble, along with two Mauser pistols. They had so much ammunition—and the weapons fired so quickly—that they had been able to fool everyone into thinking the house was defended by several desperate anarchists. It was true, however, that they belonged to a larger gang. They had a history of committing strong-arm robberies with the help of other exiles, presumably to raise money for their revolutionary cause back in Russia.

For the past two weeks the authorities had been searching for five Russians who had used Mausers to kill three policemen during a botched burglary of a jewelry shop on December 16, 1910. It soon became known as "the worst day in the history of the British police force." More than twenty bullets had been fired, with eight hitting just one of the unarmed policemen. Two more officers were hit and survived, but they were left paralyzed. No one had been prepared to deal with that kind of firepower. The lead detective investigating the murders was desperate to track down the gang before another unarmed policeman came face-to-face with the Mauser.

Churchill had attended the funerals of the slain policemen in December and understood when he raced to Sidney Street in January that the culprits would probably be using the same weapons that had already cost three lives. "The circumstances were extraordinary," he recalled of his decision to visit the scene of the gun battle, "and I thought it my duty to go and see for myself what was happening." He was right to do so, and was uncharacteristically modest about his part in helping to minimize the casualties. He never mentioned the importance of his firearms expertise, and for a hundred years no one else did.[17]

This affair should have been one of Churchill's finest moments. Instead he was ridiculed as a grandstanding egomaniac who didn't have any business inserting himself into an armed police operation. Even one of his most distinguished biographers has called the episode "Churchill's great mistake." It didn't help that he wore a top hat to the gunfight. In the newspaper photographs his hat made him look like a ballroom dancer who had wandered into a crime scene by mistake. When Eddie Marsh—who had bravely accompanied his boss to Sidney Street—went to a cinema, he was surprised to see the screen begin to flicker with newsreel images of Winston at the siege. He was even more surprised—and a little mortified—when the audience reacted with boos and shouts of "shoot him."[18]

Arthur Balfour—who knew little of the episode, and even less about Mausers—enjoyed casting Churchill as a vainglorious fool whose presence at the shoot-out put lives at risk.

In the House of Commons he said of Winston in his supercilious way: "He was, I understand, in military phrase, in what is known as the zone of fire—he and a photographer were both risking valuable lives. I understand what the photographer was doing, but what was the right hon. Gentleman doing?"

Stung by such criticism, Asquith made only a halfhearted effort to defend his Home Secretary. Winston was sitting beside him on the Front Bench when he looked at him and told the House, "My right hon. Friend, if he will forgive me for saying so, suffers from the dangerous endowment of an interesting personality." It was a memorable and amusing remark, but not particularly helpful.[19]

It was far better, however, than Rudyard Kipling's comment in a letter to a friend. A rabid opponent of Churchill, Kipling thought that Winston should have shown more gallantry and stepped in front of a bullet. "Three hours small-arms fire," he said of the Sidney Street episode, "and devil a shot where it would have done some good to the nation."[20]

Hating Winston was becoming a national pastime. Some Conservatives now saw him as the greatest traitor since Judas. Keir Hardie was continuing to paint him as a brutish reactionary, and another male supporter of the suffragettes was threatening to ambush him. In December 1910 he had received a letter from a man calling himself Alex Ballantine, who closed his three-page screed with the words "I intend to wait on you at my earliest convenience with a dog-whip to give you the chastisement you deserve." The letter was passed along to Scotland Yard for investigation, but as if that threat weren't enough, there was also a disgruntled ex-policeman blaming Winston for his dismissal from the force and suggesting that he might kill the Home Secretary to even the score. "I intend exposing Mr. Churchill's injustices," he vowed. "Must I kill my opponent with my own hand in order to force a crisis?"[21]

Winston had every reason to keep looking over his shoulder. He didn't know who might be coming after him next.

When he was asked to join a group of officials, and various lords and ladies, in a carriage procession around London to celebrate George V's coronation, he was booed as much as he was cheered. No one wanted to ride with him. When the Duchess of Devonshire and the Countess of Minto were asked to share a carriage with him, they quickly regretted accepting the offer. "It was rather embarrassing for these two Tory dames," Winston wrote Clemmie. "They got awfully depressed when the cheering was very loud, but bucked up a little around the Mansion House where there were hostile demonstrations." Incensed by the experience, the Duchess of Devonshire told Lord Balcarres she would never "again agree to drive in procession with Churchill: for she says she is sure she shared the hooting directed against the Home Secretary."[22]

Even old friends—under the increasing pressure of political differences—were showing Winston a nastier side. At four o'clock in the morning, during an all-night sitting of the House in March 1911, Linky Cecil lost his temper and turned all his fury on Winston, who was the minister in charge on the Front Bench. Lord Hugh thought that Winston had misled the opposition on some minor procedural point. He made it seem, however, as if his old friend had violated all known standards of decency.

"It is open to a Government as to any other person to break their pledged word," declared Lord Hugh, "but what is not open to them is to escape the imputation of dishonour which attaches to promise-breaking. Such a proceeding, if it involved pecuniary matters, would lead them to prison. Such a proceeding, if done in the ordinary course of private life and intercourse, would drive them from the society of gentlemen."[23]

This was the kind of rhetorical overkill that Winston and Linky had made their specialty in the Hooligan days, but at four in the morning the Home Secretary didn't want to hear it.

The reporters in the gallery came to life as Winston and the best man at his wedding fought like Cavalier and Roundhead. The press captured some of the fireworks:

Mr. Churchill, pale, heavy-eyed and rumple-haired, glared angrily at Lord Hugh.

"I am so much accustomed to the controversial methods of the noble lord," hissed the young Minister.

A storm of protesting shouts cut the sentence up. Mr. Churchill stood silently waiting at the table.

"I am so much accustomed to the controversial methods of the noble lord," persisted Mr. Churchill, "who deals always in taunts and insults—"

For five minutes he battled unsuccessfully against a torrent of protesting shouts.

Winston stayed on his feet, but he looked beaten, and a young Tory MP went in for the kill, shouting from the opposition backbenches, "This is your first attempt to lead the House of Commons, and this is how you are doing it!" To this he added in a mocking voice, "The future Prime Minister of England!"[24]

That specific taunt was another reminder that Churchill was now having to pay a heavy price for his rapid rise to power. Jealousy, resentment, spite—he was getting it all, and it was coming from friend and foe. He had wanted to be a big national figure but now was also a very big national target. Because so much had been made of his youthful flair and brilliance, it was inevitable that as a leader he would be criticized for not being brilliant enough or for showing too much flair in dramatic moments, like those in Sidney Street.

As much as he wanted to command the respect of all, he was enough of a fighter to take the hits, dust himself off, and get back in the fray. At the end of the all-night sitting—after nineteen hours of defending the government—Winston surprised the weary reporters when he strolled into the dining room smiling and acting as if he didn't have a care. He sat down at a table with Joe Chamberlain's son Austen, and the two adversaries enjoyed a pleasant breakfast of grilled sole and eggs and bacon.

Nothing seemed to slow him down for long. Just before going to breakfast he sent the king a brief report of the latest parliamentary events, as was his duty. "There has been a certain amount of ill-feeling during this prolonged debate," he wrote, "but the temperature is now again normal and the discussion is good."[25]

1

Young Titan: Winston Churchill in Boston on his speaking tour of North America, December 1900.

Victorian Beauty: Winston's mother, Jennie Churchill, in her prime.

2

Edwardian Star: Churchill in 1901 at the beginning of his political career.

3

4

Pamela Plowden was the great love of Churchill's early life. She married the Earl of Lytton in 1902, and is shown here with her first child.

The Duchess: Consuelo Vanderbilt regretted marrying the Duke of Marlborough, but was fond of his cousin Winston, whose "ardent and vital" nature she admired.

5

6

Winston Churchill fell in love with Ethel Barrymore the moment he saw her wearing this dress on the London stage.

7

House Rivals: Conservative Leaders Joseph Chamberlain (left) and Arthur Balfour were exasperated by Churchill's independence and soaring ambition.

8

Eccentric Lord Hugh Cecil joined Winston's political "hooligans" and helped him shake up the complacent Tory Party.

Rich, talented, and beautiful, Muriel Wilson once played the "muse of History" in an amateur theatrical. Winston couldn't resist her and pleaded for her to marry him.

Charm offensive: Churchill and Kaiser Wilhelm try to impress each other during German military exercises in 1906.

11

The Prime Minister's Daughter: Violet Asquith's love for Winston was unrequited, but she was a passionate friend and encouraged her father to advance young Churchill's career.

Prime Minister Herbert Henry Asquith, who welcomed Churchill's switch to the Liberal Party and brought him into the Cabinet.

12

Serious business: with his new private secretary—Eddie Marsh—at his side, Churchill begins his climb to the top by serving as a junior minister in the Colonial Office.

Looking for votes: Churchill leaving his house in London (left) to campaign in Manchester in 1908.

14

15

16

17

Slains Castle, Scotland (top): The scene of dramatic events involving Churchill and Violet Asquith near the time of his wedding to Clementine Hozier (left) in 1908.

18

Domestic battles: As Home Secretary, Churchill causes a stir when he visits the scene of a gun battle with anarchists in the East End of London, 1911 (top); and a bellringing suffragette disrupts Churchill's speech to working men in Dundee, 1908 (bottom).

19

20

"The Two Romeos": Churchill and David Lloyd George.

UNDER HIS MASTER'S EYE.

Scene—*Mediterranean, on board the Admiralty yacht "Enchantress."*

Mr. Winston Churchill. "ANY HOME NEWS?"
Mr. Asquith. "HOW CAN THERE BE WITH YOU HERE?"

21

Smooth sailing in 1913: *Punch* portrays Churchill and Prime Minister Asquith (top) on the Admiralty yacht, HMS *Enchantress.* Clementine and Churchill (bottom) leave the *Enchantress* after a voyage.

22

23

Naval Affairs: Winston Churchill, First Lord of the Admiralty, in 1914 (top); and Admiral Jacky Fisher (right), whose stormy relationship with Winston would prove disastrous.

Before the Fall: Winston in training as a pilot, 1913 (top); and strolling confidently in London just before the beginning of the First World War (bottom).

Among the ruins of his past: Prime Minister Churchill inspecting bomb damage at the House of Commons, 1941.

XXI

STORM SIGNALS

O n the Welsh island of Anglesey in April 1911 a man of thirty-six was absorbed in the solitary task of building sand models of dams and irrigation works on the beach. They were so elaborate that passersby stopped to admire them and to get a better look at their builder, wondering whether he was some brilliant architect on holiday or merely a visiting eccentric. To most people's surprise, a closer look revealed the busy builder to be the Home Secretary. The news of his presence spread quickly, and soon a little crowd had gathered, with more genteel spectators remaining at a polite distance where they could watch him through opera glasses.

"It was rather a shame that it got about," Eddie Marsh said afterward, "and he had to give it up because the cliffs were lined with people looking at him." As Eddie knew, one of Winston's favorite ways to relax was to dig in the sand, creating battle defenses or damming pretend rivers—anything that suited his ever-active imagination. Idle onlookers weren't welcome, however. This was serious work in its way, giving its builder a refreshing chance to create worlds of his own without having to ask anyone else's opinion or permission.

When he was through, he would happily leave his work to the mercy of the waves and the wind, having been reinvigorated for the real jobs ahead, where nothing else would be as easy to shape as sand. It was one of the things he liked best in the world, Eddie said of Winston's holiday digging. He would even ask Clemmie to keep an eye out for suitable beaches. "We ought to find a really good sandy beach," he wrote her one summer, "where I can cut the sand into a nicely beveled fortress—or best of all with a little stream running down—You might explore and report."[1]

This particular holiday in northwest Wales—far removed from the troubles of Tonypandy—was only a brief break for Winston before he went back to his usual marathon labors in the House and the Home Office. But for now he was enjoying a little spell of calm at the island retreat of Lord Sheffield, Venetia Stanley's father. Clemmie was with him and seemed in especially good spirits. She was expecting their second child in May and was spending most of April resting in Anglesey before going back to London for the birth. She told Winston, "I am getting rather restless & wishing for my 'Basket,'" as she called the baby. She was sure it would be a boy.[2]

Winston worked too hard at his career to have the time to be a model father, but he was a loving one and—in his fashion—an attentive one. When the second birthday of his daughter drew near in the summer, he applied all of his analytical skills to the job of finding just the right toys for her. It wasn't easy for Winston Churchill to figure out what would entertain a two-year-old girl, but after searching the shelves of a shop in London he finally settled on a set of "Noah's Ark Animals." He had a choice of buying them in white or several bright colors.

"I hovered long on the verge of buying plain white wood animals," he told Clemmie, "but decided at last to risk the coloured ones. They are so much more interesting." He doubted the shop owner's claim that the paint was harmless to children. Though he had been told of "the nourishing qualities of the paint & of the numbers sold—and presumably sucked without misadventure," he felt that he needed to caution his wife, "Be careful not to let her suck the paint off."[3]

Fortunately for his daughter's health, Churchill couldn't buy toys without approaching it like a government project that needed careful scrutiny before a decision could be reached—and then only with a special qualification attached. There were no insignificant problems once he turned his attention to them and invested them with the significance of his thought and energy. He was demanding in all things that mattered to him, which was often exhausting for others who lacked his intensity.

The son that both parents were looking forward to arrived on May 28, 1911. He was named, of course, after Winston's father. Little Randolph was a strong baby, with glowing health and handsome features. Clemmie was so pleased with him that it made her all the more confident that she had done the right thing in marrying Winston. A week after the baby's birth she told her husband, "You have so transformed my life that I can hardly remember what it felt like three years ago before I knew you."[4]

Only four days before Randolph was born, the family's neighbor in Eccleston Square—F. E. Smith—joined with his young Tory friend Lord Winterton to give a costume ball at Claridge's hotel. It was the event of the season but was also criticized as a decadent display of wealth and privilege. All the same, scores of Liberals were delighted to join the Tory festivities, and both sides tried to outdo the other in the extravagance of their costumes. The most impressive, by far, was Consuelo Marlborough. With her long neck and slender shape, she was stunning as a Dresden china shepherdess. There were the unsurprising appearances of a Henry VIII, a Cleopatra, and a Red Cross Knight. F. E. Smith came as an eighteenth-century courtier, complete with white satin and powder. But among the Cabinet ministers who attended, none wanted to compromise the dignity of office by donning a costume. They either wore ordinary evening dress or—as in Winston's case—a simple red cape.

While the fancier couples danced past midnight in the ballroom, several of the politicians stood outside smoking and talking, tugging at their capes. The highlight of the evening came when Waldorf Astor and his pretty wife, Nancy, made a surprise entrance. Nancy was dressed in pink as a ballet dancer, but it was her husband who received the greatest attention—and a good many laughs. He came dressed in the robes of a peer. A sign with the number 499 was on the front. On the back was another with the words "one more vacancy."[5]

Everybody knew what it meant. If the House of Lords failed in the coming summer to pass legislation restricting their veto—the Parliament Bill, as it was called—the Liberals would send as many as five hundred new peers to pass it for them. Though the joke was appreciated, much of the laughter was uneasy. Asquith, who was there soberly dressed in evening clothes, smiled coyly at the costume antics. He had yet to inform the opposition that he had obtained the king's pledge to create those new peers. Balfour and others were still hoping the threat was only a bluff. They would soon learn otherwise.

Though he had no way of knowing it, F. E. Smith was giving Liberals and Tories one last chance to laugh at themselves before they started a firestorm that would consume much more than the old traditional powers of the aristocracy. The friendship between Churchill and Smith would survive the political ordeal of the next few years, but many other relationships would not. What was decadent about the costume ball wasn't so much the gaudy display of wealth and privilege. It was the blithe disdain for the impending catastrophe—a lack of will to prevent a bitter fight that would divide and distract in a time of danger at home and abroad. Both sides could see that they were taking each other over a cliff, but neither seemed willing to inspect the abyss before it was too late.

Asquith's coy smiles came back to haunt him. He kept the country in the dark for so long about the king's pledge that when he revealed it in July, the opposition felt betrayed. The prime minister was accused of misleading the country and of tricking the new monarch into becoming part of an undignified political scheme. One of the most vocal critics was F. E. Smith. On Monday, July 24, he gave Asquith a much different show than the one he had staged at Claridge's in May, presenting it in ordinary dress on the floor of the Commons with a chorus of noisy backbenchers. As pure spectacle, it was much wilder than the costume ball.

On that Monday in July, London was in the grip of a heat wave, and the chamber was sweltering when Asquith rose in the afternoon to speak on the question of the Parliament Bill. He had driven to the House from Downing Street in an open car with Winston, Margot, and Violet. The streets were lined with cheering supporters, and when Margot and Violet arrived in the Ladies' Gallery, they found that the excitement was so great, some of the women were standing on chairs to get a better look at the scene below.

But as soon as Asquith opened his mouth, F. E. Smith and Linky Cecil were on their feet trying to shout him down. Half of what they said was unintelligible because of the uproar that broke out on both sides. Occasionally, through the din, Smith could be heard shouting, "the Government has degraded the political life of the country" or simply "traitor." Cecil's high-pitched voice split the air with cries of "point of order" and such disjointed phrases as "prostituted ordinary Parliamentary usage." For half an hour, F.E. and Linky kept at it, with others joining in to shout "dictator" at Asquith, as well as other terms of abuse. The prime minister could barely get a word in but he refused to sit down. The whole time Lord Hugh was so agitated that he seemed on the verge of a nervous breakdown, his face contorted and his long body twisted into awkward positions.

In a brief pause the Labour MP Will Crooks was heard to say of Linky, "Many a man has been certified as insane for less than half of what the Noble Lord has done this afternoon."[6]

Perspiring in their stuffy gallery, Margot and Violet were horrified by the verbal onslaught. Violet was torn between laughter and tears as she watched Linky taunt her father. The color had drained from Cecil's face, and he was, as Violet later put it, "gibbering execrations like a baboon, epileptic & suffragette rolled into one." Margot was so disgusted by the actions of Smith and Cecil (she called them the "cad" and the "eunuch") that she sent a message to the Foreign Secretary, Sir Edward Grey, who was sitting near her husband, to beg him to put an end to the humiliating spectacle.[7]

In office since the days of Campbell-Bannerman's premiership, Grey was the most dignified member of the Cabinet—and the most respected—partly because he kept such a low political profile. Unlike Winston, he didn't relish heated debates or public spectacles. He gave the impression that he was too fastidious and too reserved to dirty his hands in the rough-and-tumble of ordinary politics, which led one journalist to say of him, "The passions of men, the cries of the market-place, the frenzy of the conflict do not touch him. He dwells outside them in a certain grave isolation."

Instinctively, Margot turned to him as the only man who could restore peace to the House. As she recalled, "I scrawled a hasty line from our stifling gallery and sent it down to him, 'They will listen to you—so for God's sake defend him from the cats and the cads!'"[8]

They did listen to him. After Asquith had given up and sat down, and after Balfour had tried to calm his troops, Grey rebuked the opposition in his understated way. A few of the troublemakers hung their heads. Others quietly sulked.

"Never," said Grey, "did a leader of a party, with a majority in the House of Commons, have behind him more chivalrous personal loyalty and more united political support than my right hon. Friend the Prime Minister has at this moment. . . . Hon. Members opposite may easily imagine whether those feelings are less strong after the scene we have just had. So far as it was personal discourtesy to the right hon. Gentleman, the Prime Minister, every one of us resents it."

As soon as Grey sat down, F.E. shot up and tried to get a hearing, but he was shouted down, and the House adjourned in disarray. In the corridor Margot rushed to Sir Edward and embraced him like a knight of old who had just slain a dragon. "I met Edward Grey for a moment afterwards alone," she recalled, "and, when I pressed my lips to his hand, his eyes filled with tears." The prime minister didn't need Grey to defend him and may have thought it was politically advantageous to let Linky and F.E. be the faces of Tory dissent. But melodramatic Margot preferred to think that her Henry had been spared further humiliation by the lionhearted Foreign Secretary.[9]

For his part, Churchill made all the right comments about deploring "the rowdy and unreasonable disorder" of the Conservatives, but he must have secretly enjoyed watching his old Hooligan comrade and his friend F.E. make such a ruckus, especially in a lost cause. Though the Liberals were happy to play up the affront to the dignity of their leader, they knew that the Parliament Bill would pass one way or another. They had the votes, and if they lacked any, the king would have to produce more in the form of new grocer barons of a Liberal bent or even an obliging novelist baron (Thomas Hardy was on Asquith's list as a possible peer in case they needed to be mass-produced).[10]

Bowing to the inevitable—though with much rancor and protest—the House of Lords passed the bill by a narrow vote in August, ending the power of the landed aristocracy to block the work of the lower chamber but leaving them the ability to delay legislation for up to two years except in the case of money bills. This was a reasonable way of bringing the Lords into the twentieth century, but by dragging them kicking and screaming every inch of the way, the Liberals had bruised a great many powerful egos, and now many of those wounded opponents would be eagerly looking for chances to avenge their defeat.

* * *

The Liberals could handle the rhetorical bomb-throwing in the House but they were finding it increasingly difficult to cope with the violent unrest among the working classes. The heat of this summer of discontent seemed to unleash a general rebellion. Strikes broke out everywhere, but especially among the dockworkers of London and Merseyside, and among railway workers up and down the country. For about two weeks in August, chaos reigned as workers staged large protests, the transportation system broke down, and food supplies began to dwindle. Wherever possible, strikers tried to halt the movement of goods, sabotaging the rails, attacking wagon convoys, and looting warehouses.

The rioting in Liverpool was so bad that the local authorities warned Churchill that their city was "in a state of siege." They were running out of medical supplies as well as food. Alarmed, the king wired Churchill that accounts of the violence in Liverpool "show that the situation there more like revolution than a strike." He urged that if troops were used, "they should be given a free hand & the mob should be made to fear them." Churchill lost patience with the rioters and sent a full brigade of infantry and two cavalry regiments to Liverpool.[11]

The city was turned into a battlefield. When a large crowd stormed a prison van in an effort to free five comrades, a mounted policeman fired a revolver in a warning shot as a man tried to pull him from his horse. When the attack persisted, the policeman fired again and wounded the man. A cavalry escort with sabers drawn was needed to clear the street. Rioters took to the rooftops and pelted the troops and the police with pieces of bricks and chimney pots, rocks, bottles, and anything else that came to hand. More warning shots were fired by the soldiers, and as the battle raged between the two sides, tragedy struck. Two local men were killed, both shot by the military.

The next day, August 16, hundreds of soldiers and police formed a wagon convoy to bring food into the city from the docks. "It was the greatest display of force ever seen in Liverpool," noted a reporter, "and never before seen in any English town as a guard for the safe conduct of market produce."

The situation was perilous, warned the reporter. "After more than a week of anarchy, the city is in an awful plight. . . . Among the poor the most severe distress is everywhere apparent, and people are desperate. Food must be got, and men are reckless how they get it for their little ones. . . . The city streets are foul, pestilence cannot be far away. And all this is principally because the railways are at a standstill. The story of the city's last few days are heartrending."[12]

Winston had spent seven years trying to be a good Liberal, drawing up wide-ranging social reforms, promoting peace and retrenchment, and turning the other cheek to various enemies. Now the man of arms, facing massive unrest, suddenly resurfaced in full force. His Cabinet colleagues were shocked by the scale of the disturbances, but some of them felt even greater shock as they witnessed Winston's aggressive response. On August 17, Asquith's new Colonial Secretary, Lewis Harcourt, son of the old Liberal warhorse Sir William Vernon Harcourt, wrote his wife, "Fifty thousand troops are being moved all over the country tonight to protect life, property & food. . . . Winston is still mad, but a little saner than yesterday."

Loulou—as the foppish younger Harcourt was known—wasn't much of a fighting man. But he felt certain that Churchill's response to the situation was excessive. He told his wife, "Winston is much too fond of acting as Commander in Chief and moving thousands of troops about; he has already sent a warship to the Mersey with orders to land Bluejackets to work the ferries if necessary." It was indeed the case that Churchill was intent on using every means available to restore order, and to do it quickly. In the case of the warship—the cruiser HMS *Antrim*—he was responding to the request of the mayors of Liverpool and Birkenhead, who feared that they had lost control of the docks. This time he was prepared to let the military assert itself in a way that would send a strong signal of resolve. Once his old martial instincts were reawakened, he threw himself into the fight with all his energy.[13]

The deployment of so many troops carried such great risks for the government that Lloyd George was also roused to action, but as a peacemaker—the part he had scrupulously avoided playing in Tonypandy. Anxious to prevent more clashes between Winston's troops and the strikers, Lloyd George wasted no time putting his considerable skills as a negotiator to work. Much to his credit, he achieved a remarkably speedy resolution of the conflict. On August 19, after meeting all day with representatives from the railway workers and their employers, he put together an arbitration process that was acceptable to all. The railways resumed normal operations, and others on strike soon went back to work. The soldiers began returning to their barracks, goods started moving again, and even the summer heat abated.

Lloyd George was ecstatic. He went to the War Office and announced his triumph with the words "A bottle of champagne! I've done it! Don't ask me how, but I've done it! The strike is settled!"[14]

But the settlement was reached too late for the strikers in the Welsh town of Llanelli, where they halted a train, attacked the driver, and then fought with troops who tried to clear the tracks. Two strikers were shot and killed. Three more died when they attacked the station and set fire to a shed, which exploded. As it happened, the shed contained dynamite for use by the railways, and the whole town was rocked by the blast, which injured many. Several innocent civilians were severely hurt, including three women. Rioting continued for hours, and one of the local magistrates, a grocer, lost nearly everything when his business was ransacked.[15]

The newspaper owner George Riddell, who was a close friend and financial backer of Lloyd George, noted in his diaries that during the strikes Churchill was torn between the desire to show restraint and the urge to fight. "I could see that the situation was weighing upon him very seriously and that his position at the Home Office was gradually becoming intolerable to him. It was obvious that he was gradually setting his teeth, and being a soldier he would be likely to act in a thorough and drastic manner in the event of further labour troubles."

Lloyd George was worried that Churchill was becoming a liability as Home Secretary, and other Liberals felt the same way. Violet Asquith heard some of the grumbling about Winston's forceful response to the riots and knew exactly why the Liberals were so "critical and uneasy." As she recalled in old age, "They recognized, no doubt, that his action was both right and necessary, but they could not forgive the apparent gusto with which he performed it. . . . He did nothing by halves. I have seen him fling himself into the tasks of peace with the same zest and concentration."[16]

The question for Churchill was whether the conciliatory approach favored by many Liberals did more harm than good in prolonged periods of unrest. Regardless of his antagonist—whether it was a stubborn House of Lords or violent strikers—his inclination was to wage his fight with what Violet rightly described as "gusto." But such enthusiasm for battle was considered unseemly by so many in the sober Liberal ranks. Only Lloyd George could rival Winston when it came to "gusto," but he saved it for his speeches and showed more restraint in his actions. Winston tended to strike the same attitude in word and deed.

Accordingly, he didn't hesitate to make a vigorous defense of his actions when he spoke to the House on August 22. "The policy which we have pursued throughout," he said, "was wherever soldiers were sent to send plenty, so that there could be no mistake about the obvious ability of the authorities to maintain order. . . . Four or five persons have been killed by the military. The House sees these instances chronicled everywhere today. Their painful effect is fresh in our minds. What is not seen, what cannot be measured, is how many lives were saved and how many tragedies and sufferings were averted." [17]

Churchill was all the more determined to end the strikes because of an episode that clouded the horizon for most of July and August. At the very same time that the government was struggling with Lords and labor at home, the Germans decided to stir up trouble at the Atlantic port of Agadir in Morocco, southwest of Marrakech. On July 1, 1911, the *Panther*—an unimpressive German gunboat with only two small four-inch guns—steamed into the dusty port on a mission to protect German interests, which turned out to be embodied in the solitary figure of Herr Wilberg, a young Hamburg merchant. He wasn't sure why he needed protection, but he had been instructed to meet the boat, so he dutifully stood on the beach in a white suit and waved until he caught the notice of his countrymen and they "rescued" him.

The whole thing was a blatant ploy to intimidate France, which regarded Morocco as an unofficial protectorate. The German idea was to use its navy's presence in Agadir as a bargaining chip for colonial concessions elsewhere. When the German ambassador in London, Count Metternich, informed the Foreign Office of the *Panther*'s arrival in the obscure port, the few British officials acquainted with the area shook their heads in disbelief, knowing that the Germans had no reason to be there. But what began as a Gilbert and Sullivan farce soon turned into a risky standoff. France didn't want to be bullied, Germany didn't want to back down, and Britain wanted to have a say in the dispute.

Nobody cared about Agadir itself, of course, but the British Foreign Secretary was appalled by Germany's brazen power play. "The Prussians are a tiresome, cynical people," Sir Edward Grey wrote a friend. "They think the time has come for them to get something, & they will get something, but not as much as they thought." The Germans made the mistake of starting a dispute they didn't know how to end. For almost three weeks in July they kept quiet about their intentions, and their silence encouraged the British and the French to imagine the worst. "Was Germany looking for a pretext of war with France," Churchill wondered, "or was she merely trying by pressure and uncertainty to improve her colonial position?" Rumors in the press suggested that Germany wanted to develop an Atlantic fleet based at Agadir. Was this another threat to British naval superiority?[18]

For the past few months Winston had been slowly revising his old view that Germany would try to avoid a war with Britain. As Home Secretary he had learned through the Secret Service Bureau that, as he later informed Edward Grey, "We are the subject of a minute and scientific study by the German military and naval authorities, and that no other nation in the world pays us such attention." He also knew that the German army had made great improvements since he had sat astride his horse at the field exercises of 1906 in Silesia, smiling at the antique tactics. In 1909 he had slipped away from his usual ministerial duties in London to take another look at the Kaiser's troops on maneuvers, and he had noted "remarkable" advances in their training. There was less pageantry, many more machine guns, and much better use of deadly artillery batteries.

He found it hard to believe that the Germans would start a war over a port that most Europeans had never heard of. But their saber-rattling had stirred his doubts, and his anxiety grew as the standoff continued throughout the hot summer.[19]

The same doubts had begun to trouble Lloyd George. He was worried not only that the threat of Prussian militarism would drain more money away from social programs, but also that a weak France would buckle under German pressure and encourage the Kaiser's men to start more trouble. At a breakfast with Churchill and the editor of the *Manchester Guardian,* Lloyd George confided his belief that France lived in fear of "those terrible legions across the frontier. . . . They could be in Paris in a month and she knew it." With Winston's encouragement—and with the approval of the Foreign Secretary—he decided to issue a warning to the Germans.

Speaking on July 21 at a public dinner in London, Lloyd George declared, "I would make great sacrifices to preserve peace. . . . But if a situation were to be forced upon us in which peace could only be preserved by the surrender of the great and beneficent position Britain has won by centuries of heroism and achievement, by allowing Britain to be treated where her interests were vitally affected as if she were of no account in the Cabinet of nations, then I say emphatically that peace at that price would be a humiliation intolerable for a great country like ours to endure. National honour is no party question."

Not known for drawing lines in the sand on international matters, Lloyd George caught the German government off guard when the remarks appeared in print, and the Kaiser reacted angrily, devoting almost an hour to berating the British ambassador, who would recall, "He abused us like pickpockets."[20]

Late on the afternoon of July 25, Churchill and Lloyd George were walking together near Buckingham Palace when a messenger from the Foreign Office caught up with them to deliver an urgent communication. Sir Edward Grey wanted to see them right away. They rushed to his office, where they discovered that the normally unflappable Foreign Secretary was anxiously awaiting their arrival. He had just finished a tense meeting with Count Metternich, he explained, and was so concerned by the harshness of the German ambassador's response to Lloyd George's speech that he thought "the Fleet might be attacked at any moment."[21]

Such was the feverish mood of this troubled summer that Sir Edward panicked and wildly misjudged Metternich's comments. The Germans were incensed, but not enough to launch a surprise attack on the superior Royal Navy. A little calm reflection might have led Grey to reconsider his fears, but events moved too quickly. Reggie McKenna arrived from the Admiralty and agreed to send an alert to His Majesty's ships at sea. For a couple of days Britain's leaders waited in suspense, wondering whether the next incoming message from the fleet would signal the start of war.

Fortunately for all concerned, the top admirals—many of whom were on holiday escaping the summer heat—didn't regard the alert with the urgency that Sir Edward intended. Otherwise, shots fired in panic might have created a real reason for Germany to fight. It is from just such misunderstandings and hasty actions that wars are sometimes started.

But Grey's false alarm did cause Asquith and others in the Cabinet to begin taking seriously the possibility of having to defend France. High-level meetings were called to discuss strategy, maps were updated, and Churchill began churning out letters and memos full of advice. At this point, with so much uncertainty in the air, the novelist in Winston emerged from hibernation and composed a stunningly prescient work of fiction with the unpromising title of "Military Aspects of the Continental Problem." In truth, it was only a memo intended for Asquith and the Committee of Imperial Defence, but it read like an outline for a novel about the first weeks of a European war. Drawing on his considerable powers of imagination, he described what he believed would transpire in the first forty days of fighting. As he would correctly point out after the First World War, "these forecasts were almost literally verified three years later by the event."

Among other things, he predicted that the Germans would begin the war by overwhelming the Belgian army, forcing the French army to regroup to save Paris. "The balance of probability," wrote Churchill in 1911, "is that by the twentieth day the French armies will have been driven from the line of the Meuse and will be falling back on Paris and the south." The problem for the Germans, he imagined, was that "by the fortieth day Germany should be extended at full strain both internally and on her war fronts." Then the French, he believed, would have the chance to stage a counteroffensive "if the French army has not been squandered by precipitate or desperate action."[22]

Remarkably, Winston was right on target. For on September 9, 1914—the fortieth day after German mobilization—the Kaiser's over-extended army would indeed be turned back at the First Battle of the

Marne, forcing it to dig in and wage a war of attrition for the next four years. What Winston failed to foresee, however, was that this stalemate would come after the French offensive faltered, and that the resulting trench warfare would exact horrible costs from both sides. All the same, in 1911 he was the only major British leader who was thinking so far ahead about the catastrophe that awaited the world.[23]

The fears generated by the Agadir crisis soon faded as cooler heads prevailed. To allow the Germans a face-saving concession, the French handed over some African territory they didn't care much about anyway. And, after that, many in Britain felt it was safe to go back to business as usual.

But the crisis transformed Winston. Once his imagination had awakened him to the challenges of a European war, he made the subject his constant study. Such a grave threat pushed into the background almost every other problem he had been considering. He had found his great cause in the urgent need to get ready for the coming conflict. It was a cause that he felt he was born to lead. But he couldn't do it as Home Secretary. The War Office, the Admiralty, the Foreign Office, perhaps even the premiership itself—these were the places where he could serve best if he wanted to prevent the next war or to prepare Britain to win it.

While he plotted his next move, he took a long-deserved holiday with Clemmie at the seashore near Broadstairs, in Kent. One day in early September he went to the beach, armed with pail and shovel. A reporter for the *Daily Mirror* was in the area and received a tip that the Home Secretary was engaged in unusual activity on the beach. When he found Churchill, he was surprised to see him furiously at work on a series of "stout fortifications and sand castles." Sheepishly, the Home Secretary explained that it was all for the amusement of his young daughter and other children nearby.

There was an innocent article in the newspaper the next day titled "Mr. Churchill's Spade Work." But no one except his friends seemed to understand how seriously he took this work that allowed his hands to shape what he saw in his imagination. When Eddie Marsh read the article, he laughed and wrote a friend, "I wonder if the Germans heard that the Home Secretary was spending his holiday in personally fortifying the South Coast!"[24]

XXII

ARMADA

The end of September 1911 found Winston traveling to Scotland to visit his constituency and to spend a few days with the prime minister, who was staying at the same house where Margot had taken the family after Violet's "rock-affair" at Slains Castle in 1908. Loaned to Margot for the early autumn by her brother, Archerfield was a large stone house about twenty miles east of Edinburgh. To the prime minister, its greatest asset was an adjoining private golf course on the seacoast. In 1908 the magazine *Country Life* had described it as "the best private golf course in the world."

In recent months Violet had grown fonder of Clemmie, but she still wasn't entirely reconciled to losing Winston. Her face still lit up when he entered a room, and she had lost none of her desire to enjoy his company in private, pulling him away from others whenever possible so they could talk on their own. The moment he arrived at Archerfield House she swept him out to the nearby links, where, as she later wrote, "we played a lot of golf together in golden autumn sunshine with sea gulls circling overhead."[1]

There was a look of expectation in his eyes, and she knew what it meant. Political life was their mutual love, and Winston couldn't hide from her what he was thinking. In the wake of the Agadir crisis there was talk of a change being made at the Admiralty. He wanted the job, and he knew Asquith wasn't happy with Reggie McKenna's performance. The prime minister had recently sent Reggie a written rebuke, criticizing the navy's slow response to the alert recommended by Sir Edward Grey.

It was obvious that someone needed to shake up the service and prepare it for battle. One of its urgent needs was a modern naval war staff, well organized to meet the operational challenges ahead. The logical choice for the job was Richard Haldane, who had done excellent work for the past six years at the War Office, and who had just been elevated to the peerage.

It was no secret that Lord Haldane, as he was now known, wanted the job. "I felt that I was almost the only person available," he recalled, "who was equipped to cope with the problem of the Naval War Staff. I think that the Prime Minister held much the same view, but we had been careful to say nothing of impending changes."[2]

It was Violet who brought up the subject of the Admiralty. She teased Winston: "Why don't you ask my advice about it?"

He knew her mind as well as she knew his. "Between Haldane and Winston," he said, "you are not a judge—you are a barefaced partisan. Your scales are loaded by gross favoritism and emotion. . . . You are thinking how much Winston would enjoy it!"

She was also thinking of how much she would enjoy it. "I longed for Winston to go to the Admiralty," she recalled, "not only because it would give him his heart's desire, but because I felt sure that it was there that he would find his true vocation and his greatest self."[3]

Her father was inclined to agree. He had been impressed by Churchill's comments on the German threat, but he also thought it might be safer for everyone if Winston used his battle skills in the service of the navy instead of the Home Office. Working behind the scenes, Violet encouraged her father to make the change. The problem was how to explain it to Haldane. The solution that Asquith devised was clever. He decided to let Churchill and Haldane discuss their merits for the job in a meeting that would involve just the two of them. He was confident that Winston would make the stronger case for himself and soften up his colleague—a good-humored man of ample girth—for the rejection to follow.

Haldane must have known that his hopes for the job were doomed the moment he arrived for the meeting at Archerfield and saw Churchill waiting at the door to greet him, looking as if he belonged in the family. When Asquith left the two men together for their talk, Haldane realized that he had been trapped, and he would afterward describe this episode as the time "the Prime Minister shut me up in a room with [Churchill]."

Haldane did his best to argue his case, pointing out his wealth of experience at the War Office and bluntly casting doubt on Winston's skills. "I said that, to be frank, I did not think that Churchill's own type of mind was best for planning out the solution that was necessary for the problem . . . confronting us." But he was no match for Winston, who had a good response to every point. Knowing his cause was lost, Haldane beat a graceful retreat. "I parted from him at Archerfield in a very friendly spirit," he recalled.[4]

On Sunday, October 1, Winston and the prime minister took to the links and were gone for much of the afternoon. Violet was having her tea when she looked up and saw Winston come in with a big smile. He led her outside and told her the good news: "Your father has just offered me the Admiralty."

She would always remember the look he gave her at that moment. She had never seen him happier. They walked together to the sea in the fading light, and Winston talked excitedly the whole way. He was thrilled not only to have the Admiralty, but also to leave behind the burdens of the Home Office. "Look at the people I have had to deal with," he said wearily. "Judges and convicts!"

That night Violet opened her diary and described Winston's reaction to the change: "He is over the moon about it (as it has long been his Mecca in the Cabinet)—& tremendously fired by the scope & possibilities of the office."[5]

The one person who was devastated by the news was Reggie McKenna. Asquith was moving him to the Home Office, and he didn't want to go. He received word of the change on October 10 but spent almost two weeks trying to talk the prime minister out of it. He made a special trip to Archerfield to plead his case, insisting that he was needed at the Admiralty. Asquith was annoyed but tried to reason with him. He asked McKenna "if he really thought he was the only person who stood between us & a great European war." When he couldn't offer a convincing response, Reggie reluctantly agreed to the change.

"But he minded terribly," Asquith said of McKenna when he had gone, "& was rather pathetic over it."[6]

Four months later McKenna was still complaining, arguing to any and all that he was the better man for the job than Churchill. During a dinner at Number 10 in February he happened to be seated next to

Violet and decided to give her an earful, apparently unaware of her devotion to Churchill. In her diary Violet wrote, "McKenna *ranted* about Winston—to *me* of all people. He must be mad."[7]

Sooner or later, Churchill would most likely have won his coveted job as First Lord of the Admiralty, but given the competition for the position, he was fortunate to have Violet's voice in her father's ear.

Still a month shy of his thirty-seventh birthday, Winston arrived at the Admiralty in Whitehall on October 25, 1911, and took his place as the civilian head of the strongest naval force in the world. With more than five hundred ships and 130,000 men, the Royal Navy was still the pride of the British Empire and the chief instrument of its authority. In addition to the Home Fleet, there were the Atlantic, Mediterranean, and Eastern fleets, and the great dockyards scattered across the globe, from Portsmouth at home to Malta, Bombay, Singapore, Sydney, and Hong Kong. It was truly a world navy and could, theoretically, go to war anywhere, but Churchill knew that his job was to make sure that it could fight and win a battle in one particular body of water—the North Sea.

One of his first actions was to have a chart of the North Sea mounted behind his desk, where a staff officer could mark the positions of the German fleet with flags. Every morning Winston studied it, not so much to keep track of the movements, but to learn each inch of the chart by heart, and, as he later wrote, "to inculcate in myself and those working with me a sense of ever-present danger." This inhospitable stretch of water between Germany and Britain was the area he had to defend at all costs.[8]

He had reason to be grateful to McKenna for opposing him in 1909 on the dreadnought question and for building more of the giant battleships. Now he was glad to have the larger force, and he was prepared to expand it. And as a way of apologizing for his mistaken assumptions about Germany in the past, he made a point of praising McKenna in public. "We owe much to the foresight and resolution of Mr. McKenna," he told a Scottish audience in 1912.

While Lloyd George was left to complete the work of passing the landmark National Insurance Act—and to have his name forever associated with health and unemployment insurance—Winston immersed himself in the details of building faster and more potent warships to stop a German armada. The naval work left Lloyd George cold. He began complaining that whenever he saw Winston, he would hear, "Look here, David, I want to talk to you," which would be followed by a long monologue "about his blasted ships."[9]

Though he was no expert on naval tactics, Churchill did know a lot about fighting and understood a basic truth that others often overlooked. In his first year on the job he told an audience at Burlington House in London, "At the Admiralty everything contributes and converges on one single object, namely the development of the maximum war power at a given moment and at a particular point." In other words, behind all the pageantry and bureaucracy of the Admiralty, the only result that really mattered was the fleet's ability to confront an enemy with "a few minutes of shattering, blasting, overpowering force." When dreadnoughts met, the only punch worth throwing was a knockout punch. And, therefore, said Churchill, "the best way to make war impossible is to make victory certain."

Again, as Violet said of him, "he did nothing by halves." He didn't want a war; he knew it would be horrible. "If any of the great civilised and scientific nations of the world become engaged in war," he warned his Burlington House audience, "they will all be heartily sick of it long before they have got to the end." But if Germany insisted on building more ships and making more threats, he was now ready to do whatever was required to prevent a fight, or to deliver the knockout blow if necessary.[10]

The Kaiser and his admirals were given ample opportunity to renounce the arms race. A few weeks before he spoke at Burlington House, Churchill offered the Germans a "naval holiday." It was a chance for both sides to suspend their shipbuilding programs as a way of slowing the arms race, if not to end it completely. In a wonderful phrase Winston said the holiday would allow the naval rivals to "introduce a blank page into the book of misunderstanding." But the Kaiser didn't think there was any misunderstanding. As he saw it, Britain needed to be humbled so that Germany could rise. So he rejected the offer, sending a terse message "that such arrangements would only be possible between allies."[11]

Though Winston felt he needed to keep building ships, he was looking for something besides a numerical advantage. Wanting also to maintain superiority in speed and firepower, he made two of the boldest moves of his career. To give his ships greater speed, he wanted them to burn oil instead of coal. And to make sure they could outshoot the Germans, he wanted them armed with a weapon of unsurpassed power. Instead of sticking with the dreadnought's most advanced 13.5-inch guns, he opted for development of the massive new 15-inch gun that could hit targets up to twenty miles away.

The risks were considerable. For one thing, Britain lacked a reliable supply of oil. To use Winston's ornate explanation to the Commons, there was an "absence of any fresh supply of liquid fuel indigenous to these islands." As for the question of firepower, no one knew if the 15-inch gun would work because, as Churchill put it, "no such thing as a modern 15-inch gun existed. None had ever been made." But he wasn't deterred. Long before there were any clear signs that the difficulties would be overcome, he bet everything on adopting both innovations.[12]

Over the next two and a half years he would solve one problem by taking Britain into the petroleum business, arranging for the government to acquire a majority interest in the Anglo-Persian Oil Company (later British Petroleum—BP). He would tackle the problem of firepower by the simple expedient of going ahead and building the 15-inch guns with nothing more than the fervent hope they would work. If he waited for the proper tests, he would lose at least a year in the process, and he couldn't wait. "Risks have to be run in peace as well as in war," he remarked, "and courage in design now may win a battle later on."

But even as he gambled on what would turn out to be a great success, he could hear the familiar voices of his critics ridiculing him if he failed. He knew, as he later wrote, "No excuse would be accepted. It would all be brought home to me—'rash, inexperienced,' 'before he had been there a month,' 'altering all the plans of his predecessors' and producing 'this ghastly fiasco,' 'the mutilation of all the ships of the year.'" He had heard such comments so often in the past that he could easily produce specimens of it on his own that sounded like the real thing.[13]

But he was as willing as ever to make plans on a grand scale, and to be imaginative and daring when others were content to think small and go slow. Now, however, it wasn't merely his reputation or the interests of a single department that were at risk. It was the protection of the fleet and the security of the nation. For all of this to be entrusted to the judgment and skill of a young man in his mid-thirties was extraordinary, and Churchill was always aware of that, but never intimidated by it.

McKenna or Haldane would have made sure the Royal Navy was prepared to fight the growing German navy. The difference with Churchill as First Lord was that he meant to make sure the fleet won. Nothing else mattered. To that end, he got rid of incompetent officers, set out the rationale for a naval war staff and began building an efficient one, and made two appointments of crucial significance. The men who would prove to be Britain's most important admirals in the First World War—John Jellicoe and David Beatty—were given major promotions by Churchill, who went over the heads of more senior admirals to make the changes. Jellicoe became second in command of the Home Fleet, and Beatty was put in charge of the Battle-Cruiser Fleet, which Churchill liked to call "the strategic cavalry of the Royal Navy, that supreme combination of speed and power to which the thoughts of the Admiralty were continuously directed."

Beatty's appointment was inspired. Young, handsome, and courageous, he seemed to have the potential to become a twentieth-century Admiral Nelson. Yet when he came to see Churchill one day in late 1911, he was supposedly on the verge of retiring from the service. His speedy rise through the ranks had alienated some of his superiors, who complained that he had come up too fast, and Beatty felt that his career had suddenly reached a dead end. His unconventional views of naval combat and his natural spirit of irreverence had not served him well among the more traditional admirals.

But Churchill warmed to him right away. Looking up from his desk, he greeted him with the words "You seem very young to be an admiral." Three years his senior, Beatty didn't miss a beat, firing back, "And you seem very young to be the First Lord of the Admiralty."

It was significant that Beatty knew how to ride as well as sail. He was a good polo player, which meant a great deal to Churchill, who recalled of him, "He thought of war problems in their unity by land, sea and air. His mind had been rendered quick and supple by the situations of polo and the hunting-field, and enriched by various experiences against the enemy on Nile gunboats and ashore." Beatty's service on the Nile appealed to Churchill because of the remarkable coincidence that the young naval officer had fought at the Battle of Omdurman, providing gun support when Winston's cavalry regiment made their famous charge.[14]

"What did it look like?" the First Lord asked Admiral Beatty of the charge, expecting some grand description of his brave gallop through the desert sands.

"Brown currants scattered about in a great deal of suet," the admiral replied. It wasn't what Winston wanted to hear, but it made the right impression. It sounded like something he would say.[15]

On the spot he offered Beatty an appointment as his naval secretary (the First Lord's right-hand man), and the admiral accepted. When the chance came a year later to appoint a commander of the Battle-Cruiser Fleet, Winston wouldn't have to think twice about the best person to lead the navy's "cavalry."

A lifelong student of his country's history, Churchill was keenly aware of the part he had been allowed to play in the epic story of British naval power. He was following in the steps of giants who had defeated the Spanish Armada in the sixteenth century and Napoleon's navy in the nineteenth. He didn't want to be the man who let the Royal Navy be overwhelmed by the Germans, a Continental power without a great naval tradition. Speaking in Glasgow on February 9, 1912, he reminded his listeners that a powerful Royal Navy was indispensable to the defense of an island nation.

"The British Navy," he said, "is to us a necessity and, from some points of view, the German Navy is to them more in the nature of a luxury. . . . It is existence to us; it is expansion to them. We cannot menace the peace of a single Continental hamlet, nor do we wish to do so no matter how great and supreme our Navy may become."[16]

Unfortunately, in translation, this perfectly reasonable statement caused an uproar in Germany, where "luxury" was taken to mean something akin to a frivolous plaything rather than simply an expensive extra. What was intended as simply an explanation of the defensive nature of the navy was viewed in Germany as a slur on their naval force, as if it didn't merit the same consideration. Instead of settling for a blank page in the "book of misunderstanding," the German press seemed to delight in contributing whole chapters.

"The speech of Mr. Churchill contains scarcely concealed menaces against Germany," wrote one paper in Frankfurt. "We cannot be compelled by threats. The German nation would never quietly submit to a moral defeat; it would prefer to defend itself to the bitter end." Another paper complained, "We understand that it was to [Churchill's] interest to picture to his audience the naval armaments of Germany as a danger which England need hardly take seriously, and as something which England would be in a position at any time to meet."[17]

The nationalistic pride of Germany was so sensitive to perceived slights that there seemed to be a rush to condemn Churchill's words simply because he dared to make any comparison of the two navies. The assumption was that he couldn't have anything good to say about his rival. In fact, the speech was full of respectful references to Germany and its place in the world. But in the perverse reaction to his Glasgow speech there was a revealing glimpse into a militaristic culture itching for a fight.

The eagerness to twist minor episodes into major grievances started at the top. Through diplomatic channels the Kaiser didn't hesitate to make known his displeasure with what he called "Churchill's arrogant speech." He said it was "a provocation to Germany" and asked, "What apology has there been offered to us for the passage in the speech describing our fleet as an article of luxury?"[18]

The Kaiser knew better than to describe the speech as "a provocation." At the very time that Churchill was speaking in Glasgow, Lord Haldane was on a mission in Berlin to try to reduce tensions between Germany and Britain. When Winston's words reached Berlin, Haldane went out of his way to explain the remarks to the Kaiser, to read the "operative passages" directly to him and put them in the context of British policy. Only later did the Kaiser find it convenient to use the speech as a way of resisting Haldane's peace overtures and to blame Winston as the warmonger who had recklessly insulted the proud German navy. When he was president of the Board of Trade or Home Secretary, Churchill was of little concern to the German government, but as First Lord of the Admiralty he was now a figure worth undermining on even the slightest pretext.[19]

In this effort to slander Churchill as an obstacle to peace, the Kaiser and his circle may have thought he presented an especially vulnerable target at the time. The very papers that reported his speech in Glasgow were full of stories that week about how vehemently he was being reviled in his own country by those opposed to Irish Home Rule. Just one day before speaking in Glasgow, he had been under attack in Belfast, where he had gone under heavy security to promote the government's new plans for Home Rule. The time had arrived to reward the Irish Nationalists for their support of the Asquith administration, and Churchill was ready to help smooth the way for the legislation.

But the Ulster Unionists didn't want his help. One of their favorite words to describe his visit was *provocative*. They had been warning Churchill not to come, so his willingness to do so was the "provocation."

He could just as easily have stayed home and avoided controversy. For decades the whole issue of Home Rule had caused nothing but trouble for English politicians. As First Lord, Churchill didn't need to become entangled in its complexities, but as a national political figure he couldn't resist addressing the problem. Coming up with a solution seemed almost impossible, however, because the Nationalists insisted that a new Dublin parliament should have authority over all of Ireland, and the Unionists insisted that Protestant Ulster should remain under London's control. Asquith had hoped to give the Nationalists what they wanted and appease the Unionists with minor concessions, but as Churchill discovered in Belfast, there was little interest in compromise.

Hundreds of police and soldiers were called out to protect the First Lord and the six thousand people who attended his talk. The newspapers said that parts of Belfast looked like a war zone. "If, unhappily, bloodshed results from Mr. Churchill's visit," said the *Daily Mirror,* "temporary hospitals for the treatment of the wounded will be opened in various parts of the city, and a vast medical and ambulance corps will attend to the casualties." The local police were worried because of reports "that great quantities of bolts & rivets have been abstracted from the yards, and many revolvers have been taken out of pawn."[20]

Unhelpfully, George Bernard Shaw told Jennie that there might be a riot, but he didn't think Winston would be hurt. "Do not be uneasy about W," he wrote. "They will not break his head, though they may possibly break each others, with a few windows thrown in." Eddie Marsh, who traveled to Ulster with Winston, expected trouble but decided to affect a jaunty air of unconcern. "Wait and see if I am killed," he wrote his good friend the poet Rupert Brooke, "and if not write me a long letter."[21]

As Churchill's car was driving through Belfast it was in fact attacked by a mob. They tried to overturn it. Bravely, Clemmie had insisted on accompanying Winston on this dangerous visit, but when the mob surrounded the car and lifted it in the air, she was terrified. "She was not afraid of being killed," a friend recalled her saying, "but feared she might be disfigured for life by the glass of the motor being broken or by some other means."

They were rescued at the last moment by a large group of policemen who had to use their batons to break the mob's hold on the vehicle. Tragically—perhaps because of the trauma—Clemmie would suffer a miscarriage the next month. (Told the news, Churchill wrote her, "No wonder you have not felt well for the last month. Poor lamb." Clemmie replied, "It is so strange to have all the same sensations that one has after a real Baby, but with no result.")[22]

And the reason for all this animosity toward Winston? Apparently, his crime was to revise and update Lord Randolph Churchill's famous cry against Gladstone's old Home Rule Bill. If the son of Lord Randolph could reconcile himself to Home Rule, why couldn't the diehard Unionists in the Tory ranks do the same?

"It is in a different sense," Winston told the people of Belfast, "that I accept and repeat Lord Randolph Churchill's, 'Ulster will fight and Ulster will be right.' Let Ulster fight for the dignity and honour of Ireland. Let her fight for the reconciliation of races and for the forgiveness of ancient wrongs. . . . Let her fight for the spread of charity, tolerance, and enlightenment among men. Then, indeed, Ulster will fight and Ulster will be right."[23]

In their rage the Unionists didn't want to hear about forgiveness and enlightenment. They didn't want to live in peace with the Catholic majority of Ireland by sharing power in a new Dublin parliament, even if the island itself remained part of the British Empire. Instead they wanted Churchill to be the symbol of treason to the Unionist cause that Lord Randolph had once championed. It was an effective way to rally their troops. But as the passions continued to boil over in this feud, the Unionist leaders would remain stubbornly oblivious to the harm they were causing the British government, which they claimed to prefer over Home Rule.

The German leaders didn't overlook this dissension. Winston was their enemy, too. And they must have relished seeing the increasingly bitter attacks on him, which would reach a wild and vitriolic climax in April 1914, when the retired admiral and ardent Unionist Lord Charles Beresford addressed a rally in Hyde Park.

Churchill, the old admiral announced, was a "Lilliput Napoleon. A man with an unbalanced mind. An egomaniac, whose one absorbing thought is personal vindictiveness towards Ulster. He has not forgotten his reception in Belfast. . . . As long as Mr. Winston Churchill remains in office the State is in danger."[24]

XXIII

THE OLD MAN AND THE SEA

With Sir Francis Drake at his side, Winston Churchill stood on the Elizabethan dock looking up at the flag on the mainmast of the *Revenge*—the English galleon that had battled the Spanish Armada. Then he turned and, addressing a small crowd gathered nearby, heaped praise on the ships in Drake's fleet that had struck terror in the hearts of the Spanish captains. While the First Lord of the Admiralty spoke, Sir Francis gazed proudly at the crowd, clutching at his sword.

Thanks to Jennie, who was in the background standing at attention and looking like the model for a ship's prow, Winston was able for a moment to imagine that he had been transported to the dawn of the British Empire, with centuries of triumph and glory ahead of him. For that fleeting moment it didn't matter that the fleecy clouds overhead were painted on canvas, that the "Revenge" was a full-size replica in an artificial pond, or that Sir Francis Drake was a West End actor hired for the occasion. The whole thing was real enough to stir the blood and remind his listeners that the nation had conquered mighty fleets in the past, and would perhaps be forced to face another in the near future.

In an unexpected burst of energy and ambition, Jennie, at age fifty-eight, had decided to create an elaborate public fair devoted to Shakespeare's England. She had formed a limited liability company, borrowed heavily, found a few wealthy investors, promised a long run and a tidy profit, and had built a Tudor village in London at the Earls Court exhibition grounds. In addition to the ship floating in the pond with forty plaster guns "bristling defiance to the foes of England"—which occupied pride of place at the center of the fair—there was a convincing reconstruction of Shakespeare's Globe Theatre, where excerpts from Elizabethan plays were to be staged in the original manner three times a day. Cobbled lanes led to cottages, taverns, restaurants, a bookstall, "shady nooks," and "picturesque shops." A small army of actors was engaged to dress up in period costumes and parade and perform in the lanes and courtyards. Jennie didn't pinch pennies. Much of the village was designed by the best architect in Britain—Edwin Lutyens.

Jennie opened the fair on May 9, 1912, and was surrounded by all the dazzling royal guests and society darlings she could round up for the event. "Elizabethan" sailors climbed the rigging of Drake's ship and shouted down to the crowds, an acting company performed *A Midsummer Night's Dream* at the Globe, and Jennie threw an enormous party for all her friends at the "Mermaid Tavern." A series of balls took place over the next few months, and the king and queen toured the fair. Ordinary mortals had to pay a shilling for admission.[1]

The idea of holding such an educational entertainment seemed promising. The country was in the mood to reflect on its past achievements, and Jennie and Winston weren't the only ones eager to make a connection between Elizabethan naval threats and modern ones. One of the most successful theatrical events of 1912 was Louis Parker's *Drake: A Pageant-Play*, which ran for 220 performances at His Majesty's Theatre in London. The last act featured a spectacular battle scene in which the crew of the *Revenge* boarded a Spanish ship, with smoke hanging in the air and the stage "lighted up fitfully with sudden flashes of flame." The contemporary relevance of Sir Francis Drake's victory speech in the play wasn't lost on the audiences of 1912.

"We have opened the gates of the sea," Drake declaimed to a little crowd ashore in the final scene; "we have given you the keys of the world. The little spot ye stand on has become the centre of the earth. . . . See that ye hold fast the heritage we leave you. Yea, and teach your children its value: that never in the coming centuries their hearts may fail them, or their hands grow weak!"

Despite enormous publicity, Jennie's fair didn't create the kind of enthusiasm that Louis Parker's play enjoyed. It barely survived until the end of the summer. The crowds at Earls Court were appreciative but sparse, and Jennie wasted money on lavish free entertainments for her friends, most of whom seemed to expect free tickets for themselves and everyone they knew. The losses were staggering—at least £50,000—but they fell mostly on the banks and the investors, not on Jennie. British newspapers tended to underplay the disaster, but not the American press. "Fiasco at Earls Court," said the headline in the *New York Times*. "The show has been an unmitigated failure," the paper reported, adding that Jennie's "friends say that she must have spent a small fortune on the many dinner parties she has given there."[2]

But how did a woman who was in constant financial difficulties manage to raise so much money to build her Tudor village in the first place?

The answer lies in the identity of her biggest single investor, whose substantial contribution made it easier for Jennie to get bank loans and other funding. That investor was a thirty-nine-year-old widow with a million dollars. She wasn't Jennie's friend. She was one of her husband's lovers. By 1912 Jennie's marriage to the much younger George Cornwallis-West was all but finished. He had one foot out the door and wasn't making much of an effort to hide his relationships with other women, one of whom was a footloose American in Paris. Called the "Tin Plate Heiress," Nancy Stewart of Zanesville, Ohio, had already been married and divorced when she wed a wealthy manufacturer in America, who pampered her for eight years before dying in Paris in 1908 and leaving her all his fortune.

Perhaps as the price for George's indiscretions, Jennie insisted that he ask the rich widow to invest in the fair to the tune of £15,000—a sum worth about $75,000 at the time. As George blandly remarked in later years—when neither Jennie nor Nancy was alive to protest the disclosure—"I happened to be going to Paris, where [Nancy] was staying, and I put the proposition before her. . . . She consented to do it, and I am sorry to say she lost every penny, but she paid her liabilities without a murmur, and never once did she reproach me for the part I had played in the matter." Nancy went on to marry Prince Christopher of Greece. By the end of 1912 George and Jennie Cornwallis-West had agreed to separate.[3]

In retrospect, it would seem that Jennie had more reasons than one for making the "Revenge" the centerpiece of her expensive fair. At her many parties and dinners in the "Mermaid" and the Tudor banqueting hall she must have taken special pleasure in knowing that George's "friend" in Paris was footing the bill.

The future Greek princess—Nancy would style herself Princess Anastasia—may never have understood how her investment had helped to give a modest boost to the cause of the First Lord and the Royal Navy. But as soon as Jennie had squeezed all the value out of it for herself, her friends, and her famous son, she cast her eye toward her native land and wondered whether the fair would be welcome in New York. When Kate Carew, a columnist from the *New York Tribune*, interviewed her about the possibility, Jennie didn't hesitate to admit that she would welcome a new benefactor willing to move the whole thing overseas. The columnist quoted her response word for word, though it was probably said in confidence.

"Could you advise me," asked Jennie, "as to any rich man with artistic tastes who would be likely to entertain the idea of establishing the exhibition in America?"[4]

Unfortunately, when none came forward, she closed the fair, and the "Revenge" and the Globe were dismantled. Some of the Tudor cottages were moved to Bristol, where they were used to house officers when the real shooting began after 1914.

There was one man in 1912 who was pretty certain that he was the modern world's answer to Drake and Nelson, and his name wasn't Churchill. It was retired Admiral "Jacky" Fisher—now Baron Fisher—who had served more than half a century in the Royal Navy. In 1854 Lord Nelson's last surviving captain nominated young Jacky Fisher as a naval cadet. The boy was only thirteen then, and the navy he joined had not changed much since Nelson's day. Early on, he saw his mission as adapting Admiral Nelson's precepts to the changing times, and creating a modern fleet both honored and feared.

A. G. Gardiner, writing at the end of Fisher's career, said of him, "His passion for Nelson is so intense and abiding that he seems to dwell in a sort of spiritual companionship with that great man, his sayings always on his lips, his ideals always in his mind."

One of his proudest possessions was a newspaper cartoon published on the day in 1904 when he became the professional head of the Royal

Navy (the First Sea Lord). In the foreground the cartoon showed Nelson starting to climb down from his column in Trafalgar Square, with Fisher in the background striding into the Admiralty. "I was on my way down to lend them a hand myself," said the caption under Nelson, "but if Jacky Fisher's taking on the job there's no need for me to be nervous. I'll get back on my pedestal."

One of Jacky's favorite stories was about an old lady who tapped a seafaring man on the shoulder in Trafalgar Square and pointed to the massive base of Nelson's pedestal. "What are them lions a-guarding of?" she asked, munching on a penny bun. He smiled smugly and replied, "If it hadn't been for the man them lions were a-guarding of, your penny bun would cost thrupence."[5]

Without Fisher, Churchill might not have had a single dreadnought afloat in 1912. He was the father of the dreadnought fleet and the greatest naval innovator of his time. Churchill had known him well for several years and owed much to his influence. It was Fisher who had impressed on him the importance of going to war with overwhelming superiority in speed and firepower, concentrating the fleet in the North Sea for maximum effectiveness against the German threat and keeping the enemy off balance by quick, decisive thrusts. The admiral's view of war was based on his faith in what he called the three H's and three R's: "Hit first! Hit hard! Keep on hitting!" and "Ruthless, Relentless, and Remorseless." When the shooting started, total war was the only option, he believed. "If you hate, hate," he said. "If you fight, fight."[6]

He had officially retired in 1910 but he continued promoting his views as vigorously as possible through his large network of old friends. Though he was seventy when Winston became First Lord, he had lost none of his ferocious drive or combative attitude. He could be endearing to those who agreed with him, but insulting and vindictive to anyone brave enough to contradict him. With his flair for exaggeration he would shout in the hearing of his junior officers, "If any subordinate opposes me, I will make his wife a widow, his children fatherless, and his home a dunghill."[7]

In bad light, in the middle of a rant, he could look demonic, with a narrow, burning gaze, pug nose, and curled lip. When his mood was good, his taut features would soften, a twinkle would come to his eye, and then a big, disarming smile would spread across his face. At such moments he could be good company, spinning yarns and telling jokes in a hearty, fast-paced style. He had a large supply of witty epigrams and anecdotes, each tossed out with minimal introduction or logical connection to anything said before.

One moment he might be explaining that, for the average person, the navy was "a huge mystery hedged in by seasickness," and the next he would be telling the story of the stockbroker long separated from his wife who received a telegram after her sudden death abroad.

"Cremate, embalm, or bury?" the undertaker wired.

"Do all three," the stockbroker replied. "Take no risks!"

Sometimes, when carried away by a passionate point he was driving into the ground, he could be so overbearing that anyone facing him would have to keep backing away. One day at Balmoral Castle, Jacky forgot where he was and began angrily commenting on some pet peeve. "Will you kindly leave off shaking your fist in my face!" exclaimed King Edward.[8]

There was no denying Fisher's genius for engineering and design. He loved machines and was thrilled by the power they could create. But in his exuberance he would entertain possibilities that others were unwilling or unable to see. Sometimes the genius in him went awry, and he began to sound like a madman. In late 1904 he suggested to King Edward that the Royal Navy should put a quick end to Germany as an emerging naval power. Why not stage a sneak attack and destroy the ships in port? he asked. "My God, Fisher, you must be mad!" the king exclaimed.

But he meant it. "The best declaration of war," he wrote in April 1904, "would be the sinking of the enemy's fleet! That's the first they ought to know of war!"

In 1908 he suddenly began to worry that the United States might join forces with Germany and launch a joint naval attack on Britain. The more he considered it, however, the more he liked the odds. He thought it would be possible to annihilate both navies in the North Sea. It whet his appetite. "One might almost wish the United States would join Germany," he said, coldly calculating the damage his ships could do.[9]

As he grew older he became increasingly eccentric and would

proudly make declarations that left others scratching their heads. His talent for creating epigrams broke down, and he began sputtering strange battle cries. "Build more submarines," he once told Winston, "not more Lobsters!!" On another occasion he signed off, "Oil, Chauffeurs & Wireless!" [10]

Yet his wandering mind and dark imaginings also gave him prophetic visions of the slaughter that a European war would bring. He didn't think of it the way that so many of his innocent contemporaries did. They seemed to expect a series of sporting matches with only occasional casualties and civilized breaks for tea and sightseeing. Fisher saw terror, collapse, chaos, and devastation. It would be the war of wars, a cataclysm that would shake the whole world. "The Battle of Armageddon comes along in September 1914," he wrote Pamela McKenna on December 5, 1911. "That date suits the Germans, if ever they are going to fight. Both their Army and Fleet then mobilized, and the Kiel Canal finished, and their new building complete." Off by only a month, Fisher began a countdown to Armageddon, periodically reminding Winston and others of the dwindling time for preparation. [11]

Though volatile and madly fascinated by the dark arts of war, Fisher wasn't someone Winston could ignore. He had vast experience, knowledge, and vision. But it was almost impossible to separate the good Fisher from the bad. He was a whirlwind that swept into a room spouting both nonsense and wisdom. Understanding which was which became more difficult with each passing year. The one constant was the old admiral's intolerance for dissent. He preached the virtues of independent thinking, but the sermon really applied only to his thinking. He knew he was right and would highlight his views in capital letters with frequent exclamation marks, as if to give them the weight and authority of a posted command. "Compromise," he liked to say, "is the beastliest word in the English language." [12]

All of this should have encouraged Churchill to be wary of relying too much on Fisher's advice. But just as Winston had deferred too much to Lloyd George in the great campaign for Liberal reform, he was now tempted to measure his progress at the Admiralty by what Jacky Fisher thought. One person who doubted the wisdom of this new infatuation was, of all people, Lloyd George. As early as December 1911 he confided to George Riddell "that Fisher was not a very safe advisor, and that Winston would have to be cautious."[13]

It was widely known that Jacky had a habit of falling out with friends and colleagues and then blaming them for the falling-out. (His most infamous quarrel was with his fellow admiral Lord Charles Beresford, who hated Winston all the more for associating with Jacky.) To keep Fisher happy, Churchill had to resort to shameless flattery on occasion, and he was always having to phrase every communication in the most careful fashion to avoid offending him. When the inevitable blowups came, the old admiral would threaten to burn his bridges and swear that he would never deal with Churchill again.

"I am going to transfer my body & my money to the United States," Fisher vowed in April 1912 after vehemently objecting to three promotions Winston had just made. "You have betrayed the Navy in these three appointments," he said, adding, "This must be my last communication with you in any matter at all."

Time and again, Winston would gently coax him back from the edge with kindly notes, and persuade him to write or meet for a private discussion. It was a tiresome process, yet Churchill seemed to think it was worth all the insults and incoherent digressions if, in their next communication, a few flashes of insight managed to sneak through. When he was at his best—arguing, for example, in favor of risking everything on the 15-inch gun—Fisher could conjure the "romance of design," as Winston put it, and make the impossible seem suddenly achievable. "No one who has not experienced it," said Churchill of his conversations with the admiral, "has any idea of the passion and eloquence of this old lion when thoroughly roused on a technical question."[14]

To mend relations after their break over the disputed promotions, Churchill sailed to Naples for a meeting with Jacky, who was living in Italy for part of the year. As a way of emphasizing that the government needed the retired admiral's help, Asquith agreed to accompany Winston. For business of this kind, the First Lord was able to travel in great style on HMS *Enchantress*, the Admiralty's steam yacht—a sleek, well-appointed vessel with a crew of 196. Among those coming along on the voyage were Clemmie and Violet. The group left England on May 21 and went by train to Genoa, where they boarded the yacht and sailed in splendid weather to Naples.

On the overnight rail journey through France, Clemmie was ill and broke down "in tears & nerves of exhaustion." She was still suffering from the effects of her miscarriage but had resolved to make the trip anyway, thinking the cruise would do her good. As the train made its way through the mountains she stayed in bed, while Winston held forth in the next compartment on the subject of Napoleon crossing the Alps. At one point Violet went in to check on Clemmie, who asked sleepily whether Winston was talking or reading aloud. In her diary Violet noted with amusement that because Churchill's sentences rolled off his tongue in such polished fullness, even his own wife couldn't tell if the words were in print or not.[15]

When the *Enchantress* arrived in Naples on the morning of May 24, everyone left the ship to stroll along the harbor, and when they returned Admiral Fisher was waiting for them. He gave the prime minister a warm welcome but "glowered" at Winston until they visited a house belonging to one of Jacky's cronies. Once there, Fisher relaxed, began telling jokes, and by teatime his mood seemed upbeat.

"He's melting," Violet whispered to Winston, who was distracted and asked in a voice loud enough for all to hear, "What's melting?"

Thinking fast, Violet saved the day by nodding toward the table and saying, "The butter."[16]

By the evening, Winston and Jacky were old friends again, and they spent hours walking the deck of the *Enchantress* discussing the navy's problems. For the rest of the visit Fisher was on his best behavior, and gave Winston his promise to help formulate the plans for the navy's future oil supplies. Jacky was so pleased with himself that when the ship's band played on deck, he danced with Violet, lurching wildly from port to starboard. He was too full of energy and ideas to remain idle in the Italian sun, Churchill told him. He owed it to his country to be engaged in important work—otherwise, as Winston later put it, "Yr propellers are racing in air."[17]

With Fisher "recaptured," the *Enchantress* was free to make a lazy cruise home to Portsmouth by way of Malta and Gibraltar. At stops along the way Winston and company took time to swim, chase lizards,

go for picnics, recite poetry to the empty rows of an ancient amphithe-
ater, and inspect naval installations. At sea, there was ample time to relax
in the deck chairs and read or nap. The prime minister was absorbed in
Thucydides's *History of the Peloponnesian War*, reading between the lines
no doubt for guidance on how the next war might be fought.

For Winston, the one depressing experience of the cruise came when
he boarded the battleship *Cornwallis* to watch gunnery practice. With
cotton wool stuffed in his ears, he studied the horizon as the ship—
which predated the dreadnoughts—blasted away with 12-inch guns
at a distant target being towed by another vessel. Afterward he paced
the deck waiting for the results. The commander of the Mediterranean
Fleet—Admiral Edmund Poë, who had spent forty years in Queen
Victoria's navy and was now nearing retirement—had the unpleasant
duty of telling him that not a single shell had struck the target. Winston
demanded an explanation, but the response infuriated him even more.

"Well, you see, First Lord," said the admiral, "the shells seem to have
either fallen *just* short of the target or else gone just a *little* beyond it."[18]

Winston could increase the number of battleships a hundredfold, yet
it would all be in vain if victory depended on Victorian timeservers like
Admiral Poë. The First Lord had his work cut out for him, and time was
running short.

A month after Churchill's return from the Mediterranean, a political
rally was held at Blenheim Palace far surpassing in size the one that had
featured him in 1901. He wasn't welcome at this event, however. Though
he still considered Sunny a friend, the crowd of twenty thousand Conservative and Unionist faithful who swarmed the grounds on July 27,
1912, wouldn't have tolerated Winston's presence. In fact, for many of
them, the point of attending the event at Blenheim was to proclaim the
Unionist cause on his native soil. It was a way of taunting him for having
dared to speak in Belfast for Home Rule. They also wanted the rally to
serve as a reminder that Lord Randolph—and Winston—had once been
on their side.

Sunny and F. E. Smith, both of whom spoke at the rally, wouldn't
have expected Winston to see their participation as a personal betrayal.
To them, it was just politics, and they were playing the game with the

same aggressiveness that Winston himself usually showed on the political battlefield. But, given the trauma of her experience at the hands of the Unionists in Belfast, Clemmie didn't look kindly on this Blenheim gathering. It added to her growing list of reasons for wanting her husband to see less of his Tory friends. There was nothing halfhearted about Sunny's support for the rally. He spent lavishly on the event. In the house, and in the garden tents, reported the *Daily Mail*, "thousands of pounds of beef and ham and veal and hundreds of gallons of hock, claret, and beer, together with other sundries of an appetizing nature, were displayed and to be had for the asking."[19]

But this rally wasn't merely the usual excuse for a day of fun at someone else's expense. It had a sinister side that posed a danger to the nation and was embodied in the rising stars of the event—Sir Edward Carson and Andrew Bonar Law. Each used the occasion to threaten nothing less than civil war if the government pushed through Home Rule. With his long, gloomy face and slight frame, Bonar Law, who had recently taken Balfour's place as the Conservative Party's leader, looked more like a dull schoolmaster than a fiery seditionist, but his speech on the steps of Blenheim raised the possibility of an insurrection not just in Ulster but everywhere in Britain.

The government, he proclaimed, was "a revolutionary committee which has seized by fraud upon despotic power. . . . We shall use any means to deprive them of the power which they have usurped." If the Liberals insisted on a fight over Home Rule, he was sure of the consequences. "They would succeed in lighting fires of civil war which would shatter the Empire to its foundations."

The mood of discontent in these last few years had now led both the right and the left to countenance violence as a political remedy. On his own, the Tory leader wasn't likely to strike fear in Liberal hearts. The son of a backwoods Presbyterian minister in Canada, Bonar Law knew how to sound apocalyptic, but no one could imagine him on a charger leading Tory divisions into battle. What he seemed to enjoy was the religious fervor of the Ulster Protestants who saw the fight against Home Rule as God's cause. It excited him to know that "these people are in serious earnest. They are prepared to die for their convictions." But he was content to be more of a spiritual leader in this cause than a field general.[20]

Sir Edward Carson, on the other hand, talked insurrection with the cold stare of a man who looked ready to fire the first shot. A rich barrister known for his remorseless interrogations (Oscar Wilde was one of his more prominent victims), Carson was a Protestant Dubliner who had settled in England but was now obsessed by the future of Ulster. Though he had no special connection to the region, he seized the chance to become one of its champions, quickly emerging in 1910 as one of the fiercest opponents of Home Rule. Churchill's visit to Belfast had particularly enraged him. He said of the Liberal First Lord, "There is nothing that the men of the North of Ireland hate more than a turncoat."

As his private correspondence has revealed, he was expecting bloodshed from the start and reveled in the prospect of being at the forefront of the fight. In 1910 he wrote, "I like being chairman of the Ulster Unionists. . . . I feel boiling with rage & I hope there will be violence." The following year he was becoming downright trigger-happy. "I earnestly hope that all the bitterest hate of the innate savagery of the human being will be brought to play. . . . I never felt more savage." [21]

At Blenheim, while Bonar Law stood speaking for an hour to the vast crowd, Carson sat next to Sunny and leaned forward to catch every word. He wore a grim expression under his silk top hat, his big, smooth face like a block of ice, rigid and pale. When it was his turn to speak, he didn't hesitate to accept the notion of a possible insurrection, and he dared the government to put it down. "They may tell us, if they like, that [this] is treason. We are prepared to face the consequences." [22]

Lulled by his wealth and ducal isolation, Sunny didn't seem to have any idea of the consequences of civil war. Basking in the summer sunshine, surrounded by the grandeur of his palace, he applauded Carson along with everyone else in the crowd. But the hate that he was allowing the demagogue to stir up among the twenty thousand Unionists would soon have a direct consequence for Winston.

It came later that autumn, when the House of Commons was debating Home Rule. As the speeches and shouting dragged into the evening, Carson and his Ulster Unionists became increasingly angry and disruptive. By half past eight, there was so much noise that the Speaker gave up and adjourned the House, announcing "that a state of grave disorder has arisen." As members were leaving, the Unionists began throwing wads of paper at the Liberals. Amused, Churchill pulled out his hand-kerchief and waved it at the opposition benches.

This was too much for one of Carson's ardent lieutenants, Ronald McNeill, who was the most physically imposing man in the House. Standing six feet, six inches tall, he was described by a contemporary as "a big, square-jawed" fellow with "iron grey hair, brushed back from the forehead—a giant among big men." Reaching over to the table, McNeill picked up a heavy volume—the Speaker's copy of the Standing Orders of the House—then took aim and hurled it straight at Churchill. It slammed into his face, nearly knocking him down and drawing blood. As soon as Churchill had gathered his senses, he spotted McNeill and—despite the more than ten-inch difference in their heights—began to go after him. Other members restrained him, however, and McNeill walked away.[23]

Carson said nothing, but many other Tories were shocked by the violence. In disbelief, Austen Chamberlain noted, "Such a scene had not been witnessed since the fight which took place in the House in 1893 in the course of the discussion on Mr. Gladstone's Second Home Rule Bill."[24]

The next day McNeill stood up in the House and made a stiff apology. "Under the influence of a momentary loss of self-control," he confessed, "I regret to say that I discharged a missile which struck the First Lord of the Admiralty."

After a few more contrite words, "the giant," as one account put it, "sank back into his seat amid a long, low murmur of approval from both sides of the House, and Mr. Churchill, who, with bowed head, had been closely following the words of his apologist, came forward."

Winston, his cheek still bruised, was extraordinarily gracious. He refused to take the assault personally. "I thank the hon. gentleman for what he has said. I have at no time had any personal feeling in the matter, and if at any time I have had a personal feeling it would have been removed by his complete and unreserved apology."[25]

In the overheated political atmosphere of the time it was Churchill whom his enemies often portrayed as hopelessly rash and violently antagonistic. But it is difficult to imagine any other politician of the day shrugging off a physical assault as easily as Winston did on this occasion.

He made little of it, and so history has barely noted it, and over time the brutal nature of it—including the vital fact of McNeill's overwhelming size—has been obscured. But the outrage would have been enormous—and the resentment unending—if Winston had been the one to lose his temper and had flung a book with all his force across the narrow space dividing him from the opposition, striking Carson or Andrew Bonar Law in the face. After the inevitable riots, he would have been forced to resign from the Cabinet, and his career might never have recovered.

Instead, the Unionist cause emerged unblemished from this episode, and Carson—unabashed—continued to spread hate.

In the wake of his confrontation with McNeill, a story was told in the press of Winston being heckled during a speech somewhere in the north of England. A man in the back had interrupted him again and again with the cry "Liar! Liar!"

Finally, Churchill stopped speaking, peered calmly into the crowd, and announced: "If the gentleman at the back of the hall who is so anxious that this audience should know his name will kindly write it down upon a slip of paper and pass it up to the chairman, instead of bawling it out at the top of his voice, he will save himself a lot of trouble."[26]

XXIV

WINGS

While Churchill was busy preparing for war at sea and fending off attacks at home, Lloyd George had been taking two major risks of a private nature. One was financial and political, the other sexual. The first involved a dubious investment in the shares of the British Marconi Company, which stood to benefit greatly from a deal with the government to build an imperial network of telegraph stations. When the Tories learned that some of the Liberal leaders had been speculating in Marconi shares, there was great rejoicing at the thought of using the scandal to bring down the government. Lloyd George was one of the speculators, but he denied it flatly, and for a few months he was believed.

His problem was that he had told a half-truth. He had, in fact, purchased a thousand shares, but in a supposedly separate entity called the American Marconi Company. At the end of 1912 he learned that he was likely to be exposed for not telling the whole truth, and he went into a panic, fearing that his career would be ruined. For support and guidance, he turned to Asquith and Churchill, both of whom agreed to stand by him. In January 1913 he wrote to Clemmie, "I was so encouraged to hear from Winston that you took his view of my little worry. I am almost ill with worry over it."[1]

He was so upset—and apparently desperate for more sympathy—that he took another great risk, pleading with his daughter's French tutor to become his mistress. A pretty young woman of twenty-four, Frances Stevenson was staying with friends in Scotland when Lloyd George, who was a little more than twice her age, sent her a letter from London saying he needed her because "something terrible had happened." By the end of January they were lovers. She would stay at his side for the rest of his life, working as his secretary and considering herself a secret second wife. (Margaret, Lloyd George's long-suffering bride, was inclined to spend much of her time in Wales, out of the limelight.)[2]

For a man with almost as many enemies as Churchill, Lloyd George was playing a dangerous game. In March he finally admitted publicly that he had purchased shares in the American branch of Marconi, but he was able to deflect criticism by pretending an innocence of the business technicalities. The Tories, however, soon discovered that a minor official had used Liberal Party funds to speculate in Marconi shares, and the whole case blew up into a major scandal, with Lloyd George dragged into the center of a renewed controversy over political ethics. A delirious Tory backbencher was seen to put his hands together and say, "Now I am beginning to believe there really is a God."

Soon the Tory press began connecting the dots of Lloyd George's comfortable lifestyle, publishing pictures of his pleasant home in Wales, his large new house next to a golf course near Epsom Downs, the rented villa in the south of France where he had spent part of the winter, and his "sumptuous motor" driven by a chauffeur. Under a photograph of the chancellor playing golf, a caption ridiculed him for criticizing the idle rich. But there was no denying that he was living better than his official salary would have reasonably allowed, especially when wife, children, and mistress were added to the equation.[3]

Privately, Churchill was disgusted by the Marconi scandal. He later referred to it as "a squalid business" and told one of Ettie's relatives—Francis Grenfell—that Lloyd George had known what he was doing from the start and had thought he was "going to make a lot of money." It would have been relatively easy for Winston to have brought down his rival at this point. He knew, as he put it, that "Marconi has hit him terribly hard," and that Lloyd George's enemies—with a few tips and enough digging—could find other damaging information to call into question his suitability as Chancellor of the Exchequer. But Winston didn't turn against him, for at least two reasons: he thought Lloyd George's help would be crucial in obtaining more money for the navy, and he considered it his duty as a loyal friend to stick by him.[4]

He was furious, however, when the general search for culprits required him to go before a committee and declare his innocence. He resented being pulled away from his important work at the Admiralty to answer questions about things he had not done. "I lead an honourable life," he told the committee with evident pride. But when the chairman insisted that he specifically disavow any connection to the Marconi scandal, he took a deep breath and spoke, an observer noted, "with a touch of irony as well as bitterness," his eyes fixed on the committee.

"I have never, at any time," he said, "or in any circumstances, directly or indirectly, had any investment, however, it may be described, in Marconi Telegraph shares or in any other shares of that description, in this or in any other country, or in the globe."

The room broke into laughter at that last remark, but Churchill didn't smile. After a few more minutes of questioning, he rose from his seat with the words "May I assume my examination is finished?" and—without waiting for an answer or looking back—he left the room.[5]

It was Asquith who finally saved the day for Lloyd George and the Liberal Party, putting his personal prestige on the line to assure the House that there was no need to censure the chancellor for his actions. Lloyd George had made mistakes, Asquith admitted, and had been careless and imprudent, but not dishonest. There was no violation of his "public duty." The opposition wasn't convinced but decided not to press their case. Years later, Winston acknowledged that the Tories might have been able to defeat the government on the Marconi issue. "But," he explained, "some of them were too stupid and, frankly, some of them were too nice."[6]

As First Lord of the Admiralty, Winston had his own luxuries to enjoy. Besides the *Enchantress*, he also had an official residence next to the Admiralty. Clemmie called it "our Mansion," but they didn't move in for a while. The couple didn't know if they could afford to live in its three large floors. Though the space at Admiralty House came free, the Churchills were responsible for their own servants, and nine were needed to run the place properly. It wasn't until the spring of 1913—right in the middle of the Marconi affair—that they dared to make the move from Eccleston Square to Whitehall, and even then Clemmie decided to economize by closing off the first floor.[7]

Winston saved money by turning the *Enchantress* into his floating office. The more he learned about the poor readiness of the navy, the more time he spent chasing down admirals, captains, and shipbuilders to stir them to greater exertions. In the process he fell in love with the yacht—as did almost everyone who came aboard. He loved being able to use it for his quick inspections of other ships or ports, and then having the convenience of returning to work in his quarters on the ship without wasting time. Clemmie would join him occasionally, or they would meet at Admiralty House or at any convenient port as he raced around the country, looking every inch the modern First Lord in a double-breasted blue suit with a yachting cap.

Best of all, the yacht allowed him to enjoy longer cruises that combined business with pleasure. His Mediterranean voyage to confer with Jacky Fisher in 1912 was followed in May 1913 by another trip to Malta and this time also to Greece. The public purpose was to review fleet operations and discuss strategy with commanders, but ample time was left for playing in the sun. Asquith was on board again but made the mistake of bringing along both Violet and Margot, who managed to get on each other's nerves from the start. Jennie was another passenger on this cruise, and Violet was struck by the vast difference between Winston's lively, gregarious mother and the moody, snappish Margot. Everybody managed to have a good time except Margot, who complained about everything—from the food they ate on board to the steepness of the steps leading to the ancient ruins they visited.

One of Margot's pastimes on the trip was to sit back and quietly observe her fellow passengers, then criticize them in her diary at night. She was especially fascinated by the relationship between Clemmie and Winston, which she couldn't quite understand. In general she thought Winston's wife was charming, but not up to his intellectual standards. Yet she could see how much he brightened whenever she came into view. If his wife wasn't on deck when he returned from some expedition ashore, his first words were always "Where's Clemmie?"

Margot also noted that Clemmie had a short temper, but she observed that this volatile aspect of her character seemed to be part of her appeal to Winston. On a walk in Athens, Margot saw Winston push Clemmie's hand away when she tried to straighten his hat. This little gesture irritated Clemmie, who stormed off, closely pursued by Winston. When he caught up with her, she turned, and they embraced so fervently that Margot suddenly felt "ashamed" at spying on such an intimate moment.[8]

In her letters home Violet succeeded in capturing the essence of Winston's frenetic life—playing hard and working hard on a monumental scale. She concluded her description of a stop along the Albanian coast with this extraordinary sentence: "Winston stayed behind for a wild pig hunt at 3 in the morning & caught us up next day at Corfu in a destroyer."

Back in Britain there were a few complaints from members of the Labour Party that Churchill was stretching the rules "by inviting his lady friends to accompany him on yachting trips at public expense." But other political observers were more interested in the chummy relationship between the prime minister and the First Lord. Did it mean that the older man was preparing the way for the younger to succeed him? A *Punch* cartoon showed them relaxing on the deck of the *Enchantress*, with Winston pausing between puffs of his cigar to ask the prime minister, who is absorbed in a newspaper, "Any home news?" To which Asquith responds, "How can there be with you here?"[9]

It wasn't easy for anyone to keep up with Winston, but Clemmie made a heroic effort in his years at the Admiralty. She was proud of him and felt herself swept up in the passion that he felt for his work and life in this tumultuous time. But the hectic life, the pressures of office, and the seemingly never-ending political controversies also created difficulties in the marriage. The couple became more and more concerned about their finances, with Winston warning, "Money seems to flow away." At one point they were so short of cash that Clemmie, without telling Winston first, sold an expensive diamond necklace with a ruby setting. They quarreled and tears flowed.

But their misunderstandings and disagreements would rarely drag into the next day. Both had strong wills and spoke their minds plainly. After one argument Clemmie confessed that she suffered from the fault of saying too much.

"When I get excited & cross," she wrote him in early 1913, "I always say more than I feel & mean instead of less—There are never any dregs left behind."

Throughout it all, however, they remained deeply devoted to each other. "The Admiralty is a most exacting mistress," said Winston. "I have given up all others for her—except Clemmie." [10]

In romance, Winston had no desire to follow Lloyd George's lead, and even if he had been tempted to do so, he was far too busy to keep up with a wife and another woman. Whenever he wanted to bask in the intense light of Violet's admiration, she was always willing to listen to his troubles and encourage his hopes. She was becoming a convincing substitute for the sister he never had, and her relationship with Clemmie was also becoming like that of a sister. On the cruise in 1913 Violet finally fell completely under Clemmie's spell.

"Clemmie is most smooth & serene & delicious to live with," Violet concluded. "And looking more beautiful than I have ever seen her." [11]

In London, when Winston was working late or was aboard the Admiralty yacht, Violet proved to be a good companion to his wife. She practically lived next door, so close was Number 10 to Admiralty House. And, on weekends, Clemmie was often the guest of the Asquiths at their new country cottage in the little village of Sutton Courtenay—"The Wharf."

At any rate, the Churchills worked hard at making their marriage a success, trying to iron out their differences and allowing room for compromises. They needed no reminders of the miseries that attended a marriage gone bad. Jennie could provide them more than enough evidence of that.

With her beauty faded, and her Elizabethan fair a dismal failure, Jennie was now facing the harsh glare of publicity in the divorce court. F. E. Smith represented her, and though the proceedings were short, they were humiliating. A private detective was called to the witness box to provide the sordid evidence of George Cornwallis-West's adultery, and even a hotel chambermaid appeared as a supporting witness.

"Louisa Minton," the press reported, "chambermaid at the Great Western Hotel, Paddington, said she recollected a lady and gentleman staying at the hotel at the latter end of March 1913 as Captain and Mrs. West."

F. E. Smith pointed at Jennie and asked the chambermaid, "Was the lady who stayed at the hotel the lady that is sitting below?"

"No," came the reply, and the case wrapped up in ten minutes. The other "Mrs. West" wasn't identified, but George, apparently, had many to choose from. Jennie was given her divorce, and it was announced that she "would in future be known as Lady Randolph Churchill."

Winston wasn't sorry to see the back of George Cornwallis-West, and not just for his mother's sake. In the past, when stories had appeared of George's difficulties with his finances or his marriage, the press would invariably bring up Winston's name as Jennie's "famous son." Not surprisingly, "Mother of First Lord" appeared in the headlines announcing her divorce on July 16. It was the kind of attention Winston didn't need, for his mother's embarrassing misfortunes merely gave his enemies more reasons to laugh at him and to deride his ambitions.[12]

Perhaps the greatest strain on Winston's marriage at this time came from his decision to take flying lessons. Fearless as always, and fascinated by the possibilities of naval aviation, he thought he should know firsthand the risks and advantages of flight. And they were considerable at this early stage. Churchill compared it to the uncertain performance of George Stephenson's steam locomotives near the dawn of the Victorian age. "We are in the Stephenson age of flying," he used to say. "Now our machines are frail. One day they will be robust, and of value to our country."

The historian G. M. Young recalled seeing in his youth a man point at one of the new biplanes and ask, "Can these things carry machine guns," to which another man replied, "My dear fellow, they can't carry themselves yet."[13]

Clemmie was stricken with fear over Winston's adventures in the air and found it almost impossible to accept this dangerous activity as he took greater risks. Some of his adventures were indeed perilous, and every time he went up in one of the navy's primitive flying machines she feared he wouldn't return alive.

It didn't start out that way. In the late summer of 1913, when he began flying a lot, Clemmie insisted on taking a ride in one of the planes—a daring thing for a woman of her position to do in those days.

Winston said no, but she disobeyed the First Lord and climbed into one of the two seats in a Sopwith biplane, and in a few minutes she was in the air with one of the navy's new pilots—Lieutenant Spenser Grey. They went up about a thousand feet and did a few lazy circles over Southampton.

Winston couldn't bear to follow her progress in the sky. With his gaze fixed on the ground, he paced the field anxiously the whole time she was gone.

When the plane landed, she emerged with her hair blowing in all directions and her cap in hand. She had almost lost the cap on takeoff when it came loose in the wind. Smiling, she said of the flight, "It was beautiful!"

Winston shook his head. "I have been on thorns ever since you went up," he said.

As they walked away from the field, he kept repeating, "Never again!"

Writing to Jennie afterward, Clemmie let her mask of bravery slip. "It was a wonderful sensation," she said, "but a very terrifying one. . . . It felt such a frail structure & every moment I thought we should be dashed to the ground." [14]

Her worries about the flying machines increased as winter approached and Winston kept going back up in various models—some of them new and untried—and in all kinds of weather. He was slowly learning how to fly, but he also wanted a better idea of what the planes could do when conditions were less than ideal—as was bound to be the case in war. On one occasion he was in a seaplane that made a landing in the Thames estuary in a driving rain with winds blowing fifty miles an hour.

Much of his flying was done from an airfield in Kent at Eastchurch, near Sheerness, where he would mingle with the other pilots as they tinkered with their machines before taking off. In his leather flying jacket and airman's cap, he was almost indistinguishable from the others, and he always made an effort to fit in, behaving more like a junior officer than the First Lord. Once aloft, when he was able to look around from this area at altitudes of a few thousand feet, he learned something invaluable. In an age when such aerial views were rare, he was able to give himself a tour of the naval battlefield he would have to defend in case of war—the waters separating England from the French and Belgian coasts. On clear days he could see the outline of those coasts and study them carefully. It would give him an advantage over so many other commanders content to rely on maps and surface views.

Though he didn't start the process of developing the navy air wing, he did throw so much support behind it that he was able to make it independent from the army wing. The Royal Naval Air Service was his creation, and he turned it into a first-class force with some of the best airmen in the world. He also rechristened a new kind of plane—one that used floats to take off and land on the water. "Hydroaeroplanes," everyone had been calling them. "That's a beastly word," he said when he first heard it. Turning to a group of flyers, he announced, "Let's give them a better name. Let's call them seaplanes." [15]

Because he didn't need to fly solo to accomplish most of his goals in the air, his instructors conspired to keep shifting him from pilot to pilot, and to avoid having anyone take responsibility for sending him up alone. "No one will risk letting him solo," one instructor told another. "If anything happened to [Churchill], the career of the man who had allowed him a solo flight would be finished." [16]

In November he began flying with a young pilot of twenty-six who had only a year of experience, and who had already suffered a tragedy in his training. In April he had accidentally killed another airman, who was helping him start his plane and didn't get out of the way in time. The propeller struck the man, who died from his injuries two hours later. An inquest cleared the pilot of any wrongdoing.

The pilot's name—Captain Wildman-Lushington—may not have inspired confidence in some, but Churchill liked him and trusted him. They went flying together several times at Eastchurch in a plane with dual controls. On Saturday, November 29, they spent about three hours in the air together, and his instructor said he "showed great promise." At five hundred feet he took over the controls and flew the plane for an hour. That night they dined together on board the *Enchantress*, which was anchored in Sheerness harbor.

On Tuesday afternoon, December 2, Churchill was at the Treasury in a meeting with Lloyd George when a messenger gave him a note. He opened it and stared in disbelief at the news. His new instructor had been killed earlier that day in a crash at Eastchurch. The plane had stalled on its approach, and he fell to earth, breaking his neck. He had just been engaged, and Churchill wrote a note of sympathy to the young woman. (Fifty years later she wrote his official biographer, "What a mercy for England that Sir W's flight was not the fatal one.")[17]

At home, Winston found Clemmie distraught, her mind tormented by thoughts that Winston might have been the one who died. It was from that moment that she began telling him what he had told her, "Never again!" Other friends chimed in. "Why do you do such a thing as fly repeatedly?" asked F. E. Smith. "Surely it is unfair to your family, your career & your friends."[18]

Two days after the fatal crash Churchill did take the sensible precaution of instructing Eddie Marsh to check on his life insurance policy, which was in the amount of £10,000. Was he covered in case of an accident in the air? To everyone's relief, the family lawyer wrote back immediately, "I am of the opinion that the policies cover the risk of death caused by accident in connection with aviation."[19]

But that was cold comfort to Clemmie, who would spend the next few months trying in vain to get her husband to stop flying. He considered it his duty to fly from time to time, but as he later admitted, "I continued for sheer joy and pleasure." Suspecting as much, she tried to frighten him with melodramatic accounts of her bad dreams, and her fear that every time a telegram arrived, "I think it is to announce that you have been killed." She ended one letter to him, "Goodbye Dear but Cruel One."

She would complain of his reckless fascination with planes to anyone who would listen. At a dinner party that took place just before the war broke out in 1914, she shared her concerns with an elderly, white-haired novelist sitting next to her. He was so sympathetic that she confided to him that the First Lord had finally relented a little after learning that she was now pregnant with their third child. Writing of the dinner shortly afterward, Thomas Hardy noted, "Mr & Mrs Winston Churchill came. I had her next me. He has promised her not to fly again till after a certain event [the birth], but he won't promise *never* to fly again."[20]

XXV

COUNTDOWN

On a damp November morning in 1913 a burly man in a bowler hat stood at the entrance of the Ritz hotel in London waiting for a taxi. He had dark eyes, a long black mustache, and a distinctly foreign air. He might have been a Continental banker on holiday or a diplomat in town negotiating a minor treaty. But he didn't have any important business to conduct today. It was his last day in London, and he was free to spend it as he pleased. When the taxi arrived, the doorman helped him get in and told the driver to take his passenger to Harrods.

There, the Archduke Franz Ferdinand—heir to the throne of the Austro-Hungarian Empire—whiled away the morning wandering happily through the great emporium, picking out a few gifts to be sent home. He attracted little notice from the other shoppers, most of whom probably wouldn't have known who he was anyway. There had been a few articles in the press about his private visit to Britain as guest of His Majesty the King, but hardly anyone paid much attention to such things. There were only two foreign potentates who could cause a real stir in London—the Kaiser or the Czar. The rest were just hazy figures in magazine pictorials of crowned heads and their families.[1]

Yet, in little more than seven months, the death of this unremarkable shopper would start a chain of events that would topple empires and kill millions. The crowned heads seemed to have been looking for an excuse to win a little glory in a brief but spectacular clash of arms, and Franz Ferdinand's assassination by Serbian nationalists on June 28, 1914, would provide the necessary spark. Great armies and navies would mobilize, ultimatums would be sent, and then—as Jacky Fisher predicted—Armageddon. But on this ordinary November day in 1913, among the well-stocked shelves of Harrods, the idea that this one man could start a world war would have seemed laughable.

What was more difficult to dismiss was Germany's continuing preparation for war. Who was their target? France? Russia? Britain? Did the Germans really think that they could send their battleships into the North Sea and sweep the British fleet off the map? For many in Britain, the idea of these two highly civilized nations staging a naval Armageddon, with one group of dreadnoughts blasting away at the other, was almost unthinkable, especially now that both sides had enough of these well-armed leviathans to make a conflict seem insane to any reasonable person.

Looking back at the determined push for more dreadnoughts in 1909, or the panic started by the little *Panther's* arrival at Agadir, many were now thinking that the dangers had been exaggerated, and that the time had arrived to bring the arms race to an end—or at least to slow it to a manageable crawl. Let the diplomats sort it out, the thinking went, so that Britain can concentrate on defusing some of the ticking time bombs at home. Women needed to be able to vote, workers needed to be able to earn a decent living, the poor needed a way to escape the misery of the slums, and the old problem of Irish Home Rule needed to be settled peacefully.

A landmark book of 1913, *The Six Panics*, by Francis Hirst, editor of *The Economist*, dismissed the arms race as much ado about nothing and wondered why the Liberals "pandered to the guilty passion for naval and military extravagance." It was time, Hirst argued, for Liberals to go back to the good work of promoting peace and prosperity. Lord Loreburn— recently retired from the Liberal Cabinet—gave his support to *The Six Panics*, declaring confidently, "Time will show that the Germans have no aggressive designs against us, nor we against them; and then foolish people will cease to talk of a future war between us, which will never take place."[2]

Seeing the pendulum swing, David Lloyd George seized the opportunity to command a new "peace offensive." He decided that his earlier flash of belligerence in the Agadir crisis had been politically unwise, and he now hastened to show Hirst and other Liberal opinion-makers that he had learned his lesson and was returning to his antiwar roots.

On New Year's Day 1914 he fired the first metaphorical shot in this new offensive. In an interview published that day by the *Daily Chronicle* the chancellor made it clear that he was weary of having to find more and more money for armaments and was leaning toward a return to the time-honored Liberal principle of retrenchment.

The threat that had seemed so ominous in 1911 was no longer a cause for concern, he said. Relations with Germany were "infinitely more friendly than they had been for years." Both sides better understood the other's concerns, he insisted, and "sanity has now been more or less restored on both sides of the North Sea." He thought there was little chance of a naval war between the two powers because the Germans now understood that they couldn't win such a fight. As he expressed it, "Even if Germany ever had any idea of challenging our supremacy at sea, the exigencies of the military situation must necessarily put it completely out of her mind."

So, under these new circumstances, he had come to the only logical conclusion. It was time, he announced, to stop the "feverish efforts" to add to the Royal Navy's already overwhelming strength. Indeed, in his view, it was dangerous to continue the expansion, because it would "wantonly provoke other nations." He conceded that Germany was continuing its military expansion but believed that they had a legitimate excuse. "The country has so often been invaded, overrun and devastated by foreign foes that she cannot afford to take any chances in that direction."[3]

There was no evidence to support Lloyd George's sunny view of Anglo-German relations, nor his assumption that the Kaiser's admirals wouldn't go to war in the North Sea. But he wanted to believe these things because there was much he admired about Germany, and there were many reasons why he thought reason would prevail. Politically, at this point, there was little advantage to him to say anything else. But it is worth noting that he would argue almost the same view more than twenty years later when he went to Germany to visit Hitler, then returned to tell the readers of the *Daily Express* that the growing military of the Third Reich was merely a defensive force.

"What Hitler said at Nuremberg is true," wrote Lloyd George in 1936. "The Germans will resist to the death every invader of their own country, but they have no longer the desire themselves to invade any other land." In the aftermath of his chat with Hitler—whom he praised as "the George Washington of Germany"—Lloyd George even managed the audacious feat of reversing himself to repeat himself when he declared, "The establishment of a German hegemony in Europe, which was the aim and dream of the old pre-war militarism, is not even on the horizon of Nazism."[4]

As in 1914, when he was eager to discount that "old pre-war militarism," so in 1936 he was equally quick to discount the prospect of widespread Jewish persecution by the Nazis. "The German temperament takes no more delight in persecution than does the Briton," he explained, "and the native good humour of the German people soon relapses into tolerance after a display of ill-temper."[5]

For good measure, on his way out of Germany in 1936, Lloyd George would warn the Nazi leaders Rudolf Hess and Joachim von Ribbentrop to be wary of Churchill, "who had no judgment."[6]

While Lloyd George was promoting his new, more understanding view of German militarism at the beginning of 1914, Winston and his family—including Jennie—were spending their holidays on the southwest coast of France at a chateau belonging to the Duke of Westminster. There were several other guests present, and one of them, Francis Grenfell, kept a diary while he was there. It makes fascinating reading because it contains some revealing comments from Churchill in this crucial period leading up to war. A soldier, Grenfell had obvious reasons for sounding Winston out on the prospects for war, but they were also old friends and had much to discuss. Grenfell's brother Robert fought with Churchill at Omdurman and was killed there. (Francis himself would die in 1915, but not before distinguishing himself in battle and winning the Victoria Cross.)

At lunch on Christmas, Churchill was harshly critical of Lloyd George, which was an unusual thing for him. Among other names he called him "a peasant with peasant's ideas." Churchill had been counting on Lloyd George to support his efforts to keep ahead of the German navy, but by the end of 1913 he knew that the chancellor was trying to undermine those efforts, and that many others in the Cabinet were lining up to do the same.

In fact, the very next day a messenger arrived at the chateau with a Cabinet memorandum from Lloyd George, written on December 24. It was a clear statement of opposition to Winston's plans for four new battleships. The number would have to be reduced, he insisted.[7]

"To commit the country," wrote the chancellor, "to new expenditure of millions, unless it is abundantly clear that it is necessary in order to maintain the security of our shores, would . . . lay the Government open to a serious charge of extravagant folly."[8]

Winston knew now that he would have an explosive fight on his hands. If two leading Cabinet members went head-to-head over an issue of this importance, it was likely that one of them would end up yielding or resigning. Winston wasn't going to yield.

"Very pensive and moody all day," Grenfell wrote of Churchill. "Worked in evening but hardly spoke a word at dinner and sat all of a heap."

But then, in typical style, Winston suddenly came to life late in the evening and began to talk in great detail about the kind of war that was coming, and the best way to fight it. What others sometimes saw in him as depression was often simply the intense concentration of his brooding mind. From time to time these retreats into himself—and the grinding of his mental gears, when he couldn't see a clear way forward—would cast a cloud over him, and then he would suffer bouts of what he called his "Black Dog."

When the words began to flow from the newly energized Winston, Francis Grenfell followed it avidly and later tried to recapture some of it in his diary: "W. then talked freely about Franco-German war—which he thinks is bound to come." Churchill wasn't sure how the war would start, but he believed that Britain was certain to get involved because "we could never see France crushed by Germany." He knew the French dreaded the fight, but also that their lack of respect for the Kaiser's military abilities gave them one great hope—"the Germans might suffer from unexpected reverses if [the] German Emperor tries to run things himself."

As for Britain, Winston said, "The action of England depends on 4 or 5 men." Presumably, he considered himself one of those men, because he was sure of the best way for the army to enter the fight. "England should be on a flank," he said, "so that the command can be separate [from the French], and the communication maintained with the sea."

But, to win, the leaders of the fight needed men who knew how to fight. And that was still something of a problem with the navy, he told Grenfell. He was astonishingly candid, and more than a touch arrogant for someone who had fought as a soldier, but not as a sailor. "The Navy are very bad at War. Their one idea is to fight bull-headed. For example, if 3 ships meet 4 German [ships], the Navy would go bull-headed instead of collecting 7 or 8 other ships."[9]

What men like Lloyd George—who had never been in battle—failed to understand was that in the event of war the navy would have to do much more than contend with the German fleet in open seas—an immense challenge in itself. It would also have to protect that vulnerable army flank on the Continent with ships that could cruise offshore and fire their guns far inland. The regular British Army was small compared to the German army, which could field millions of men. An expeditionary force—as Churchill had argued in his first year as an MP—couldn't possibly defeat a Continental force on its own. But if it went to the assistance of the French, fighting on the flank nearest the sea, it might help to turn the tide of a battle. If not, the Royal Navy could always come to the rescue. But only, Churchill reasoned, if its command of the seas was vastly superior to that of any other navy.

This kind of thinking, however, anticipated events that went far beyond what the Cabinet was ready to consider. If Lloyd George's new views were correct, there would be no war, and therefore no need to think about flanks and sea power along the French and Belgian coasts. Instead of four more battleships, two would be more than enough—which is the number many in the Cabinet considered reasonable.

That word *reasonable* was the key. Winston's opponents never tired of saying that he was unreasonable. He wouldn't listen to reason, they said; he wouldn't compromise. He was still too much of the boy, a spoiled child demanding more than he deserved. In the middle of the fight over the new battleships, Lloyd George told his friend George Riddell, "Winston has acted like an extravagant boy placed in possession of a banking account for the first time" (an interesting criticism coming from a man who had recently endangered his career over a financial scandal).[10]

The Liberal critics of the arms race were right to think that such a buildup defied reason. At the outset Winston had opposed it on the grounds that it did indeed seem unreasonable in the absence of a clear German threat. But all that changed once he perceived that the threat was real. After he had made reasonable overtures to Germany for a "Naval Holiday"—he repeated the offer in October 1913—and the offer was spurned, then he thought it was only reasonable to prepare for war.

There was a terrible, inescapable logic to the problem. If Germany attacked France, if Britain would not allow her to be "crushed," if a British expeditionary army stood ready to be sent to France, and the Cabinet agreed to send it, then Winston could easily imagine the horrors that would follow in the wake of those developments. As First Lord of the Admiralty, he was left with a clear choice: resign and work for peace at any price, or stay put and prepare for total war. Faced with such options, he followed one of Jacky Fisher's cherished—and perhaps most reasonable—slogans: "If you fight, fight."

Lloyd George, however, wanted to fight and not fight. He wanted to defend France if necessary, but not anytime soon. He wanted Britain to have a superior navy, but not too superior. Instead of four battleships or no battleships, he was content to have two. For better or worse, it was otherwise with Winston. If he fought, he fought.

Accordingly, when Winston wrapped up his stay in France, he returned to London with his war paint on. "LG is accustomed to deal with people who can be bluffed and frightened," he said privately, "but he will not bluff or frighten me! He says that some of the Cabinet will resign. Let them resign!"[11]

For the next two months he fought for his ships, and everything else of military value that he could squeeze into the Navy Estimates. The cost was enormous. The figures were always in dispute and shifting, but the final sum was over £50 million. But he did what he vowed to do. He held firm against Lloyd George, resisting the Cabinet's calls for naval economy with the same forcefulness that he had once used against Reggie McKenna's dreadnoughts. Now the two men had reversed their positions. Reggie was on Lloyd George's side. "You know I am a big navy man," Reggie told a friend, "but I am against waste."[12]

When the dispute dragged on too long for Asquith's patience, he put an end to it, handing Winston his four battleships and much else in March, and forcing Lloyd George to accept the agreement or resign. The prime minister felt sure that his chancellor wouldn't resign, and he was right.

As soon as this battle of the battleships was won, Winston wanted to resume his old friendly relations with Lloyd George. But there was a chill in the chancellor's attitude toward him now, and a lingering resentment that Winston had prevailed in the Cabinet debate. "Really if it wasn't for Winston's affectionate quality and good temper," Lloyd George later confided to Margot, "I sometimes think I can hardly do with him! . . . He's as you say, such a child!"[13]

Lloyd George's very public expressions of a conciliatory attitude toward Germany revealed to the British public—and to the German military— the deep opposition within the Cabinet to Churchill's ambitious plans for the navy. Asquith tried to present something of a united front, but he did so only belatedly, and not very convincingly. Inside the Cabinet, Asquith was almost alone in his support for Winston. In January 1914 an Admiralty civil servant wrote privately, "The fact is the cabinet is sick of Churchill's perpetually undermining & exploiting its policy and are picking a quarrel with him. As a colleague he is a great trial to them. But their battleground is very ill-chosen as in consequence of their indolence he has probably got chapter & verse for every item of the Naval Programme."[14]

After all the political blood spilled over budgets and vetoes, the government was weakened, and vulnerable. Before Germany had a chance to take advantage of this weakness, another well-armed force decided to test the government's will. As the Home Rule Bill was being thrashed out in 1913–14, Edward Carson and his Ulster Unionists were preparing to show that their talk of civil war had teeth to it. They had shown a genius for organization, raising a 100,000-man militia—the Ulster Volunteer Force—and had endowed the whole movement with a cultish passion for political and religious freedom, with half a million people signing a "Solemn Covenant" to defeat Home Rule and defend Ulster.

In 1914 the force began aggressively trying to arm itself with

smuggled rifles. It was not lost on the German military that the out-
break of an insurrection in Ulster would divert British troops and
provide a fine opening for a quick Prussian offensive against France.
As Lord Haldane recalled in his memoirs, "The Germans appeared to
be taking an uncomfortably vivid interest in the troubles of the British
Army in Ireland." The Austrian embassy in London sent a diplomat to
Belfast to report on the situation. What he found frightened him. He
had no doubt that the Unionists were preparing for an epic fight.

"I found Ulster in a state of feverish ferment," the Austrian diplomat
George Franckenstein recalled after the war. "Ulster's grim determination to offer armed resistance was brought home to me in Belfast, where
I saw Protestant clergy in full canonicals bless the colours of the volunteers to the accompaniment of prayers and hymns. Many thousands of
these volunteers . . . marched by with a detachment of nurses, while Carson, his face hewn out of granite, looked the very symbol of unbending
resolve, as he towered above the crowd and spoke of their determination
to stop at nothing rather than be forced out of the Union." [15]

Carson was so "unbending," and so immersed in his dark dreams of
an Ulster bloodbath, that he refused every effort by Asquith to create
some amendment to the Home Rule Bill that would make it more acceptable. One proposal was to delay carrying out the law in Ulster for six
years, but this produced a howl of indignation. It was nothing more than
a "sentence of death with a stay of execution for six years," said Carson. [16]

The Ulster Unionists were placing the British government in an impossible position, and if the prime minister had been a stronger, more
confrontational figure, he might have chosen this moment to stand up
to Carson and to find a way to isolate him. But in this crisis the Cabinet
turned to Winston for help. Resented only weeks earlier for his unreasonable demands, he was suddenly the Cabinet's favorite bulldog to put
the Unionist leader in his place. Lloyd George decided that he had been
too hard on Winston after all, and he was now inspired to speak warmly
to his old friend. "You can make a speech which will ring down the corridors of history," he told him.

The flattery hit its mark. Churchill gave a speech in the North, at
Bradford, that dared the Unionists to back up their threats. "If all the
loose, wanton and reckless chatter we have been forced to listen to these

many months is in the end to disclose a sinister and revolutionary purpose, then I can only say to you: Let us go forward and put these grave matters to the proof." He wanted to shame them into retreating, but they held firm. He made the mistake of allowing them to create what the Germans, quietly watching from afar, must have been hoping for—a domestic crisis that was an even greater distraction than before.[17]

Over the next four months the government was utterly absorbed in an effort to subdue the Ulster unrest. Misunderstandings proliferated. Thinking that they were going to be sent to fight the Unionists in Belfast, a few dozen army officers at a camp near Dublin—the Curragh—threatened to resign their commissions, which created fears of widespread mutinies. Believing that supplies of arms and other military equipment in Ulster might be at risk from a sudden attack, Churchill sent destroyers to help move army reinforcements to the area. When the opposition learned of his action, he was subjected to a rhetorical bombardment far out of proportion to what he had done. The Unionists whipped up hate against him as the leader of a secret plot to storm Ulster and institute a "pogrom." On the basis of rumors alone, Edward Carson sought to portray Churchill as a would-be Ulster czar bent on massacre. He condemned him as "Lord Randolph's renegade son who wanted to be handed down to posterity as the Belfast butcher."[18]

To his critics throughout his career, Churchill always presented a tempting half-finished portrait that they could touch up as desired. With the right brushstrokes and shading they could turn him into a snarling demon capable of any crime. In large part it was the aristocrat in him that so many of his critics couldn't forgive. It was convenient to ignore the fact that, surrounded by political contemporaries who eagerly accepted grand titles as their just reward, he remained plain Winston for so much of his career. But none of that mattered when one of his detractors was determined to find a mad duke, a strutting prince, or a tyrannical emperor lurking somewhere inside Churchill.

At the height of the Ulster crisis the *Fortnightly Review* gave this portrait: "Mr. Churchill reminds one more and more of other aristocratic demagogues in history . . . their immense ability, the Claudian insolence of manner, recklessness of speech, and colossal swagger. Courage, eloquence, unbounded self-confidence, limitless ambition, but not an ounce of scruple."[19]

As it happened, the threatened civil war over Ulster was merely a long series of uncivil verbal duels. The feud was still raging on June 28, 1914, when that bland London tourist of the autumn was shot down, the victim of another conflict over nationalist aspirations. Just as Archduke Franz Ferdinand had not attracted much attention on his London visit, so now his death was slow to sink into the consciousness of the British public. The reaction of the Tory MP who owned Chequers, Arthur Lee, was typical: "The news that an Austrian archduke (one of so many, and none of them known to us) had been murdered at a place called Sarajevo (which was equally unfamiliar) made little impression upon our minds, apart from the fact that the Court Ball to which we had been looking forward had to be cancelled on account of Court mourning."[20]

What did it matter to an empire struggling to avoid civil war if an obscure assassin gunned down an archduke in a Balkan backwater? But, as would soon become clear, this was the opening scene of a long tragedy that would quickly overshadow the Ulster question and leave it to drift back, as Churchill said, "into the mists and squalls of Ireland." As soon as war was declared, Ulster did indeed fight, but against Germany, along with the rest of the empire.[21]

XXVI

LAST STAND

I t didn't take long for war to spread. Austria threatened the Serbs, Russia prepared to fight the Austrians, and Germany seemed hostile to almost everyone except the Austrians. The ultimatums flew, the elder statesmen huddled and spoke in hushed tones, armies mobilized, the battleships of the Royal Navy steamed out to sea, and anxious vigils were held as deadlines loomed. Lusting for conquest and nursing obscure grievances, Germany had been looking for an excuse to fight and now had found it, supporting Austria against the Russian czar and his ally in the West, the French.

As Winston had predicted, the British couldn't abide the possibility of a French defeat, and the German decision to attack France through the neutral territory of Belgium made it easy to join the fight. In London, on the warm evening of August 4, 1914, Churchill waited in the Admiralty, his eye fixed on the clock. Germany had until eleven that night to answer the British demand that Belgium's neutrality be respected.

The minutes ticked away, no answer came, and at eleven he heard through an open window the chimes of Big Ben striking. "As the first stroke of the hour boomed out," he recalled, "a rustle of movement swept across the room. The war telegram, which meant 'Commence hostilities against Germany,' was flashed to the ships."[1]

Still only thirty-nine, Winston was now at the center of a world war, with a heavy responsibility for the largest navy in the world, and a duty to protect the shores of his island nation. It had taken him only thirteen years to rise from a parliamentary backbencher to one of the top posts in an empire at war. After all the struggles, after all the political fights and name-calling, he now had the chance to change the course of world history, and to prove the worth of his heroic view of life.

At this dramatic moment a figure out of his past wrote him an encouraging note. It was someone who knew all too well how much his success meant to him, and how long he had waited for it. On August 10, Pamela Lytton wrote him, "I think you must feel your dreams and capabilities are all fulfilled today by your position as head of England's Navy, and of England's naval battles in this greatest war." [2]

In the early days of the war many in Britain assumed that it would end in a few months, and that the best commanders would come home covered in glory. How could it be otherwise for a powerful empire with a long tradition of military greatness? The idea that the war would resemble a kind of sporting event was so pervasive that the brutality of it was easily overshadowed at the start by thrilling fantasies of rivers crossed, towns overrun, and soldiers captured after relatively bloodless charges and stealthy maneuvers. Like gentlemen prizefighters, some British strategists seemed to think they would win on points, forcing the Kaiser's surrender by completely outsmarting the much larger German army. While superior British troops drove the invaders from the battlefield, the Royal Navy would make quick work of the German fleet and set up a punishing blockade. Or so many in Britain hoped as they watched the "summer war" begin.

At the Admiralty, Winston enjoyed an enormous advantage, for this was his hour—the arrival of the war he had seen coming, and had prepared himself to fight, whether by land, sea, or air. He couldn't suppress his excitement, and this unsettled some of those around him, who thought he shouldn't be so pleased to wage war.

Others rejoiced that Winston had worked so hard to make sure that a strong navy could command the seas. One of his unexpected admirers was the biographer and essayist Lytton Strachey, who gave no hint of irony when he said in September 1914, "God has put us on an island, and Winston has given us a navy, and it would be absurd to neglect those advantages." [3]

At the outset Churchill found the challenge exhilarating, though he knew it meant death and destruction for so many. "Everything tends towards catastrophe & collapse," he wrote Clemmie. "I am interested, geared-up & happy. Is it not horrible to be built like that? The preparations have a hideous fascination for me."[4]

A telling moment came during the Cabinet debates over whether to go to war. On August 1, Lewis Harcourt—who had been arguing in earlier months that Britain was unlikely to fight on the Continent—noted with amazement and disgust in his journal, "Churchill wants to mobilise the whole navy: very violent." Faced with German armies preparing to invade Belgium, Churchill was indeed "violent," and Harcourt was so removed from the realities of the crisis that he couldn't understand why.[5]

For the British, what would help to turn the war into such a long and bitter slog was the halfhearted way in which Harcourt, Lloyd George, Asquith, and other Liberals threw the nation into the fight and then failed for so long to pursue it vigorously. In the beginning they seemed to regard the war as a subcontracted affair—nice work for the military but not much of a business to occupy them. Ten days after the war began, Churchill's Cabinet rival Reggie McKenna was spending his Saturday playing golf and complaining sourly to a friend that Winston was getting too much attention at the Admiralty. "He talks well," Reggie said of Churchill, "but has never done anything big." He continued in this vein for some time, completely blind to the irony that he was golfing while Churchill was hard at work as First Lord.

One of the few Cabinet members who had the good sense to resign after admitting that he had no desire to prosecute a war was old John Morley. He had long outstayed his welcome in politics and was ready to retire, and he wasn't afraid to oppose the decision to go to war. To Winston, he gave a forthright explanation of his position: "I should be no use in a War Cabinet. I should only hamper you. If we have to fight, we must fight with single-hearted conviction. There is no place for me in such affairs."[6]

The prime minister was more like Morley than he would have wanted to admit. His decision to vote for war served only to illustrate how wise his colleague was to resign, and how wrong he was to stay. For, once the fighting started, Asquith began to grow increasingly disengaged from it, and he would spend hours each day writing to young Venetia Stanley for comfort and diversion. Though she was thirty-five years his junior, he had developed a passion for her that grew ever stronger in the early months of the war. A typical letter to her in this period ended with the words "Most dear—never more dear—I love you with heart & soul."

He knew little of war, and what he knew came mostly from books. He was never going to embarrass himself by appearing happy or violent at a Cabinet meeting, but he was also not going to fight the war with conviction and purpose—not to mention daring. In the hectic and crucial first weeks of the fighting, the prime minister was often absorbed in his old routine of attending dinner parties, giving speeches, and taking naps after drinking too much. One day in September, while Lord Kitchener—the new head of the War Office—and Churchill were immersed in battle plans, Asquith was in a deep sleep, lost in a dream about Venetia and the pleasures of other worlds. "After I had slept a little," he wrote her, "or rather dreamt over your dear letter in a kind of Kubla Khan mood, I again confronted stern realities in the shape of Kitchener & Winston—the latter just returned from his flying & secret visit to [Admiral] Jellicoe somewhere in the North of Scotland."[7]

Asquith was so besotted with Venetia that he routinely divulged top-secret war plans to her in his letters. "This is very secret," he would write, and then give the details of some confidential mission or troop movement, jeopardizing lives by his indiscretion. Indeed, his many letters to her are filled with passages that discuss the war as if it happened to be a mildly diverting parlor game, but one being reported to him secondhand like the moves in a long-distance chess game.

He had no business fighting a war. Worried that the Royal Navy wasn't getting into enough fights on the high seas, he issued a less than inspiring war command that made him sound more like an elderly aunt bossing a nephew than a leader directing vast armies: "As I told Winston last night . . . it is time that he bagged something, & broke some crockery."[8]

But if the prime minister couldn't lead, who could? Of course, it didn't take Winston long to decide that he would have to step in and fill the void. He had everything that his Cabinet colleagues lacked for war—youthful energy, battlefield experience, and the will to win. And some of them conceded that these were indeed his advantages, at least early on. In the opening months of the war when he seemed to be everywhere at once—meeting with an admiral here, discussing strategy with a general there—Lord Haldane wrote him, "Asquith said to me this afternoon that you were the equivalent of a large force in the field & this is true."[9]

Churchill took this praise to heart. He shocked the military, and most of the nation, when he abruptly decided to throw himself into combat as a field commander in all but name. As First Lord of the Admiralty, he wasn't supposed to be on the bridge of a battleship under fire, much less commanding troops on the front lines. But on October 3, when he went to the Belgian port of Antwerp to observe the fierce fighting there, he ended up staying three days and leading the beleaguered forces as if he had suddenly been transformed into a general. He was under continuous and heavy fire, and the sheer violence of it—as well as the drama of a last stand against an overwhelming German force—awakened every fighting instinct in his body. Serving alongside Belgian troops as well as Royal Marines and units of the Royal Naval Division—which he had established in August—Churchill was determined to hold the city until reinforcements could arrive.

He was so caught up in the mad energy of the moment that he seemed to forget everything else but the battle. An Italian war correspondent recalled seeing him moving among the troops dressed in a cloak and yachting cap and seemingly oblivious to the heavy shrapnel falling on all sides. Lacking sleep but with his mind spinning relentlessly, he came up with all kinds of ideas for defending the city—some good and some bad. The worst came when he wired Asquith requesting that he be allowed to resign as First Lord and be given "full powers of a commander of a detached force in the field." In the heat of battle he lost all sense of priorities, thinking that holding Antwerp was everything. But the only priority that mattered to him at that second was winning.

He was lucky to get out alive when a senior officer arrived to take command, enabling him to make his way back to London. The reaction to this adventure among his colleagues in the Cabinet ranged from disbelief to soaring admiration. Sir Edward Grey was bursting with pride. He wrote to Clemmie, "I feel a glow imparted by the thought that I am sitting next a Hero. I can't tell you how much I admire his courage & gallant spirit & genius for war."[10]

Though Antwerp was later taken by the Germans, the battle delayed their advance toward the French coast, and they were prevented from seizing the Channel Ports. All the same, Antwerp's fall soon took away the "glow" of Winston's heroics, leaving him a figure of fun in some eyes. His exuberance in battle had misled him into thinking he alone could save the city, and his critics were quick to condemn him for leaving his work at the Admiralty to wage a hopeless fight in a Belgian port. H. A. Gwynne, the editor of the *Morning Post*, led an effort to hold Churchill solely responsible for what the paper called the "Antwerp blunder." Gwynne and others were convinced that the First Lord had rushed into the battle and had placed British troops in danger to serve his own personal ambition for glory.

"The whole adventure," Gwynne wrote, was "a Churchill affair and does not seem to have been considered or thought over, or consented to, by the Cabinet." The outraged editor sent letters to the prime minister and other Cabinet members demanding Winston's dismissal. To the proprietor of his paper, he wrote of the First Lord, "Imagine our Fleet being commanded by a man of this caliber. A man who gets an idea into his head and without waiting to consider or think . . . involves us in a quite new expedition; and this at a time when every man we have to spare is wanted at the front." [11]

In fact, Churchill had gone to Antwerp after consulting closely with Kitchener and Grey, both of whom had agreed that it was vital to keep the Germans from entering the city for as long as possible. Churchill's job had been to persuade the Belgians to keep up the fight, and in support of his mission, Kitchener had pledged to supply up to fifty thousand troops. When Asquith learned of the plan, he backed it entirely. "The intrepid Winston set off at midnight & ought to have reached Antwerp by about 9 this morning," the prime minister had told Venetia on October 3. "If he is able to do himself justice in a foreign tongue, the Belges will have listened to a discourse the like of which they have never heard before. I cannot but think that he will stiffen them up to the sticking point."

For a while Churchill's presence in the city was instrumental in maintaining the Belgian resistance to the Germans. "Winston succeeded in bucking up the Belges, who gave up their panicky idea of retreating," wrote Asquith on October 5. But by the time Churchill left Antwerp on the sixth, the resolve of the exhausted Belgian army was already crumbling, and the city fell four days later. Asquith didn't find any fault with

Winston's efforts, placing the blame on the Belgian forces, and on the French for failing to provide more support.[12]

In later years Churchill defended his actions at Antwerp but admitted that "had I been ten years older, I should have hesitated long before accepting so unpromising a task."[13]

History is full of leaders who send others to die without facing the fire themselves, yet some of Winston's fiercest critics singled him out for ridicule for doing the opposite. At the time of the battle for Antwerp, however, those Cabinet ministers who were fully aware of the facts felt nothing but admiration for Churchill's courage and resourcefulness. "He is a wonderful creature," Asquith said of him on October 7, "with a curious dash of schoolboy simplicity . . . and what someone said of genius—'a zigzag streak of lightning in the brain.'"[14]

The Royal Navy that Churchill helped to build in his thirties suffered its share of setbacks, but it held its own against the German naval threat and would emerge triumphant at the end of the First World War. In many ways the early months of the war posed the greatest danger. A weak navy might have been caught off guard and marginalized early on; the landings of the British Expeditionary Force in France might have come under attack, and the troops pushed back into the sea. But by the end of 1914 the risk of sudden and catastrophic knockout blows had been eased by the barbed-wire standoff on the Western Front.

Afraid of risks, many of the generals and politicians running the war were content to let the stalemate play out, and to hope that by some stroke of luck, or perhaps the occasional sacrifice of thousands in an attack of brute force, they would create a breakthrough. Churchill hated this kind of grinding warfare and wanted to do something innovative in its place. He was looking for a dramatic way to shift the battle lines and deliver decisive blows instead of pinpricks. Unimpressed with many of the leaders at the top, he decided to seek help from someone whose unconventional views he admired—Jacky Fisher.

Over the initial objections of the king, who thought he was too old and too erratic, Admiral Fisher returned to active service at Churchill's invitation in late October 1914. Bringing him back to the Admiralty would turn out to be Winston's worst decision of the war. The king's fears were justified. Age was starting to catch up with Fisher, who was nearly seventy-four, and was as difficult as ever—if not more so. By the beginning of 1915 some of his subordinates were beginning to wonder what he could possibly contribute to the war effort.

"In reality he does nothing," Captain Herbert Richmond wrote of Fisher in January 1915. "He goes home and sleeps in the afternoon. He is old and worn-out and nervous. It is ill to have the destinies of an empire in the hands of a failing old man, anxious for popularity, afraid of any local mishap which may be put down to his dispositions. It is sad."[15]

Churchill may have thought he needed Fisher's advice, but it would take him longer than Captain Richmond to realize that the old admiral was "worn-out." Meanwhile, Churchill thought that he had stumbled on a great plan for changing Britain's fortunes in the war. As was so often the case, Asquith felt it necessary to share the latest top-secret developments with Venetia. "His volatile mind," Asquith said of Winston on December 5, 1914, "is at present set on Turkey & Bulgaria, & he wants to organize a heroic adventure against Gallipoli and the Dardanelles."[16]

At first, Asquith was firmly set against the idea. The narrow Turkish strait of the Dardanelles was a long way from the Western Front. There were advantages to subduing Turkey (Germany's ally) and then enabling Russia (Britain's ally) to move freely through the Dardanelles and into the Mediterranean. It was the kind of grand diversion that was meant to force Germany to shift its attention away from the Western Front. But what if it didn't do much to improve Russia's fortunes, or to threaten Germany? Though the strait was only thirty-eight miles long, the Turks could be expected to defend every mile with all the force they could muster. They were well aware that if an enemy fleet ever managed to get through, it could quickly reach Constantinople and attack the city at will.

Churchill himself soon had second thoughts. At the end of December he suggested another target closer to home—the little German island of Borkum, in the North Sea, just off the coast of the mainland. A surprise invasion of it was sure to shake things up, he told Asquith. "Its retention by us would be intolerable to the enemy, and would in all probability bring about the sea battle." Something new had to be tried, he emphasized. "Are there not other alternatives than sending our armies to chew barbed wire in Flanders?"[17]

For the next couple of weeks Winston promoted the Borkum attack, while Jacky Fisher and Lord Kitchener took up the Dardanelles idea. On January 12, Fisher wrote a friend that a combined land and sea assault on the strait and the Gallipoli peninsula could work so well—especially with a large commitment of troops—that "we could count on an easy and quick arrival at Constantinople." But Winston decided to be more cautious and suggested to Fisher that they give up the Dardanelles idea. It didn't matter whether it would be easier to fight the Turks than the Germans, he said. "Germany is the foe," he wrote, "& it is bad war to seek cheaper victories & easier antagonists."[18]

Churchill would have done well to stick to that view, but over the next few days Fisher won him over to the Dardanelles plan when he suggested that the brand-new battleship HMS *Queen Elizabeth* could take part in the assault. She was armed with the 15-inch guns that Winston was so proud of, and he liked the idea that these guns could be tested at long range on the Turkish forts defending the strait. It made all the difference to him because he doubted that the Turks would stand fast after witnessing the damage that a powerful barrage from the Royal Navy's mightiest warship could inflict on their forts. In this he was influenced by his experience in Antwerp, where the constant fire from German artillery had been so effective in breaking the will of the Belgian defenders.

In a secret memo prepared for the Grand Duke Nicholas of Russia, Churchill wrote that the plan would involve "the systematic & deliberate reduction of the forts by the long range fire of the 15" guns of the Queen Elizabeth, followed up by direct attacks by old battleships. It is expected that the operation will take 3 or 4 weeks, & it is hoped that it may be similar in character to the methods by which the Germans destroyed . . . the forts of the outer line at Antwerp."[19]

On January 13 Winston gave his Cabinet colleagues an explanation of how the navy could take out the forts "one by one" and establish control over the strait. Lloyd George was the first to respond, saying he "liked the plan." Kitchener said "it was worth trying." Then Asquith gave his approval, and soon a fleet of more than a dozen battleships—most of them older vessels—were being readied for the assault.

Almost immediately Fisher began to reconsider the plan, worried that it might fail. But others in the government began to grow more enthusiastic about its chances for success. Near the end of January, Edward Grey thought that "the Turks would be paralyzed with fear when they heard that the forts were being destroyed one by one." In late February the prime minister was ready to take "a lot of risks," as he told Venetia, to make the plan work. "I am strongly of the opinion," he wrote her, "that the chance of forcing the Dardanelles, & occupying Constantinople, & cutting Turkey in half, and arousing on our side the whole Balkan peninsula, presents such a unique opportunity that we ought to hazard a lot elsewhere rather than forgo it."[20]

He was wrong. It was a disaster from start to finish. The *Queen Elizabeth*'s guns performed well in February, but when the older battleships moved into the strait on March 18 to attack additional forts they ran into mines, and three were lost in a matter of a few hours. As the situation went from bad to worse in the next few months, mistake after mistake was made, by both the navy and especially the army, which tried to clear Gallipoli of Turkish troops who proved to be far more disciplined and determined than the British had been willing to believe.

Beginning on April 25, Australian and New Zealand troops joined a large French and British force to fight the Turks, and though both sides showed extraordinary bravery, they found themselves bogged down in the same kind of standoff that prevailed on the Western Front. Tens of thousands died as the fighting dragged through the rest of the year. The rugged terrain, harsh weather, and military incompetence turned Asquith's "unique opportunity" into one long misadventure that did nothing to change the course of the war.

The blame for this tragic campaign was widely shared, but it was Churchill who was made to pay the price of failure. The young titan had pushed his luck too far. So, too, had others, but this setback was so big that a suitably big scapegoat was needed, and Winston was it. As soon as things began to go wrong, little time was wasted in pointing the finger of blame in his direction. It was in May 1915 that his colleagues and rivals began turning on him.

As prime minister, Asquith had been the one to decide that the risk was worth taking. It was his responsibility to accept the consequences of failure. But he evaded it, as did Kitchener, who mishandled the Gallipoli campaign. As for Jacky Fisher, he would later pretend that he had been opposed to the Dardanelles plan all along. Because of his youth and his reputation for taking risks, Winston made a more convincing military bungler to a public unaware of the deliberations leading up to the disaster. It was easier to assume that he was at fault rather than such old hands as Asquith, Kitchener, and Fisher.

Jacky was the first to turn on him. The admiral lost his nerve after the battleship HMS *Goliath* was torpedoed by the Turks on May 13, with the loss of five hundred men. The old admiral didn't want merely to argue for a change of strategy or a complete withdrawal. He wanted to disassociate himself from the whole affair. On May 15 he sent Winston and Asquith his letter of resignation. Winston begged him to return, but he refused, writing melodramatically, "You will remain. I SHALL GO."

Then Fisher turned nasty and set out to destroy Winston by feeding incendiary comments to his enemies. "HE'S A REAL DANGER!" Fisher said of Churchill in a letter to the Tory leader Andrew Bonar Law. "W.C. MUST go at all costs! AT ONCE." He warned that "a great national disaster was in the making" because of the failure in the eastern Mediterranean, and he laid all the blame at Winston's feet, saying, "I refuse to have anything to do with him."[21]

Churchill could have seen this coming. Everything that he had worked so hard for was jeopardized by the trust he had placed in the crusty old admiral, and by his failure to see the dangers lurking in a poorly conceived expedition far from the main center of action. But it was too late. He had made a dire mistake in war, and the consequence of such a mistake was usually fatal on the battlefield. In his case it meant disgrace, which was a kind of death to him, proud as he was.

With astounding suddenness, his meteoric rise flamed out. The crash turned everything upside down. Under pressure for the government's failures, Asquith was ready to do anything to save his premiership. His Conservative foes knew he was vulnerable, and they knew that Fisher's resignation had exposed the flaws in the wartime government. "Suddenly the Ministerial edifice has crumbled," wrote Lord Curzon on May 18, "kicked over by old Jack Fisher."[22]

Lloyd George didn't see any sentimental reason for helping Winston. Sacrificing him meant that Asquith and Lloyd George could hold on to power. "Churchill will have to go," the chancellor told his mistress on May 15. "He will be a ruined man." As for his own responsibility in the crisis, Lloyd George insisted that it was only "very unwillingly" that the Cabinet had given its "consent to a bombardment of the Dardanelles forts."

King George welcomed the change. He had grown weary of Churchill the upstart. "The Prime Minister is going to have a National Govt.," the king remarked; "only by that means can we get rid of Churchill from [the] Admiralty."

Winston tried to plead with Asquith not to replace him, but it was all in vain. "I am finished," he lamented to George Riddell on May 20. "Finished in all I care for—the waging of war, the defeat of the Germans." By this point he didn't expect any help from the prime minister, whom he called "[t]erribly weak—supinely weak. His weakness will be the death of him." [23]

Even Violet couldn't help Churchill this time. She was caught between wanting to serve her friend's best interests and wanting to see her father survive this crisis. She chose to stand by her father and to make excuses for his decisions. There was a tearful discussion between Violet and Winston in his office on the nineteenth. "I think your father might perhaps have stuck to me," he told her as he sat looking at the floor, enveloped in gloom. "I felt heart-broken for him," she confessed in her diary, but there was little she could do except urge her father to find another suitable position for him. Asquith promised her that he would do his best, but in the end he was, as Churchill now knew, too weak to stand up for anyone but himself. [24]

In the last week of May, the prime minister entered into a wartime coalition with the Tories, who had no use for Winston and wanted him out of the Cabinet. The reversal of fortunes couldn't have been more shocking. Balfour was brought back from obscurity to take over the Admiralty, and two of Churchill's worst enemies—the Unionists Edward Carson and Bonar Law—were given positions in the government. Winston was humiliated not only by the loss of his job as First Lord, but also by the offer of nothing better than a minor position as chancellor of the duchy of Lancaster. Reluctantly, he took it until he could make sense of what had happened and decide how to deal with it.

But the change was hard to justify. A year earlier he had been at the forefront of the preparations for war, when Carson and Bonar Law had been trying to start one. What was even more incomprehensible, Carson—the man who had threatened to break every law if necessary to defend Ulster—was now the attorney general of Great Britain. For good reason, Winston's enemies were jubilant. He had seemed untouchable, and now they were having their revenge for all his moments of defiance and impudence. Fisher's comments to Bonar Law were echoed in the Tory press. "The truth is that Winston Churchill is a danger to this country," said H. A. Gwynne's *Morning Post*.

The war was not even a year old—and still had three years to go—but with stunning speed Churchill had become one of its early political casualties. Like Lord Byron, young Winston met tragedy in a fight against the Turks.

Perhaps the people who were happiest over Churchill's fall were the Germans. Their newspapers were full of taunting remarks and jokes. It was said in jest that Germany had lost one of her "most valuable allies." Some of his well-known phrases were now used against him. Gloating, one paper remarked, "The coiner of the phrase 'Germany's deluxe fleet' seems himself to have become an expensive luxury for his country." But Churchill was warned not to enter the battlefield and risk capture. "If he falls into German hands we mustn't take his sword of honor, for he has broken it."[25]

He felt betrayed not only by Fisher, but by his Cabinet colleagues who had supported the Dardanelles mission and then had pretended that it wasn't their problem. Lloyd George's failure to support him was especially discouraging, though he pretended to be sympathetic to Winston's plight. Speaking of Churchill's loss of the Admiralty, he said, "The Unionists would not, and could not in the circumstances, have assented to his retention in that office. But it was quite unnecessary in order to propitiate them to fling him from the masthead whence he had been directing the fire, down to the lower deck to polish the brass." Asquith's excuse for his shoddy treatment of his close associate was that, given the political hostility to Churchill, he really couldn't have kept him at the Admiralty. Inasmuch as Asquith was now something of a Tory hostage, that was true.[26]

* * *

For a long time Winston was in a state of shock. He wandered around like a man half alive. "The wound bleeds but does not smart," he later said of his feelings at this time. Now forty, he suddenly looked older than his years. He walked with a more pronounced stoop, and his eyes grew dull. A war correspondent visiting London was shocked when he saw Winston at a dinner party, and wrote, "I am much surprised at the change in Winston Churchill. He looks years older, his face is pale, he seems very depressed, and to feel keenly his retirement from the Admiralty."[27]

It was not simply his misfortune that weighed on him. It was the abrupt loss of purpose. He was like a complex piece of machinery that had been roaring away for ages and was suddenly cut back to a slow spin. "I'm afraid Winston is very sad at having nothing to do," said Jennie. "When you have had your hand at the helm for four years it seems stagnation to take a back place and for why?" Moreover, because he still held a minor place in the government, he felt tortured by the experience of watching from the sidelines while others blundered ahead with the doomed land battles in the east and west.

"I had to watch the casting away of great opportunities," he would recall, "and the feeble execution of plans which I had launched, and in which I heartily believed. One dwelt in a sort of cataleptic trance, unable to intervene, yet bound by the result."

When asked in her old age what had been the greatest strain of her husband's life, Clemmie replied without hesitation, "The Dardanelles. I thought it would break his heart."[28]

He could have taken encouragement from the fact that he was still alive, with a devoted wife and now three small children to love and care for. Sarah Churchill—with a good head of fiery red hair—had been born in October 1914 and was beautiful. And Clemmie was so fiercely loyal that she seized every opportunity to defend his reputation. She even wrote a long letter detailing the reasons why he deserved a second chance and sent it to the prime minister. Understanding Winston as well as she did, she told Asquith that her husband had three invaluable qualities that the government couldn't afford to waste—"the power, the imagination, the deadliness to fight Germany." Relieved to have his scapegoat, the prime minister was unmoved by her letter, dismissing it as "the letter of a maniac."[29]

Much as Winston loved his family, he was still his old impatient self and wanted to be useful in a larger sphere of action. In wartime there was a simple cure for a restless man with nothing to do. He wanted to fight, but didn't relish the kind of fighting that trench warfare had become. He wanted a command of some kind and was willing to go almost anywhere and do almost anything to take charge of some promising war effort. But Asquith refused to give him anything of significance. For about five months he was more or less idle, waiting for opportunities that never came. As a way of simply keeping himself occupied in this long lull, he suddenly developed an interest in the art of painting. With a little help from a family friend, he began painting basic portraits and landscapes in oil, and he discovered that he had a talent for it.

Churchill found the work so absorbing that he could forget his troubles at least for a while. Like his passion for building sand castles, painting gave him a way to exercise his imagination in a form that he could control and shape on his own. No Jacky Fisher or Lloyd George could intrude and alter his view of a line of trees, a garden, or a country lane. He saw what he wanted to see and captured it on canvas in his own fashion. He would never have the luxury in public life of such complete authority. Painting became his lifelong passion. As he would later say of the activity, "Every day and all day is provided with its expedition and its occupation—cheap, attainable, innocent, absorbing, recuperative."[30]

But in his darkest moments of 1915 even the pleasures of painting would sometimes fail to lift his spirits. Wilfrid Scawen Blunt visited him in August and was surprised to find him in a deep despair. He thought that the only thing keeping Winston sane was the love of Clemmie. At one point as Blunt was watching him struggle to complete a painting, Winston suddenly turned to him with a sad expression and held up his fingers. "There is more blood than paint upon these hands," he said. "All those thousands of men killed. We thought it would be a little job, and so it might have been if it had been begun in the right way." And then his voice trailed off.[31]

As the summer ended, and the landscapes he was painting turned somber and gray, he knew that he needed to make a change. He made up his mind to start his career all over again at forty. He still held his commission in the Queen's Own Oxfordshire Hussars. He would go out to the front as an ordinary major if that was the best position he could find. People would laugh at the thought of the once grand First Lord, with his yacht, now reduced to a major standing in a muddy trench waiting to be killed. But people had been laughing at him all along, and there was nothing he could do about that.

On November 11, 1915, he resigned from his do-nothing job in the government, explaining in a letter to Asquith that he did not "feel able in times like these to remain in well-paid inactivity."

His resignation was announced in the press, along with the news that he was going to fight in France. Before he left, he received a letter from Muriel Wilson. It was a simple but heartfelt farewell. It ended with the words "I just wanted to tell you how much I admired you for your courage."[32]

In a war that left so many of its combatants maimed or traumatized for life, Churchill was lucky to escape with merely a wounded career. But he couldn't be sure at the time that the wound would ever heal and allow him to resume his rise to the top. Because he had been so sure of himself, and had risen so quickly, he was so unprepared for his precipitous fall that few options were left open to him. In peacetime he might have appealed to the country for support, arguing his case in speeches and newspaper articles. But in wartime that kind of personal campaign was unseemly. He was not only out of power, but was effectively silenced—at least for the time being.

It was a surprising turn in a life that had always seemed rich in possibilities. Until the war came along, he had been able to soar from one triumph to the next with a reasonable expectation that something would always catch his fall. As a peacetime hero, he had been ready to suffer many political deaths, knowing that he would fight again. But now the war had left the fallen hero with no place to turn but the very real battlefields of France, where failure was usually fatal. Like a Byronic figure in a novel that he might have written about his own political adventures, he was suddenly confronted with the possibility that he had reached the last chapter, and must now fight or die.

He couldn't take any comfort from the story of his father's life, for Lord Randolph had never managed to revive his own career after falling from power in his late thirties. Winston must have been haunted by that fact, and have wondered whether he was simply repeating a family tragedy. His father lingered too long and suffered a slow death. Winston would take his chances in the trenches.

In the middle of November there was a small party to say good-bye to Winston. Clemmie did her best to hold back her tears, Eddie Marsh wept openly, and Jennie was sad but also angry that her "brilliant son" was "being relegated to the trenches." Perhaps to Winston's surprise, Margot and Violet came. Henry didn't. There was food and drink; Winston tried on his uniform and promised to write.[33]

His star had grown so dim that he didn't think his reputation could suffer much more. From this point, it seemed that he could only rise, if he survived. Ever the gambler, he was willing to throw the dice once more and risk everything for another chance to restore his fortunes. He arranged for a letter to be given to Clemmie "in the event of my death." It had been written earlier in the summer and concerned some insurance details and other financial information, but it closed with a brief attempt to affirm what he really valued in his life, now that the bright lights and storms of his first forty years were behind him. It was supposed to be the voice of a ghost speaking to Clemmie in case his story had reached its end without the chance to add one more chapter.

"Do not grieve for me too much," said the letter. "I am a spirit confident of my rights. Death is only an incident, & not the most important which happens to us in this state of being. On the whole, especially since I met you my darling one I have been happy, & you have taught me how noble a woman's heart can be. If there is anywhere else I shall be on the look out for you. Meanwhile look forward, feel free, rejoice in Life, cherish the children, guard my memory. God bless you. Good bye. W."[34]

Epilogue

T hough Churchill survived his time in the trenches and slowly succeeded in rebuilding his career, he lost something in 1915 that he never regained. At forty, youth begins to slip away from most people, but what Winston lost was not merely a matter of looks or energy. It was a spirit that had once seemed so vital and inexhaustible, a lively spark that had served him well from crisis to crisis. But it flickered and went out in 1915 and Churchill was never the same.

He remained a romantic at heart, a great patriot, and a courageous fighter, and he persevered in politics until his moment in the sun came again in 1940. But by that time he was a harder, much less exuberant character, whose boyish innocence and earnestness survived only in the occasional mischievous smile and thoughtful frown. He had learned the tough lessons of a long life lived at a high level—that even the best plans go awry, that even the best friends prove unreliable, and that even the best intentions may be misunderstood. It was better for the world that he had known failure and suffered moments of self-doubt, but the magical, sparkling qualities of vision and leadership that so many of his Edwardian contemporaries had found in him were mostly muted or absent after the First World War.

What took the place of this glamorous charm was the cumulative force of a character that had been tested and strengthened over time. Balfour, Chamberlain, Lloyd George, and Asquith had taught young Churchill invaluable lessons. Often, a politician who fights on equal terms with such giants is already in his prime, and will be too old to apply the lessons of his experience in a second career like that which Churchill enjoyed as prime minister in the 1940s. But having matched wits with the best of the Edwardian statesmen, he brought to his position of mature leadership a level of skill and understanding that few politicians could rival. And there was still enough drive left in him to keep him from becoming a fossilized figure like Lloyd George, whose views were largely irrelevant in the days of Winston's premiership.

For twenty-five years after the end of his first rise to power, Churchill was frustrated to sit and watch as others reached the top while he seemed to languish in lesser positions or with no ministerial authority at all. He was forced to learn patience, and to ponder the meaning of his early experiences by writing about them in various volumes, including *My Early Life* and his works on the history of the First World War. One by one, the old giants faded as he waited. Asquith lost power in 1916 and was replaced by Lloyd George, who used all his wiles to remain prime minister for almost six years. Asquith died in 1928, and Lloyd George lived until 1945. Balfour died in 1930.

Winston the Liberal politician died in the mid-1920s and a Conservative Winston was reborn to take his place. Of course, he was attacked for changing his stripes once again, but the combined efforts of Lloyd George and Asquith had reduced the Liberals to a minor party with little future. There were good reasons to think that Churchill was fooling himself to believe that he could heal the deep wounds created during his Liberal battles against the Tories, but he refused to accept that the promise of his early career was dead and gone. He continued to guard that legacy even when few believed it was worth guarding. His treasure was his past, and he always came back to it, cherishing it on the hope that others would one day see its value.

His old enemy Edward Carson seemed to understand that there was something in Churchill's character that simply wouldn't allow him to give up. At a dinner not long after Winston was dismissed as First Lord of the Admiralty, a journalist asked Carson, "What is the trouble with Churchill?"

The unsentimental Carson thought for a second and shot back a perceptive reply that would have made Winston smile:

"He is a dangerous optimist."[1]

ACKNOWLEDGMENTS

I doubt whether this book would have been written if I had not had the good fortune to join forces with two literary dynamos—my agent, Molly Friedrich, and my editor, Priscilla Painton. Both gave me the enthusiastic support and encouragement that were crucial to transforming an idea into a finished work. Molly is a passionate champion of her authors, and Priscilla is the kind of editor every writer hopes to find—knowledgeable, insightful, and scrupulous.

For their expert assistance and kind attention, I also want to thank Lucy Carson and Molly Schulman of the Friedrich Agency. At Simon & Schuster I am grateful for the hard work and thoughtful advice of Michael Szczerban, Tom Pitoniak, and Mike Jones.

In Britain, my good friend Adrian Clark helped enormously to ease my research burdens, generously tracking down information in various archives. I am immensely grateful for his tireless efforts.

At the Bodleian Library, University of Oxford, Colin Harris was especially helpful in introducing me to the remarkable archives housed in the Department of Special Collections, where he serves as Supervisor of the Reading Rooms. I very much appreciate his useful suggestions, and I was encouraged by his eagerness to answer my questions.

Among those at my university who helped, I am happy to thank the President of Indiana State, Dan Bradley; the dean of the library, Alberta Davis Comer; the chair of my department, Robert Perrin; and the following colleagues: Cheryl L. Blevens, Keith Byerman, Tom Derrick, Mary Ann Duncan, Kathy Edwards, Kit Kincade, and Holli Moseman.

For support of various kinds, I am grateful to Joe and Nancy Fisher, Lee and Maria McKinley, Wes and Mary Burch Ratliff, John Seavey, and June Shelden.

I treasure the love of my daughters, Sarah and Vanessa, and would never have made any progress worth mentioning without the love of my wife, Sue.

ILLUSTRATION CREDITS

Author photograph: 16

Author's collection: 20

Bain News service, personal collection: 18

Harold Begbie, *Master Workers* (1905): 24

Bibliothéque nationale de France: 25

The Bystander (1906): 9

The Bystander (1908): 14, 15

Violet Bonham Carter, *Lantern Slides* (1996): 11

Corbis: 27

Country Life (1904), 4

Library of Congress: 1, 5, 6, 8, 10, 12, 17

The Illustrated London News (1908): 19

Ernest William Loxley Mainprice, Fleet Paymaster, Royal Navy, died May 31, 1916: 22

Menpes, *War Impressions* (1901): 3

Painting by Sydney Prior Hall, 1895: 7

Photographer unknown: 13

Punch: 21

A. McCullum Scott, *Winston Spencer Churchill* (1905): 2

The Times Book of the Navy (1914): 23

NOTES

Abbreviations

CHAR   Chartwell Papers, Churchill Archives Centre, Churchill College, Cambridge. Microfilm edition, Gale/Cengage Learning, 2001–2005.

CS   *Winston S. Churchill: His Complete Speeches, 1897–1963.* 8 vols. Ed. Robert Rhodes James. New York: Chelsea House, 1974.

CV   Churchill, Randolph, and Martin Gilbert. *Winston S. Churchill: Companion Volume.* 5 vols. Boston: Houghton Mifflin, 1966–79.

NYT   *New York Times*

WSC   Winston S. Churchill

Prelude: The Prime Minister

1. WSC to Randolph Churchill, June 8, 1941 (*The Churchill War Papers: The Ever Widening War, 1941*, 766). For background on the attacks of May 10–11, see "Air-Raid Deaths and Damage," House of Lords, May 13, 1941, *Hansard;* Robert P. Post, "London Is Hard Hit," *NYT*, May 12, 1941; "British Commons Will Meet on Time," *NYT*, May 13, 1941; Fell, *The Houses of Parliament*, 34; "Nazis Wreck Great Monuments of English Culture," *Life*, June 2, 1941; Colville, *The Fringes of Power*, 385–86; WSC, *The Second World War: The Grand Alliance*, 46–47.
2. Moran, *Diaries*, 131.
3. "War Situation," House of Commons, May 7, 1941, *Hansard;* Eden, *Portrait of Churchill*, 64. "We shape our buildings and afterwards our buildings shape us," said WSC when he made his formal request that "the late Chamber" be "restored in all essentials to its old form, convenience and dignity" ("House of Commons Rebuilding," Oct. 28, 1943, *Hansard*). The restoration was completed in 1950.
4. WSC to Pamela [Plowden] Lytton, Oct. 20, 1950 (Private Collection).

Introduction: The Young Titan

1. WSC, Philomathic Society, Liverpool, Nov. 21, 1901, *CS*, 110; "Sketches in Parliament," *Black & White*, June 29, 1907; "Winston Churchill in the Commons," *American Monthly Review of Reviews*, May 1905; Hassall, *A Biography of Edward Marsh*, 565.

2. Aneurin Bevan, "War Aims Begin at Home," *Tribune*, Oct. 4, 1940; WSC, *Marlborough*, 1:15 and 493; *Churchill by Himself*, 339.

3. For a sampling of WSC's fondness for Byron's verse, see Sarah Churchill's recollections in *A Thread in the Tapestry*, 78; Sandys, *Chasing Churchill*, 11; Colville, *The Fringes of Power*, 282; Moran, *Diaries*, 324; WSC, *The Second World War: The Grand Alliance*, 605, and *The Story of the Malakand Field Force*, 234. Also, see "His Majesty's Government," House of Commons, May 13, 1940, *Hansard*, for "blood, toil, tears and sweat." For WSC's membership in the Byron Society, see Trueblood, *Lord Byron*, 10. Byron's "a fever at the core" is from *Childe Harold's Pilgrimage*, as is the phrase "united nations." WSC's 1906 purchase of Byron's *Works* is recorded in "Account from James Roche, Bookseller, London, Mar. 12, 1906" (CHAR 1/63/22). In British history two prime ministers have written Byronic novels—WSC and Disraeli, whose *Venetia* (1837) features a character closely based on Byron himself.

4. WSC, "Riches of English Literature," Nov. 2, 1949, *CS*, 7883; "Mr. Winston Churchill and Democracy," *Westminster Review*, Jan. 1906.

5. "Lord Randolph Churchill," *Saturday Review*, Jan. 26, 1895. Frank Harris, the editor of the *Saturday Review* in 1895, discusses his authorship of the article and WSC's view of it in Harris, *Contemporary Portraits*, 90. For more on Harris's article see "Lord Randolph Churchill," *Review of Reviews*, March 1895, and chap. 9 of this biography.

6. Gardiner, *Prophets, Priests and Kings*, 104; and Bonham Carter, *Churchill*, 6.

7. In *Churchill: The Unruly Giant*, Rose argues that WSC was "going through the motions" in his "lackadaisical" attitude toward romance, 60. Manchester makes the extraordinary claim that, "outside his home," WSC didn't "genuinely" like women and "was never really comfortable in the company of women" (*The Last Lion: Visions of Glory*, 366–67). Brendon says that WSC revered women "from afar" and was "largely oblivious to the possibilities of intimate friendship" (*Winston Churchill*, 41–42). In *The Churchills*, Lovell states flatly, "With women [WSC] was inept" (200). For accounts of WSC's "maiden speech" at the Empire Theatre, see Davis, *Real Soldiers of Fortune*, 82–83, and WSC, *My Early Life*, 50–59. An extended discussion of the anti-vice campaign against the Empire Theatre can be found in Faulk, *Music Hall & Modernity*, which notes that a staunch defender of the theater confessed, "'Every sane man knew vice had been prominent in the Empire promenade'"(79).

8. The three women were Pamela Plowden, Ethel Barrymore, and Muriel Wilson. His intimate friend Violet Asquith said that he was such a "conspicuous figure" that he was "assailed and pursued by importunate hostesses" (Bonham Carter, *Churchill*, 113–14). Balsan, *The Glitter and the Gold*, 55.

9. Bonham Carter, *Churchill*, 107 and 173.

10. E. J. Moyle, "Witty Retorts of Politicians," *Chambers's Journal*, Nov. 17, 1900. The story of WSC's wordplay on Christopher Marlowe's line about "the face

that launched a thousand ships" exists in several versions, including Hassall, *A Biography of Edward Marsh*, 131, and Bibesco, *Sir Winston Churchill*, 109–10.

11.　"Assails Churchill As Public Danger," *NYT*, Apr. 27, 1915; "German Gibes at Churchill," *NYT*, Nov. 14, 1915.

I: A New World

1.　WSC to Pamela Plowden, Nov. 28 [1898], *CV* 1:2, 989; Cynthia Asquith, *Diaries*, 154. WSC to Pamela Plowden, July 23 [1898] and March 6, 1899 (Private Collection).

2.　WSC to Pamela Plowden, Nov. 18 [1899], *CV* 1:2, 1074. Pamela Plowden to Jennie Churchill, Dec. 22, 1899, *CV* 1:2, 1093. WSC to Jennie Churchill, Sept. 3, 1899, *CV* 1:2, 1045. WSC acknowledges the fiftieth anniversary of his proposal in WSC to Pamela [Plowden] Lytton, Oct. 20, 1950 (Private Collection); see also Colville's statement: "Churchill told me he proposed to [Pamela] in a punt when they were both staying at Warwick Castle. She said no" (*The Fringes of Power*, 591). The Countess of Warwick recalls the couple visiting her together in 1900 (*Life's Ebb and Flow*, 258).

3.　WSC to Jennie Churchill, Jan. 1, 1901, *CV* 1:2, 1224. For the promotion of WSC's Winnipeg lecture, see the *Manitoba Morning Free Press*, Jan. 21, 1901. Davis, *Real Soldiers*, 88–89; WSC to Pamela Plowden, Jan. 21, 1901 (Private Collection).

4.　J. P. Brabazon to Mrs. John Leslie, [? Oct. 1900], *CV* 1:2, 1209; Marsh, *A Number of People*, 154; Balsan, *The Glitter and the Gold*, 57.

5.　Moran, *Diaries*, 348.

6.　WSC to Pamela Plowden, March 6, 1899 (Private Collection).

7.　WSC to Jennie Churchill, Jan. 22, 1901, *CV* 1:2, 1231; Strachey, *Queen Victoria*, 423; Ponsonby, *Recollections of Three Reigns*, 128.

8.　WSC to Pamela Plowden, Jan. 21, 1901 (Private Collection).

9.　WSC, *My Early Life*, 362; "Had Thrills in It: Winston Spencer Churchill's Lecture at the Lyceum," *Minneapolis Journal*, Jan. 19, 1901.

10.　E. J. Moyle, "Witty Retorts of Politicians," *Chambers's Journal*, Nov. 17, 1900.

11.　Twain to William Dean Howells, Jan. 25, 1900, *Selected Letters*, 345. (Twain introduced WSC's lecture at the Waldorf-Astoria on Dec. 12, 1900.) WSC to Jennie Churchill, Jan. 1, 1901, *CV* 1:2, 1224; Ellsworth, *A Golden Age of Authors*, 252.

12.　"Great Dominion," *Globe and Mail* (Canada), May 5, 2005; James B. Pond's notes, Dec. 27 [1900], Russell Theatre, Ottawa (Special Collections, University of Delaware Library); "War Lecturer Goes on Strike," *Daily Mail and Empire* (Toronto), Dec. 29, 1900.

13.　WSC to J. B. Pond, Jan. 9, 1901 (Special Collections, University of Delaware Library); WSC to Jennie Churchill, Jan. 1, 1901, *CV* 1:2, 1224.

14.　"On a Very High Horse," *St. Paul Globe*, Jan. 22, 1901; "Explains It All Away," *St. Paul Globe*, Jan. 25, 1901. For a selection of TR's comments on young WSC, see *Theodore Roosevelt's History of the United States*, 296–97.

As the *NYT* reported on Sunday, Dec. 9, 1900, "On Monday Mr. Churchill will dine with Gov. Roosevelt at Albany." For "bully pulpit," see *Outlook*, Feb. 27, 1909. Jenkins, *Churchill*, 70.

15. "Great Dominion," *Globe and Mail* (Canada), May 5, 2005; WSC to Jennie Churchill, Jan. 22, 1901, *CV* 1:2, 1231.

16. "Winston Churchill on the War," *Manitoba Morning Free Press*, Jan. 22, 1901; WSC, London to Ladysmith, 189; WSC to Jennie Churchill, Jan. 22, 1901, *CV* 1:2, 1231.

17. WSC to Jennie Churchill, Jan. 22 and Jan. 1, 1901, *CV* 1:2, 1231 and 1225.

18. "Discipline in Army Brings Disasters: Winston Churchill Thinks Each Fighter Must Act for Himself," *NYT*, Dec. 9, 1900.

II: A Family Affair

1. Wells, *The New Machiavelli*, 10; WSC, *My Early Life*, 363.

2. Gardiner, *Prophets, Priests and Kings*, 27.

3. Ibid., 105; Lucy, *The Balfourian Parliament*, 64.

4. "The Scaffolding of Rhetoric," *CV* 1:2, 816–21; James, *Churchill*, 15; Smalley, *Anglo-American Memories*, 92.

5. Macdonagh, *The Book of Parliament*, 225; "Parliamentary Sketch," *Yorkshire Post*, Feb. 19, 1901.

6. "Address in Answer to His Majesty's Most Gracious Speech," House of Commons, Feb. 18, 1901, *Hansard*.

7. "Under the Clock," *Daily Telegraph*, and "Mr Churchill's Spellbinding," *Daily Express*, Feb. 19, 1901; "Parliament in Perspective," *Echo*, Feb. 19, 1901; Gilbert, *Churchill: A Life*, 135.

8. WSC to Marlborough, Sept. 29, 1898 (Library of Congress). For more on the skin graft for Richard Molyneux, see WSC, *My Early Life*, 197–98, and Moran, *Diaries*, 556. WSC to W. Murray Guthrie, Feb. 18, 1901, *CV* 2:1, 22.

9. Ward, *The Coryston Family*, 3–4; Cornwallis-West, *Reminiscences*, 120–21.

10. "The Ladies' Gallery: Resolution," House of Commons, March 30, 1885, *Hansard*.

11. Michael Macdonagh, "The New House of Commons," *Living Age*, May 14, 1910; Cornwallis-West, *Reminiscences*, 123.

12. "The Progress of the World," *American Monthly Review of Reviews*, May 1905.

13. WSC, *My Early Life*, 151–52; WSC to Jennie, Feb. 16, 1898, *CV* 1:2, 882.

14. Rossmore, *Things I Can Tell*, 107; Marie, Queen of Romania, *The Story of My Life*, 74; Asquith, *Autobiography*, 49–50; Anne Morton Lane, "A Special Interview with Mrs. George Cornwallis-West," *Good Housekeeping*, January 1902.

15. In his posthumously published *Memoirs of a Tattooist* (1958), the legendary George Burchett (1872–1953) recalls Tom Riley telling him that he gave Jennie the tattoo "when he was in America and she was visiting New York" (102). R. J. Stephen credits Riley for Jennie's tattoo in the *Harmsworth*

Magazine, December 1898. See also "Pen Portrait of a Lady," *NYT*, June 28, 1908, and "The Most Influential Anglo-Saxon Society Woman in the World," *Current Literature*, December 1908.

16. Cornwallis-West, *Reminiscences*, 60 and 381–82.
17. Wilde, *Complete Letters*, 566–67. The quotation is from Wilde's *A Woman of No Importance*.
18. WSC, *My Early Life*, 4; Moran, *Diaries*, 637.
19. Cornwallis-West, *Edwardian Hey-Days*, 102 and 119; "Lady Churchill Married," *Manitoba Morning Free Press*, July 30, 1900; Smyth, *What Happened Next*, 285 (quoted in Sebba, *American Jennie*, 230).
20. "Lady Churchill Now Mrs. West," *Chicago Tribune*, July 29, 1900; WSC to Jennie Churchill, Sept. 3, 1899, *CV* 1:2, 1045.
21. WSC to Jennie Churchill, March 26, 1901, *CV* 2:1, 49.

III: Born for Opposition

1. WSC, *Great Contemporaries*, 23; Trollope, *Autobiography*, 138–39; WSC, *The World Crisis: 1911–1914*, 20.
2. Paul Smith, "Cecil, Robert Arthur Talbot Gascoyne, Third Marquess of Salisbury," *Oxford Dictionary of National Biography*; Malcolm, *Vacant Thrones*, 8; Lindsay, *The Crawford Papers*, 65.
3. "An Unreal Conversation," *Punch*, Nov. 6, 1901; Cecil, *The Cecils of Hatfield House*, 236; Gilmour, *Curzon*, 128; WSC, *My Early Life*, 370.
4. Young, *Arthur James Balfour*, xii; Lucy, *The Balfourian Parliament*, 7.
5. D'Este, *Warlord*, 155; Kenneth Rose, "Cecil, Hugh Richard Heathcote Gascoyne, Baron Quickswood," *Oxford Dictionary of National Biography*; "Notes," *Saturday Review*, May 16, 1896; WSC, *Thoughts and Adventures*, 53; Gardiner, *Pillars of Society*, 71; Rose, *The Later Cecils*, 231.
6. WSC, *Lord Randolph Churchill*, 312; WSC to Lord Rosebery, June 10, 1902, *CV* 2:1, 146; Griffith-Boscawen, *Fourteen Years in Parliament*, 198; Balsan, *The Glitter and the Gold*, 114; Cecil, *The Cecils of Hatfield House*, 303.
7. Stuart, *Dear Duchess*, 58; Wolcott, *Heritage of Years*, 276; Kate Carew, "England's Man of the Hour," *New York World*, July 11, 1901. Lady Helen Stewart was the only daughter of the 6th Marquess of Londonderry.
8. The Duchess of Sutherland refers to her nickname and her desire to be an agitator in "Duchess Recalls Changes," *NYT*, July 7, 1912. WSC defended the duchess in "Peat-Reek and Harris Tweeds," *Times* (London), Sept. 9, 1901. Millicent's recollection of the letters from Cecil and WSC is quoted in Bibesco, *Sir Winston Churchill*, 111–12.
9. WSC to Lord Rosebery, July 24, 1901, and July 25, 1902, *CV* 2:1, 76 and 163; "The Hooligans" to Lord Rosebery, Aug. 6 [1901], *CV* 2:1, 77.
10. Begbie, *Master Workers*, 161; WSC, *Great Contemporaries*, 16–17.
11. WSC to Lord Rosebery, Sept. 4, 1901, and Lord Rosebery to WSC, Sept. 5, 1901, *CV* 2:1, 78–79; Bill Glauber, "Saving a Portrait of U.S. History," *Baltimore Sun*, March 2, 2001. Rosebery's picture of Napoleon was acquired in 1961 by the National Gallery of Art in Washington, D.C. The

Lansdowne portrait of Washington found a permanent home at the Smithsonian National Portrait Gallery.

12. Ian Malcolm, "In and Out of Parliament," *Living Age*, Jan. 15, 1910. Roy Jenkins's biography suggests that WSC wanted his group to be known as the "Hughligans," but provides no supporting evidence (*Churchill: A Biography*, 76–77).

13. WSC, *Thoughts and Adventures*, 53–56; Gilbert and Sullivan, *Iolanthe*.

14. "Marriage with a Deceased Wife's Sister's Bill," House of Commons, April 24, 1901, *Hansard*; Byron, *Don Juan*, Canto XV.

15. Wells, *The Wife of Sir Isaac Harman*, 292–93; WSC to Alfred Milner, March 17, 1901 (quoted in Addison, *Churchill on the Home Front*, 17); Pakenham, *The Boer War*, 109 and 572; "Service Horses and Mules," House of Commons, Dec. 13, 1900, *Hansard*. William Manchester and others have mistakenly attributed Healy's comment to WSC (*The Last Lion: Visions of Glory*, 348).

16. "Army Organisation," House of Commons, May 13, 1901, *Hansard*; William Harcourt to WSC, May 14, 1901, *CV* 2:1, 69.

17. Curzon, *Lady Curzon's India*, 93; "The Passing Hour," May 18, 1901, *Black & White*; "Policy and Armaments," *Westminster Budget*, May 17, 1901; WSC, *Lord Randolph Churchill*, 56.

18. "Mr. Punch's Sketchy Interviews," *Punch*, Sept. 10, 1902.

IV: The Duke's Smile

1. WSC to Jennie Churchill, March 13, 1901, *CV* 2:1, 46.

2. Curzon, *Lady Curzon's India*, 81, 93, and 106.

3. Davenport-Hines, *Ettie*, 4, 82, and 67; Beerbohm, *Seven Men*, 63; Fox, *Five Sisters*, 113.

4. Lee, *Jean, Lady Hamilton*, 46.

5. "Miss Plowden Engaged," *NYT*, Feb. 2, 1902; Davenport-Hines, *Ettie*, 123; Leslie, *Lady Randolph Churchill*, 299; George Cornwallis-West to Jennie Churchill, Aug. 24, 1899 (CHAR 28/35/62); Cynthia Asquith, *Diaries: 1915–1918*, 154. Lady Curzon was shocked to hear in August 1901 that Pamela—whom Lord Lytton was then courting—was romantically involved with Asquith. In a letter to Lord Curzon, she wrote that Asquith had "fallen in love with Pamela Plowden & gone to her room at night! . . . Can you conceive of anything more grotesque than Henry in the role of a lover of girls!" Curzon replied that he had never dreamed the politician was capable of making "mid-night visits to virginal chambers" (*Lady Curzon's India*, 123 and 128).

6. Mosley, *Julian Grenfell*, 175–76.

7. Wheeler, *Cherry*, 267; Holmes, *The Essential Holmes*, 86.

8. Davenport-Hines, *Ettie*, 65–66 and 161; "The Four-in-hand Club Meet in Hyde Park on Monday," *Black & White*, July 20, 1901; Hugh Cecil to WSC, Aug. 31, 1903, *CV* 2:1, 222.

9. Balsan, *The Glitter and the Gold*, 161; Davenport-Hines, *Ettie*, 93, 161–62, and 363.

10. WSC, *Marlborough*, 2:754.
11. Ibid., 2:28.
12. Cornwallis-West, *Reminiscences*, 86.
13. "The Gathering of the Unionist Clans," *Westminster Budget*, Aug. 16, 1901.
14. Representative articles on the rally include "Unionist Demonstration at Blenheim," *Times* (London), Aug. 12, 1901; "Great Unionist Gathering at Blenheim," *Daily Express*, Aug. 12, 1901; "The Blenheim Fete," *Primrose League Gazette*, Sept. 2, 1901; "Unionists at Blenheim," *Lloyd's Weekly*, Aug. 11, 1901.
15. Balsan, *The Glitter and the Gold*, 89. (In her account of the Blenheim rally Consuelo gives the wrong date, but other details clearly indicate 1901.) WSC, *Marlborough*, 2:1039.

V: Empire Dreams

1. WSC, *My Early Life*, 359–60, and *Great Contemporaries*, 64; Mackintosh, *Joseph Chamberlain*, 257.
2. Malcolm, *Vacant Thrones*, 96; Arthur Balfour to Lady Elcho, Mar. 15, 1892, quoted in Zebel, *Balfour*, 79; Brett, *Journals and Letters*, 1:319.
3. WSC, *Great Contemporaries*, 72; Gardiner, *Pillars of Society*, 41; Elletson, *The Chamberlains*, 53.
4. Austen Chamberlain, *Politics from Inside*, 367; Marsh, *Joseph Chamberlain*, 324–26 and 667.
5. "Young Men in Commerce," *Puritan*, October 1899; WSC, *Great Contemporaries*, 73.
6. Elletson, *The Chamberlains*, 135; John Foster Fraser, "The New House of Commons," *Living Age*, March 16, 1901.
7. "Riot in Birmingham at Pro-Boer Meeting," *NYT*, Dec. 19, 1901; "Mr. Lloyd-George at Birmingham," and "The Rioting in Birmingham," *Times* (London), Dec. 19 and 20, 1901.
8. WSC to J. Moore Bayley, Dec. 19, 1901, *CV* 2:1, 103.
9. "Birmingham and Free Speech," *Echo*, Dec. 19, 1901; Elletson, *The Chamberlains*, 136; " 'I Withdraw Nothing,'" *Daily Mail*, Jan. 13, 1902.
10. "Mr. Lloyd-George at Birmingham," *Times* (London), Dec. 19, 1901. A printer by trade, Joseph G. Pentland served on the Birmingham School Board, and later on the town council.
11. WSC to Shane Leslie, Oct. 2, 1920 (Gilbert, *Churchill*, 425–26); WSC to J. Moore Bayley, Dec. 23, 1901, *CV* 2:1, 104.
12. WSC, Conservative Association Meeting, Blackpool, Jan. 9, 1902, *CS*, 114; WSC to Lord Rosebery, Jan. 17, 1902, *CV* 2:1, 114.
13. WSC, Conservative Club Dinner, Manchester, March 19, 1902, *CS*, 135.
14. "Detention of Mr. Cartwright," House of Commons, April 24, 1902, *Hansard*.
15. Malcolm, *Vacant Thrones*, 95 and 97; WSC, *My Early Life*, 371; Gardiner, *The Pillars of Society*, 47–48.
16. The dialogue at the Hooligan dinner is taken from the two surviving eyewitness accounts in Malcolm, *Vacant Thrones*, 97–98, and WSC, *My Early*

Life, 371–72. For an earlier version of Malcolm's account, see his "In and Out of Parliament," *Living Age*, Jan. 15, 1910.

17. Marsh, *Joseph Chamberlain*, 307 and 425.
18. Lindsay, *The Crawford Papers*, 67.
19. WSC to Ernest Fletcher, Nov. 14, 1902, and to Jennie Churchill, Dec. 19, 1902, *CV* 2:1, 174–75. Gilbert (*Churchill*, 153) says that WSC left England for Egypt on November 20, but "The Assouan Dam," *Echo*, Nov. 18, 1902, notes that Cassel and WSC left on November 18.
20. WSC, *Thoughts and Adventures*, 52; Bonham Carter, *Churchill*, 77.
21. WSC to Jennie Churchill, [Dec. 9, 1902], *CV* 2:1, 176.

VI: The Great Rift

1. Herbert Vivian, "Studies in Personality: Winston Churchill," *Pall Mall Magazine*, April 1905.
2. Chamberlain, *Imperial Union and Tariff Reform*, 18; "Duty of Empire," *Daily Express*, May 16, 1903.
3. Herbert Vivian, "Studies in Personality: Winston Churchill," *Pall Mall Magazine*, April 1905.
4. WSC, Free Trade, Hoxton, May 21, 1903, *CS*, 191; WSC to J. Moore Bayley, May 20, 1903, *CV* 2:1, 183. The old saying about goods and frontiers is sometimes attributed to Frédéric Bastiat, the French philosopher of classical liberalism.
5. Margot Asquith, *Autobiography*, 228; Elletson, *The Chamberlains*, 144.
6. WSC, *Great Contemporaries*, 249; Balfour to WSC, May 26, 1903, *CV* 2:1, 185.
7. "Sugar Convention Bill" and "Consolidated Fund," House of Commons, July 29 and Aug. 14, 1903, *Hansard*.
8. WSC to Jennie Churchill, Aug. 12, 1903, *CV* 2:1, 218.
9. Joseph Chamberlain to WSC, Aug. 15, 1903, *CV* 2:1, 219–20.
10. "Sugar Convention Bill," House of Commons, July 29, 1903, *Hansard*.
11. MacKenzie, *The Fabians*, 126, and Hunt, *Building Jerusalem*, 366.
12. Holroyd, *Bernard Shaw*, 1:263–64.
13. Webb, *The Diary of Beatrice Webb*, 2:287–88 and 326. Beatrice Webb to WSC, [July 14, 1903], *CV* 2:1, 213. The appendix Webb recommended to WSC by a shortened title is in the 1902 one-volume edition of her *Industrial Democracy*.
14. WSC to Jennie Churchill, Sept. 11 [1903], CHAR 28/27/18; "Resignation of Mr. Chamberlain," *Daily Mail*, Sept. 18, 1903; Marsh, *Joseph Chamberlain*, 590–91.
15. WSC to Hugh Cecil, Oct. 24, 1903 (not sent), and WSC to Lord Cranborne (Salisbury), Nov. 2, 1903, *CV* 2:1, 243 and 248.
16. "Cecil and Churchill," *Daily Express*, Nov. 10, 1903; "Angry Birmingham," *Daily Mirror*, Nov. 11, 1903; WSC to Hugh Cecil, Nov. 3, 1903, *CV* 2:1, 248.
17. "Free Trade Meeting," *Daily Express*, Nov. 12, 1903; "Free Fooders Speak in Chamberlain's City," *NYT*, Nov. 12, 1903.

18. WSC, Town Hall, Birmingham, Nov. 11, 1903, *CS*, 220–24.
19. Jennie's tears are noted in a sardonic description of the Birmingham speech on the front page of the *Saturday Review*, Nov. 14, 1903.
20. "Our Celebrities," *Daily Mirror*, Nov. 16, 1903.
21. In his excellent *Churchill by Himself: The Definitive Collection of Quotations* (2008), Richard M. Langworth includes part of this sentence but says that its source has not been identified: "Many references cite this remark but without attribution." Its correct source is Harold Begbie, "Master Workers: Mr. Winston Churchill, MP," *Pall Mall Magazine*, September 1903. Begbie later reprinted the interview in his *Master Workers*, 161–77.
22. Ibid.
23. "London Theatrical and Musical News," *NYT*, July 13, 1902. Barrymore discusses her close friendship with the Duchess of Sutherland in *Memories*, 106 and 124–27. For Millicent's plan to stage a play with Ethel, see "Court & Society," *Daily Mail*, Aug. 27, 1902. For the one-night London performance of *Captain Jinks*, see Ethel's comments in *"Oceanic's* Passengers Praise Ship's Officers," *NYT*, Aug. 15, 1901. For Ethel's comment on the first time WSC saw her, see Ogilvy, *An Autobiography*, 63–64.
24. Landor, *Everywhere*, 2:81; Geoffrey C. Ward, "The Desperate Barrymores," *American Heritage*, December 1990.
25. Barrymore, *Memories*, 125. In 1903 Henry James seems to have been on very close terms with Millicent (see James, *Henry James: A Life in Letters*, 392–93).
26. Ethel B. [Ethel Barrymore] to WSC, [late October 1903], filed among "unknown" correspondents in CHAR 1/25, but the handwriting matches Barrymore's, the West Fifty-ninth Street address on the letter is her New York apartment in 1903 (see Peters, *The House of Barrymore*, 549), and several internal references point to a date in October shortly after the Broadway opening of her play *Cousin Kate* on October 19.

VII: Departures

1. "Adjournment of the House (Easter)," House of Commons, March 29, 1904, *Hansard*; "Parliament in Perspective," *Echo*, March 30, 1904.
2. On April 2, 1904, in "News of the Week," the *Spectator* mentioned Balfour's excuse of a prior engagement. See "The Adjournment," *Lloyd's Weekly*, April 3, 1904, for the criticism of Balfour's "schoolboy antics."
3. WSC to Hugh Cecil, Oct. 24, 1903, *CV* 2:1, 243.
4. Hugh Cecil to WSC, December [1903], *CV* 2:1, 267–68; *Scotsman*, March 12, 1904.
5. "Free Food," House of Commons, May 18, 1904, *Hansard*; "The Outlook: Parliament in Perspective," *Echo*, May 19, 1904; "Chamberlain Called Coward in Commons," *NYT*, May 19, 1904.
6. WSC to Hugh Cecil, Oct. 11, 1904, *CV* 2:1, 364. Other quotations taken from Richard A. Rempel, "Lord Hugh Cecil's Parliamentary Career,

1900–1914," *Journal of British Studies*, May 1972.

7. WSC, Philomathic Society, Liverpool, Nov. 21, 1901, *CS*, 110; J. L. Wanklyn to WSC, Feb. 5, 1904, *CV* 2:1, 311.

8. WSC to Lord Rosebery, Oct. 10, 1902, *CV* 2:1, 168.

9. WSC to J. Moore Bayley, Dec. 23, 1901, *CV* 2:1, 104; Morley, *Recollections*, 2:255; Margot Asquith, *Autobiography*, 251.

10. J. L. Wanklyn to David Lloyd George, Jan. 1, 1904 (quoted in Grigg, *Lloyd George: The People's Champion*, 65).

11. *The Times*, Jan. 17, 1899 (quoted in A. J. A. Morris, "Sir Henry Campbell-Bannerman," *Oxford Dictionary of National Biography*).

12. "Trade Unions and Trades Disputes Bill," House of Commons, April 22, 1904, *Hansard;* "Moving Incident in the House," and "Mr. Churchill's Health," *Daily Mirror*, April 23 and 25, 1904.

13. Ethel's arrival on April 28, 1904, was announced in the *Daily Mirror* under the headline "Over for the Season."

14. WSC pocket engagement diary for 1904, CHAR 1/48/1. Quotations about WSC's romance with Barrymore are taken from Moir, *I Was Winston Churchill's Private Secretary*, 78; and Randolph Churchill, *Winston S. Churchill*, 244.

15. "Wyndham's Theatre," *Times*, May 17, 1904; Peters, *The House of Barrymore*, 93; "*Cynthia* to Go," *Daily Express*, June 3, 1904.

16. Blanche Partington, "Ethel Barrymore," *San Francisco Call*, July 17, 1904.

17. Peters, *The House of Barrymore*, 101.

18. "A Precarious Majority," *Manchester Guardian*, June 1, 1904; Hugh Cecil to WSC, Jan. 13, 1904, *CV* 2:1, 299.

VIII: The Bachelor and the Heiress

1. Herbert Vivian, "Studies in Personality: Winston Churchill," *Pall Mall Magazine*, April 1905.

2. "Politicians and Caricaturists," *Westminster Budget*, Sept. 2, 1904; "According to Cocker," *Black & White*, July 2, 1904; "Character Sketch," *Review of Reviews*, July 1904; "Characters in Outline," *Speaker*, Aug. 27, 1904.

3. Wilson, *CB*, 419.

4. WSC, Carnarvon, Oct. 18, 1904, *CS*, 368.

5. *Times* (London), Oct. 19, 1904 (quoted in Toye, *Lloyd George & Churchill*, 33); WSC, Carnarvon, Oct. 18, 1904, *CS*, 368.

6. Lloyd George to Margaret Owen, [c. 1885], quoted in Kenneth O. Morgan, "George, David Lloyd, first Earl Lloyd-George of Dwyfor," *Oxford Dictionary of National Biography*.

7. Grigg, *Lloyd George: The People's Champion*, 66 and 155.

8. WSC to Bourke Cockran, June 19 [1904]. See McMenamin and Zoller, *Becoming Winston Churchill*, 194, for the full text and an excellent discussion of Cockran's influence on WSC.

9. Martin Gilbert, "Churchill's London: Spinning Top of Memories of

Ungrand Places and Moments in Time," International Churchill Society, London, Sept. 17, 1985.

10. On Sept. 24, 1904, WSC wrote his mother that he had visited Chamberlain two days earlier (*CV* 2:1, 456). See also WSC to J. Moore Bayley, Oct. 17, 1904, and Joseph Chamberlain to WSC, *CV* 2:1, 366–67 and 457; and WSC, *Great Contemporaries*, 73–74.

11. "Small-Talk of the Week," *Sketch*, Dec. 7, 1904.

12. Lionel Barrymore, *We Barrymores*, 291; Attwood, *The Wilsons of Tranby Court*, 219; "Well-Known Women," *London Journal*, June 8, 1901; *Cassell's Magazine*, June 1900. For discussions of Muriel Wilson's acting career, and for photos of her as allegorical figures, see Leo Trevor, "Recollections of the Chatsworth Theatricals," *Pall Mall Magazine*, November 1903; George A. Wade, "Amateur Theatricals," *Lady's Realm*, November 1901; Credland, *The Wilson Line*, 74.

13. WSC to Muriel Wilson, n.d. [1904], and Dec. 25, 1904 (Private Collection). Muriel's letters from WSC were sold by Christie's in 1994. For quotations, see the sale catalog or Dalya Alberge, "Churchill Letters Show Torment of Unrequited Love," *Independent* (UK), April 28, 1994.

14. Brook-Shepherd, *Uncle of Europe*, 144–45.

15. Muriel Wilson to WSC, [August 1907], CHAR 1/66/82; WSC to Muriel Wilson, n.d. [1904].

16. "Winston at Mombasa," *Bystander*, Dec. 4, 1907.

17. "Winston Churchill May Wed Miss Muriel Wilson," *San Francisco Call*, Oct. 8, 1905.

IX: Fortunate Son

1. WSC, *Lord Randolph Churchill*, 32.

2. Ibid., 242.

3. Blunt, *My Diaries*, 1:142. For Blunt's obsession with Byron, see MacCarthy, *Byron*, 562.

4. Blunt, *My Diaries*, 2:104.

5. Foster, *Lord Randolph Churchill*, 177 and 127; Rosebery, *Lord Randolph Churchill*, 113.

6. WSC, *Lord Randolph Churchill*, 803 and 818.

7. Rosebery, *Lord Randolph Churchill*, 72, 71, and 114; Foster, *Lord Randolph Churchill*, 218.

8. Leslie, *Lady Randolph Churchill*, 201.

9. WSC to Jennie Churchill, Nov. 2 [1894], *CV* 1:1, 531.

10. Moran, *Diaries*, 394.

11. Harold Begbie, "Master Workers: Mr. Winston Churchill, MP," *Pall Mall Magazine*, September 1903. Gardiner, *Prophets, Priests and Kings*, 104.

12. WSC to Hugh Cecil, Nov. 30, 1905, *CV* 2:1, 407.

13. Frank Harris to WSC, Oct. 7, 1905, *CV* 2:1, 466.

14. Quoted in Holroyd, *Bernard Shaw*, 1:407. The *Saturday Review* essay on Lord Randolph appeared in 1895 as a leading article under Harris's

editorship, and his authorship of it was no mystery. For confirmation see "Lord Randolph Churchill," *Review of Reviews*, March 1895.

15. Harris, *Contemporary Portraits*, 90 and 95–96.

16. "Business of the House," House of Commons, March 15 and July 31, 1905, *Hansard.*

17. Master of Elibank to WSC, July 27, 1905; WSC to Lord Rosebery, Nov. 1, 1905; and Sidney Greville to WSC, Jan. 2 [1906], *CV* 2:1, 399, 425, and 480.

18. Marsh, *Joseph Chamberlain*, 625.

19. *Manchester Guardian*, Dec. 6, 1905 (quoted in Wilson, *CB*, 441). A summary of Cabinet suggestions is given in "Loaves and Fishes," *Daily Mail*, Dec. 5, 1905. WSC to Jennie Churchill, Dec. 4, 1905, *CV* 2:1, 409; Cortissoz, *The Life of Whitelaw Reid*, 2:317.

X: Winners and Losers

1. Wilson, *CB*, 425–26.

2. Byron, *Childe Harold's Pilgrimage*, Canto II; *Punch*, Apr. 25, 1906. In a letter to Hugh Cecil, Dec. 16, 1905, *CV* 2:1, 416, WSC explained that he chose the Colonial Office over the Treasury, but didn't offer a reason why. "On Politicians," *Penny Illustrated Paper*, Dec. 17, 1910.

3. Hugh Cecil to WSC, [?18 Dec. 1905], *CV* 2:1, 417; Pamela [Plowden] Lytton to WSC, Sept. 14 [1907], CHAR 1/66/27.

4. Marsh, *A Number of People*, 148–49.

5. Ibid., 143.

6. Gilbert (*Churchill: A Life*, 174) and others seem to have been confused by an ambiguous reference Marsh makes to "Lady Lytton" in an early account of his relationship with WSC (see Marsh, *A Number of People*, 149). Consequently, the quotation has been attributed to Pamela. But as Christopher Hassall—Eddie's close friend—makes clear in his *A Biography of Edward Marsh* (119–20), the comment about WSC's faults and virtues was made by Edith, the Dowager Countess of Lytton.

7. Hassall, *A Biography of Edward Marsh*, 120.

8. Marsh, *A Number of People*, 151.

9. Hastings, *The Secret Lives of Somerset Maugham*, 424–25.

10. Hassall, *A Biography of Edward Marsh*, 19.

11. WSC, *Thoughts and Adventures*, 220. Gilbert (*Churchill: A Life*, 175) has WSC arriving in Manchester on January 4, but WSC gave his first speech of the campaign the night before in the city.

12. WSC, Cheetham Hill, Jan. 10, 1906, *CS*, 545.

13. The most colorful accounts of the campaign are found in a series of *Daily Mail* articles by Charles Hands under the headlines "Winston," "Manchester," "The Fight for Manchester," and "Manchester's Excitement," on Jan. 5, 11, 12, and 13, 1906.

14. "Lord Randolph Churchill," *Spectator*, Jan. 6, 1906.

15. WSC, *Thoughts and Adventures*, 219.

16. Marsh, *A Number of People*, 149–50.

XI: The World at His Feet

1. Dorothy O. Helly and Helen Callaway, "Dame Flora Louise Lugard, Lady Lugard," *Oxford Dictionary of National Biography*.
2. Flora Lugard's visit with WSC at the Colonial Office is described in Perham, *Lugard*, 237–41.
3. See Pakenham, *The Scramble for Africa*, 651–53, for an excellent summary of Lugard's actions in West Africa and WSC's comments on them.
4. Carland, *The Colonial Office and Nigeria*, 96.
5. Perham, *Lugard*, 271.
6. Lugard's use of force in Abeokuta is discussed in D. C. Dorward, "British West Africa and Liberia," *The Cambridge History of Africa*, 7:429.
7. Perham, *Lugard*, 276–78.
8. "King's Speech," House of Commons, Feb. 22, 1906, *Hansard*.
9. For an account of the Sekgoma episode, see Ronald Hyam, "At the Colonial Office, 1905–8," in Stansky, ed., *Churchill: A Profile*, 24–26.
10. The original source for WSC's comment to Elgin, "These are my views," is Austen Chamberlain's *Politics from Inside*, 459. The other examples of banter between WSC and Elgin are quoted in Perham, *Lugard*, 269–70.
11. Minutes, WSC and Elgin on Lugard, Jan. 3, 1906, Colonial Office, quoted in Perham, *Lugard*, 248–49.
12. Addison, *Churchill on the Home Front*, 54.
13. Arnold White, "The British System of Colonial Government," *Harper's Monthly Magazine*, January 1900; Hyam, "At the Colonial Office, 1905–8," 29.
14. Details of the purchase and repairs to 12 Bolton Street are given in Lumley & Lumley to WSC, Jan. 25, 1906, CHAR 1/59/2–3. Incorrectly, Manchester (*The Last Lion: Visions of Glory*, 392) says WSC was renting.
15. "South Africa (High Commissioner)," House of Commons, March 21, 1906, *Hansard*.
16. "Civil Services and Revenue," House of Commons, April 5, 1906, *Hansard*.
17. Frederick Ponsonby to WSC, Aug. 20, 1906, *CV* 2:1, 566.
18. Mencken, *Newspaper Days*, 239.
19. Richard Harding Davis to WSC, May 4 [1906], CHAR 1/56/15–16.

XII: Private Lives

1. WSC to Edward Marsh, Aug. 21, and to Jennie Churchill, Sept. 1, 1906, *CV* 2:1, 571 and 579.
2. Gardiner, *Prophets, Priests and Kings*, 78.
3. Henry Campbell-Bannerman to WSC, Aug. 25, 1906, *CV* 2:1, 574.
4. WSC, *Thoughts and Adventures*, 80.
5. WSC to the German emperor, Jan. 26, 1908, CHAR 1/72/23.
6. The photo of WSC and Wilhelm pointing with his sword was published in the *Daily Mirror*, Sept. 24, 1906. It has often been misdated (see Manchester, *The Last Lion: Visions of Glory*, 425). The parody appeared in *Punch*, Sept. 19, 1906.

7. WSC, *Thoughts and Adventures*, 79 and 76.
8. Stuart, *Consuelo and Alva Vanderbilt*, 269; "Marlborough Row Jars England," *Boston Journal*, Oct. 22, 1906; Hayden Church, "Drear Christmas in Woodstock," *Chicago Tribune*, Dec. 23, 1906.
9. Jennie Churchill to Consuelo Marlborough, Nov. 2, 1906, CHAR 28/78/45.
10. Cornwallis-West, *Edwardian Hey-Days*, 119; Jennie Churchill to WSC, May 7 [1907], CHAR 1/65/40.
11. Consuelo Marlborough to WSC [Dec. 1906], CHAR 1/57/24; Hugh Cecil to WSC, [Oct. 1906], *CV* 2:1, 588; WSC to Consuelo Marlborough, Dec. 22, 1906, CHAR 1/57/57.
12. Balsan, *The Glitter and the Gold*, 103.
13. Davis, *Real Soldiers of Fortune*, 84.
14. WSC to Richard Harding Davis, April 20, 1907 (Special Collections, University of Virginia Library); "Good Journalism," *Black & White*, April 13, 1907.
15. Birkenhead, *Churchill*, 112–13.
16. "The Mystery of England's Winston Churchill," *Current Literature*, June 1908; Henry Campbell-Bannerman to WSC, Jan. 22, 1907, *CV* 2:1, 624.
17. Wilson, *CB*, 590.
18. Ibid., 590–92.
19. Farr, *Reginald McKenna*, 92.

XIII: The Political Maiden

1. Bennett, *Margot*, 209.
2. Bonham Carter, *Lantern Slides*, 127–28 and 130; Davenport-Hines, *Ettie*, 162.
3. Bonham Carter, *Winston Churchill*, 115 and 7.
4. D. W. Brogan, "He Gave His Best in Their Finest Hour," *NYT*, May 30, 1965.
5. Bonham Carter, *Winston Churchill*, 4 and 356.
6. Margot Asquith, *Autobiography*, 202. For Margot's opinion of Winston and Violet in 1907, see the entry for August 23 in the full manuscript of her diary, Bodleian MS 3206–3207.
7. Clifford, *The Asquiths*, 148 and 200.
8. Balsan, *The Glitter and the Gold*, 165–66; Moran, *Diaries*, 201; Margot Asquith, *Autobiography*, xxx.
9. Clifford, *The Asquiths*, 167.
10. Dorothy Parker, "Re-enter Margot Asquith," *New Yorker*, Oct. 22, 1927; Hyde, *Lord Reading*, 221. There are several versions of Margot's comment to Harlow, including the one quoted here from *Bartlett's Book of Anecdotes*, but the original source seems to be Oliver Wendell Holmes, *The Holmes-Einstein Letters* (359), where Margot says, "The final 't' in my Christian name is silent, unlike your family name." For a description of Margot's voice, see her *Autobiography*, xxxii.

11. Margot Asquith, *Autobiography*, xxiii; Bonham Carter, *Winston Churchill*, 6.
12. Clifford, *The Asquiths*, 9.
13. WSC to Sir Walter Runciman, Dec. 30, 1907, *CV* 2:2, 735.
14. *Daily Mail* and *Manchester Chronicle* to WSC, Apr. 27, 1907, CHAR 1/65/37–38; "The Misses Botha," *Daily Mail*, April 25, 1907; Muriel Wilson to WSC, [May 2, 1907], *CV* 2:1, 656. Jan Smuts, among others, later confirmed that Botha was leading the force that captured WSC (see *Life*, April 3, 1944).
15. WSC to Jennie Churchill, Aug. 21, 1907, *CV* 2:1, 669; "Transvaal Loan (Guarantee) Bill," House of Commons, Aug. 19, 1907, *Hansard*; WSC to Lord Knollys, Aug. 22, 1907, *CV* 2:1, 665. For a tense debate between WSC and the opposition on the subject of the diamond, see "Commons' Hot Debate: Mr. Churchill and the Cullinan Diamond," *Daily Mail*, Aug. 20, 1907. Marsh, *A Number of People*, 152.

XIV: A Place in the Sun

1. WSC to Pamela [Plowden] Lytton, Sept. 19, 1907, *CV* 2:2, 679.
2. Lord Elgin to Lord Crewe, May [?], 1908; and Jennie Churchill to WSC, Oct. 21, 1907, *CV* 2:2, 797 and 689. *Punch*, Oct. 2, 1907.
3. Sir Francis Hopwood to Lord Elgin, Dec. 16 and 27, 1907, *CV* 2:2, 724 and 730.
4. Hassall, *A Biography of Edward Marsh*, 134.
5. WSC, *My African Journey*, 88, 86, and 94; King Daudi Chwa to WSC, Jan. 22, 1908, *CV* 2:2, 748.
6. WSC, *My African Journey*, 38, 63, 209, and 64.
7. Ibid., 1, 14, and 166.
8. Hassall, *A Biography of Edward Marsh*, 134 and 139.
9. WSC, *My African Journey*, 208.
10. WSC to H. H. Asquith, March 14, 1908, *CV* 2:2, 755–56.
11. "The King's Speech," House of Commons, Feb. 10, 1904, *Hansard*.
12. Masterman, *C. F. G. Masterman*, 97–98.
13. Bonham Carter, *Lantern Slides*, 151; Bonham Carter, *Winston Churchill*, 123.
14. Wharton, *A Backward Glance*, 214–15.
15. Lee, *"A Good Innings,"* 97. For information on the Lugards in Hong Kong, see Perham, *Lugard*, 297.
16. Hassall, *A Biography of Edward Marsh*, 346; Longford, *A Pilgrimage of Passion*, 387.
17. Wilson, *CB*, 626; John Morley to WSC, April 8, 1908, *CV* 2:2, 766.
18. Gilbert, *David Lloyd George*, 1:332–34.
19. Clifford, *The Asquiths*, 139.
20. *Winston and Clementine*, 7.

XV: Best-Laid Plans

1. "Life and Letters," *Academy*, May 2, 1908; "Automobiles Serve as Political Rostrums," *Motor World*, May 14, 1908.

2. WSC, Manchester, April 22, 1908, *CS*, 1004.
3. Pankhurst, *My Own Story*, 52.
4. WSC, *Thoughts and Adventures*, 222; Toye, *Lloyd George & Churchill*, 81.
5. "Woman Suffrage: The Assault on Mr. Churchill" and "Woman Suffrage: A Suffragist's Whip," *Times* (London), Nov. 16 and Dec. 23, 1909; "Mr. Churchill Assaulted," *Lloyd's Weekly News*, Nov. 14, 1909.
6. "Mobbed by Women" and "Assault on First Lord," *Daily Mirror*, Nov. 28, 1910, and March 17, 1914. Also see Soames, *Clementine Churchill*, 79–80, and "More Suffragette Outrages," *Lloyd's Weekly News*, Feb. 23, 1913.
7. "Manchester Today," *Daily Mirror*, April 24, 1908; "Mr. Churchill Out," *Daily Mail*, April 25, 1908; H. G. Wells to an Elector in Manchester, [April 13, 1908?], *CV* 2:2, 780.
8. Pankhurst, *My Own Story*, 106–7.
9. Cortissoz, *The Life of Whitelaw Reid*, 2:402.
10. "Routed by a Suffragette," *Daily Mail*, May 5, 1908; "Winston Churchill's Fight for a Seat," *Penny Illustrated Paper*, May 9, 1908.
11. Addison, *Churchill on the Home Front*, 67.
12. "The By-Elections," *Scotsman*, May 11, 1908.
13. Gardiner, *Prophets, Priests and Kings*, 104–5.
14. WSC, Kinnaird Hall, Dundee, May 4, 1908, *CS*, 1029, 1033, and 1035.
15. WSC, *Great Contemporaries*, 141; R. Hyam, "Bruce, Victor Alexander, Ninth Earl of Elgin," *Oxford Dictionary of National Biography*; Bonham Carter, *Lantern Slides*, 157.
16. Margot Asquith, *Autobiography*, 250; Bonham Carter, *Winston Churchill*, 131.
17. "Will Winston Marry?," *Bystander*, May 13, 1908; Farr, *Reginald McKenna*, 121 and 123.
18. Bonham Carter, *Winston Churchill*, 126.
19. Birkenhead, *Churchill*, 112. For WSC's intention to visit Violet in Scotland on Aug. 17, 1908, see Bonham Carter, *Lantern Slides*, 162.

XVI: The Castle

1. "Fires at Country Houses: Mr. Churchill's Narrow Escape," *Times* (London), Aug. 7, 1908; *Winston and Clementine*, 11.
2. Soames, *Clementine Churchill*, 59 and 62.
3. Lady Airlie to WSC, Aug. 20, 1908, *CV* 2:2, 811; Soames, *Clementine Churchill*, 60; *Winston and Clementine*, 16.
4. Muriel Wilson to WSC, Aug. 15, 1908; Joseph Chamberlain to WSC, Aug. 24, 1908; Ian Malcolm to WSC, Sept. 8, 1908; and Hugh Cecil to WSC, Sept. 5, 1908, *CV* 2:2, 804, 813, 817, and 816; Evan Charteris to Jennie Churchill [1908], CHAR 28/78/70.
5. Bonham Carter, *Lantern Slides*, 162.
6. Browne, *Long Sunset*, 145.
7. Hill, *Footsteps of Dr. Johnson*, 125; "Mr. Churchill," *Daily Mirror*, Aug. 25, 1908; "Mr. Churchill's Wedding," *Daily Mail*, Aug. 25, 1908. WSC's return

from Scotland by rail to King's Cross in London was reported in the *Scotsman* on Friday, Aug. 28, 1908, in an untitled article on p. 4.

8. Soames, *Clementine Churchill*, 63; Birkenhead, *Churchill*, 178.

9. "Mr. Churchill's Wedding," *Daily Mail*, Aug. 28, 1908.

10. Venetia Stanley to Violet Asquith, Aug. 26, 1908, Bodleian Library, University of Oxford.

11. Bonham Carter, *Winston Churchill*, 172–73. Margot mentions WSC's August visit in her diary entry, "Slains Castle August & Sept. 1908," Bodleian Library, University of Oxford.

12. Violet Asquith to Venetia Stanley, [September 1908], Bodleian Library, University of Oxford.

13. "Mr. Churchill's Wedding," *Times* (London), Sept. 14, 1908; "Mr. Churchill's Wedding," *Scotsman*, Sept. 14, 1908; *Daily Mirror*, Sept. 12, 1908.

14. Davenport-Hines, *Ettie*, 162–63; "Mr. and Mrs. Winston Churchill," *Bystander*, Sept. 16, 1908; Longford, *A Pilgrimage of Passion*, 386.

15. For Margot's dramatic account of Violet's misadventure on September 19, see her diary entry, "Slains Castle August & Sept. 1908," Bodleian Library, University of Oxford. (She noted Winston's visit in August but made no comment about it except to disparage Clemmie's intellect.) Newspaper stories offered various accounts. See the front-page story in the *Daily Mirror*, Sept. 22; "Illness of Miss Asquith," *Times* (London), Sept. 22; "Miss Asquith's Adventure," *Lloyd's Weekly News*, Sept. 27, 1908. Colin Clifford includes helpful information in his excellent *The Asquiths*, but because there is no discussion of Winston's visit to Slains, or of his complicated history with Violet, the account underestimates his importance in the events of 1908.

16. Bonham Carter, *Lantern Slides*, 166.

17. Margot Asquith diary, "Slains Castle August & Sept. 1908," Bodleian Library, University of Oxford (Clifford, *The Asquiths*, 143). For Bram Stoker's connection to Cruden Bay, see Belford, *Bram Stoker*, 233–34 and 255.

18. Bonham Carter, *Lantern Slides*, 170.

19. Clifford, *The Asquiths*, 143.

20. Bonham Carter, *Lantern Slides*, 171.

21. WSC, *Great Contemporaries*, 139.

22. Soames, *Clementine Churchill*, 85.

XVII: Eminent Edwardian

1. "Engagement of Mr. Churchill," *Daily Mirror*, Aug. 15, 1908; Gardiner, *Prophets, Priests and Kings*, 109; Douglas, *Adventures in London*, 216.

2. Mary McDowell, "The National Women's Trade Union League," *Survey*, Oct. 16, 1909.

3. "I don't think I could press my Unemployment Insurance plan," WSC wrote Asquith on Dec. 26, 1908, "until Lloyd George has found a way of dealing with infirmity or (which is possible) has found that there is no way"

(*CV* 2:2, 860). See also WSC, Cabinet Memorandum, April 17, 1909, *CV* 2:2, 883–84.

4. Toye, *Lloyd George & Churchill*, 58. WSC to Clementine Churchill, April 22, 1911, *CV* 2:2, 1069.
5. Gilbert, *David Lloyd George*, 1:323; Koss, *Lord Haldane*, 56.
6. Chamberlain, *Politics from Inside*, 127; Hobhouse, *Inside Asquith's Cabinet*, 73.
7. Addison, *Churchill on the Home Front*, 69.
8. Bonham Carter, *Winston Churchill*, 132.
9. Webb, *The Diary of Beatrice Webb*, 3:100–1.
10. WSC to H. H. Asquith, Dec. 29, 1908, *CV* 2:2, 863; H. H. Asquith to WSC, Jan. 11, 1909, *CV* 2:2, 869–70.
11. "Trade Boards Bill," House of Commons, April 28, 1909, *Hansard*.
12. WSC to H. W. Massingham, Jan. 22, 1909, *CV* 2:2, 873; WSC, Kinnaird Hall, Dundee, Oct. 9, 1908, *CS*, 1097 and 1099; "Mr. Churchill at Dundee," *Scotsman*, Oct. 10, 1908.
13. "The Launch of HMS *Dreadnought*," *Bystander*, Feb. 14, 1906; "The Navy," *Edinburgh Review*, July 1909.
14. "Battleship Armament," House of Commons, Dec. 17, 1909, *Hansard*.
15. Farr, *Reginald McKenna*, 155.
16. WSC, Albert Hall, Swansea, Aug. 14, 1908, *CS*, 1085–86.
17. Farr, *Reginald McKenna*, 165.
18. Lloyd George to WSC, Dec. 21, 1908, *CV* 2:2, 937.
19. Farr, *Reginald McKenna*, 161.
20. Lloyd George to WSC, Jan. 3 [1909], *CV* 2:2, 938.
21. "Our Threatened Sea Power," *Lloyd's Weekly*, March 21, 1909.
22. Williams, *Defending the Empire*, 171; Blunt, *My Diaries*, 2:240. For more on the naval expansion, see Michael Howard, "The Edwardian Arms Race," in Read, ed., *Edwardian England*, 145–61.
23. "Dreadnought Building" and "Final Balance Sheet," House of Commons, April 29, 1909, *Hansard*.
24. WSC to Clementine Churchill, April 28 [1909], *CV* 2:2, 887.
25. WSC, "Why I Believe in Free Trade," *Tom Watson's Magazine*, July 1905; WSC, City Liberal Club, Walbrook, London, June 28, 1909, *CS*, 1273.
26. Spender, *Life, Journalism and Politics*, 1:231.
27. "Final Balance Sheet" and "Naval Problem," House of Commons, April 29, 1909, *Hansard*. At least £11 million of the £16 million increase went to dreadnoughts and old-age pensions (Gilbert, *David Lloyd George*, 1:368). Naval expenditures increased from £36 million in 1909–10 to £43 million in 1911–12 (*The Naval Annual*, 1913, ed. Viscount Hythe, 457). Historians haven't always given Asquith the credit he deserves for developing the legislation for old-age pensions, but his contemporaries widely recognized him as the driving force behind the plan. See Sidney Brooks, "Old-Age Pensions in England," *Harper's Weekly*, June 20, 1908.
28. WSC, *Thoughts and Adventures*, 57.
29. Gilbert, *David Lloyd George*, 1:15–16.

30. WSC to the Duke of Marlborough, Jan. 22, 1916, Library of Congress; Hobhouse, *Inside Asquith's Cabinet*, 121; Masterman, *C. F. G. Masterman*, 173.
31. Gilbert, *David Lloyd George*, 1:354.

XVIII: Sound and Fury

1. *Winston and Clementine*, 22.
2. Masterman, *C. F. G. Masterman*, 137.
3. Randolph Churchill, *Winston S. Churchill*, 284.
4. *Winston and Clementine*, 33.
5. Blunt, *My Diaries*, 2:271 and 284; Longford, *A Pilgrimage of Passion*, 386.
6. For WSC's investments, see the letters to him from Cassel on Nov. 3 and Dec. 4, 1908, CHAR 1/78/17 and 25. Manchester incorrectly says of WSC, "The money he had invested with Cassel was gone" (*The Last Lion: Visions of Glory*, 402).
7. Masterman, *C. F. G. Masterman*, 144.
8. John Campbell, "Smith, Frederick Edwin, First Earl of Birkenhead," *Oxford Dictionary of National Biography*; Smith, *F.E.*, 98 and 73; Campbell, *F. E. Smith*, 257.
9. Iain Sproat, "Women Behind the Great Men of Parliamentary History," *Scotsman*, April 18, 2004.
10. Smith, *F.E.*, 175; "Mr. F. E. Smith's Attack," *Daily Mirror*, Feb. 23, 1910.
11. Batt, *Dr. Barnardo*, 161–62.
12. David Lloyd George, "The Budget & the People: A Speech Delivered for the Budget League at the Edinburgh Castle, Limehouse, London, on July 30th, 1909," Parliamentary Archives, LG/C/33/2/11.
13. "Budget Battle," *Daily Mail*, Aug. 2, 1909; "The House of Commons," *Fortnightly Review*, Nov. 1, 1909. The repeal of the land taxes is discussed in Jenkins, *Churchill*, 159.
14. "Chancellor & Landlords," *Daily Mail*, Aug. 3, 1909.
15. WSC, Free Trade Hall, Manchester, May 22, 1909, *CS*, 1258.
16. WSC, St. Andrew's Hall, Norwich, July 26, 1909; Colston Hall, Bristol, Nov. 13, 1909; Liberal Club, Branksome, July 31, 1909, *CS*, 1293, 1346, and 1300; Randolph Churchill, *Winston S. Churchill*, 314–15.
17. WSC, Palace Theatre, Leicester, Sept. 4, 1909, *CS*, 1314–24.
18. "Mr. Churchill Flouts the Premier" and "Twelve Titled Relatives," *Daily Express*, Sept. 6 and 8, 1909.
19. Bonham Carter, *Winston Churchill*, 131.
20. Soames, *Clementine Churchill*, 109 and 127.
21. Edwards, *David Lloyd George*, 1:311.
22. Grigg, *Lloyd George: The People's Champion*, 220.
23. Gilbert, *David Lloyd George*, 1:393.
24. Farr, *Reginald McKenna*, 185. For Lloyd George's prediction of a ninety-seat majority, see Gilbert, *David Lloyd George*, 1:403.

25. Addison, *Churchill on the Home Front*, 89; WSC, *Liberalism and the Social Problem*, xxiii; Gilbert, *David Lloyd George*, 1:465.
26. WSC, Palace Theatre, Leicester, Sept. 4, 1909, *CS*, 1319.

XIX: Life and Death

1. "Mr. Lloyd George in Danger," *Lloyd's Weekly News*, Jan. 16, 1910; "Mr. Lloyd George and the People of Grimsby: Over a Wall," *Daily Express*, Jan. 17, 1909 (see also the cartoon, "Still Running," in this issue).
2. WSC, Torquay, Devon, Jan. 21, 1910, *CS*, 1477.
3. Margot Asquith to WSC, Feb. 12, 1910, *CV* 2:2, 1134; Clifford, *The Asquiths*, 165.
4. WSC to H. H. Asquith, Feb. 5, 1910, *CV* 2:2, 1133.
5. Lee, *Jean, Lady Hamilton*, 197.
6. "The Burnley Child Murder" and "Refusal of Reprieve," *Times* (London), Jan. 12 and Feb. 21, 1910. News reports identified the murdered child as a boy, not—as Jean Hamilton's diary recorded—a girl.
7. Home Office, "Capital Sentence Schedule," CHAR 12/13/1–5. A researcher for Randolph Churchill counted forty-three cases (*Winston S. Churchill*, 396).
8. "Suspension of Death Penalty for Murder," House of Commons, July 15, 1948, *Hansard;* "Reprieved Man's Suicide," *Lloyd's Weekly News*, Sept. 4, 1910.
9. Lee, *King Edward VII*, 2:676; Jennie Churchill to Queen Alexandra, May 9, 1910, CHAR 28/78/73.
10. Jennie Churchill to WSC, Aug. 25, 1906, CHAR 1/56/34–38.
11. "The Creation of Peers," *Times* (London), Sept. 11, 1909. Knollys's comment has sometimes been described as part of a letter to the *Times* (Gilbert, *Churchill*, 206), but the national newspaper was merely reprinting a report in the *Glasgow Herald*. WSC to Clementine, Sept. 12, 1909, *CV* 2:2, 908–9.
12. Randolph Churchill, *Winston S. Churchill*, 319 and 327; "Duration of Parliament," House of Commons, March 31, 1910, *Hansard*.
13. Lindsay, *The Crawford Papers*, 153; Hassall, *A Biography of Edward Marsh*, 156.
14. Asquith, *Fifty Years in Parliament*, 86–88.
15. Lytton, *Prison and Prisoners*, 213–66; Earl of Lytton to WSC, March 18, 1910, CHAR 12/2/21; Hassall, *A Biography of Edward Marsh*, 162.
16. Mosley, *Julian Grenfell*, 176.
17. Addison, *Churchill on the Home Front*, 130.
18. WSC, "Memorandum," Home Office, July 19, 1910, *CV* 2:3, 1447–48; "Plot to Kidnap a Cabinet Minister," *Daily Mirror*, May 14, 1913; *Dundee Advertiser*, Dec. 2, 1910, *CV* 2:3, 1466.
19. Toye, *Lloyd George & Churchill*, 83.

XX: Valiant

1. Wood, *Nineteenth Century Britain: 1815–1914*, 435; Smith, *The Making of Scotland*, 401.
2. "Suspension of Death Penalty for Murder," House of Commons, July 15, 1948, *Hansard*.

3. *Colliery Strike Disturbances in South Wales*, 4.
4. "Prime Minister (Engagements)," House of Commons, Nov. 30, 1978, *Hansard*.
5. "A State of Siege," *Times* (London), Nov. 9, 1910.
6. *Colliery Strike Disturbances in South Wales*, 4–5; "Coal Owners and Mediation," *Times* (London), Nov. 11, 1910.
7. James, *Churchill: A Study in Failure*, 44; House of Commons, Nov. 24, 1910, *CS*, 1619.
8. Public Record Office, Home Office 144/1553/199768, cited in Anthony Mòr O'Brien, "Churchill and the Tonypandy Riots," *Welsh History Review/ Cylchgrawn Hanes Cymru*, June 1994.
9. *Colliery Strike Disturbances in South Wales*, 48; O'Brien, "Churchill and the Tonypandy Riots."
10. Addison, *Churchill on the Home Front*, 71.
11. WSC to Lloyd George, Nov. 13, 1910, *CV* 2:2, 1211.
12. Lloyd George, *Family Letters*, 153.
13. Randolph Churchill, *Winston S. Churchill*, 331; WSC to Asquith, Jan. 3, 1911, *CV* 2:2, 1032.
14. *Winston and Clementine*, 42.
15. WSC, *Thoughts and Adventures*, 68.
16. WSC, *My Early Life*, 193; "Mr. Churchill in Command," *Daily Mirror*, Jan. 4, 1911.
17. Andy McSmith, "Siege of Sidney Street," *Independent* (UK), Dec. 11, 2010; "Inquest on the Bodies of Two Unknown Men," January 1911, CHAR 12/11/3. The three policemen weren't murdered in January, as stated in Gilbert, *Churchill*, 223.
18. Jenkins, *Churchill*, 200; Hassall, *A Biography of Edward Marsh*, 171.
19. "His Majesty's Most Gracious Speech," House of Commons, Feb. 6, 1911, *Hansard*.
20. Kipling, *The Letters of Rudyard Kipling: 1911–19*, 10.
21. CHAR 12/3/62–64 and CHAR 12/7/9–11. John Syme, an ex-inspector of police, was charged with threatening WSC's life (*Times*, Aug. 3, 1911).
22. Soames, *Clementine Churchill*, 92; Lindsay, *The Crawford Papers*, 189.
23. "Clause 9," House of Commons, March 9, 1911, *Hansard*.
24. "Angry Scenes in House of Commons," *Daily Mirror*, March 11, 1911.
25. WSC to the King, March 10, 1911, *CV* 2:2, 1057.

XXI: Storm Signals

1. Hassall, *A Biography of Edward Marsh*, 172; *Winston and Clementine*, 111.
2. *Winston and Clementine*, 43.
3. Soames, *Clementine Churchill*, 95.
4. Ibid., 91.
5. "Society in Costume," *Lloyd's Weekly News*, May 28, 1911; "Fancy Dress Ball at Claridge's," *Times* (London), May 25, 1911.
6. "Parliament Bill," House of Commons, July 24, 1911, *Hansard*. Unlike

some fanciful accounts of this debate, mine is based primarily on the parliamentary transcript.

7. Bonham Carter, *Lantern Slides*, 274; Clifford, *The Asquiths*, 185.

8. Gardiner, *Prophets, Priests and Kings*, 90; Margot Asquith, *Autobiography*, 276.

9. "Parliament Bill," House of Commons, July 24, 1911, *Hansard*; Margot Asquith, *Autobiography*, 276.

10. WSC to the King, July 24, 1911, *CV* 2:2, 1101; Tuchman, *The Proud Tower*, 393.

11. Lord Derby to WSC; and the King to WSC, Aug. 15 and 16, 1911, *CV* 2:2, 1274.

12. "Fighting in Liverpool," *Lloyd's Weekly News*, Aug. 20, 1911.

13. Lewis Harcourt to Mary "Molly" Harcourt, Aug. 16 and 17, 1911, Bodleian Library, University of Oxford.

14. Austen Chamberlain, *Politics from Inside*, 437.

15. "Strike Calamity," *Lloyd's Weekly News*, Aug. 20, 1911.

16. Riddell, *Diaries*, 25; Bonham Carter, *Winston Churchill*, 180.

17. House of Commons, Aug. 22, 1911, *CS*, 1875.

18. Robbins, *Sir Edward Grey*, 243; WSC, *The World Crisis: 1911–1914*, 40. Harold Nicolson identified the lone German in Agadir as Herr Wilberg (*King George the Fifth*, 186).

19. WSC to Edward Grey, Nov. 22, 1911, CHAR 13/1/25 (Andrew, *Defend the Realm*, 37); WSC, *Thoughts and Adventures*, 83.

20. Gilbert, *David Lloyd George*, 1:450–54.

21. WSC, *The World Crisis: 1911–1914*, 44–45.

22. Ibid., 58–62.

23. On Sept. 4, 1914, the Kaiser believed that the war was won. "It is the thirty-fifth day," he said. "We are besieging Rheims, we are thirty miles from Paris" (Keegan, *The First World War*, 112).

24. *Daily Mirror*, Sept. 5, 1911; Hassall, *A Biography of Edward Marsh*, 174.

XXII: Armada

1. *Country Life*, Jan. 18, 1908; Bonham Carter, *Winston Churchill*, 187.

2. Haldane, *An Autobiography*, 245. Asquith sent his criticisms to McKenna on Sept. 18, 1911 (Farr, *Reginald McKenna*, 210).

3. Bonham Carter, *Winston Churchill*, 187.

4. Haldane, *An Autobiography*, 246–47.

5. Bonham Carter, *Winston Churchill*, 188, and *Lantern Slides*, 285.

6. Farr, *Reginald McKenna*, 217–18.

7. Bonham Carter, *Lantern Slides*, 306.

8. WSC, *The World Crisis: 1911–1914*, 71.

9. WSC, Glasgow, Feb. 9, 1912; *CS*, 1912; Toye, *Lloyd George & Churchill*, 119.

10. WSC, Burlington House, London, May 4, 1912, *CS*, 1961–62.

11. WSC, *The World Crisis: 1911–1914*, 111–12.

12. WSC, House of Commons, March 26, 1913, *CS*, 2082; and *The World Crisis: 1911–1914*, 126.

13. Ibid., 127–28.
14. Morgan, *Churchill*, 322; WSC, *The World Crisis: 1911–1914*, 87–88.
15. WSC, *My Early Life*, 196.
16. WSC, Glasgow, Feb. 9, 1912, *CS*, 1910.
17. "Mr. Churchill's Speech: German Comment," *Times* (London), Feb. 12, 1912.
18. Huldermann, *Albert Ballin*, 183.
19. WSC, *The World Crisis: 1911–1914*, 103.
20. "Black Outlook in Belfast," *Daily Mirror*, Feb. 5, 1912; Alexander Murray [Elibank] to WSC, Jan. 31, 1912, *CV* 2:3, 1390. For an example of the use of "provocative" to describe WSC's visit, see "Mr. J. H. Campbell and Mr. Churchill," *Times* (London), Feb. 10, 1912.
21. George Bernard Shaw to Jennie Churchill, Jan. 20, 1912, CHAR 28/81/4–8; Hassall, *A Biography of Edward Marsh*, 184.
22. Soames, *Clementine Churchill*, 105; *Winston and Clementine*, 61–62.
23. WSC, Belfast, Feb. 8, 1912, *CS*, 1909.
24. "Mr. Balfour in the Park," *Daily Mail*, April 6, 1914.

XXIII: The Old Man and the Sea

1. For a superb account of Jennie's fair, see Marion F. O'Connor, "Theatre of the Empire: 'Shakespeare's England' at Earl's Court, 1912," in Howard and O'Connor, eds., *Shakespeare Reproduced*, 68–98.
2. "Fiasco at Earl's Court," *NYT*, Aug. 4, 1912.
3. Cornwallis-West, *Edwardian Hey-Days*, 163–64.
4. Kate Carew, "Mrs. Cornwallis-West Interrupts a Busy Day to Chat with Kate Carew," *New York Tribune*, Sept. 8, 1912.
5. Gardiner, *The War Lords*, 306; Fisher, *Memories*, 208–9 and 163.
6. Ibid., 274; Begbie, *Master Workers*, 38.
7. WSC, *Great Contemporaries*, 337.
8. Fisher, *Memories*, 110 and 116; Mackay, *Fisher*, 289.
9. Ibid., 319, 320, and 403.
10. Lord Fisher to WSC, Dec. 10, 1911, and April 24, 1913, *CV* 2:3, 1927 and 1939.
11. Mackay, *Fisher*, 434–35.
12. Fisher, *Memories*, vi.
13. Riddell, *Diaries*, 28.
14. Lord Fisher to WSC, April 22, 1912, *CV* 2:3, 1545–46; WSC, *The World Crisis: 1911–1914*, 126.
15. Bonham Carter, *Lantern Slides*, 316.
16. Bonham Carter, *Winston Churchill*, 202.
17. WSC to Lord Fisher, June 11, 1912, *CV* 2:3, 1929.
18. Bonham Carter, *Winston Churchill*, 217.
19. "Unionist Gain at Crewe," *Daily Mail*, July 29, 1912.
20. Adams, *Bonar Law*, 108–9 and 101.
21. Gardiner, *Pillars of Society*, 121. Carson's unpublished letters are quoted in

Thomas C. Kennedy, "Troubled Tories: Dissent and Confusion Concerning the Party's Ulster Policy, 1910–1914," *Journal of British Studies*, July 2007, 574.

22. "Conservative Fete at Blenheim," *Lloyd's Weekly News*, July 28, 1912.

23. There are various accounts of the assault on WSC in the House of Commons, but few note how serious the impact would have been from a large book thrown by a "giant." For McNeill's height, see his obituary in the *Times* (London), Oct. 13, 1934. For my account I have drawn on Lewis Harcourt's description in his journal entry of Nov. 13, 1912 ("Book thrown by McNeill . . . at Winston, hit on cheek and drew blood."), Bodleian Library, University of Oxford; and the reports in the *Times*, Nov. 14, 1912, and the *Daily Mirror*, Nov. 15, 1912. McNeill's name is incorrectly given as "O'Neill" in Gilbert, *Churchill*, 250.

24. Austen Chamberlain, *Politics from Inside*, 491.

25. "Speaker's Plan to Restore Peace," *Daily Mirror*, Nov. 15, 1912.

26. "Silenced," *Penny Illustrated Paper*, Nov. 30, 1912.

XXIV: Wings

1. Toye, *Lloyd George & Churchill*, 95.

2. Frances Lloyd George, *The Years That Are Past*, 53.

3. Gilbert, *David Lloyd George*, 2:45; "Doing Himself Well," *Primrose League Gazette*, March 1, 1913.

4. Moran, *Diaries*, 168; Diary of Francis Octavius Grenfell, Dec. 25, 1913, Centre for Buckinghamshire Studies, Aylesbury.

5. "The Anger of Mr. Winston Churchill," *Daily Mirror*, April 29, 1913.

6. "Marconi's Wireless Telegraph Company," House of Commons, June 19, 1913, *Hansard;* Cooper, *Old Men Forget*, 46.

7. Buczacki, *Churchill & Chartwell*, 51–52.

8. On Aug. 25, 1913, Margot copied into her diary the notes that she had taken on the cruise in May (Bodleian Library, University of Oxford, and Clifford, *The Asquiths*, 208).

9. Bonham Carter, *Lantern Slides*, 384–85; "Churchill in Collision with Labor Members," *New York Tribune*, May 28, 1913.

10. *Winston and Clementine*, 85 and 70; WSC to the Duke of Marlborough, Nov. 6, 1912, Library of Congress.

11. Bonham Carter, *Lantern Slides*, 383.

12. "Mrs. Cornwallis-West Gets Divorce," *Daily Mirror*, July 16, 1913.

13. Randolph Churchill, *Winston S. Churchill*, 681; Briggs, ed., *They Saw It Happen*, 27.

14. Clementine Churchill to Jennie Churchill, Sept. 3 [1913], CHAR 28/80/6–7 (misidentified as 1912). Clemmie said that she flew in an "aeroplane," not a "sea-plane," but press accounts were confusing on this matter. See "Mrs. Churchill in a Waterplane," *Daily Mirror*, Sept. 5, 1913, and "Mrs. W. Churchill Flies," *NYT*, Sept. 5, 1913.

15. Davies, *Sailor in the Air*, 83.

16. Randolph Churchill, *Winston S. Churchill*, 682.

17. "The Eastchurch Aeroplane Accident," *Times* (London), April 24, 1913; Wildman-Lushington to Airlie Hynes, Nov. 30, 1913, *CV* 2:3, 1889; WSC, *Thoughts and Adventures*, 196; "Naval Air Accident," *Times* (London), Dec. 3, 1913; "First Lord As Air Pilot," *Daily Mail*, Dec. 2, 1913; Airlie Madden to Martin Gilbert, Jan. 6, 1963, *CV* 2:3, 1895.
18. F. E. Smith to WSC, Dec. 6, 1913, *CV* 2:3, 1893.
19. Theodore Lumley to Edward Marsh, Dec. 4, 1913, CHAR 1/108/42.
20. WSC, *Thoughts and Adventures*, 195; *Winston and Clementine*, 91; Thomas Hardy to Florence Henniker, July 17, 1914, *Selected Letters*, 285.

XXV: Countdown

1. "The Archduke at Windsor," *Daily Mail*, Nov. 18, 1913.
2. Hirst, *The Six Panics*, 6; Roch, *Mr Lloyd George and the War*, 74.
3. Ibid., 78–79; Grigg, *Lloyd George: From Peace to War*, 134–35.
4. David Lloyd George, "I Talked to Hitler," *Daily Express*, Sept. 17, 1936.
5. Ibid.
6. Toye, *Lloyd George & Churchill*, 318.
7. Diary of Francis Octavius Grenfell, Dec. 25, 1913, Centre for Buckinghamshire Studies, Aylesbury.
8. Gilbert, *David Lloyd George*, 2:72.
9. Diary of Francis Octavius Grenfell, Dec. 26 and 28, 1913, Centre for Buckinghamshire Studies, Aylesbury.
10. Riddell, *Diaries*, 77.
11. Ibid., 79.
12. Farr, *Reginald McKenna*, 255.
13. Toye, *Lloyd George & Churchill*, 136.
14. Sir Francis Hopwood to Lord Stamfordham, Jan. 5, 1914, *CV* 2:3, 1842.
15. Haldane, *An Autobiography*, 287; Briggs, ed., *They Saw It Happen*, 170.
16. Adams, *Bonar Law*, 152.
17. Toye, *Lloyd George & Churchill*, 115; "Lest We Forget," *Nineteenth Century*, March 1919.
18. Randolph Churchill, *Winston S. Churchill*, 484.
19. "Personalities of the Session," *Fortnightly Review*, May 1, 1914.
20. Lee, *"A Good Innings,"* 132.
21. WSC, *The World Crisis*, 205.

XXVI: Last Stand

1. WSC, *The World Crisis*, 246.
2. Pamela Lytton to WSC, Aug. 10, 1914, CHAR 1/112/13.
3. Holroyd, *Lytton Strachey*, 308.
4. *Winston and Clementine*, 96.
5. Lewis Harcourt Journal, Aug. 1, 1914, Bodleian Library, University of Oxford.
6. Riddell, *Diaries*, 89; WSC, *Great Contemporaries*, 105.
7. Asquith, *Letters to Venetia Stanley*, 365 and 247.

8. Ibid., 309.
9. Lord Haldane to WSC, Sept. 3, 1914, *CV* 3:1, 79.
10. WSC to H. H. Asquith, Oct. 5, 1914, and Sir Edward Grey to Clementine Churchill, Oct. 7, 1914, *CV* 3:1, 163 and 178.
11. Gwynne, *The Rasp of War*, 39.
12. Asquith, *Letters to Venetia Stanley*, 260 and 262.
13. WSC, *The World Crisis*, 388.
14. Asquith, *Letters to Venetia Stanley*, 266–67.
15. Mackay, *Fisher of Kilverstone*, 488.
16. Asquith, *Letters to Venetia Stanley*, 327.
17. WSC to H. H. Asquith, Dec. 29, 1914, *CV* 3:1, 344.
18. Lord Fisher to William Tyrrell, Jan. 12, 1915, and WSC to Lord Fisher, Jan. 4, 1915, *CV* 3:1, 407 and 371. Fisher also advocated the "naval advantages of possession of Constantinople" in a letter to WSC of Jan. 4, 1915 (*CV* 3:1, 372).
19. WSC to the Grand Duke Nicholas, Jan. 19, 1915, *CV* 3:1, 430.
20. "Meeting of the War Council," Jan. 13 and Jan. 28, 1915, *CV* 3:1, 409–10 and 464; Asquith, *Letters to Venetia Stanley*, 445–46.
21. Mackay, *Fisher of Kilverstone*, 498.
22. Williams, *Defending the Empire*, 232.
23. Gilbert, *David Lloyd George*, 2:192 and 197; Koss, *Asquith*, 195.
24. Bonham Carter, *Champion Redoubtable*, 53.
25. Quotation in *Morning Post* taken from "Assails Churchill as Public Danger," *NYT*, April 27, 1915; "German Gibes at Churchill," *NYT*, Nov. 14, 1915.
26. Lloyd George, *War Memoirs*, 1:139.
27. Soames, *Clementine Churchill*, 161; Ashmead-Bartlett, *The Uncensored Dardanelles*, 121.
28. Leslie, *Lady Randolph Churchill*, 356 and 358; Coombs, *Sir Winston Churchill*, 107.
29. Soames, *Clementine Churchill*, 162.
30. Coombs, *Sir Winston Churchill*, 115.
31. Longford, *A Pilgrimage of Passion*, 409.
32. WSC to H. H. Asquith, Nov. 11, 1915, and Muriel Wilson to WSC, Nov. 16, 1915, *CV* 3:2, 1249 and 1274.
33. Leslie, *Lady Randolph Churchill*, 362.
34. *Winston and Clementine*, 111.

Epilogue

1. Marcosson, *Adventures in Interviewing*, 154.

SELECTED BOOKS
BY WINSTON S. CHURCHILL

Great Contemporaries. Chicago: University of Chicago Press, 1973 [1937].

Liberalism and the Social Problem. London: Hodder & Stoughton, 1909.

London to Ladysmith Via Pretoria. London: Longmans, Green, 1900.

Lord Randolph Churchill. 1 vol. edition. London: Macmillan, 1907 [1906].

Marlborough: His Life and Times. 2 vols. Chicago: University of Chicago Press, 2002 [1933–38].

My African Journey. Toronto: William Briggs, 1909 [1908].

My Early Life: 1874–1904. New York: Touchstone/Simon & Schuster, 1996 [1930].

The River War: An Account of the Reconquest of the Sudan. New York: Carroll & Graf, 2000 [1899].

Savrola: A Tale of the Revolution in Laurania. London: Longmans, Green, 1900.

The Second World War: The Grand Alliance. Boston: Houghton Mifflin, 1950.

The Story of the Malakand Field Force: An Episode of Frontier War. London: Longmans, Green, 1901 [1898].

Thoughts and Adventures. Ed. James W. Muller. Wilmington, DE: ISI Books, 2009 [1932].

The World Crisis: 1911–1914. New York: Scribner's, 1923.

BIBLIOGRAPHY

Adams, R. J. Q. *Bonar Law*. Stanford: Stanford University Press, 1999.

Addison, Paul. *Churchill: The Unexpected Hero*. Oxford: Oxford University Press, 2005.

———. *Churchill on the Home Front: 1900–1955*. London: Pimlico, 1993.

Andrew, Christopher. *Defend the Realm: The Authorized History of MI5*. New York: Knopf, 2009.

Ashmead-Bartlett, Ellis. *The Uncensored Dardanelles*. London: Hutchinson, 1928.

Asquith, Herbert Henry. *Fifty Years in Parliament*. London: Cassell, 1926.

———. *H. H. Asquith: Letters to Venetia Stanley*. Ed. Michael and Eleanor Brock. Oxford: Oxford University Press, 1982.

Asquith, Lady Cynthia. *Diaries: 1915–1918*. London: Hutchinson, 1968.

Asquith, Margot. *The Autobiography of Margot Asquith*. Ed. Mark Bonham Carter. Boston: Houghton Mifflin, 1963.

Attwood, Gertrude M. *The Wilsons of Tranby Croft*. Beverley, East Yorkshire, UK: Hutton Press, 1988.

Balsan, Consuelo Vanderbilt. *The Glitter and the Gold*. Maidstone, Kent, UK: George Mann, 1973 [1953].

Barrymore, Ethel. *Memories: An Autobiography*. New York: Harper & Brothers, 1955.

Barrymore, Lionel. *We Barrymores*. New York: Appleton-Century-Crofts, 1951.

Batt, John Herridge. *Dr. Barnardo: The Foster-Father of "Nobody's Children."* London: Partridge, 1904.

Baxendale, Alan S. *Winston Leonard Spencer Churchill: Penal Reformer*. Oxford: Peter Lang, 2010.

Beerbohm, Max. *Seven Men*. New York: Knopf, 1920.

Begbie, Harold. *Master Workers*. London: Methuen, 1905.

Belford, Barbara. *Bram Stoker: A Biography of the Author of Dracula*. New York: Knopf, 1996.

Bennett, Daphne. *Margot: A Life of the Countess of Oxford and Asquith*. London: Victor Gollancz, 1984.

Bibesco, Marthe. *Sir Winston Churchill: Master of Courage*. New York: John Day, 1959 [1957].

Birkenhead, Frederick. *Churchill: 1874–1922*. Ed. John Colville. London: Harrap, 1989.

Blunden, Margaret. *The Countess of Warwick: A Biography*. London: Cassell, 1967.

Blunt, Wilfrid Scawen. *My Diaries: Being a Personal Narrative of Events, 1888–1914*. 2 vols. New York: Knopf, 1921.

Bonham Carter, Violet. *Champion Redoubtable: The Diaries and Letters of Violet Bonham Carter, 1914–1945.* Ed. Mark Pottle. London: Phoenix Books, 1999.

———. *Lantern Slides: The Diaries and Letters of Violet Bonham Carter, 1904–1914.* Ed. Mark Bonham Carter and Mark Pottle. London: Phoenix Books, 1997.

———. *Winston Churchill: An Intimate Portrait* [*Winston Churchill As I Knew Him*]. New York: Konecky & Konecky, 1999 [1965].

Bordes, Philippe. *Jacques-Louis David: Empire to Exile.* New Haven, CT: Yale University Press, 2005.

Brendon, Piers. *Winston Churchill: An Authentic Hero.* London: Methuen, 1985.

Brett, Reginald. *Journals and Letters of Reginald, Viscount Esher.* 4 vols. London: Nicholson & Watson, 1934–38.

Briggs, Asa, ed. *They Saw It Happen: An Anthology of Eye-witnesses' Accounts of Events in British History, 1897–1940.* Oxford: Basil Blackwell, 1960.

Brook-Shepherd, Gordon. *Uncle of Europe.* London: Collins, 1975.

Browne, Anthony Montague. *Long Sunset: Memoirs of Winston Churchill's Last Private Secretary.* London: Cassell, 1995.

Buchan, John. *Francis and Riversdale Grenfell: A Memoir.* London: Thomas Nelson & Sons, 1920.

Buczacki, Stefan. *Churchill & Chartwell: The Untold Story of Churchill's Houses and Gardens.* London: Frances Lincoln, 2007.

Campbell, John. *F. E. Smith, First Earl of Birkenhead.* London: Jonathan Cape, 1983.

Cannadine, David. *The Decline and Fall of the British Aristocracy.* New York: Vintage Books, 1999 [1990].

———. *In Churchill's Shadow: Confronting the Past in Modern Britain.* New York and Oxford: Oxford University Press, 2003.

Cannadine, David, and Roland Quinault, eds. *Winston Churchill in the Twenty-First Century.* Cambridge and London: Cambridge University Press and the Royal Historical Society, 2004.

Carland, John M. *The Colonial Office and Nigeria, 1898–1914.* Stanford, CA: Hoover Institution Press, 1985.

Carter, Miranda. *George, Nicholas and Wilhelm: Three Royal Cousins and the Road to World War I.* New York: Vintage Books, 2011.

Cecil, David. *The Cecils of Hatfield House: An English Ruling Family.* Boston: Houghton Mifflin, 1973.

Chamberlain, Austen. *Politics from Inside: An Epistolary Chronicle, 1906–1914.* New Haven, CT: Yale University Press, 1937.

Chamberlain, Joseph. *Imperial Union and Tariff Reform: Speeches Delivered from May 15 to Nov. 4, 1903.* London: Grant Richards, 1903.

Churchill, Randolph S. *Winston S. Churchill: Young Statesman, 1901–1914.* Boston: Houghton Mifflin, 1967.

Churchill, Sarah. *A Thread in the Tapestry.* New York: Dodd, Mead, 1967.

Churchill by Himself: The Definitive Collection of Quotations. Ed. Richard M. Langworth. New York: PublicAffairs, 2008.

The Churchill War Papers: The Ever-Widening War, 1941. Ed. Martin Gilbert. New York: Norton, 2001.

Clews, Graham T. *Churchill's Dilemma: The Real Story Behind the Origins of the 1915 Dardanelles Campaign.* Santa Barbara, CA: Praeger, 2010.

Clifford, Colin. *The Asquiths.* London: John Murray, 2002.

Colliery Strike Disturbances in South Wales: Correspondence and Report. London: His Majesty's Stationery Office, 1911.

Colville, John. *The Fringes of Power: 10 Downing Street Diaries, 1939–1955.* New York: Norton, 1986.

Coombs, David, and Minnie S. Churchill. *Sir Winston Churchill: His Life and His Paintings.* Lyme Regis, Dorset, UK: Ware House, 2011.

Cooper, Diana. *The Rainbow Comes and Goes.* Boston: Houghton Mifflin, 1958.

Cooper, Duff. *Old Men Forget.* New York: E. P. Dutton, 1954.

Cornwallis-West, George. *Edwardian Hey-Days or A Little about a Lot of Things.* New York: Putnam's, 1931.

Cornwallis-West, Mrs. George [Jennie Churchill]. *The Reminiscences of Lady Randolph Churchill.* New York: Century, 1908.

Cortissoz, Royal. *The Life of Whitelaw Reid.* 2 vols. New York: Scribner's, 1921.

Credland, Arthur G. *The Wilson Line.* Stroud, Gloucestershire, UK: Tempus, 2000.

Curzon, Mary. *Lady Curzon's India: Letters of a Vicereine.* Ed. John Bradley. New York: Beaufort Books, 1986.

Dangerfield, George. *The Strange Death of Liberal England.* Stanford, CA: Stanford University Press, 1997 [1935].

Davenport-Hines, Richard. *Ettie: The Life and World of Lady Desborough.* London: Phoenix, 2009.

Davies, Richard Bell. *Sailor in the Air.* Barnsley, UK: Seaforth, 2008 [1967].

Davis, Richard Harding. *Real Soldiers of Fortune.* New York: Scribner's, 1906.

D'Este, Carlo. *Warlord: A Life of Winston Churchill at War, 1874–1945.* New York: Harper Perennial, 2009.

Donaldson, Frances. *The Marconi Scandal.* New York: Harcourt, Brace & World, 1962.

Douglas, James. *Adventures in London.* London: Cassell, 1909.

Edel, Leon. *Henry James: The Master, 1901–1916.* New York: Avon Books, 1978 [1973].

Eden, Guy. *Portrait of Churchill.* London: Hutchinson, 1945.

Edwards, J. Hugh. *David Lloyd George: The Man and the Statesman.* 2 vols. New York: Sears, 1929.

Elletson, D. H. *The Chamberlains.* London: John Murray, 1966.

Ellsworth, William Webster. *A Golden Age of Authors: A Publisher's Recollection.* Boston: Houghton Mifflin, 1919.

Farr, Martin. *Reginald McKenna: Financier among Statesmen, 1863–1916.* New York: Routledge, 2008.

Faulk, Barry J. *Music Hall & Modernity: The Late-Victorian Discovery of Popular Culture.* Athens: Ohio University Press, 2004.

Fell, Bryan H. *The Houses of Parliament: An Illustrated Guide to the Palace of Westminster.* London: Eyre & Spottiswoode, 1961.

Ferguson, Niall. *The Pity of War*. New York: Basic Books, 1999.

Fisher, John Arbuthnot. *Memories*. London: Hodder & Stoughton, 1919.

Foster, R. F. *Lord Randolph Churchill: A Political Life*. Oxford: Clarendon Press, 1981.

———. *W. B. Yeats: A Life*. 2 vols. Oxford: Oxford University Press, 1997–2003.

Fowler, Marian. *Blenheim: Biography of a Palace*. London: Penguin Books, 1991.

Fox, James. *Five Sisters: The Langhornes of Virginia*. New York: Simon & Schuster, 2000.

Frances, Countess of Warwick. *Discretions*. New York: Charles Scribner's Sons, 1932.

———. *Life's Ebb and Flow*. New York: William Morrow, 1929.

Fussell, Paul. *The Great War and Modern Memory*. New York: Oxford University Press, 1977 [1975].

Gardiner, A. G. *The Pillars of Society*. New York: Dutton, 1916 [1913].

———. *Prophets, Priests and Kings*. London: Alston Rivers, 1908.

———. *The War Lords*. London: Dent, 1915.

Gilbert, Bentley Brinkerhoff. *David Lloyd George: A Political Life*. 2 vols. Columbus: Ohio State University Press, 1987–92.

Gilbert, Martin. *Churchill: A Life*. New York: Henry Holt, 1991.

———. *Churchill and America*. New York: Free Press, 2005.

———. *Winston S. Churchill: The Challenge of War, 1914–1916*. Boston: Houghton Mifflin, 1971.

Gilmour, David. *Curzon: Imperial Statesman*. New York: Farrar, Straus & Giroux, 2003.

Gollin, Alfred. *The Impact of Air Power on the British People and Their Government, 1909–1914*. Stanford, CA: Stanford University Press, 1989.

Griffith-Boscawen, Arthur. *Fourteen Years in Parliament*. London: John Murray, 1907.

Grigg, John. *Lloyd George: From Peace to War, 1912–1916*. Berkeley: University of California Press, 1985.

———. *Lloyd George: The People's Champion, 1902–1911*. Berkeley: University of California Press, 1978.

Gwynne, H. A. *The Rasp of War: The Letters of H. A. Gwynne to The Countess Bathurst, 1914–1918*. Ed. Keith Wilson. London: Sidgwick & Jackson, 1988.

Haldane, Richard Burdon. *An Autobiography*. Garden City, NY: Doubleday, Doran, 1929.

Hardy, Thomas. *Selected Letters*. Ed. Michael Millgate. Oxford: Clarendon Press, 1990.

Harris, Frank. *Contemporary Portraits: Third Series*. New York: Author, 1920.

Hassall, Christopher. *A Biography of Edward Marsh*. New York: Harcourt, Brace, 1959.

Hastings, Selina. *The Secret Lives of Somerset Maugham: A Biography*. New York: Random House, 2010.

Hill, George Birkbeck. *Footsteps of Dr. Johnson (Scotland)*. London: Sampson Low, 1890.

Hirst, F. W. *The Six Panics and Other Essays*. London: Methuen, 1913.

Hobhouse, Charles. *Inside Asquith's Cabinet: From the Diaries of Charles Hobhouse.* Ed. Edward David. New York: St. Martin's Press, 1978.

Holmes, Oliver Wendell. *The Essential Holmes: Selections from the Letters, Speeches, Judicial Opinions and Other Writings of Oliver Wendell Holmes, Jr.* Ed. Richard A. Posner. Chicago: University of Chicago Press, 1996.

Holmes, Oliver Wendell, and Lewis Einstein. *The Holmes-Einstein Letters: Correspondence of Mr. Justice Holmes and Lewis Einstein, 1903–1935.* Ed. James Bishop Peabody. New York: St. Martin's Press, 1964.

Holroyd, Michael. *Bernard Shaw.* 3 vols. New York: Random House, 1988–91.

———. *Lytton Strachey: The New Biography.* New York: Farrar, Straus & Giroux, 1995.

Howard, Jean E., and Marion F. O'Connor, eds. *Shakespeare Reproduced: The Text in History and Ideology.* New York and London: Methuen, 1987.

Huldermann, Bernhard. *Albert Ballin.* Translated by W. J. Eggers. London: Cassell, 1922.

Hunt, Tristram. *Building Jerusalem: The Rise and Fall of the Victorian City.* New York: Metropolitan Books, 2005.

Hyde, H. Montgomery. *Lord Reading: The Life of Rufus Isaacs, First Marquess of Reading.* New York: Farrar, Straus & Giroux, 1967.

James, Henry. *Henry James: A Life in Letters.* Ed. Philip Horne. London: Allen Lane, 1999.

James, Robert Rhodes. *Churchill: A Study in Failure, 1900–1939.* London: Weidenfeld & Nicolson, 1970.

———. *Lord Randolph Churchill: Winston Churchill's Father.* New York: Barnes, 1960.

Jenkins, Roy. *Churchill: A Biography.* New York: Plume/Penguin, 2002.

Jolliffe, John. *Raymond Asquith: Life and Letters.* London: Collins, 1980.

Keegan, John. *The First World War.* New York: Vintage Books, 2000.

Kelly, Patrick J. *Tirpitz and the Imperial German Navy.* Bloomington: Indiana University Press, 2011.

Kipling, Rudyard. *The Letters of Rudyard Kipling: 1911–19.* Ed. Thomas Pinney. Iowa City: University of Iowa Press, 1999.

Koss, Stephen E. *Asquith.* New York: St. Martin's Press, 1976.

———. *Lord Haldane: Scapegoat for Liberalism.* New York: Columbia University Press, 1969.

Lambert, Nicholas A. *Sir John Fisher's Naval Revolution.* Columbia: University of South Carolina Press, 2002.

Landor, Arnold. *Everywhere: The Memoirs of an Explorer.* 2 vols. New York: Frederick A. Stokes, 1924.

Larson, Erik. *Thunderstruck.* New York: Crown, 2006.

Lee, Arthur. *"A Good Innings": The Private Papers of Viscount Lee of Fareham.* Ed. Alan Clark. London: John Murray, 1974.

Lee, Celia. *Jean, Lady Hamilton: 1861–1941.* London: Celia Lee, 2001.

Lee, Celia, and John Lee. *The Churchills: A Family Portrait.* New York: Palgrave Macmillan, 2010.

Lee, Sidney. *King Edward VII: A Biography*. 2 vols. London: Macmillan, 1925.

Lees-Milne, James. *The Enigmatic Edwardian: The Life of Reginald, 2nd Viscount Esher*. London: Sidgwick & Jackson, 1986.

Leslie, Anita. *Lady Randolph Churchill: The Story of Jennie Jerome*. New York: Scribner's, 1969.

Lindsay, David. *The Crawford Papers: The Journals of David Lindsay, Earl of Crawford*. Ed. John Vincent. Manchester, UK: Manchester University Press, 1984.

Lloyd George, David. *Family Letters: 1885–1936*. Ed Kenneth O. Morgan. Cardiff and London: University of Wales Press and Oxford University Press, 1973.

———. *War Memoirs*. London: Odhams Press, 1938.

Lloyd George, Frances. *The Years That Are Past*. London: Hutchinson, 1967.

Longford, Elizabeth. *A Pilgrimage of Passion: A Life of Wilfrid Scawen Blunt*. London: Tauris Parke, 2007 [1979].

Lovell, Mary S. *The Churchills: In Love and War*. New York: Norton, 2011.

Lucy, Henry W. *The Balfourian Parliament: 1900–1905*. London: Hodder & Stoughton, 1906.

Lytton, Constance. *Prisons & Prisoners: Some Personal Experiences*. Ed. Jason Haslam. Buffalo, NY: Broadview Editions, 2008 [1914].

MacCarthy, Fiona. *Byron: Life and Legend*. New York: Farrar, Straus & Giroux, 2002.

Macdonagh, Michael. *The Book of Parliament*. London: Isbister, 1897.

Mackay, Ruddock F. *Balfour: Intellectual Statesman*. Oxford: Oxford University Press, 1985.

———. *Fisher of Kilverstone*. Oxford: Clarendon Press, 1973.

MacKenzie, Norman, and Jeanne MacKenzie. *The Fabians*. New York: Simon & Schuster, 1977.

Mackintosh, Alexander. *Joseph Chamberlain: An Honest Biography*. London: Hodder & Stoughton, 1906.

Malcolm, Ian. *Vacant Thrones: A Volume of Political Portraits*. London: Macmillan, 1931.

Manchester, William. *The Last Lion, Winston Spencer Churchill: Alone, 1932–1940*. Boston: Little, Brown, 1988.

———. *The Last Lion, Winston Spencer Churchill: Visions of Glory, 1874–1932*. New York: Delta/Dell, 1989 [1983].

Marcosson, Isaac. *Adventures in Interviewing*. London: John Lane, the Bodley Head, 1920.

Marie, Queen of Roumania. *The Story of My Life*. New York: Scribner, 1934.

Marsh, Edward. *A Number of People: A Book of Reminiscences*. New York: Harper & Brothers, 1939.

Marsh, Peter T. *Joseph Chamberlain: Entrepreneur in Politics*. New Haven, CT: Yale University Press, 1994.

Massie, Robert K. *Castles of Steel: Britain, Germany, and the Winning of the Great War at Sea*. New York: Random House, 2003.

———. *Dreadnought: Britain, Germany, and the Coming of the Great War.* New York: Ballantine, 1992.

Masterman, Lucy. *C. F. G. Masterman: A Biography.* London: Frank Cass, 1968 [1939].

McCarthy, Justin. *British Political Portraits.* New York: Outlook, 1903.

McKinstry, Leo. *Rosebery: Statesman in Turmoil.* London: John Murray, 2005.

McMenamin, Michael, and Curt Zoller. *Becoming Winston Churchill: The Untold Story of Young Winston and His American Mentor.* New York: Enigma Books, 2009.

Mencken, H. L. *Newspaper Days: Mencken's Autobiography, 1898–1906.* Baltimore: Johns Hopkins University Press, 2006 [1941].

Menpes, Mortimer. *War Impressions.* London: Adam & Charles Black, 1901.

Meredith, George. *Letters of George Meredith.* 2 vols. New York: Scribner's, 1912.

Moir, Phyllis. *I Was Winston Churchill's Private Secretary.* New York: Wilfred Funk, 1941.

Moorehead, Alan. *Gallipoli.* New York: Perennial, 2002 [1956].

Moran, Charles. *Churchill: Taken from the Diaries of Lord Moran.* Boston: Houghton Mifflin, 1966.

Morgan, Ted. *Churchill: Young Man in a Hurry, 1874–1915.* New York: Simon & Schuster, 1982.

Morley, John. *Memorandum on Resignation: August 1914.* London: Macmillan, 1928.

———. *Recollections.* 2 vols. New York: Macmillan, 1917.

Morrell, Ottoline. *Ottoline at Garsington: Memoirs of Lady Ottoline Morrell, 1915–1918.* Ed. Robert Gathorne-Hardy. New York: Knopf, 1975.

Mosley, Nicholas. *Julian Grenfell: His Life and the Times of His Death, 1888–1915.* New York: Holt, Rinehart & Winston, 1976.

Nel, Elizabeth. *Mr. Churchill's Secretary.* New York: Coward-McCann, 1958.

Nicolson, Harold. *King George the Fifth: His Life and Reign.* Garden City, NY: Doubleday, 1953.

Ogilvy, David. *An Autobiography.* New York: Wiley, 1997.

Pakenham, Thomas. *The Boer War.* London: Macdonald, 1982.

———. *The Scramble for Africa: 1876–1912.* New York: Random House, 1991.

Pankhurst, Emmeline. *My Own Story.* London: Eveleigh Nash, 1914.

Parker, Louis N. *Drake: A Pageant-Play.* London: John Lane, the Bodley Head, 1913.

Perham, Margery. *Lugard: The Years of Authority: 1898–1945.* London: Collins, 1960.

Peters, Margot. *The House of Barrymore.* New York: Touchstone/Simon & Schuster, 1991.

———. *Mrs. Pat: The Life of Mrs. Patrick Campbell.* New York: Knopf, 1984.

Ponsonby, Frederick. *Recollections of Three Reigns.* New York: Dutton, 1952.

Priestley, J. B. *The Edwardians.* New York: Harper & Row, 1970.

Rauchbauer, Otto. *Shane Leslie: Sublime Failure.* Dublin: Lilliput Press, 2009.

Read, Donald, ed. *Edwardian England.* New Brunswick, NJ: Rutgers University Press, 1982.

Riddell, George. *The Riddell Diaries: 1908–1923*. Ed. J. M. McEwen. London: Athlone Press, 1986.

Rideing, William H. *Many Celebrities and a Few Others: A Bundle of Reminiscences*. Garden City, NY: Doubleday, Page, 1912.

Robbins, Keith. *Sir Edward Grey: A Biography of Lord Grey of Fallodon*. London: Cassell, 1971.

Roch, Walter. *Mr Lloyd George and the War*. London: Chatto & Windus, 1920.

Roosevelt, Theodore. *Theodore Roosevelt's History of the United States*. Ed. Daniel Ruddy. New York: HarperCollins, 2010.

Rose, Kenneth. *The Later Cecils*. New York: Harper & Row, 1975.

Rose, Norman. *Churchill: The Unruly Giant*. London: Tauris Parke, 2009 [1995].

Rosebery, Lord. *Lord Randolph Churchill*. London: Arthur L. Humphreys, 1906.

Rossmore, Lord. *Things I Can Tell*. New York: George H. Doran, 1912.

St. Aubyn, Giles. *Edward VII: Prince and King*. New York: Atheneum, 1979.

Sandys, Celia. *Chasing Churchill: The Travels of Winston Churchill*. London: HarperCollins, 2003.

Scott, C. P. *The Political Diaries of C. P. Scott, 1911–1928*. Ed. Trevor Wilson. Ithaca, NY: Cornell University Press, 1970.

Sebba, Anne. *American Jennie: The Remarkable Life of Lady Randolph Churchill*. New York: Norton, 2007.

Smalley, George W. *Anglo-American Memories*. 2nd series. New York: Putnam, 1912.

Smith, Frederick Winston Furneaux. *F.E.: The Life of F. E. Smith, First Earl of Birkenhead*. London: Eyre & Spottiswoode, 1959.

Smith, Robin. *The Making of Scotland: A Comprehensive Guide to the Growth of Its Cities, Towns, and Villages*. Edinburgh: Canongate, 2001.

Smyth, Ethel. *What Happened Next*. London: Longmans, Green, 1940.

Soames, Mary. *Clementine Churchill: The Biography of a Marriage*. New York: Paragon House, 1988 [1979].

———. *Family Album: A Personal Selection from Four Generations of Churchills*. Boston: Houghton Mifflin, 1982.

Spender, J. A. *Life, Journalism and Politics*. 2 vols. London: Cassell, 1927.

Stafford, David. *Churchill and Secret Service*. New York: Overlook Press, 1998.

Stansky, Peter, ed. *Churchill: A Profile*. New York: Hill & Wang, 1973.

Strachey, Lytton. *Queen Victoria*. New York: Harcourt, Brace, 1921.

Stuart, Amanda Mackenzie. *Consuelo and Alva Vanderbilt: The Story of a Daughter and a Mother in the Gilded Age*. New York: HarperCollins, 2006.

Stuart, Denis. *Dear Duchess: Millicent, Duchess of Sutherland, 1867–1955*. London: Gollancz, 1982.

Sturgis, Matthew. *Walter Sickert: A Life*. London: Harper Perennial, 2005.

Terraine, John. *The Life and Times of Lord Mountbatten*. London: Hutchinson, 1968.

Thompson, Paul. *The Edwardians: The Remaking of British Society*. 2nd ed. London and New York: Routledge, 1992.

Tirpitz, Alfred von. *My Memoirs*. 2 vols. New York: Dodd, Mead, 1919.

Toye, Richard. *Churchill's Empire: The World That Made Him and the World He Made*. New York: Henry Holt, 2010.

———. *Lloyd George & Churchill: Rivals for Greatness*. London: Pan Macmillan, 2008.

Trollope, Anthony. *Autobiography*. New York: Dodd, Mead, 1905 [1883].

Trueblood, Paul Graham. *Lord Byron*. Boston: Twayne, 1977.

Tuchman, Barbara W. *The Guns of August*. New York: Ballantine, 1994 [1962].

———. *The Proud Tower*. New York: Ballantine, 1996 [1966].

Twain, Mark, and William Dean Howells. *Selected Mark Twain–Howells Letters, 1872–1910*. Ed. Frederick Anderson, William M. Gibson, and Henry Nash Smith. Cambridge, MA: Belknap Press of Harvard University Press, 1967.

Ward, Mrs. Humphry. *The Coryston Family: A Novel*. New York: Harper & Brothers, 1913.

Webb, Beatrice. *The Diary of Beatrice Webb*. 4 vols. Ed. Norman and Jeanne MacKenzie. Cambridge, MA: Belknap Press of Harvard University Press, 1982–85.

Wells, H. G. *The New Machiavelli*. New York: Duffield, 1910.

———. *The Wife of Sir Isaac Harman*. New York: Macmillan, 1914.

Wharton, Edith. *A Backward Glance*. New York: Touchstone/Simon & Schuster, 1998 [1934].

Wheeler, Sara. *Cherry: A Life of Apsley Cherry-Garrard*. New York: Modern Library, 2003.

Wilde, Oscar. *The Complete Letters of Oscar Wilde*. Ed. Merlin Holland and Rupert Hart-Davis. New York: Henry Holt, 2000.

Williams, Rhodri. *Defending the Empire: The Conservative Party and British Defence Policy, 1899–1915*. New Haven, CT: Yale University Press, 1991.

Williamson, Samuel R. *The Politics of Grand Strategy: Britain and France Prepare for War, 1904–1914*. Cambridge, MA: Harvard University Press, 1969.

Wilson, John. *CB: A Life of Sir Henry Campbell-Bannerman*. London: Constable, 1973.

Winston and Clementine: The Personal Letters of the Churchills. Ed. Mary Soames. Boston: Houghton Mifflin, 1998.

Wolcott, Frances M. *Heritage of Years: Kaleidoscopic Memories*. New York: Minton, Balch, 1932.

Wood, Anthony. *Nineteenth-Century Britain: 1815–1914*. Harlow, Essex, UK: Longman, 1982.

Young, Kenneth. *Arthur James Balfour: The Happy Life of the Politician, Prime Minister, Statesman, and Philosopher, 1848–1930*. London: G. Bell & Sons, 1963.

Zebel, Sydney H. *Balfour: A Political Biography*. Cambridge: Cambridge University Press, 1973.

INDEX

ABOUT THE AUTHOR

Michael Shelden is the author of four previous biographies. His *Orwell: The Authorized Biography* was a Pulitzer Prize finalist. For twelve years he was a features writer for *The Daily Telegraph* (London) and a fiction critic for *The Baltimore Sun*. He is currently a professor at Indiana State University.